The Perennial Philosophy

Series

World Wisdom
The Library of Perennial Philosophy

The Library of Perennial Philosophy is dedicated to the exposition of the time-less Truth underlying the diverse religions. This Truth, often referred to as the *Sophia Perennis*—or Perennial Wisdom—finds its expression in the revealed Scriptures as well as the writings of the great sages and the artistic creations of the traditional worlds.

A Christian Pilgrim in India: The Spiritual Journey of Swami Abhishiktananda (Henri Le Saux) appears as one of our selections in the Perennial Philosophy series.

The Perennial Philosophy Series

In the beginning of the twentieth century, a school of thought arose which has focused on the enunciation and explanation of the Perennial Philosophy. Deeply rooted in the sense of the sacred, the writings of its leading exponents establish an indispensable foundation for understanding the timeless Truth and spiritual practices which live in the heart of all religions. Some of these titles are companion volumes to the Treasures of the World's Religions series, which allows a comparison of the writings of the great sages of the past with the perennialist authors of our time.

Swami Abhishiktananda at Jyotiniketan, Easter 1969

A CHRISTIAN PILGRIM IN INDIA

The Spiritual Journey of
Swami Abhishiktananda
(Henri Le Saux)

by

Harry Oldmeadow

World Wisdom

A Christian Pilgrim in India: The Spiritual Journey of Swami Abhishiktananda
(Henri Le Saux)
© 2008 World Wisdom, Inc.

Library of Congress Cataloging-in-Publication Data

Oldmeadow, Harry, 1947-
  A Christian pilgrim in India : the spiritual journey of Swami Abhishiktananda (Henri
le Saux) / by Harry Oldmeadow.
     p. cm. -- (The library of perennial philosophy) (The perennial philosophy series)
  Includes bibliographical references and index.
  ISBN 978-1-933316-45-1 (pbk. : alk. paper) 1. Abhishiktananda, Swami, 1910-1973.
2. Spiritual biography. I. Title.
  BX4705.A214O53 2008
  261.2'45092--dc22
  [B]
                                                                        2007035476

Cover: Abhishiktananda, Indore, October 1973
Nicholas Roerich, *Path to Shambhala*, 1933; courtesy of the Nicholas Roerich
Museum, New York

Printed on acid-free paper in Canada.

For information address World Wisdom, Inc.
P.O. Box 2682, Bloomington, Indiana 47402-2682

www.worldwisdom.com

Let the athlete of the spirit ever integrate himself
Standing in a place apart,
alone, his thoughts and self restrained,
Devoid of earthly hope, possessing nothing.
(*Bhagavad Gītā* VI.10)

The Spirit of God is living in you.
(*Romans* VIII.9)

The conditions of a solitary bird are five:
The first, that it flies to the highest point;
the second, that it does not suffer for company,
not even of its own kind;
the third, that it aims its beak to the skies;
the fourth, that it does not have a definite color;
the fifth, that it sings very softly.
(*San Juan de la Cruz*)

What if all the tumult of the body were to quiet down, along
with all our busy thoughts about Earth, sea, and air? What
if this very world should stop, and the mind cease thinking
about itself, go beyond itself and be quite still? What if all the
fantasies that appear in dreams and imagination should cease,
and there be no speech, no sign . . . so that we should hear the
voice of the One who made all things, not through any symbol,
but we might hear the One whom in these things we love,
might hear that very Self without these? And what if it could
be continued on, and all other visions be withdrawn, and this
one ravish, and absorb, and wrap up its beholder amid inward
joys? And what if life could be forever like this single breathless
moment of illumination!
(*St Augustine*)

I know him, that great Puruṣa
Of the color of the sun,
Beyond all darkness.
He who has known him
Goes beyond death.
There is no other way.
(*Śvetāśvatara Upanishad* III.8)

CONTENTS

Illustrations

China

Pakistan

Tibet

Gangotri
Uttarkashi
Rajpur
Rishikesh
Haridwar
Delhi
Bareilly
Lucknow
Vrindaban
Ganges River
Allahabad
Yumana River
Varanasi

Nepal

Bhutan

Bangladesh

Burma

INDIA

Indore

Nagpur

Calcutta

Bombay
Poona

Bangalore
Kavery River
Tiruvannamalai
Tirukoyilur
Kulitali
Trichinopoly
Madurai

Madras

Sri Lanka

Colombo

India

The map shows places significant in
Abhishiktananda's life. Names which
were current in his lifetime are used—for
instance, Madras rather than Chennai.

Map of India

Introduction

It is early in the morning, late in June, 1973. We find ourselves on the banks of India's most holy river, Mother Ganga, a short distance from the Sivananda Ashram of Rishikesh. We notice three men in the river. One is evidently an Indian swami; there is a bearded and elderly European, also clothed in the garb of an Indian renunciate; the third man, another European, is very much younger. Having discarded all his clothing the young man is being plunged under the water as the other two recite strange chants. At the end of what is apparently a religious ceremony in which all three are quite rapt, the young man is enveloped in a fire-colored cloth, given a bowl and, it seems, told to depart. Who are these people and what are they doing? The Indian is Swami Chidananda, successor to Swami Sivananda at the nearby ashram which bears his name; the somewhat wild-looking and disheveled older man—who seems to have fallen into an ecstatic state—is Swami Abhishiktananda, a Benedictine monk who had arrived in India nearly a quarter of a century earlier; the young man is a French seminarian, Marc Chaduc. They are conducting a "trans-religious" Hindu/Christian initiation ceremony from which the young man will emerge as a *sannyāsī* (renunciate) and with the new name of "Swami Ajatananda."

How did Henri Le Saux, raised in an atmosphere of fervent Catholic piety in a small provincial town in Brittany, come, on this June morning, to be chanting Sanskrit mantras and reciting the *mahavākyas* (great sayings) from the *Upanishads*? This is one of the questions addressed in the present volume. Abhishiktananda was one of the spiritual luminaries of the last century. Through his many years in the land of the Vedic rishis he undertook an intrepid journey of spiritual exploration. His quest for "the secret of Arunachala," initiated by his contacts with Ramana Maharshi and glimpsed during his sojourns in the caves of the Holy Mountain, attained its goal in the last years of his life when, in the deepest recesses of the "cave of the heart," he experienced fully that inner awakening to the mystery of the Self which the Upanishadic sages had extolled millennia before. In his last years he found, too, the resolution of the acute existential tensions arising out of the "dual presence" in his heart of the Christian Gospel and the *Upanishads*.

The reader will find in these pages a sketch of the remarkable life of this indefatigable pilgrim of the Absolute. However, the book is not primarily a biographical study; our governing purpose is to draw attention to certain spiritual *leitmotiv* in Abhishiktananda's life and his extensive writings. Abhishiktananda confronted many of the challenges which face the spiritual wayfarer in our own crepuscular era, in particular the problem of religious pluralism and the inter-relations of the world's integral traditions. Abhishiktananda was immediately concerned with the encounter of Christianity and Hinduism, but his experiences and his ever-deepening reflections on this subject illuminate a range of more far-reaching issues.

This book is squarely addressed to seekers who might find in Abhishiktananda's life and work a light to help guide them on their way, no matter on which particular path they might be traveling. In an age when we are surrounded by the clamor of false prophets on all sides it is my hope that readers will find inspiration (in-the-spirit-ness) in the example of this obscure, humble, and immensely courageous French monk. His own perplexities and contradictions, his foibles and idiosyncrasies, remind us that Abhishiktananda was a very human figure with his feet on the ground, so to speak. He would certainly have been appalled by any attempt at a hagiography. I hope this will also be a book in which scholars and theologians (who may well also be pilgrims!) will find something of interest, even though it deliberately bypasses some of the more technical theological and philosophical debates which have accumulated around Abhishiktananda's work—some of which would no doubt have irritated him! With some years of scholarly writing behind me, I am increasingly wary of any treatment of spiritual and religious subjects which has no apparent purpose other than to maintain the endless turning of the academic mills. Even more alarming is the lamentable fact that much academic activity nowadays stands at radical odds with the purpose for which the Academy was originally founded—the practice of *philo-sophia*, the love and pursuit of wisdom.

Readers will not venture very far in these pages without noticing frequent references to the works of traditionalist authors such as René Guénon, Frithjof Schuon, Ananda Coomaraswamy, and Marco Pallis, to mention only a few. These figures formed the vanguard of the traditionalist or perennialist "school," dedicated to the elucidation of the metaphysical and cosmological principles which comprise "the perennial philosophy" and which inform the manifold religious forms of traditional civilizations. The traditionalist writers understand the spiritual treasures of the East in the light of the *sophia perennis*, and thus help to protect them from the profanations of ill-equipped Western scholars and popularizers alike. In the later chapters of this book we will give some sustained attention to the explication of certain subjects by such exponents of the Wisdom of the Ages; their metaphysical and doctrinal intellectuality at times serves as a corrective to certain confusions and inadvertencies in Abhishiktananda's own thinking, while at other times Abhishiktananda's consonance with traditionalist thought brings the subject at hand into sharper focus. If this book serves to introduce readers to these perennialist masters as well as directing them to Abhishiktananda's own luminous works, it will have served two worthy purposes.

*

An undertaking such as the present volume owes much to those who have gone before. Our study draws directly on Abhishiktananda's own writings—more than a dozen published books and monographs, some fifty-odd articles, the voluminous private journals he maintained from his arrival in India until a few weeks before his death, and his prodigious correspondence. That these writings are now available in accessible form and in English translation is due in no small part to the tireless labors of several people who were friends of "Swamiji." I pay tribute and acknowledge my considerable debts to Odette Baumer-Despeigne, Raimon Panikkar, James Stuart, David Fleming, Bettina Bäumer, and others whose names will be found in the pages following. The draft of this book was completed before the appearance of Shirley du Boulay's biography, *In the Cave of the Heart*, which now stands as the definitive biography.

A Note on Terminology, Quotation, and Documentation

- The spelling of Sanskrit and other Eastern terms has been made uniform throughout, even within quotations. (Abhishiktananda himself was by no means consistent in this regard.) Apart from those words which have by now found a home in English (examples: yoga, Vedanta, guru), such terms are italicized. Sanskrit terms have been used as sparingly as possible. (A short glossary is provided on pp. 289-290.) Indian names have not been accented.
- The titles of Scriptures and other texts are invariably italicized, even within quotations.
- The volume and issue numbers of journals have been standardized in English numerals.

- Only author names and titles, sometimes abbreviated, are cited in footnotes: full bibliographical details are provided in the listed Sources.
- When letters are cited from sources other than James Stuart's *Abhishiktananda: His Life Told through His Letters*, this is usually because the letter in question does not appear in Stuart's work. Likewise with excerpts from his journals.

*

Small portions of this book have previously appeared in two earlier books, *Traditionalism: Religion in the Light of the Perennial Philosophy* (Colombo: Sri Lanka Institute of Traditional Studies, 2000) and *Journeys East: 20th Century Western Encounters with Eastern Religious Traditions* (Bloomington: World Wisdom, 2004), and in *Australian Religions Studies Review* (Sydney) and *Sacred Web: A Journal of Tradition and Modernity* (Vancouver). I am grateful to the respective publishers and editors for permission to reproduce this material.

*

The epigraph from St Augustine's *Confessions* on p. v, is a passage freely rendered by Beatrice Bruteau, and is taken from her article, "In the Cave of the Heart: Silence and Realization," *New Blackfriars*, July-August 1984, 306.

List of Abbreviations of Works by Abhishiktananda

(dates are of editions consulted)

BA   *A Benedictine Ashram* (written with Jules Monchanin), Douglas: Times Press, 1964.

D (Diary)   *Ascent to the Depth of the Heart: The Spiritual Diary (1948-1973) of Swami Abhishiktananda (Dom Henri Le Saux)*, ed. Raimon Panikkar, tr. David Fleming and James Stuart, Delhi: ISPCK, 1998.

DD   "The Depth Dimension of Religious Dialogue," *Vidjayjoti*, 45:5, 1981, 202-221.

EG   "Experience of God in Eastern Religions," *Cistercian Studies,* 9:2-3, 1974, 148-157.

EL   *The Eyes of Light*, ed. A. Gozier and J. Lemarié, Denville, NJ: Dimension, 1983.

FS   *The Further Shore*, Delhi: ISPCK, 1975.

GD   *Guru and Disciple*, tr. Heather Sandeman, London: SPCK, 1974.

HC   *Hindu-Christian Meeting Point*, tr. Sara Grant, Delhi: ISPCK, 1976.

L (Letters) *Swami Abhishiktananda: His Life Told through His Letters*, by James Stuart, Delhi: ISPCK, 2000.

ML   *Mountain of the Lord: Pilgrimage to Gangotri*, Delhi: ISPCK, 1990.

Pr   *Prayer*, London: SPCK, 1974.

RC   *Towards the Renewal of the Indian Church*, Bangalore: Dharamaran College, 1970.

SA   *The Secret of Arunachala: A Christian Hermit on Shiva's Holy Mountain*, Delhi: ISPCK, 1997.

SC   *Saccidananda: A Christian Approach to Advaitic Experience*, Delhi: ISPCK, 1984.

The following works are referred to in the endnotes by author's name only:

Baumer-D   Odette Baumer-Despeigne, "The Spiritual Journey of Henri Le Saux-Abhishiktananda," *Cistercian Studies*, 18, 1983, 310-329.

du Boulay   Shirley du Boulay, *The Cave of the Heart: The Life of Swami Abhishiktananda*, Maryknoll, NY, 2005 (Foreword by Raimon Panikkar).

Friesen   John Glenn Friesen, *Abhishiktananda's Non-Monistic Advaitic Experience*, PhD thesis, University of South Africa, Cape Town, 2001. (Page numbers in text refer to the on-line version.)

Kalliath   Antony Kalliath, *The Word in the Cave*, New Delhi: Inter-cultural Publications, 1996.

Panikkar   Raimon Panikkar, "Letter to Abhishiktananda," *Studies in Formative Spirituality*, 3:3, 1982, 429-451.

Stephens   Robert Stephens, *Religious Experience as a Meeting-Point in Dialogue: An Evaluation of the Venture of Swami Abhishiktananda*, MA thesis, Sydney University, 1984.

Vattakuzhy   Emmanuel Vattakuzhy, *Indian Christian Sannyasa and Swami Abhishiktananda*, Bangalore: Theological Publications in India, 1981.

Swami Abhishiktananda

I

"Consecrated to God"

The Life and Work of Abhishiktananda

"Like you, I come from God; like you,
it is to him that I am going; apart from
that, nothing else matters."

1

A Biographical Sketch

The monk is a man who lives in the solitude
(Greek: *monos*) of God, alone in the very alone-
ness of the Alone. . . . He does not become a monk
in order to do social work or intellectual work or
missionary work or to save the world. The monk
simply consecrates himself to God.

Abhishiktananda[1]

The monk is a man who, in one way or another,
pushes to the frontiers of human experience and
strives to go beyond, to find out what transcends
the ordinary level of existence.

Thomas Merton[2]

The "Irresistible Call"

Henri Hyacinthe Joseph Marie Le Saux was born on August 30, 1910,
in St. Briac, a small town on the north coast of Brittany, not far from
Saint-Malo.[3] He w as the first of seven children born to Alfred Le Saux
and Louise Sonnefraud. His parents ran a small grocery business. The
last of the siblings, Marie-Thérèse, later to become the confidante to
whom Henri sent many letters, was not born until 1930. The young
boy breathed in Catholic piety in the very atmosphere of the family
home and the early signs that he might be destined for the priesthood
were encouraged. At age ten he was sent to the Minor Seminary at
Châteaugiron. Three years later his mother nearly died in childbirth.
When she fell pregnant again the following year Henri vowed that if
she survived he would go "even to the most distant mission" in God's
service—perhaps to follow in the footsteps of an uncle who had gone to
China as a missionary a year or two earlier. The year 1926 saw him enter
the Major Seminary at Rennes where, under the influence of a friend
who had died, he determined to become a Benedictine. His thirst for
the monastic life and for God is evident in a letter from the young seminarian to the Novice Master of the Abbey of Saint Anne de Kergonan:

> What has drawn me from the beginning and what still leads me on, is
> the hope of finding there the presence of God more immediately than
> anywhere else. I have a very ambitious spirit—and this is permissible,

is it not? when it is a matter of seeking God—and I hope I shall not be disappointed. . . . I feel an irresistible call.[4]

But the path to the monastery was not without obstacles: parental opposition; the reluctance of the Archbishop; the problem of his compulsory military service. Nor was Henri without his own doubts. But in 1929 he entered the Abbey where he was to remain for the next two decades. In 1931 he made his first profession and soon after completed his military service before returning to the Abbey where he was ordained as a priest in December 1935. He assisted with novices and served as the Abbey librarian, and during these years immersed himself in the Patristical and mystical literature of the Church, especially the Desert Fathers, as well as reading about the spiritual traditions of India. He was particularly taken by the work of St Gregory Nazianzen and his "Hymn to God Beyond All Names" which struck a theme which was to "accompany him all the way till his death":

You who are beyond all, what other name befits you?
No words suffice to hymn you. Alone you are ineffable.
Of all beings you are the End, you are One, you are all, you are none.
Yet not one thing, nor all things. . . .
You alone are the Unnamable.[5]

Among his other favorite authors were Athanasius, Cyril of Alexandria, and Gregory Palamas.[6] By 1942, when Le Saux came to write a manuscript for his mother, *Amour et Sagesse*, he was already familiar with some of the Hindu literature and closed each chapter of this work with the sacred syllable OM. Other subjects of Abhishiktananda's later writings adumbrated in *Amour et Sagesse* are the doctrine of the Trinity and apophatic mysticism.

In 1939 he was called up for military service. His unit was captured by the Germans. Whilst his captors were registering the names of the prisoners, Le Saux took advantage of a momentary distraction to slip away and hide in a cornfield. A nearby garage-keeper gave him a pair of workman's overalls and a bicycle on which Le Saux was able to make his way home where he went into hiding before eventually returning to the monastery. After the war Fr Henri taught novices at Kergonan and also served as Master of Ceremonies, a duty he discharged with some relish.

From one of his letters written many years later it seems that he first heard the call of India in 1934, by which time he was already feeling "deep dissatisfaction" with his life at Kergonan.[7] In a 1947 letter to Fr Jules Monchanin, Le Saux spoke of his thirteen-year old dream of a

Christian monastic life in India, which had in recent years been "continually in my thought and prayer."[8] However, despite his frustrations at Kergonan he remained attached to the Rule of St Benedict and to the monastery right up to the time of his death. In his last year he wrote, "Kergonan has been the background of all that I have been able to do here."[9] The family ties with the monastery continued when, soon after his departure for India, Marie-Thérèse entered the Abbey of St Michel, sister-abbey to Kergonan.

Fr Henri's vision of a monastic life in India was not to come to fruition for fifteen years. As he was later to write of his frustrations and disappointments in these long years of waiting, "I have looked squarely in the face of a good number of them as well as at a good number of obstacles."[10] It was not until after the war that his abbot gave him permission to launch inquiries about the possibilities of a move to India, but even then the wheels turned slowly. In 1947 Le Saux wrote to Msgr James Mendonça, the Bishop of Tiruchchirappalli (Trichinopoly) in South India, stating that he aspired to "the contemplative life, in the absolute simplicity of early Christian monasticism and at the same time in the closest possible conformity with the traditions of Indian *sannyāsa*." The Bishop was himself a man of considerable vision.[11] The answer Le Saux was praying for came in a letter written on behalf of the Bishop by Fr Jules Monchanin, thus initiating one of the most important relationships of Le Saux's life and clearing the way for his momentous passage to India. From Monchanin's letter:

> Your letter came to me as an answer from God. . . . If you come his Lordship is very willing for us to begin together a life of prayer, poverty, and intellectual work. Learn as much English as you can. You will have no objection to a purely vegetarian diet (essential for the life of the *sannyāsī*). You will need unshakable courage (because you will have disappointments), complete detachment from the things of the West, and a profound love of India. The Spirit will give you these three gifts.[12]

On July 26, 1948, Abhishiktananda left his homeland, never to return. He was to join Fr Monchanin in setting up a Christian Ashram at Kulittalai on the Kavery River, there to achieve his "most ardent desire." Fr Bede Griffiths was later to describe an ashram this way:

> An ashram must above all be always a place of prayer where people can find God, where they can experience the reality of the presence of God in their lives and know that they were created not merely for this world but for eternal life.

Furthermore, "An ashram is a place which should be open to all such seekers of God, or seekers of Self-realization, whatever their religion or without any religion."[13]

Father Jules Monchanin

Let us pause for a moment to consider the manner of the man with whom Le Saux was to be so closely associated for the next decade. The first forty years of Jules Monchanin's life were quite unexceptional for a provincial French priest.[14] He was born near Lyons in 1895, decided at an early age to enter the priesthood and completed his theological training in 1922. Despite his intellectual distinction he did not complete his doctoral studies but instead asked to be sent to a miners' parish in a poor suburb of Lyons. He served in three parishes before serious illness led to less demanding appointments as a chaplain, first in an orphanage and then at a boys' boarding school. Throughout these years he continued to move in an academic milieu and applied himself to a range of studies. Since boyhood he had felt an attraction to India which now steered him towards Sanskrit, and Indological and comparative religious studies. From the early 1930s Monchanin was exploring the possibility of living some sort of Christian monastic life in India, no easy task for someone bound to Mother Church. It took many years of negotiations before Monchanin finally received the approval of the Bishop of Tiruchirapalli to work amongst the scattered Indian Christians in the region, evangelized centuries before by both Francis Xavier and Roberto Nobili. Monchanin left Marseilles for India in May 1939. For the next decade Monchanin was immersed in pastoral work in India. These were years of social deprivation, physical hardship, and acute loneliness, preparatory to the contemplative life for which he yearned.

Swami Arokianadar, who taught Monchanin Tamil, and later became his disciple, testifies to Monchanin's infectious enthusiasm and erudition in all matters Indian:

> I noticed that he was very much interested in Indian philosophy, Indian history, art and literature, and social customs and manners. He taught me also to appreciate them and I could say that I learnt about India more from him than from anybody else. He gave me books on India. He helped me to understand the mystical meaning even of poems like *Gītā Govinda* or of myths like Kali. He was very much pleased when he saw me taking interest in the *Bhagavad Gītā*. It is amazingly true that he was able to talk on any subject that pertains to India, be it religious or philosophical, social or cultural, philological or ethical. In short he was an indologue.[15]

In Monchanin we find a formidable intellect, vast erudition, a refined sensibility with a deep appreciation of Europe's cultural heritage, and an ability to relate to ordinary folk. As one of his contemporaries wrote, he had a gift for understanding both ideas and souls:

> This gave him the opportunity to make intimate contacts at once with the most learned as well as the humblest, to assimilate with an extraordinary rapidity the philosophical and the scientific works of the specialists and to share the artistic emotion of painters, poets, and musicians; finally to receive with full love those who wanted to make him the confidant of their personal hopes and difficulties.[16]

Monchanin might easily have fashioned a splendid academic or ecclesiastical career; we have the testimony of some of the leading French Indologists of the day to this effect,[17] whilst Abhishiktananda said of him,

> He was one of the most brilliant intellects among the French clergy, a remarkable conversationalist, at home on every subject, a brilliant lecturer and a theologian who opened before his hearers marvelous and ever new horizons.[18]

Instead, Monchanin surrenders all to plunge himself into the materially impoverished life of the Indian villager and the life of the monk lived in the fashion of the *sannyāsī*. In 1941 he had written in his journal, "May India take me and bury me within itself—in God."[19] It was a noble ideal. Now, at last, in 1950, he was able to establish a monastic hermitage on the banks of the Kavery River.

Shantivanam: A Christian Ashram

On arrival in India, via Colombo, Le Saux was captivated by India—by its color and vitality, its history, its people, its temples and ashrams, but above all by the vibrant spiritual life pervading the whole culture. He immediately set about learning Tamil and was able to preach his first sermon in that language on Christmas Day, only a few months after his arrival. He traveled extensively in Tamil Nadu, familiarizing himself with the people, the language, the customs, with all aspects of Hinduism, and with the Indian Church with which he was now associated. He also took on his Indian name, Abhishiktananda ("Bliss of the Anointed One"), the name we will use henceforth.[20]

By early 1950 Abhishiktananda and Monchanin were ready to establish their ashram, variously known as *Eremus Sanctissimae Trinitatis* (Hermitage of the Most Holy Trinity), *Shantivanam* (Grove of Peace), and *Saccidananda Ashram* (after the Vedantic ternary Being-Awareness-Bliss). Appropriately enough, the ashram was formally opened on the Feast of St Benedict, 21 March, 1950. Monchanin and Abhishiktananda articulated their agenda:

> Our goal: to form the first nucleus of a monastery (or rather a *laura*, a grouping of neighboring anchorites like the ancient laura of Saint Sabas in Palestine) which buttresses the Rule of Saint Benedict—a primitive, sober, discrete rule. Only one purpose: to seek God. And the monastery will be Indian style. We would like to crystallize and transubstantiate the search of the Hindu *sannyāsī*. *Advaita* and the praise of the Trinity are our only aim. This means we must grasp the authentic Hindu search for God in order to Christianize it, starting with ourselves first of all, from within.[21]

In short: Vedantic philosophy, Christian theology, Indian lifestyle. The hope was that "what is deepest in Christianity may be grafted on to what is deepest in India."[22] This was not a syncretic exercise which would issue forth some kind of religious hybrid, but an attempt to fathom the depths of Christianity with the aid of the traditional wisdom of India which, in the monks' view, was to be found in Vedanta and in the spiritual disciplines of the renunciate. However, whilst India had "her own message to deliver," it would only be "after finding her own achievement in Christ, the Truth, the Way and the Life (*John* 14.6) that she [would] be able to radiate to the world her message, imprinted, by the Word and the Spirit, in the very depth of her own culture."[23] The bridge between Indian spirituality and the Church was to be monasticism, "the plane whereon they may feel themselves in consonance with each other."[24] They looked forward to the day when God would send to the hermitage many "true sons of India, sons of her blood and sons of her soul,"

> priests and laymen alike, gifted with a deep spirit of prayer, an heroic patience, a total surrender, endowed with an iron will and right judgment, longing for the heights of contemplation, and equipped, too, with a deep and intimate knowledge of Christian doctrine and Indian thought.[25]

The lifestyle at the ashram was to be thoroughly Indian: meditation, prayer, study of the Scriptures of both traditions, a simple vegetarian diet, the most Spartan of amenities. Each donned the ochre cloth of the *sannyāsī* and lived Indian style—sleeping on the floor, dispensing with almost all furniture, eating with the hands rather than with "those strange implements that the West substitutes in a disgraceful way for the natural implements given by the Creator."[26] The skimpy bamboo and thatch shelters which were their first abode soon had to be abandoned because the snakes, scorpions, and monkeys, perhaps claiming the rights of prior occupation, disturbed their sleep and their meditations.[27]

Monchanin had alluded earlier to the case of Dom Joliet, a French naval officer in China who became a Benedictine in 1897 and waited thirty years to realize his dream of founding a Christian monastery in the Far East. Monchanin had written, "Will I someday know the same joy, that in India too—from its soil and spirit—there will come a [Christian] monastic life dedicated to contemplation?"[28] The dream was not to be fully realized in Monchanin's own lifetime. On the face of it, the efforts of the French monks were less than successful: it was a constant struggle to keep the ashram afloat; there was little enthusiasm from either European or Indian quarters; there were endless difficulties and hardships; not a solitary Indian monk became a permanent member of the ashram. Abhishiktananda felt weighed down by practical responsibilities to which Monchanin remained quite indifferent. As James Stuart remarked, "For Fr Monchanin, study, thought, and prayer were everything, and he was content to leave the future entirely in the hands of God. If God willed, the ashram would develop; if not, he was perfectly happy to remain a hermit."[29] Abhishiktananda's personality was more dynamic, impetuous, and volatile, and he felt impatient with the failure of the ashram to attract Indian monks as permanent residents. The arrival in September 1955 of the Belgian monk, Fr Francis Mahieu, introduced new tensions into the small community, and by the end of the following year, Mahieu had left Shantivanam to establish Kurisumala Ashram (Kerala) with Bede Griffiths.[30] By the time of Monchanin's death in 1957 there seemed little to show for the hard years behind them. Monchanin was not able even to realize his desire to die in India as he had been sent to Paris for medical treatment. But the seeds had been sown. As Bede Griffiths later wrote, "It was Monchanin's vocation not to reach the goal to which he aspired, but to open the way to it for others."[31]

If the ashram did not meet the early hopes of its founders in attracting a stable community of Indian monks, it played a vital and exemplary role in the eventual flowering of the Christian Ashram movement. Furthermore, for many years it provided both a physical and spiritual hospitality, the effects of which are not easily gauged, but which surely left its mark on its beneficiaries. In the next chapter we shall meet some of the visitors to Shantivanam. During Abhishiktananda's time there they included H.W.J. Poonja ("Harilal," disciple of Ramana), Harold Rose (ex-Trappist novice with interests in Sufism and

Advaita), Raimon Panikkar (Spanish-Indian priest and scholar), Murray Rogers (English Anglican priest), John Cole (American Presbyterian missionary), Bettina Bäumer (Austrian student), Fr Klaus Klostermaier (German missionary and scholar), Vinoba Bhave (Gandhi's most well-known disciple), C.T. Venugopal (Protestant convert and railway official), Sachit Dhar (ex-Marxist Bengali), Fr Lazarus (English Orthodox priest), Devananda (Singhalese Anglican, founder of an ashram in Sri Lanka), Swami Kaivalyananda (Hindu monk), Fr Dharmanadhan (who at one time was to stay permanently but eventually moved on), Frs Dominique van Rollenhagen and Emmanuel de Meester (Belgian Benedictines), Ilsa Friedeberg (Swiss convert to the Orthodox Church), Jean Sullivan (French novelist), Philippe Franchette (Mauritian priest), Max Thurian (from the Taizé Community), Olivier Clément (Orthodox theologian), Mme Malou Lanvin (one of Abhishiktananda's many correspondents in France), as well as various church dignitaries and a host of other Indians who no doubt found some spiritual sustenance there. Nor should we forget the role that the ashram played in the religious life of the Christian villagers in the parish in which it was situated, many of them regularly attending services there. Then, too, there were many conferences, seminars, retreats, study groups and the like which took place under the aegis of the ashram, both at Shantivanam and elsewhere. It was also during the Shantivanam years that Abhishiktananda took on his life-long role as a spiritual father to the Carmelites of Bangalore, an "invisible ministry" which was highly significant both in his own development and in the lives of those to whom he ministered.[32]

A decade after Monchanin's death Fr Bede Griffiths and two Indian monks left their own ashram at Kurisumala and committed themselves to Shantivanam. There were to be many difficult years still ahead but Monchanin's dream finally came to fruition under the husbandry of Bede Griffiths who later wrote of Monchanin's mission:

> The ashram which he founded remains as a witness to the ideal of a contemplative life which he had set before him, and his life and writings remain to inspire others with the vision of a Christian contemplation which shall have assimilated the wisdom of India, and a theology in which the genius of India shall find expression in Christian terms.[33]

There are today something like fifty Christian ashrams in India, owing much to the pioneering efforts of Frs Monchanin, Le Saux, and Griffiths. Many of these ashrams are peopled entirely by indigenous Christians who continue the task of seeking out and living a distinctively Indian form of Christianity. Amongst the most enduring of these ashrams, along with Saccidananda and Kurisumala, are Christukula, established by two Anglican missionaries in the early 1930s, Christa Prema Seva Ashram, founded by John Winslow in 1927 in Shivajinagar (Mumbai region), Jyotiniketan near Bareilly, and the Christi Panti Ashram in Varanasi. Many of the ashrams established in the last fifty years owe their inspiration to Shantivanam and to Monchanin, Abhishiktananda, and Bede Griffiths. Whether one regards this legacy as beneficent depends on one's point of view. The Christian Ashram movement in general and the "Trinity from Tannirpalli" in particular, have come under vituperative attack from some Hindu quarters—a matter to which we will return in a later chapter. The Christian Ashram movement still awaits a thorough phenomenological analysis,[34] but what can be said here without fear of contradiction is that Shantivanam and the pioneering work of Monchanin, Abhishiktananda, and Bede Griffiths had broken the trail for this movement.

"Unknown Harmonies": Ramana, Arunachala, and Gnanananda

However, Abhishiktananda was soon to find himself moving in another direction. The die was cast as early as January 1949 when Monchanin took him to Arunachala, the *liṅga*-mountain of Lord Shiva, and to visit Bhagavān Sri Ramana Maharshi, one of the most remarkable saints and sages of modern times—or, indeed, of any times. So potent was the impact of the Sage and of Abhishiktananda's several sojourns on Arunachala that by early 1953 he was writing,

> Shantivanam henceforth interests me so little. Arunachala has caught me. I have understood silence.... Now *sannyāsa* is no longer a thought, a concept, but an inborn summons, a basic need; the only state that suits the depths into which I have entered.[35]

In other words, Abhishiktananda was no longer primarily motivated by the ideal of a monastic Christian witness in India but was now seized by the ideal of *sannyāsa* as an end in itself. It can fairly be said that from the early 50s onwards Abhishiktananda's life was a sustained attempt to live out this ideal.

Although Abhishiktananda's first sightings of Ramana left him somewhat dissatisfied and with a sense of distaste for the way in which the devotees venerated him, it was not long before Abhishiktananda felt the mesmerizing *darśana* of the gentle saint:

> Even before my mind was able to recognize the fact, and still less to express it, the invisible halo of this Sage had been perceived by something in me deeper than any words. Unknown harmonies awoke in my heart.... In the Sage of Arunachala of our own time I discerned

the unique Sage of the eternal India, the unbroken succession of her sages, her ascetics, her seers; it was as if the very soul of India penetrated to the very depths of my own soul and held mysterious communion with it. It was a call which pierced through everything, rent it in pieces and opened a mighty abyss.[36]

One can find any number of testimonies of this kind. Monchanin himself wrote of the meeting, "I did not for a moment cease to be lucid, master of myself. And I was nevertheless captivated. . . . There is a mystery in this man, who has rediscovered the *one essence* of Indian mysticism."[37] For the moment we will restrict ourselves to juxtaposing Abhishiktananda's words with Frithjof Schuon's strikingly similar account of the Maharishi's nature and significance:

In Sri Ramana Maharshi one meets again ancient and eternal India. The Vedantic truth—the truth of the *Upanishads*—is brought back to its simplest expression but without any kind of betrayal. It is the simplicity inherent in the Real, not the denial of that complexity which it likewise contains. . . . That spiritual function which can be described as the "activity of presence" found in the Maharishi its most rigorous expression. Sri Ramana was as it were the incarnation, in these latter days and in the face of modern activist fever, of what is primordial and incorruptible in India. He manifested the nobility of contemplative "non-action" in the face of an ethic of utilitarian agitation and he showed the implacable beauty of pure truth in the face of passions, weaknesses, and betrayals.[38]

Abhishiktananda had no real "relationship" with Ramana in the normal sense of the word—for instance, he was never in his presence alone but only as part of a group. His encounters with the Sage were few and rather fleeting, and his hopes of more sustained contact were thwarted by Ramana's passing in January 1950. But assuredly the meeting with Ramana precipitated a series of radically transformative experiences for Abhishiktananda.

In the years following Ramana's death Abhishiktananda spent two extended periods as a hermit in one of Arunachala's many caves. He wrote of an overwhelming mystical experience while in retreat on the mountain, an experience of non-duality (*advaita*), and stated that he was "truly reborn at Arunachala under the guidance of the Maharishi,"[39] understanding "what is beyond silence: *śūnyatā* (voidness)." "Ramana's *Advaita* is my birthplace. Against that all rationalization is shattered."[40]

He who receives this overwhelming Light is both petrified and torn apart; he is unable to speak or to think anymore; he remains there, beyond time and space, alone in the very solitude of the alone. It is a fantastic experience, this sudden irruption of the fire and light of Arunachala.

Ramana and Arunachala alike had, he said, "become part of my flesh, they are woven into the fibers of my heart."[41]

Abhishiktananda's last extended stay at Tiruvannamalai was in December 1955, one with momentous consequences. During this period, accompanied by his friend Harold Rose, he also visited Tirukoyilur, some thirty miles to the south. From a letter written on Christmas Eve:

> I have met . . . through an unforeseen combination of circumstances, an old Hindu *sannyāsī* (they say is 120 years old; 70 or 150, what does it matter?), before whom, for the first time in my life, I could not resist making the great prostration of our Hindu tradition, and to whom I believe I might give myself over completely.[42]

The "old Hindu *sannyāsī*" in question was Swami Sri Gnanananda, or to give him the full treatment, Paramahamsa Parivrajaacharya Varya Sri Gnanananda Giri Swami, disciple of Paramahamsa Parivrajaacharya Varya Sri Sivaratnagiri Swami, belonging to the Kashmir Jyotir Mutt Peetam of the lineage of Adi Sankara Bhagavat Pada! Here is Abhishiktananda's first impression:

> He had short legs and his body was half shrouded in an orange *dhotī*, which left one shoulder bare, while one end was draped over his head. He was unshaven. On his forehead there was no trace of his hundred and twenty years!—only the three lines of ash worn by devotees of Shiva and the vermillion mark in the center. But from this deeply peaceful face shone eyes filled with immense tenderness.[43]

Interestingly, Abhishiktananda remarks that upon meeting Gnanananda he *automatically* yielded his allegiance to him, something which he had never previously done.[44] Here is his third-person account from *Guru and Disciple* (in which "Vanya" is Abhishiktananda himself):

> [Vanya] had often heard tell of gurus, of the irrational devotion shown to them by their disciples and their total self-abandonment to the guru. All these things had seemed utterly senseless to him, a European with a classical education. Yet now at this very moment it had happened to him, a true living experience tearing him out of himself. This little man with his short legs and bushy beard, scantily clad in a *dhotī*, who had so suddenly burst in upon his life, could now ask of him anything in the world.[45]

Abhishiktananda had spontaneously become a disciple of Gnanananda. In February and March of the following year, at the swami's invitation, Abhishiktananda returned to his ashram at Tapovanam, there to give himself over to Gnanananda and to experience nearly three weeks "which have been among the most unforgettable of my life."[46] As Gnanananda is much less well-known than Ramana, we must here say a few words about him.

Like most such figures, Gnanananda was reticent about his own biography but we can assemble a few facts which were gleaned from scattered and off-hand remarks made by the swami himself. It is believed that he was born at Managalapuri near Gokarna in the west of Karnataka. As a boy he was attracted to Pandharpur, the famous pilgrimage center in Maharashtra and it was there that he met Sri Sivarathna of Jyotir Mutt, who was to become the guru under whom Gnanananda underwent his spiritual apprenticeship at Srinagar, in Kashmir. After his guru departed this life Gnanananda spent many years as an ascetic in the Himalayas, including many years at Gangotri (close to the site of Abhishiktananda's own Himalayan hermitage) before embarking on travels which took him to all parts of the sub-continent, including Nepal, Burma, and Sri Lanka. During these travels he came into contact with many of the leading lights of the day, including Ramana, Sai Baba of Shirdi, Ramakrishna, Vivekananda, and Aurobindo. (Whether he physically met these figures is a matter of some conjecture, some of his followers suggesting that he was able to "know" them by virtue of his powers as a *trikāljñānī*—one who moves freely through past, present, and future.[47])

Eventually Gnanananda settled near the temple city of Tirukoyilur in Tamil Nadu, where an ashram grew up around him. The area, within the benign aura of Arunachala, had been the abode of many Tamil saints over the centuries. Gnanananda spent the rest of what, by all accounts, was an extraordinarily long life in this region, eventually passing away in 1974. (The consensus amongst his followers, including several sober-minded scholars, seems to be that Gnanananda lived for about 150 years.[48]) Gnanananda was proficient in many languages and was said to have a prodigious memory. Contrary to Abhishiktananda's assertions in *Guru and Disciple* that Gnanananda "exhibits no trace of anything extraordinary, [n]o ecstasies, no *siddhis*"[49] he was also believed to have the powers of telepathy, astral travel, astrological prediction, and various other wonder-working faculties.

Gnanananda's ashram at Tapovanam remains a lively spiritual center to this day, and is now presided over by Swami Nityananda Giri, one of the founders, in 1978, of the Abhishiktananda Society.[50] Abhishiktananda later wrote in some detail about his experiences at

Arunachala and at Sri Gnanananda's ashram at Tapovanam in *The Secret of Arunachala* and *Guru and Disciple*.[51] These fateful experiences will be considered in more detail in the next two chapters.

On the Christian-Hindu Frontier

From the early 50s onwards Abhishiktananda faced a daunting problem: how to reconcile the advaitic insight which Ramana, Arunachala, and Gnanananda had brought him with his own deep Christian commitment and his vocation as a priest and a monk. In September 1953 we find him articulating the dilemma in his diary, in all its fully-felt pain:

> What does it mean, this agony of having found one's peace far from the place and form of one's original commitments, at the very frontiers of Holy Church? What does it mean, to feel that the only obstacle to final peace and *ānanda* [joy] is one's attachment to that place, that form, that *mythos*? Who is there on either side of the frontier to whom I can cry out my anguish—who, if he belongs to this side, will not take fright and anathematize me, and if he is on the other side, will not take an all too human delight because I am joining him?[52]

He was also troubled in these early years by the failure of his abbot to seek the renewal of his indult of exclaustration (the ecclesiastical authority to live outside his monastery), and thought about going himself to Rome:

> What use would it be to go to Europe? What use in going to Rome in search of ecclesiastical authorization? When Saint-Exupery had lost his way and was flying a course between Orion and the Great Bear, he could laugh a Claudelian laugh when a petty airport official radioed to him that he was fined because he had banked too close to the hangars. ... So it is with the letters of Fr Abbot.[53]

But it was the interior problem which was most acute. He agonized over it for many years—to put his problems before Rome? to abandon his Christian faith? to turn his back on *advaita*? There was no simple answer and it was not until his last years that the dilemma was fully resolved. In our explorations of Abhishiktananda's thought, his writings, his spiritual experience, we will find him confronting these questions again and again. Here is one of many tormented cries from his journal: "Therefore I am full of fear, plunged in an ocean of anguish whichever way I turn. ... And I fear risking my eternity for a delusion. And yet you are no delusion, O Arunachala."[54] Nor was his predicament eased by his growing disenchantment with many aspects of the institutional church:

If only the Church was *spiritually radiant*, if it was not so firmly attached to the formulations of transient philosophies, if it did not obstruct the freedom of the spirit . . . with such niggling regulations, it would not be long before we reached an understanding.[55]

He was deeply troubled by the thought that he might be "wearing a mask of Christianity, out of fear of the consequences" (of taking it off).[56]Abhishiktananda's spiritual crisis was at its most intense in the years 1955-56, and was to the fore during his month-long silent retreat at Kumbakonan.[57]

For the moment we can say that Abhishiktananda, with heroic audacity, chose to live out his life on that very frontier, neither forsaking Christianity nor repudiating the spiritual treasures which he had found in such abundance in India: "I think it is best to hold together, even though in extreme tension, these two forms of a unique faith until the dawn appears."[58] It was a position which was to cause him much distress and loneliness, and a good many difficulties with some of his fellow Christians, be they ecclesiastical authorities, priests and scholars, or acquaintances—though we should also note that many of his Christian friends, far from anathematizing him, showed a remarkable level of understanding of Abhishiktananda's predicament, an unwavering love of the man himself and a deep respect for the path he had chosen.

Here is Abhishiktananda in later years, pondering his journey and the two traditions which had nurtured him, both of which he loved profoundly:

> Whether I want it or not, I am deeply attached to Christ Jesus and therefore to the *koinonia* of the Church. It is in him that the "mystery" has been revealed to me ever since my awakening to myself and to the world. It is in his image, his symbol, that I know God and that I know myself and the world of human beings. Since I awoke here to new depths in myself (depths of the self, of the *ātman*), this symbol has marvelously developed. Christian theology had already revealed to me the eternity of the mystery of Jesus in the bosom of the Father. Later India revealed to me the cosmic wholeness of this mystery. . . . Moreover I recognize this mystery, which I have always adored under the symbol of Christ, in the myths of Narayana, Prajapati, Siva, Puruṣa, Krishna, Rama etc. The same mystery. But for me, Jesus is my *sadguru*.[59]

In another letter he wrote this:

> It is precisely the fact of being a bridge that makes this uncomfortable situation worthwhile. The world, at every level, needs such bridges. The danger of this life as "bridge" is that we run the risk of not belonging to

either side; whereas, however harrowing it may be, *our duty is to belong wholly to both sides.* This is only possible in the mystery of God.[60]

He had few companions on this path. Until the Church was much more widely pervaded by contemplative awareness and open to the experience of *advaita*, ". . . there is only the loneliness of the prophet . . . and the impossibility of being at one's ease anywhere except with those few people who have an intuition of this 'transcendent' level— like traveling faster than sound, or escaping from earth's gravity, to use physical metaphors."[61]

From the Kavery to the Source of the Ganges

Monchanin's death in 1957 left Abhishiktananda in charge of Shantivanam and he struggled on with his various duties there as best he could, as if cultivating a piece of land he no longer owned.[62] Towards the end of 1958 he wrote to his friend in France, Fr Lemarié, "I no longer have any desire for a monastic institution; it is too heavy a responsibility."[63] More critical than the burden of responsibility was his growing conviction that "the completion in Christ of the mystical intuition of *advaita* is the fundamental ontological condition for the building up not in statistics, not in masonry, but in reality of the Church in India."[64] Increasingly he found himself allured to the holy sites of Hinduism and spent more and more of his time on such pilgrimages and peregrinations. Before his last years at Gyansu, when he withdrew from the world as far as he was able, he journeyed thousands of miles all over India, always traveling third class—often being able to get in or out of the astonishingly crowded carriages only through the window! Robert Stephens has characterized him as "the hermit who could not stay put."[65] He refused to fly anywhere as he believed that such a mode of travel was quite incongruous for a *sannyāsī* vowed to poverty.

It was not until 1968 that Abhishiktananda formally relinquished the leadership of Shantivanam to Fr Bede Griffiths. After this hand-over he never returned to Shantivanam. He formalized his Indian citizenship in 1960—he had long been a spiritual citizen—and built a small hermitage on the banks of the Ganges at Gyansu, a tiny hamlet near Uttarkashi, in the Himalayas. His friend Murray Rogers gives us a picture of the humble habitation which was thenceforth to be Abhishiktananda's "home":

> It was a one-roomed house built of stones gathered from the hillside, covered with mud plaster; the upstairs portion, reached by a rickety ladder, was an attic or loft which served as a chapel and box-room; at

the back there was a lean-to for a kitchen and, by the time I visited him, there was in front another little cell for infrequent visitors, made largely of bamboo netting and a covered porch. Here Swamiji often worked at a table. This porch was wide open towards the Ganga. . . . Except in the eyes of Swamiji himself there was apparent disorder, books and papers, pots, a lantern, a screwdriver and hammer, some dal and bengan. . . . I told him that in a previous incarnation he must surely have been related to Heath Robinson, for I swear that paper and string have never had so much to do with holding a building together.[66]

Here Abhishiktananda plunged ever deeper into the *Upanishads*, realizing more and more the Church's need of India's timeless message. He also consolidated his grasp of Sanskrit, Tamil, and English, and often participated in retreats, conferences, seminars, and the like. How appropriate that most of his books were written here, near the source of the holy river!

It was only in the last few years of his life that he resolved the tension between his Christian commitments and his advaitic experience, becoming ever more firmly convinced that the meeting place of the two traditions was not to be found in any doctrinal or philosophical formulations but in the lived reality of *sannyāsa*:

Believe me, it is above all in the mystery of *sannyāsa* that India and the Church will meet, will discover themselves in the most secret and hidden parts of their hearts, in the place where they are each most truly themselves, in the mystery of their origin in which every outward manifestation is rooted and from which time unfolds itself.[67]

In his journal he wrote of himself as "at once so deeply Christian and so deeply Hindu, at a depth where Christian and Hindu in their social and mental structures are blown to pieces, and are yet found again ineffably at the heart of each other."[68] As Frithjof Schuon has remarked,

When a man seeks to escape from "dogmatic narrowness" it is essential that it should be "upwards" and not "downwards": dogmatic form is transcended by fathoming its depths and contemplating its universal content, and not by denying it in the name of a pretentious and iconoclastic "ideal" of "pure truth."[69]

Abhishiktananda never denied or repudiated the doctrines or practices of either Christianity or Hinduism, nor did he cease to observe the Christian forms of worship and to celebrate the sacraments; rather, he came to understand their limitations as religious *signs*. His own "statements" on doctrinal matters, he said, were to be regarded as "no more than working hypotheses" and as "vectors of free inquiry."[70] Religious forms and structures (doctrines, rituals, laws, etc.) were *signposts* to the

Absolute but should never be invested with any absolute value themselves.[71] In this insight he again echoes Schuon who writes:

> Exoterism consists in identifying transcendent realities with the dogmatic forms, and if need be, with the historical facts of a given Revelation, whereas esoterism refers in a more or less direct manner to these same realities.[72]

It is true that Abhishiktananda many times referred to the tensions arising out of the simultaneous "presence of the *Upanishads* and the Gospel in a single heart"[73] and that he sometimes used the language of fulfillment when addressing Christians; on occasions this would seem, at least in his later years, to have been a case of *upāya*, "skilful means" as the Buddhists have it, or what Schuon calls "saving mirages."[74] As Schuon also observes, "In religious exoterisms, efficacy at times takes the place of truth, and rightly so, given the nature of the men to whom they are addressed."[75] In Abhishiktananda's case we can trace through his writings a move *away* from all notions of Christian exclusivism and triumphalism, *through* the theology of fulfillment, *towards* the *sophia perennis*.

All the evidence suggests that Abhishiktananda did indeed undergo the plenary experience and see that Light that, in Koranic terms, is "neither of the East nor of the West." In communicating that experience, and the knowledge that it delivers, Abhishiktananda freely resorts to the spiritual vocabulary of both theistic Christianity and non-dualistic Hinduism. Take, for instance, passages such as these:

> The knowledge (*vidyā*) of Christ is identical with what the *Upanishads* call divine knowledge (*brahmavidyā*). . . . It comprises the whole of God's self-manifestation in time, and is one with his eternal self-manifestation.[76]

> Step by step I descended into what seemed to me to be successive depths of my true self—my being (*sat*), my awareness of being (*cit*), and my joy in being (*ānanda*). Finally nothing was left but he himself, the Only One, infinitely alone, Being, Awareness, and Bliss, *Saccidānanda*.[77]

In 1971, in his Introduction to the English edition of *Saccidananda*, Abhishiktananda had this to say:

> Dialogue may begin simply with relations of mutual sympathy. It only becomes worth while when it is accompanied by full openness . . . not merely at the intellectual level, but with regard to [the] inner life of the Spirit. Dialogue about doctrines will be more fruitful when it is rooted in a real spiritual experience at depth and when each one understands

that *diversity does not mean disunity, once the Center of all has been reached.*[78]

Abhishiktananda makes an interesting contrast with Monchanin insofar as he gave primacy to his own mystical realization over the theological doctrines to which he was formally committed as a Christian. As he somewhere remarked, "Truth has to be taken from wherever it comes; that Truth possesses us—we do not possess Truth," thus recalling St Ambrose's dictum that "All that is true, by whosoever spoken, is from the Holy Ghost."[79] On the basis of his own testimony and that of those who knew him in later years we can say of Abhishiktananda that through the penetration of religious forms he became a fully realized *sannyāsī*—which is to say, neither Hindu nor Christian, or, if one prefers, both Christian and Hindu, this only being possible at a mystical and esoteric level where the relative forms are universalized. As he wrote in *The Further Shore*, "The call to complete renunciation cuts across all *dharmas* and disregards all frontiers . . . it is anterior to every religious formulation."[80]

Vocation and Eucharist

There are two persistent motifs in Abhishiktananda's life in India which deserve mention here: his unwavering adherence to his vocation as a monk and to the celebration of the Eucharist. Whatever his uncertainties about where he stood in relation to Christianity and Vedanta, he was completely free of doubts about his role as a monk, a man of God. As Fr Vattakuzhy remarks in his study,

> The center of Abhishiktananda's life was his monastic consecration to which he was experientially and existentially committed. He came to India, not because he was a Christian, but because he was a monk.[81]

Raimon Panikkar addressed him on this issue in his "Letter to Abhishiktananda" (written on the second anniversary of his death):

> The center of your life was your monastic vocation. . . . You were tortured by the apparent incompatibility between Christianity and *Advaita*. Experientially and existentially committed to both, you could not solve the tension between the two, except perhaps at the very end of your life. . . . You doubted whether, out of loyalty to yourself, you should quit the Church; you hesitated to give yourself fully to *Advaita*, but you never for a moment questioned your monastic consecration, your way of life. . . . Your support was your life of a monk, and we must pay tribute to that pure and clear surrender of your existence which

allowed you to become a *kurukṣetra* (a battlefield), while the outcome of the war was still totally undecided.[82]

Similarly, he cleaved to the Eucharist which was an unending source of spiritual rejuvenation. However troubled he sometimes felt about the Church, even about Christianity as a whole, he never relinquished his faith in the efficacy of the rite. It may well be that it provided a kind of anchorage which could stabilize some of his psychic tensions. The editor of his journal has accented this

> often overlooked aspect of Dom Le Saux's spirituality—his Eucharistic devotion, that is to say, his rootedness in the earth, his ascent to the depth of matter—matter transfigured, divinized. It was the Mass that linked him to the Church whose function, as he said, was to preserve the Eucharist.[83]

This sacrament, Panikkar suggests, kept Abhishiktananda grounded and acted as a counterbalance to his aspiration to become an "acosmic"—which is to say "without birth, with no place, no goal, nothing."[84] Abhishiktananda himself believed there was a fundamental affinity between the Eucharistic mystery and the ideal of *sannyāsa*, and that the sacrament itself could be "a sign beyond signs," which is to say one infinitely surpassing the historical and religious context in which it first appeared.[85] Murray Rogers recalls celebrating the Eucharist daily with Abhishiktananda in his hermitage at Gyansu, in the last year of his life:

> And when I went to stay with him, Swamiji just rejoiced to celebrate the Eucharist every day. We spent hours at it! We'd go up the ladder in his *kutiya* [hut] to his chapel in the attic. It would be in complete chaos, boxes and trunks and pieces of rock. There in the middle was a little table a few inches from the floor and all his treasures were underneath so they were close by, incense and camphor and brass dishes. His stone chalice and paten bought in the bazaar at Haridwar. . .[86]

Of the Eucharist Abhishiktananda himself wrote in his journal:

> The Mass is not for getting anything whatever . . . it is like the expression of my being, like the expectation of and approach of the moment that comes in the moment that now is, in the same way as I draw breath in the power of this actual moment, bringing about also my presence to the moment which is coming.[87]

The sacrament also played a vital role in Abhishiktananda's deepening understanding of the "cosmic theophany." In *Saccidananda* he wrote:

The basis of the Eucharist and also of the whole sacramental character of the Church is to be found in the ascent of the whole cosmos—matter and spirit—towards its Lord. The Eucharist is the *anamnesis*, or memorial of all that has been and all that will be. It is the memorial of the Passion, also of the Incarnation, and so of the Creation.[88]

Last Years

In his last years Abhishiktananda assumed the role of guru to his only real disciple (using that word in its strict sense), the young French seminarian Marc Chaduc, who was given a joint Christian-Hindu initiation (*dīkṣā*) by Abhishiktananda and Swami Chidananda. Abhishiktananda spent a good deal of time at the Sivananda Ashram in his last years and became a close friend of Chidananda. Abhishiktananda's early advaitic experience at Arunachala and Tapovanam was deepened and enriched by further experiences in the two years before his death in 1973. One particular advaitic experience must be noted, as recounted by Marc Chaduc:

> It was on the way to Pulchatti that the grace erupted. In these mountains which have sheltered so many contemplatives, overwhelmed by the interior vision, the Father was seized by the mystery of the purely acosmic one who leaves all in response to the burning invitation of God. The blessed one who receives this light, the Father told me, is paralyzed, torn asunder, he can no longer speak nor think, he remains there, immobile outside of time and space, alone in the very solitude of the Alone. Absorbed in this way, the Father relived—lived again—the sudden eruption of the infinite Column of fire and the light of Arunachala.[89]

One measure of Abhishiktananda's mystical extinction in advaitic non-dualism, and the problems this posed for some of his Christian contemporaries (and for all rigidly theistic theologies), is evident in the manuscript of a talk he prepared in the last months of his life:

> In this annihilating experience [of *advaita*] one is no longer able to project in front of oneself anything whatsoever, to recognize any other "pole" to which to refer oneself and to give the name of God. Once one has reached that innermost center, one is so forcibly seized by the mystery that one can no longer utter a "Thou" or an "I." Engulfed in the abyss, we disappear to our own eyes, to our own consciousness. The proximity of that mystery which the prophetic traditions name "God" burns us so completely that there is no longer any question of discovering it in the depths of oneself or oneself in the depths of it. In

the very engulfing, the gulf has vanished. If a cry was still possible—
at the moment perhaps of disappearing into the abyss—it would be
paradoxically: "but there is no abyss, no gulf, no distance!" There is
no face-to-face, for there is only That-Which-Is, and no other to name
it.[90]

This passage, reminiscent of Eckhart, can take its place amongst the
most exalted of mystical commentaries; it also dispels any doubts as to
the validity of Abhishiktananda's own mystical annihilation, called by
whatever name.

The last decade of Abhishiktananda's life saw the publication of a
series of books bearing the fragrance of his long years of prayer, meditation, study, and spiritual awakening, his "literary apostolate" as it has
been called.[91] The English-language versions of these books are: *The
Mountain of the Lord* (1966), an account of his pilgrimage to Gangotri,
Prayer (1967), *Hindu-Christian Meeting Point* (1969), *The Church in
India* (1969), *Towards the Renewal of the Indian Church* (1970), *Saccidananda: A Christian Experience of Advaita* (1974), probably his most
mature theological work, *Guru and Disciple* (1974) in which he recalls
his experiences with Ramana and with Gnanananda, and *The Further
Shore* (1975), his deepest meditation on the *Upanishads* and the ideal
of *sannyāsa*. *The Secret of Arunachala* (1979) and a collection of several
essays, *The Eyes of Light* (1983), appeared posthumously.

As his works became known in Europe he was several times invited
to return to the West. Raimon Panikkar recalls one such occasion:

> A course was to be given on Indian metaphysics, especially yoga, and
> you were asked to preside as the "key figure," even the "guru." You
> could not deny the gravity of the invitation nor the possible good you
> might do. Moreover, you agreed that a visit to the West after so many
> years of absence would give you not only an insight into a changed
> Occident but a new perspective on India and her spiritual message. Yet
> you refused. I vividly remember our conversations and letters on the
> subject. You had an almost physical aversion to, and mistrust of, the
> idea of yourself as a "key figure" on a temporal mission. Instinctively
> you rejected the part, feeling in your heart that it would betray the
> plunge you had taken into an experience allowing of no return. . . . You
> resisted playing the *jīvanmukta*, the accomplished saint. . . . You did not
> accept or ever play such a role.[92]

Abhishiktananda never figured himself to be anyone special—just a
humble monk. As his sixtieth birthday approached, some of his friends
canvassed the idea of a special tribute with which to mark the occasion.
His response in a letter to one of its proponents:

The interest that I arouse is restricted to a very limited circle. My withdrawal to the Himalayas perhaps adds a mythical touch to my personality. In any case, I cannot imagine where you have "fished up" this idea of a commemorative volume. . . . It would be a betrayal of all that I stand for, solitude, silence and monastic poverty. . . . Nothing else remains for me but to be a hermit for good, not a mere salesman of solitude and monastic life.[93]

Mother Yvonne Lebeau, with whom Abhishiktananda became friendly at the Sivananda Ashram, has left us with a snapshot of Abhishiktananda in his later years:

Nothing seemed to vex him; he was always smiling and happy. I treated him as my pal. He was lucid. . . . He did things without ill-feeling or criticism. . . . He was pure like a child, and strikingly honest.[94]

John Alter, the son of some friends at the Rajpur Retreat and Study Center, recorded his impressions of Abhishiktananda in early 1972:

His eyes twinkled. That struck me immediately. His bright, sparkling gaze. And the comical nimbus of white hair. A jester in the court of God . . . with his disorganized simplicity. The first glance deepened, of course. . . . As the days opened around us, his silence—the sadness which sometimes enveloped him—his spiritual authority and experience—the realism of his instructions—his very real and practical affection for each of us as fellow pilgrims on the long path home—his delight in the day and the moment—enriched and affirmed this first impression. Nothing was denied. At the mouth of the *guha* Swamiji did know mirth. The encounter deep within the speechless silence of himself did not eclipse or deflate the garrulous human reality. . . . Swamiji knew that paradox, the comical disproportion between advaitic experience and the ordinary, daily world . . . what he made manifest in his human, often less than royal, way was the vow of "insecurity" he had taken. It was a vow which committed him to an almost unimaginable loneliness. Out of that solitude he returned to us, with a twinkle in his eye.[95]

Knocking on Heaven's Door

Early on the morning of June 30, 1973, a small group of people gathered on the banks of the Ganges, close to the Sivananda Ashram at Rishikesh. We have arrived back at the scene at which we started—Chaduc's initiation, in which Swami Chidananda "co-opted him into the host of monks and seers of India" and Abhishiktananda "united him with the succession of monks that goes back to the desert Fathers, and behind that to Elijah," and from which he emerged as Swami Ajatananda ("Bliss of the Not-born"), immediately to set off as a wandering beggar.[96] In a letter to Murray Rogers Abhishiktananda wrote,

> Marc has received *sannyāsī* in the Ganga from Chidanandaji and myself. Very simple ceremony, but it was simply too beautiful. The three of us were simply radiant. Deep in the Ganga he pronounced the old formula of renunciation. I join him; he plunges into (the) water; I raise him up, and we sing our favorite mantras to the *Puruṣa*. He discards all his clothes in (the) water, and I receive him as from the maternal womb. We envelop him in the fire-colored dress. We communicate to him the *mahavākyas*, and I give him the "envoi": "Go to where there is no return.". . .[97]

This lovely ceremony on the banks of India's most holy river, in the company of his disciple and the Hindu holy man, was to be one of the last formal events of Abhishiktananda's life. Soon after he wrote to Ajatananda,

> It was too wonderful that morning of June 30. . . .
> Your *dīkṣā* moved me
> To the depths of my being,
> stealing me away from myself,
> losing me in infinite space, where I no longer know anything,
> where I look for myself in vain! OM![98]

In the fortnight following, he spent three days with Ajatananda in complete isolation, without food, at a Shaivite temple at Ranagal, close to Rishikesh. James Stuart describes this experience as one of "holy inebriation," "like that of the *keśī* (hairy ones) of the *Rig-Veda*."[99] Ajatananda wrote of Abhishiktananda at this time:

> These were days when Swamiji discovered ever deeper abysses of the soul. . . . The inbreaking of the Spirit snatched him away from himself, and shone through every inch of his being, an inner apocalypse which at times blazed forth outwardly in a glorious transfiguration.[100]

On July 14th, in the Rishikesh bazaar, shopping for groceries before returning to Ranagal, Abhishiktananda was felled to the ground. Mother Yvonne Lebeau, his compatriot and friend from the Sivanananda Ashram, happened to be passing and was able to come to his assistance. He had, in his own words, been "brushed by Siva's column of fire," an experience he described as his definitive "awakening," his discovery of the Grail, whose physiological accompaniment was a massive heart attack:

Really a door opened in heaven while I was lying on the pavement. But a heaven which was not the opposite of earth, something which was neither life nor death, but simply "being," "awakening" . . . beyond all myths and symbols. . . . That coronary attack was only a part, but an essential one, of a whole process of grace.[101]

He wrote in one of his last letters, "the quest is fulfilled."[102] As Confucius said, "one who has seen the way in the morning can gladly die in the evening"—but, to his own surprise, Abhishiktananda lingered on for several months, concluding that the only possible reason for this "extension" was the opportunity to share something of his final awakening with his friends. He was taken to Rajpur and thence to Indore to be cared for by the Franciscan Sisters in the Roberts Nursing Home where he found "a homely atmosphere, medical attention, suitable food, and all that 'for the love of God.'"[103] In a letter to Ajatananda on October 9th he feels the time is near to abandon this "old garment"[104] and writes to his beloved sister Marie-Thérèse a fortnight later: "When the body no longer responds to the guidance of the spirit, then you understand St Paul's agonized desire to be relieved of it."[105] Finally, on December 7th, after a day during which he had spent much time contemplating an icon of Elijah, and with prayerful friends at his bedside, Abhishiktananda crossed to the further shore.

*

We will bring this sketch towards its conclusion with a few personal reminiscences from three women. The first, Bettina Bäumer, met Abhishiktananda in 1963, at Shantivanam, and later spent a good deal of time with him on his visits to Varanasi. In her reflections about Abhishiktananda she draws attention to several aspects of his personality and character which could only be fully appreciated by those knew him intimately:

He had the gift of drawing out the best in a person and lifting her up to his own level . . . his great simplicity of life, and his indomitable faith in the spirit of India . . . he was never discouraged from the path he had chosen, and he never lost faith. In fact, there were not too many who could understand him and he passed through phases of loneliness. . . . Another sign of his true contemplative spirit was his love for nature. . . . Another aspect of the human side . . . was his sense of humor. He could laugh at himself and did not take himself too seriously. Unlike some spiritual persons, he did not mix up the seriousness of his concerns and ideals with his own person.[106]

An unnamed Sister of the Sacred Heart, a participant in a 1972 seminar on ashram life, remembered Abhishiktananda this way:

> He could be "a child among children.". . . To me he was the embodiment of what "Unless you become as little children. . ." means. His joy, spontaneity, and total inner freedom made us feel completely at home with him.[107]

Early in 1973 Abhishiktananda took great pleasure in the visit of an American friend with whom he had corresponded for fifteen years. She was Mrs Ann-Marie Stokes, also a Breton but for many years resident in New York where she was deeply involved with Dorothy Day and the Catholic Worker movement. After meeting her in Delhi he took her to Haridwar and Rishikesh and to the retreat center in Rajpur. Later they met up with Marc Chaduc. After Abhishiktananda's passing Mrs Stokes wrote a small recollection for a memorial volume which eventually found its way, in truncated form, into James Stuart's biography. There are no metaphysical flights in the piece, no theological ruminations, no weighing up of Abhishiktananda's significance—rather, some deeply affectionate memories of the person himself. From a few excerpts we can catch some further glimpses of Abhishiktananda's personality:

> Fifteen years of correspondence create both friendship and an image, but the living image was slightly different, more subtle, more shaded, harsher, more imperative. And then the little personal touches—using beautiful stilted French, memories of his humanities as he entered the monastery, he would sometimes interject a slang word, common to college boys of his time, that added great flavor to his conversation. Impossible feats were his daily bread, but the usual little materialistic things became great undertakings and filled him with misgivings. Whilst traveling, he was agitated and constantly in a hurry; and I can still remember those scalding cups of tea taken by the roadside. . . . His asbestos-lined throat had absorbed them while we were still wetting our lips. . . . He slept on the ground on a blanket in a corner among his books, his only possessions. . . . Simone Weil and her ardent wish to be a bridge between cultures and religions was often quoted, and also her magnificent thoughts on the Holy Grail. . . . We differed a good deal about suffering and its impact, and suddenly he said an extraordinary thing: "I do not know either suffering or evil.". . . Little by little I discovered his tremendous intelligence—how beautiful a gift he had surrendered—and his eminently poetic personality, not only as a poet—"Arunachala" is a great poem—but in his poetic view of things. There too I discovered his absolute poverty and his insecurity by probing (he never complained), worn like a splendid mantle and embellished by the immense value he gave to the "invaluable.". . .

The bazaar fascinated him with its handicrafts, and he gravely gave advice on my purchases. And then we made our way to Rishikesh, to Sivananda Ashram. Its director, Chidanandaji, was a deeply admired friend. The mutual relationship of these two men was a joy to behold. . . . Several times it happened that Swamiji would say: "Now I can go, my message has been heard," his Nunc Dimittis. All his modest desires had been granted in this world, and the other unlimited one seized upon him from time [to] time.[108]

*

It can hardly be doubted that, in the words of his friend Raimon Panikkar, Abhishiktananda was "one of the most authentic witnesses of our times of the encounter in depth between Christian and Eastern spiritualities."[109] One measure of this was the considerable esteem in which Abhishiktananda was held in some Vedantic circles. Father Gispert-Sauch recounts a visit to the Sivananda Ashram where he discovered that not only had Abhishiktananda's writings on *sannyāsa* (later published as *The Further Shore*) been serialized in the ashram's monthly publication, but that they were obligatory reading for all of the novices, and that the novices discussed these essays with Swami Chidananda who regarded them as giving "beautiful expression to the authentic meaning of *sannyāsa* in the Indian tradition."[110] Abhishiktananda himself came to embody and to live this ideal. There can be no more fitting epitaph for Swamiji than one of his favorite Upanishadic verses, to which he returned again and again:

> I know him, that great *Puruṣa*
> Of the color of the sun,
> Beyond all darkness.
> He who has known him
> Goes beyond death.
> There is no other way.
> (*Śvetāśvatara Upanishad*, III.8.)

Notes

1. From Abhishiktananda, "Le Père Monchanin," quoted in A. Rawlinson, *Book of Enlightened Masters*, 148. An almost identical passage can be found in Abhishiktananda, *Swami Parama Arubi Anandam*, 28.
2. From "Renewal and Discipline," quoted in T. Conner, "Monk of Renewal," 183.
3. On his ordination as a priest in 1935 he also took on the name "Briac" in

honor of his hometown.

4. L 4.12.28, 2-3.

5. P. Coff, "Abhishiktananda," 2. For another translation of this passage and some commentary by Abhishiktananda, see *Swami Parama Arubi Anandam*, 98-99.

6. L 7.

7. L 13.2.67, 12.

8. L 18.8.47, 15.

9. L 22.9.73, 312.

10. Letter to Fr Monchanin, 18.8.47, in EL 11.

11. As well as supporting the radical experiment proposed by Monchanin and Le Saux, the Bishop made many decisions which, in the context of the times, were courageous and controversial—permitting these priests to don the garb of the Hindu *sannyāsī*, for instance, or encouraging their visits to Ramana Maharshi's ashram. On the question of visiting Hindu ashrams and the like, see du Boulay, 64.

12. L 7.8.47, 14-15.

13. From a pamphlet on Saccidananda Ashram and from an article in *Clergy Monthly*, August 1971, both quoted in Stephens, 115.

14. The biographical information following is taken from J.G. Weber, *In Quest of the Absolute*, and from S. Rodhe, *Jules Monchanin*, after *Swami Parama Arubi Anandam* the two best sources available in English.

15. Swami Arokianadar, "He Taught Me to Appreciate my Motherland," in Abhishiktananda (ed), *Swami Parama Arubi Anandam*, 107.

16. Dr Biot, quoted by E. Duperray, "A Sign of the Spirit," in Abhishiktananda (ed), *Swami Parama Arubi Anandam*, 99-100.

17. J.G. Weber, *In Quest of the Absolute*, 16.

18. Abhishiktananda, *Swami Parama Arubi Anandam*, 2.

19. J.G. Weber, *In Quest of the Absolute*, 56.

20. On this name see Friesen, 1, and L 40.

21. In J.G. Weber, *In Quest of the Absolute*, 73.

22. Bede Griffiths quoted in J.G. Weber, *In Quest of the Absolute*, 2.

23. BA 24.

24. BA 27.

25. BA 90.

26. Abhishiktananda quoted in du Boulay, 63.

27. See Abhishiktananda, *Swami Parama Arubi Anandam*, 18-19.

28. J.G. Weber, *In Quest of the Absolute*, 21-22.

29. J. Stuart in L 52.

30. For a clear-eyed and sensitive account of some of the difficulties in the inter-relations of Abhishiktananda, Monchanin, Mahieu, and Griffiths, see du Boulay, 153-155.

31. Quoted in S. Rohde, *Jules Monchanin*, 67.

32. The phrase "invisible ministry" is Bettina Bäumer's.

33. Quoted in J.G. Weber, *In Quest of the Absolute*, 3.

34. For some material on the Christian ashram movement see H. Ralston, *Christian Ashrams: A New Religious Movement in Contemporary India* (1987); Sister Vandana Mataji, *Gurus, Ashrams, and Christians* (1978), and "Spiritual Formation in Ashrams in Contemporary India" (1990); Sister Vandana Mataji (ed), *Christian Ashrams: A Movement with a Future?* (1993); Philipos Thomas, "Christian Ashrams and Evangelization of India," *Indian Church History Review*, 11, 1977.

35. Quoted in M. Rogers, *Abhishiktananda*, 2.

36. SA 9.

37. Quoted in S. Rohde, *Jules Monchanin*, 33.

38. F. Schuon, *Language of the Self*, 44, and *Spiritual Perspectives*, 122; the passage quoted here is a combination of two translations in these volumes.

39. Quoted in J.M.D. Stuart, "Sri Ramana Maharshi and Abhishiktananda," 170.

40. Quoted in Baumer-D, 316.

41. Quoted in Baumer-D, 315, 317.

42. L 24.12.55, 87.

43. GD 23.

44. J.E. Royster, "Abhishiktananda: Hindu-Christian Monk," 311.

45. GD 27.

46. L 14.3.56, 89.

47. See Friesen, 100.

48. See C.T. Indra et al, *Swami Gnanananda*, 2.

49. GD 15.

50. For an article by the swami on Gnanananda, see "Sadguru Sri Gnanananda," *Monastic Interreligious Dialogue*, Bulletin 64, May 2000; website. Includes detailed reference to Abhishiktananda.

51. See also Baumer-D, 314.

52. D 19.9.53, 73.

53. D 19.9.53, 73.

54. This translation from Panikkar, 438—a better translation than the one in D 180.

55. L 24.10.1960, 132.

56. D 12.4.1957, 204.

57. For a detailed account of Abhishiktananda's inner travail during this period, see du Boulay, chs. 9, 11.

58. 1970 letter quoted in Baumer-D, 314.

59. L 23.7.71, 331-2. (*Sadguru*: "real guru" or, sometimes, "root guru.")

60. B. Bäumer, "Swami Abhishiktananda," website (italics mine).

61. Abhishiktananda uses this image in reference to his former life. D 27.8.55, 118.

62. L 5.7.66, 182.

63. Quoted in S. Visvanathan, *An Ethnography of Mysticism*, 72.

64. Quoted in S. Visvanathan, *An Ethnography of Mysticism*, 73.

65. Stephens, 44.

66. M. Rogers, "Swamiji the Friend," 24.
67. GD 162.
68. Diary 30.6.64, quoted in J.M.D. Stuart, "Sri Ramana Maharshi and Abhishiktananda," 173.
69. F. Schuon, *Stations of Wisdom*, 16.
70. Baumer-D, 320.
71. SA 47.
72. F. Schuon, *Logic and Transcendence*, 144.
73. Letter to Odette Baumer-Despeigne, January 1969, quoted in Baumer-D, 310
74. F. Schuon, *Survey of Metaphysics and Esoterism*, 185, n2.
75. F. Schuon, *The Transfiguration of Man*, 8.
76. GD xi.
77. SAC 172.
78. SAC xiii (italics mine).
79. St Ambrose quoted in A.K. Coomaraswamy, *Selected Letters*, 108.
80. FS 27.
81. Vattakuzhy, 210.
82. Panikkar, 446.
83. R. Panikkar, *Introduction to Ascent to the Depth of the Heart*, xxi.
84. R. Panikkar, *Introduction to Ascent to the Depth of the Heart*, xx.
85. See FS 50-52.
86. M. Rogers, *Abhishiktananda*, 15.
87. D 1.12.1970, 324.
88. SAC 59.
89. Quoted in Friesen, 154.
90. EG 152.
91. Vattakuzhy, 82.
92. Panikkar, 435-436.
93. L 11.12.69, 223.
94. Quoted in Vattakuzhy, 91-92.
95. Quoted in L 266n.
96. L 6.7.73, 303.
97. L 3.7.73, 302.
98. Quoted in Baumer-D, 327.
99. James Stuart in L 305.
100. Quoted in M. Rogers, *Abhishiktananda*, 34. (The fact that this kind of language is used indiscriminately about all manner of dubious "gurus" should not blind us to the fact that, in some cases—and this is one—such language is perfectly appropriate.)
101. L 10.9.73, 311.
102. Letter to Odette Baumer-Despeigne, October 1973, quoted in Baumer-D, 329.
103. L 28.8.73, 309.
104. L 9.10.73, 315.

105. L 22.10.73, 317.
106. B. Bäumer, "Abhishiktananda," website.
107. Quoted in L 264.
108. Quoted in L 287-289.
109. Panikkar quoted in J.E. Royster, "Abhishiktananda: Hindu-Christian Monk," 308.
110. G. Gispert-Sauch, "The Spirituality of Abhishiktananda" in Vandana (ed), *Swami Abhishiktananda*, 70.

2

Friends and Influences

Charity respects and brings together in a higher
unity the twofold mystery of the person—his individual uniqueness and also his reciprocal presence
to others.

Man is a social being. . . . Man discovers himself,
realizes himself only in meeting with others.

Abhishiktananda[1]

We now turn to the principal influences which helped to shape Abhishiktananda and to a few jottings on some of those people with whom
Abhishiktananda had significant relationships. These will yield further
insights into Abhishiktananda's life and personality.

Family and French Catholicism

One refrain in Abhishiktananda's life is his unwavering love of Brittany
and of his family. To the very end of his life he revered the memory of
his mother to whom he was intensely devoted, cherished his recollec-
tions of childhood and family life, and took the closest interest in the
welfare of his siblings and their families. He also retained a passionate
love for Brittany and in later years wrote that he had never returned
because he doubted whether he could "bear it emotionally" and feared
that he might be unable to return to his "role" in India. In the same
letter he writes,

> The Himalayas are splendid, and Arunachala is greater still; yet what
> can be compared to the sea of my Emerald Coast. . . . All this belongs
> to the depth of my being. It is like those Tridentine Masses and the
> Gregorian chant of the monasteries, which I would doubtless put on
> again like a glove, even after having lived the marvelous experience of
> "spontaneous" Masses or those Masses in the Upanishadic tradition
> which I celebrate each morning and which help me to carry on.[2]

In his now well-known "Letter" Raimon Panikkar wrote:

> You were one of the most authentic "Western" spirits ever to expose
> himself to the genuine "Indian" experience. You had a truly Western
> character and a profound Western formation. *Only a man equipped*

*with all the traditional Western resources could have done what you did. .
. . I have just gone through your manuscript, Amour et Sagesse, written
in 1942 for your mother. It is a moving confession of your traditional
Catholic faith. It also shows a command of Scripture, Tradition, and
Theology that many a highly placed professor might envy.*[3]

We have already noted Abhishiktananda's remark, close to his
death, that "Kergonan has been the background of all that I have been
able to do here."[4] Throughout his life he retained close ties not only to
his family but with the Abbey where he had spent his formative years
and where he had drunk deeply from the well-springs of the Judeo-
Christian tradition, particularly the Patristic and mystical literature.
Joseph Lemarié, who entered Kergonan in 1935, was to remain a close
friend and correspondent. In his final years, after a quarter of a century
on the sub-continent, Abhishiktananda momentarily entertained the
idea of returning to Kergonan.[5] Whilst it is true that the "call to India"
was impelled partly by a "deep dissatisfaction"[6] with various aspects
of monastery life in France it would be a grave error to suppose that
Abhishiktananda's immersion in Hindu spirituality was, even at the
unconscious level, an attempt to "escape" from or to abandon his Christian faith. Even the most cursory reading of his journal and letters makes
this clear. No, the experiences of India were not only to modify but
to enrich his Christian faith and to synthesize it with *advaita* in lived
experience. Abhishiktananda didn't jettison his Christian heritage when
he embarked for the sub-continent—how could he? It was woven into
the fabric of his being, as were his family and home-place.

Abhishiktananda's Reading

Like many Europeans of an intellectual bent, Abhishiktananda was
addicted to reading; even during his sojourns on Arunachala, much to
the astonishment of some of his fellow anchorites (and to the anger of
a few!), he remained an inveterate reader. One of the hermits asked
him why he bothered with these books: "You open them, and you
close them. What is that, compared with the book of the heart?"[7] And
on another occasion, "There is only one book, the 'living' book that is
within you. . .".[8] The editor of his journal tells us that he was seriously
shaken and somewhat ashamed when a *sannyāsī* visiting his hermitage
at Gyansu expressed amazement over the number of books Abhishiktananda had in his possession.[9] He was at least half-persuaded that books
themselves, even religious ones, were an obstacle to the final realization—but he couldn't help himself and remained a voracious reader.

On leaving Shantivanam Abhishiktananda had given away most of his books but at the time of his death he still owned several hundred, now in a dusty room of the Vidyajyoti College Library in Delhi. Amongst these are to be found, unsurprisingly, the *Gītā*, several editions of the *Upanishads*, writings by Sankara, Ramanuja and various poet-saints, Sanskrit dictionaries, and the *Dhammapada*. Modern Hindu writers are represented by Aurobindo, Gandhi, Radhakrishnan, Ramana, Ramdas, and Sivananda whilst traditional Western writers include Plato, Plotinus, Augustine, Aquinas, Eckhart, St John of the Cross, St Teresa of Avila, Rhenish mystics such as Tauler and Ruysbroeck, Pascal and Thomas Merton, as well as *The Cloud of Unknowing* and *The Way of a Pilgrim*. Modern philosophers and Indologists in the collection include Barth, Bultmann, Henri de Lubac, Eliade, Gilson, Heidegger, Jaspers, Kierkegaard, Louis Renou, Rudolf Otto, Simone Weil, and Heinrich Zimmer. The only fictional literature comes from Tolstoy and Dostoevsky. There are also significant runs of several Catholic journals such as *La Vie Spirituelle, Verbum Caro, Concilium,* and *Carmel* as well as Indian publications like *Saiva Siddhanta* and *The Mountain Path* (the journal of the Ramana Ashram). We find in Abhishiktananda's diary and letters countless references to other books and authors. But the list above provides a fair sample though it is perhaps worth noting that Abhishiktananda was more widely read in Buddhism than it suggests; his writings include references to the works of such expositors as D.T. Suzuki, and he refers several times in *Guru and Disciple* to the ways in which Gnanananda himself helped him better to understand the Buddha's teachings on *anātman* (no-soul), *śūnyatā* (voidness), and the imperatives of *dhyāna* (meditation). In his late years Abhishiktananda was also much impressed by his meetings with Fr Oshida, a Japanese Dominican who combined "in a marvelous harmony" his ancestral Zen and his Christian faith. The Orthodox Christian mystics are also somewhat under-represented in the list above, as are the early Church Fathers who had such an influence on him during the years in the Abbey and to whom he often referred in later years. Ignatius of Antioch was one of his favorites. Even a selective catalogue of Abhishiktananda's reading must also include the works of Olivier Lacombe, Indologist and Professor of Comparative Religion at the Sorbonne; it was from his works that Abhishiktananda derived some of his understanding of Ramana's teachings. He was also influenced, for a time, by Lacombe's "fulfillment theology."[10] Among many other contemporary books and authors to whom he refers in his letters and journals we find Jean Herbert, Lanzo del Vasto, Claudel, Buber, Camus, Jung, Hans Küng, Rilke, Rimbaud, John Robinson, Jean Daniélou, Schillebeeckx, Teilhard de Chardin, Tillich, and Lossky. We can surmise that Abhishiktananda's reading focused on theological, philosophical, mystical, and Indological works with the occasional foray into more literary creations. But we should not imagine that Abhishiktananda suffered from that bugbear of modern intellectual life—the notion that profane "research" is an end in itself. René Guénon properly remarked that

> The passion for research taken as an end in itself [is] . . . mental restlessness without end and without issue. . . . This substitution of research for knowledge [i.e., the knowledge of higher things] is simply giving up the proper object of intelligence.[11]

In recalling Abhishiktananda's reading let us also not forget his own heartfelt observation that

> No religious man indeed wants to develop and feed his mind simply for the mind's sake alone. As the ancient authors put it, there is no knowledge which should not pass into love. There is no knowledge which should not go beyond the mind and reach to the very source of the mind—the heart—the "heart" understood in its Indian meaning (which was Pascal's too) as the center of being, the place where God abides.[12]

Fr Jules Monchanin

In the last chapter mention was made of the personality, the work, and the influence of Fr Jules Monchanin, particularly as the co-founder of Shantivanam. Here we will reflect a little further on Monchanin's influence on Abhishiktananda, and compare their positions on the central issue with which they were mutually concerned in the Shantivanam years, the relationship of Christianity and Hinduism, and the role of Christian contemplatives in India.

The annals of Christian missionizing are replete with stories of heroic self-sacrifice, of dedication to tireless, often thankless work in arid fields, an exacting and lonely life in the service of Christian ideals—precisely, the pursuit of a vocation. Monchanin, however, is a fascinating case because in him the missionary dilemma, if one may so express it, becomes fully and acutely self-conscious. The poignancy and tragedy of Monchanin's life in India is that he was unable to find his way out of the quandary. Here is a telling passage from Alain Daniélou's autobiography:

> Then there was the curious little ashram of Père Montchanin (sic). This priest . . . had been deeply influenced by Hinduism and wanted

to combine the two religions. He wore the draped orange cloth of Hindu monks, but obviously did not perform the ritual ablutions. . . . He lived in a hermitage with a few followers and exerted a great influence on that special brand of foreigner who, while acknowledging the spiritual, philosophical, and moral superiority of Hinduism, still insists on Christian supremacy. . . . . Instead of mellowing through Hinduism, Montchanin and his devotees remained frustrated, neurotic, ill at ease, and, on the whole, rather disagreeable people. . . . The word ashram, which is literally "a place of rest" has come to mean "a pseudo-spiritual gathering place for maladjusted Westerners with a craving for exoticism."[13]

This passage is itself somewhat "disagreeable," lacking in charity, tainted with that condescension which is often the mark of the Western convert and oblivious to Monchanin's saintly qualities (which any number of people—Hindus, Christians, and others alike—have attested). Nonetheless, it is insightful. It is perfectly clear from Monchanin's own writings that he intuitively understood "the limits of religious expansionism" (to borrow a phrase from Schuon). He was intelligent enough to see that insofar as Christians were bent on converting Indians, the enterprise was doomed to failure, the odd individual convert only being the exception that proves the rule. He rightly sensed that devout Hindus found the idea of conversion abhorrent—"a betrayal, cowardice."[14] Shortly before his death he wrote,

The root of the matter is that Hindus are not spiritually uneasy. They believe they possess supreme wisdom and thus how could they attach any importance to the fluctuations or investigations of those who possess lesser wisdom. Christ is one among *avatāras*. Christianity in their eyes is a perfect moral doctrine, but a metaphysics which stops on the threshold of the ultimate metamorphosis.[15]

Monchanin was also, as Daniélou intimates, well-equipped to appreciate the vast storehouse of Indian spirituality. But throughout he felt bound to the conventional Christian belief in the ultimate superiority of his own faith, a position to which he was theologically committed by the weight of the centuries. His friend Père Henri de Lubac had characterized Monchanin's task this way: "to rethink everything in the light of theology, and to rethink theology through mysticism."[16] The problem was that the theology and the mysticism were pulling in opposite directions, the tension arising out of a dogmatic literalism and an ossified exoterism in the Catholic Church which insisted on the *exclusive* truths of Christianity and, *ipso facto*, on its *superiority* to other faiths. During a near-fatal illness in 1932 Monchanin had vowed that, if he were to recover, he would devote himself to the salvation of India:[17] his years in India taught him, at least sub-consciously, that India (insofar as it still abided in Hindu orthodoxy) was in no need of salvation! In the early 50s he wrote, "I confess, the more I deal with Hindus, the less I see my way," and "To speak of *christianizing Hinduism* is no doubt improper."[18] Eventually he returned to his earlier position, claiming that, "Our task . . . is the same as that of the Greek fathers: to accept that which is compatible, to reject that which is incompatible with Christianity. And the rest is vertigo or betrayal."[19] Consider a sample of quotes from Monchanin's writings:

> India has stood for three millennia, if not longer, as the seat of one of the principal civilizations of mankind, equal to if not greater than that of Europe and China.

> India has received from the Almighty an uncommon gift, an unquenchable thirst for whatever is spiritual. Since the time of the *Vedas* and the *Upanishads*, countless numbers of its sons have been great seekers of God.

> Century after century there rose up seers and poets singing the joys and sorrows of a soul in quest of the One, and philosophers reminding every man of the supremacy of contemplation.

Cheek-by-jowl with lofty passages such as these we find quite contradictory ones:

> Unfortunately Indian wisdom is tainted with erroneous tendencies. . . . Outside the unique revelation and the unique Church man is always and everywhere incapable of sifting truth from falsehood and good from evil.

> So also, confident in the indefectible guidance of the Church, we hope that India, once baptized into the fullness of its body and soul and into the depth of its age-long quest for Brahma, will reject its pantheistic tendencies and, discovering in the splendors of the Holy Spirit the true mysticism and finding at last the vainly longed-for philosophical and theological equilibrium between antagonistic trends of thought, will bring forth for the good of humanity and the Church and ultimately for the glory of God unparalleled galaxies of saints and doctors.

> We cannot hide [Hinduism's] fundamental error and its essential divergence in terms of Christianity. Hinduism must reject its *ātman-brahman* equation, if it is to enter into Christ.[20]

How much easier Monchanin's life would have been had the Vatican II renovation of Catholic attitudes to other religions taken place two decades earlier. (Vatican II was, in common parlance, "a mixed bag" but the mitigation of centuries of rigid Christian exclusivism was a significant step in the right direction.) How much agonizing he might also have been spared by recourse to the works of traditionalists such as his compatriot René Guénon. Seyyed Hossein Nasr has stated the problem in a nutshell:

> The essential problem that the study of religion poses is how to preserve religious truth, traditional orthodoxy, the dogmatic theological structures of one's own tradition, and yet gain knowledge of other traditions and accept them as spiritually valid ways and roads to God.[21]

This was the problem which Monchanin could never quite resolve. His successor, Bede Griffiths, was able to at least partially resolve the dilemma by discerning that the task at hand was not to "Christianize" Hinduism—an undertaking to which the Indians themselves remained, for the most part, supremely indifferent—but to "Hinduize" Christianity, that is, to recover the mystical and contemplative dimension of the Christian tradition, by recourse to India's sapiential wisdom and a more or less intact spiritual methodology, still comparatively untouched by the ravages of modernity.

Abhishiktananda had a more natural affinity for the actual practices of Hindu spirituality than did Monchanin and was less troubled by the *doctrinal* tensions between the two traditions which he was seeking to bridge. It is surely significant that it was Abhishiktananda who was able to surrender to the extraordinary *darśana* of Ramana. It is also suggestive that of the three Benedictines most closely associated with Shantivanam, only Le Saux became universally known under his Indian name. Unlike Monchanin, he became the *chelā* of a Hindu guru, and was at home in the pilgrimage sites and dharamsalas, the maths and ashrams of India, mixing freely with swamis and *sādhus* over the length and breadth of the subcontinent. One also gets the impression from reading the writings of the two men (including their more intimate letters and journals) that Abhishiktananda suffers little of Monchanin's angst about their missionizing. Indeed, he affirms quite explicitly that the true monk has no essential function but to *be*.[22]

In the early days of their association Monchanin had written, "As the days pass in his company, I admire more and more the scarcely believable *convergences* of his views with my own aspirations. And this is all the more *striking* because on the humanist plane . . . we differ so much."[23] But, as Panikkar has observed, it was inevitable that the divergences in both personality and theological outlook should in time lead to some estrangement. Panikkar himself summed up these differences by likening Monchanin to *logos* and Abhishiktananda to *pneuma*, by which terms he was no doubt alluding to the "Greek" rationalism of the former, compared with Abhishiktananda's more intuitive and experiential approach. After the first few years of their association Monchanin became increasingly troubled by Abhishiktananda's mystical excursions into *advaita* and yoga, and disapproved of his travels to Rishikesh, "a place where *sādhus*, real or supposedly so (both kinds no doubt) devote themselves to delusive exercises, verging on mirage."[24] In a letter to Abbé Edouard Duperray in 1955, referring to Abhishiktananda, Monchanin confided that

> The institutional Church is a burden to him (to him who was earlier devoted to Canon Law and Liturgy!); he suffers from its narrowness, realized through his contact with Hinduism. Basically he comes from a *rigorist* and even *integrist* theology: the change is too sudden. . . . I react in a contrary direction; never have I felt myself intellectually more *Christian* and also, I must say, more *Greek*. I experience a growing horror at the forms of muddled thinking in this "beyond thought" which most often proves to be only a "falling short of thought," in which everything gets drowned.[25]

Abhishiktananda echoed these thoughts when he wrote, in 1954, that Monchanin

> is too Greek to go to the depths. India presses relentlessly beyond concepts, beyond *manas* [mind]; how will the Greek, even if a follower of Plotinus, ever make the sacrifice of his *nous*? And yet, neither the self, nor therefore India, will ever be reached through concepts.[26]

In some undated notes Monchanin wrote,

> It seems to me more and more doubtful that the essence of Christianity can be found by going through *Advaita* (the non-dualism of Sankara). *Advaita*, like yoga and more than yoga, is an abyss. Whoever dizzily plunges into it cannot know what he will find in its depths. I fear it may be *himself* rather than the living, triune God.[27]

It was a measure of Abhishiktananda's respect for his companion that he took these misgivings to heart and for many years was troubled by the possibility that he might surrender his faith for a "mirage." In later years Abhishiktananda himself referred to Monchanin's skepticism about any reconciliation of Christianity and Vedanta, and spoke of Monchanin's fear that his Christian faith might be overwhelmed by Vedanta as it had nearly been earlier by Greek rationalism.[28] Some hard words on these subjects were exchanged at Shantivanam but their mutual respect and deep affection withstood the strain imposed by these disagreements.[29]

All this said, Abhishiktananda's debt to Monchanin was massive. Monchanin played a crucial role in Abhishiktananda's passage to India and in the establishment of the ashram which would allow each to fulfill the dream of a contemplative Christian life rooted in the culture of India. His fellow-monk provided Abhishiktananda with a living example of someone who, as part of his Christian vocation, was intent on fathoming the spiritual depths of the Indian tradition. Monchanin also introduced Abhishiktananda to the writings of many "Christian *jñānīs*" (Ruysbroeck, Suso, Tauler, Eckhart, Hadewijch of Anvers, the authors of *The Cloud of Unknowing* and *The Mirror of Simple Souls* among them) who gave him "an irreplaceable preparation for a sound intellectual understanding of Indian religious thought and a comprehensive approach to Indian mystical experience."[30] It was Monchanin who took Abhishiktananda on the fateful trip to Ramana and the Mountain of Shiva, and it was he who seems to have first introduced Abhishiktananda to the audacious and formative idea that all religious forms (Scriptures, doctrines, etc.) are relative (which makes Monchanin's resistance to *advaita* somewhat puzzling on the purely intellectual plane—perhaps Monchanin's resistances were rather of an emotional and psychological kind). We should also not underestimate Monchanin's role as a kind and faithful friend, whatever their theological differences might have been, nor, in Abhishiktananda's own words, "his uncommon quality of humility, gentleness, peace, and poverty of spirit."[31] We have no reason to doubt the sincerity of Abhishiktananda's generous tributes to Monchanin. From the Memorial Address:

> A soul contemplative both by nature and by grace, nourished on the Greek Fathers, the mystics of the West, and above all the mediaeval Rhinelanders, he was in all respects ready to penetrate that secret of contemplation which is at the root of all the most fundamental institutions of India, both philosophical and religious, that mystic center of her being from which all her civilization has sprung.[32]

If, in the end, we believe that it was actually Abhishiktananda rather than Monchanin who penetrated to the "mystic center," this should not detract from the heroic spiritual odyssey of Monchanin himself.

Brahmabandhav Upadhyay

Abhishiktananda begins his memoir of Monchanin with a reference to Brahmabandhav Upadhyay (1861-1907), a Bengali Brahmin, pupil of

Ramakrishna, friend of Vivekananda and Tagore, and convert to Christianity, baptized into both Anglican and Roman Churches in 1891.[33] After entering the Christian fold he boldly proclaimed that he would be "the first Indian to sing the praises of the same triune *Saccidānanda* in the sacred tongues of the rishis." In 1894 he became a *bhikṣu* (wandering beggar), wearing the *kavi* dress of the *sannyāsī*, but pitching up for worship in Catholic Churches. In 1900, in Hyderabad, Upadhyay established the journal *Sophia* in which he developed his ideas about "Christian Vedanta," "Christian *sannyāsa*," *advaita*, the Trinity, monasticism, and an Indian theology—precisely the themes which were to preoccupy Abhishiktananda throughout his years in India. He envisaged the founding of a *maṭha* where "Hindu Catholics" could be trained to the monastic life and to a life of *sannyāsa*:

> The contemplative monks will give the lie to the prevalent notion that meditative life is idleness, show by their steady contemplation of the Infinite Goodness that it is possible to live the life of God on earth and to repair by their self-immolation the injury done to human nature by the ravages of sin. The itinerant monks will issue forth from the central *Maṭha* and carry the torch of Catholic faith to the darkest nooks and corners of India. The proposed institution shall be imbued with the spirit of ancient monasticism. . . . It shall be conducted on strictly Hindu lines. There shall not be the least trace of Europeanism in the mode of life and living of the Hindu Catholic monks.[34]

In 1900 Upadhyay and three disciples established just such a Christian *maṭha* on the banks of the Narmada at Jabalpur, where they put this ideal into practice.

> Here in the midst of solitude and silence [Upadhyay wrote] will be reared up true Yogis to whom the contemplation of the Triune *Saccidānanda* will be food and drink. . . . In this hermitage, will the words of the Eternal word be strung in the hymns of eastern melody, in this holy place will transcendent Catholic devotions be clothed in Hindu garb. Here on the banks of the classic river will the children of India sit at the feet of the Angelic and Seraphic Doctors to drink deep of Divine Science; here will the Vedanta philosophy be assimilated to universal truths.[35]

Upadhyay traveled and lectured throughout India, arguing that Christian theology must be freed from the grip of Aristotelian scholasticism and recast in the language of the Vedanta, and that "the last end of man is the vision and enjoyment of the Divine Essence."[36] Writing on such themes, he became a regular contributor to a well-known Hindu journal, *Twentieth Century*.

In the end Upadhyay proved too much of a handful for the Church authorities. The apostolic delegate, Msgr Zaleski, prohibited the faithful from reading *Sophia*, the Jabalpur ashram was closed down, and Upadhyay stopped writing on the themes which had scandalized the ecclesiastical hierarchy. He remained obedient to the Church and resolute in his commitment to Christ, writing a canticle in praise of the Trinity and a hymn to Jesus a few months before his death. He died in 1907 but was refused a Christian burial—a shameful page in the history of the Catholic Church in India! Writing in 1956 Abhishiktananda said of Upadhyay, "Some sixty years ago, the intuition of what Indian Christian monasticism ought to be gushed out of the heart of Brahmabandhave Upadhyay."[37] Even from the brief jottings above it is not difficult to discern in this "powerful, fearless, detached, and unselfish" Christian *sannyāsī*, a heroic exemplar who pioneered a trail to be followed by men like Monchanin and Abhishiktananda half a century later.

Ramana and His Followers

We have already called attention to the dramatic impact of Ramana Maharshi on the French monk during his two visits to Tiruvannamalai in January and July 1949—"Ramana's *Advaita* is my birthplace. Against that all rationalization is shattered."[38] Writing of Ramana some twelve years later Abhishiktananda described the sage's significance in the most simple and direct terms:

> "It is in his saints above all that the Lord shows his wonders.". . . We should simply thank God in deepest humility when we happen to meet any such sage or saint, no matter to which *dharma* he may outwardly belong, and be ready to accept with open heart his witness and message. . . . One of these sages was with us in fact not very long ago. His life was passed entirely in the clear light of day and could be observed by anyone who wished. It was a quite simple and unpretentious life, which indeed was the strongest guarantee of its authenticity. Many of those who visited him or lived with him are still alive. Not a few consider him to be the most manifest embodiment in our time of that experience which has been handed down in India from the days of the rishis; and certainly most of those who met him claim to have recognized in him the unquestionable sign of the Presence and to have received from him an inspiration which has for ever illuminated and transformed their life.[39]

And so it was with Abhishiktananda himself.

The first visit to Tiruvannamalai was cut short by illness. Following his return to Shantivanam, Abhishiktananda recalls that, "in my feverish dreams . . . it was the Maharshi who unremittingly appeared to me . . . the Maharshi bringing the true India which transcends time and of which he was for me the living and compelling symbol." He goes on to add, tellingly,

> My dreams also included attempts—always in vain—to incorporate in my previous mental structures, without shattering them, these powerful new experiences which my contact with the Maharshi had brought to birth; new as they were, their hold on me was already too strong for it ever to be possible for me to disown them.[40]

On his second visit Abhishiktananda was much more receptive to the Maharshi's *darśana* as well as now taking a serious and sustained interest in his teachings, his writings, and his followers. As we have seen, all this led to his retreats in the caves of Arunachala.

It is by no means the case that Ramana introduced Abhishiktananda to *Advaita* Vedanta; he had already been studying the *Upanishads* and their central message—*Tat tvam asi* ("That thou art") for some years past. He refers to some of these studies in a letter of 1954:

> Deep contacts with Hindu thought, books, and people. Even before I came here, they had already made a mark on me. A hidden spiritual sympathy, this sense of the Unity, of the ONE, of God at the source of my being, of the fading out of this "ego" as soon as you penetrate into the interior of yourself so as to reach the unique "I."[41]

Abhishiktananda was to write, two decades after his brief meetings with Ramana,

> My deepest ideal—that to which unconsciously everything in me is referred—is that of Ramana, who is such a perfect example of Vedanta; and this ideal of Ramana could never have rooted itself at this depth in my psyche if there had not been a meeting with an obscurely felt call, a "surfacing," an "awakening."[42]

Ramana's role, in this case as in so many others, was primarily one of presence—as a radiant embodiment of the wisdom of the *Upanishads*, a living exemplar of *Advaita*, a vibrant symbol of eternal India.

Abhishiktananda's intercourse with Ramana's followers, his close study of the slender corpus of the Maharshi's writings, and his own retreats into "the cave of the heart," crystallized the advaitic message. There was to be no turning back. However, although both Ramana and Arunachala struck Abhishiktananda lightning-like, and although he was to speak of them and the experiences they brought him with the deepest reverence for the rest of his life, we should not conclude that Abhishiktananda emerged from Arunachala as a fully-fledged *jñānī* for whom all problems, contradictions, and tensions had been resolved once and for all. Far from it. Decisive as the encounter was, the rest of his life was a long and sometimes painful struggle to integrate "the secret of Arunachala."

Both the biography of the Sage of Arunachala and the main contours of *Advaita* Vedanta are too well known to rehearse here. Recall that Ramana's teaching revolved around an apparently simple question: "Who am I?". Frithjof Schuon writes,

> The great question "Who am I?" appears, with him, as a concrete expression of a reality that is "lived," if one may so put it, and this authenticity gives to each word of the sage a flavor of inimitable freshness—the flavor of Truth when it is embodied in the most immediate way. In the Maharshi's question, "Who am I" all the Vedanta is summed up. The answer is the Inexpressible.[43]

Suffice it to offer a small sample of Abhishiktananda's own efforts to formulate the simple yet mystery-filled lessons of self-inquiry (*vichāra*) which he derived from his experiences at Tiruvannamalai:

> [Ramana's teaching] is simply to go back to the source of myself and to grasp (but not intellectually) that the authorship, the *Aham*, which governs our corporal and mental activity, cannot be divided into two—God and myself. Understand this as best you can!

> *Advaita* is neither a doctrine nor a system. It is the supreme experience here below, one which forbids giving an absolute meaning to the form of multiplicity which marks everything in the world that comes before our senses or our mind. . . . *Advaita* is the fundamental dimension of being.

> It is for the Self to find the way to the Self. The intellect can merely give assistance; it is not able to open the door. It makes preparations, but only the Self opens the door of the Self. Lightning, thunder. . . !

> The guru, Ramana, Arunachala, and the rest, they are the outward projection of the Self, who hides himself in order to be found.[44]

As an aside it is worth noting John Glenn Friesen's suggestion that Ramana inflected the Vedanta in several ways which distinguished his teachings from that of other advaitins, and that these in turn influenced Abhishiktananda. In this context Friesen flags three distinctive aspects of Ramana's message: his use of the *Vivekacūḍāmani* (*The Crest-Jewel of Discrimination*), attributed to Sankara, which allows the world a qualified reality—and thus Ramana's emphasis on "seeing *Brahman* in all things"; the assimilation of the teachings of the *Yoga Vāsiṣṭha*, attributed to Valmiki and possibly dating back to the sixth/seventh century AD, in which the question "Who am I?" is pivotal to the spiritual method prescribed and in which the notion of *śakti* (divine energy) is foregrounded; and Ramana's indebtedness to both the *Rihu Gītā* (an extract from the epic *Śivarahasya*) and the *Tripura Rahasya*, a tantric text about the Supreme Goddess, and which Ramana apparently considered to be "one of the greatest works of *advaita*" and which he regretted was not available in English.[45]

*

Abhishiktananda learned much from several of Ramana's followers from whom he also drew both inspiration and support. Here we may mention a few of the more significant. Ethel Merstone, an Englishwoman of Jewish descent, friend of Gurdjieff and Ouspenski, and a convert to Hinduism, helped him to overcome his initial resistance to Ramana by urging him to "empty" himself of preconceptions and expectations— this a prelude to the evening when his encounter with the sage "opened a mighty abyss." Merstone also intervened on Abhishiktananda's behalf on his second visit when other visitors were being turned away from the ashram because of Ramana's illness. Because Ramana was unable to converse, it was also she who alerted Abhishiktananda to the temple and mountain as channels of grace to which he could turn for inspiration and guidance. Merstone also introduced Abhishiktananda to several of the Sage's other followers with whom he discussed *advaita*.[46]

H.W.L. Poonja, referred to by Abhishiktananda as "Harilal," was an industrial entrepreneur and one of Ramana's most faithful followers. He argued an uncompromising line of *advaita* and challenged Abhishiktananda in many of his ideas and in his relentless reading and study.[47] (In the 70s Poonja had a vision of "the Cosmic Christ" and for a while devoted himself to the path of *bhakti* which he had previously spurned. Later still he set up as a guru, apparently returning to a radical form of *advaita*.)[48] Another Indian disciple of Ramana was A. Shastri who helped Abhishiktananda integrate Patanjali's yoga with Ramana's Vedanta, while Dr Dinshaw K. Mehta, a Parsee follower of the Maharshi and one-time doctor to Mahatma Gandhi, introduced him to certain psychological models and techniques of meditation, some of them reminiscent of the theories of C.G. Jung. Abhishiktananda was for a time influenced by Mehta and met with him several times in the years 1955-1967, but seems to have eventually become disenchanted with his ideas—which, it must be said, often veered away from the teachings of Ramana and were contaminated by certain scientific ideas of the most dubious kind.[49] Others whom Abhishiktananda mentions with respectful affection in *The Secret of Arunachala* were three women, Sundarammal, Lakshmi Devi, and Radhabai Ammeyar; the Brahmin Sri Kuppusami Aiyar who arranged for Abhishiktananda to take up residence in one of the mountain's caves; S.S. Cohen with whom Abhishiktananda enjoyed several stimulating discussions; Sujata, a Buddhist nun who was impressed by the brightness of his "halo," and who lent him several books by D.T. Suzuki and expatiated on Zen Buddhism; and Dr T.M.P. Mahadevan, professor of philosophy at Madras University, and author of one of the more authoritative books on the Maharshi.[50]

Gnanananda

Gnanananda's teaching was akin to that of Ramana, and similarly influenced by the *Vivekacūḍāmani* and the *Yoga Vāsiṣṭha*. He was insistent on the centrality of meditation for the advanced aspirant but, as Swami Nityananda observes, he also "underlined the importance of *Karma* Yoga and *Bhakti* Yoga and held the traditional view that only one who has attained purity of heart, single-minded concentration, and desirelessness by cultivating intense devotion to God, is qualified for intense study of Vedanta and Self-inquiry."[51]

We shall leave Abhishiktananda's impressions of Gnanananda and the recounting of his experiences at Tapovanam for the next chapter and here simply touch on several aspects of Gnanananda's influence on Abhishiktananda. First and foremost, here was a living guru, more immediately accessible than Ramana (who in his later years was often surrounded by a squad of followers and ashram functionaries of one sort and another). Without any fanfare, Gnanananda accepted Abhishiktananda as a *chelā* and to him Abhishiktananda could spontaneously surrender in the practice of *guru-bhakti*. From a letter written immediately after his time at Tapovanam:

> I have been totally "caught."... People prostrate before him with a veneration which fills their whole heart, and at his feet they feel close to him, enveloped in his fatherly affection and animated towards him with childlike love and trust.... If that man [Gnanananda] were to ask me tomorrow to set out on the roads naked and silent like Sadashiva Brahman, I would be unable to refuse. The mysterious ways of Providence!... In him I have felt the truth of *advaita*.[52]

Further,

> One felt that with Gnanananda all distinction, *bheda*, had been overcome and had vanished. It was the true personality, the self alone, the *ātman*, in each person which was immediately perceived by him.[53]

This, then, is Gnanananda's primary significance in Abhishiktananda's life, as a living guru who exhibited those supra-personal qualities of *being* that are the very hallmark of the genuine master. Abhishiktananda:

> The guru is one who has himself first attained the Real and who knows from personal experience the way that leads there; he is capable of initiating the disciple and of making well up from within the heart of the disciple, the immediate ineffable experience which is his own—the utterly transparent knowledge, so limpid and pure, that quite simply "he is."[54]

Abhishiktananda stresses that it was not a question of learning "new ideas" from Gnanananda; insofar as the guru was intellectually important it was in the way in which he enabled Abhishiktananda to understand old ideas anew for "what the guru says springs from the very heart of the disciple." Indeed,

> What does it matter what words the guru uses? Their whole power lies in the hearer's inner response. . . . When all is said and done, the true guru is he who, without the help of words, can enable the attentive soul to hear the "Thou art that," *Tat-tvam-asi* of the Vedic rishis; and this true guru will appear in some outward form or other at the very moment when help is needed to leap over the final barrier.[55]

And so it was with Gnanananda and Abhishiktananda, though perhaps the final barrier was not altogether cleared until Abhishiktananda's last days.

With these reflections in mind, it is worth noting a few aspects of Gnanananda's teaching and his example which perhaps gave Abhishiktananda's own understanding a different coloration, so to speak. Friesen suggests that it was primarily through Gnanananda that Abhishiktananda was exposed to several currents of Kashmiri Saivism, subsequently evident in his own experiences and writings: the devotion to Siva and the appreciation of the dense symbolic world of Saivism (to which Abhishiktananda always felt more attuned than to the Vaisnavite); the rich symbolism of the heart, inspired by the *Śvetāśvatara Upanishad* which enjoys a privileged position in Kashmiri Saivism; the emphasis on the creative cosmic force of *śakti* mirrored in the human microcosm by *kundalini*; the joyful Tantric affirmation of the world, a useful counter-balance to the austere renunciation extolled in many of the *Upanishads*; the elevation of direct experience over all conceptual knowledge, and the suspicion of language as a vehicle of understanding.[56] All of these themes are indeed on display in *Guru and Disciple* and in many of

Abhishiktananda's other writings. Here is an illustrative instance, this one concerning *śakti*:

> In fact, there is probably nowhere else in the world where the mystery of the Presence has been felt as intensely as it has in India since the remotest Vedic times—and that as a supremely active presence, the whole sphere of the divine *Śakti* which somewhat resembles the *shekinah* of Jewish tradition. It is a presence that is immanent in every being that has issued from the hands of the Creator, and in every phase of the life of man and the universe, the daily, monthly, and yearly cycles each of which depends on the phases of the heavenly bodies in which spiritual and uncreated Light manifests itself materially for the benefit of men.[57]

Murray Rogers and the Jyotiniketan Group

Mary and Murray Rogers went to India as Anglican missionaries for the Church Missionary Society in 1946. A few years later they accepted an invitation to join Mahatma Gandhi's ashram at Sevegram, "an experience which changed their lives and attitudes, and eventually led to their severing their institutional ties with the West."[58] In 1954 they established the ecumenical Christian ashram of Jyotiniketan in the village of Kareli, near Bareilly (Uttar Pradesh). In later years Murray and Mary Rogers lived for a time in the Garden of Gethsemane, a Russian Orthodox monastery in Jerusalem, and in Hong Kong and Canada, before retirement in Oxford.

At the end of April 1959 Abhishiktananda set off from Shantivanam on a journey which would take him almost the full length of the subcontinent, culminating in the Himalayas. One of his many stopovers was at Jyotiniketan where he met Murray and Mary Rogers, Heather Sandeman, and John Cole, an American Presbyterian missionary. Later he wrote to his sister that these were the most "excellent" of his contacts with Protestants in India.[59] Heather Sandeman and Mary Rogers were to translate several of Abhishiktananda's books.

Here is Murray Rogers' account of Abhishiktananda's arrival at the ashram:

> It was a dark night and the little group of us were in the Chapel for Night Prayers, Compline. . . . Having received and given the Peace, we turned to face the open door, and the last one gave the Peace to our neighbors in the two near-by villages who, though not present in their bodies, were always there in our hearts. That night, as she took a step or two towards the door, we saw in the light of the kerosene

lanterns a figure—it was our first glimpse of Swamiji. He had been an hour or more wandering in the groves, quite unable to see the ashram buildings until the gathering of lights for Compline gave him a hint of our whereabouts; and there he was—the saffron *khadi*, the old bag that became so familiar, at least a couple of other bags hanging from his neck, and the smile.[60]

This was the first of many visits and the beginnings of a close communion with the Jyotiniketan ashram—one in which the participants sought not only to bridge the gulf between Christian and Indian traditions but to heal the divisions within Christianity itself. Interesting to note that Abhishiktananda at first struck Rogers as "an old style French priest, rather proper and 'entrenched,' at least so it seemed."[61] Abhishiktananda confided to Rogers that he had practically no experience of non-Catholic Christians and still had difficulty in conceiving of them as Christians at all! Abhishiktananda's stay at Jyotiniketan inaugurated a fruitful series of meetings with Protestants of various stripe. Because of illness, the Jyotiniketan folk sent Abhishiktananda to recuperate with the Quakers Laurie and Kuni Baker, who ran a hospital in the Himalayas. On returning, he commented to Rogers: "Mooray, I am amazed! I am amazed. They believe hardly anything that they are supposed to, but they are among the deepest Christians I have ever met."[62] To his friend Anne-Marie Stokes he wrote, "What Pharisees we Catholics often are, and how the Lord sometimes delights in making us aware that Love (the essential thing) is sometimes found in greater measure outside the Church than within it."[63]

Abhishiktananda's friends at Jyotiniketan were soon being invited to Shantivanam for a week of study and prayer, followed by a series of retreat/seminars concerned with Hindu-Christian encounter. John Cole and Murray Rogers were to become two of Abhishiktananda's closest friends, both visiting him for extended periods at Shantivanam and Gyansu.[64] Rogers was to play an important role in facilitating the publication of several of Abhishiktananda's works, and later contributed a piece to the memorial volume, *Swami Abhishiktananda: The Man and His Message* (1986). In 2003 he published a short and charming tribute in *Abhishiktananda: A Memoir of Dom Henri Le Saux*. It is worth quoting Rogers at some length for his insights into Abhishiktananda's personality and the pain he suffered in his attempt to harmonize his Christianity and his Indian experiences:

> I can still hear his roar of laughter when I first diagnosed him as Don Quixote and Sancho Panza rolled into one! As we sat under the tree listening to Swamiji expounding the way of the rishis, the way to "the

cave of the heart," or, later, as we read parts of his writings, we knew him as the bravest of men tilting at windmills, daring everything for the sake of his vision. . . . And simultaneously, all part of the same "old Swamiji"—as we called him affectionately—there was a sense of the practical, an interest in the preparation of food and its arrival on time on the table, an almost competitive pride in his knowledge of railway timetables, a fund of uproarious stories and much pulling of our (British) legs. He was a man of tensions, struggling to be free. . . . In conversation and discussion, at some conference or smaller meeting about the Church and the marvelous treasures which God had entrusted to his Hindu children, he was no fool. He could speak out of his own experience as very few, if any, others could—and yet—until, I think, the last six months of his life—he never succeeded in ridding himself of painful feelings of inferiority. Little did most people know how much courage it needed for Swamiji to share what he knew and saw, and little did they know how he was hurt when theologians and thinkers, better trained intellectually no doubt than he himself was, proceeded to dissect and analyze his words and experience in cerebral terms, after the cocksure fashion of western theological thought. He himself, struggling as he was to express the inexpressible, was often taken beyond traditional Christian formulations; and when someone . . . failed to trust his Christian integrity and feared for his orthodoxy, Swamiji was almost shattered.[65]

Rogers, who spent a good deal of time with Abhishiktananda not only at Jyotiniketan but also at Gyansu, provides many other sympathetic insights into Abhishiktananda's personality and his spiritual growth: his lifelong attachment to his family and to France; the tension between his thirst for solitude and the need for human companionship; his changing relationship with non-Catholic Christians; his enthusiasm for pilgrimage; his love of the natural order.

The Cuttat Circle

The intra-religious dialogue which flowed from Abhishiktananda's meeting with the Jyotiniketan group was loosely formalized in the "Cuttat Circle." In 1961 Dr Jacques-Albert Cuttat, the Swiss ambassador to India and a man with an abiding interest in Oriental spirituality, took a leading role in sponsoring and organizing a series of meetings at Rajpur (April 1962), Nagpur (December 1963) and Jyotiniketan (April 1964 and January 1966). Cuttat was born in Switzerland in 1909, did his tertiary studies in Berne and Paris, and taught at the universities of Bogata and Columbia, and at the Sorbonne. He had served as a diplomat in several Latin American countries, and been a consultant to the Vatican Secretariat for Non-Christians. In his book *The Encounter of Religions* (1964) Cuttat himself articulated a theme which circulated through many of Abhishiktananda's own writings: ". . . the more deeply I go into my own religion, the more I become capable of penetrating and assimilating the core, the really positive content, of other religious perspectives."[66] It was Cuttat who introduced Abhishiktananda to the "phenomenological" ideas of *epochê* and *eidetic vision*: the provisional bracketing or suspension of one's own beliefs in the face of the thing itself (the religious phenomenon being investigated) in order to let it "speak," to reveal its essence. From time to time Abhishiktananda refers to these notions in his own writings.[67]

The Cuttat Circle consisted primarily of Catholic monks such as Abhishiktananda and Bede Griffiths but also included a member of the Church of South India and an Orthodox archimandrite, as well as John Cole, a Congregationalist, and the Anglican Murray Rogers. Abhishiktananda stopped attending after the Nagpur gathering as he felt the dialogue was becoming too academic. He had also been deeply wounded by a remark in which Dr Cuttat himself seemed to question his Christian integrity—always a very raw nerve with Abhishiktananda in these years.[68] Nonetheless, he had found the meetings with the various participants in the Cuttat group immensely stimulating and they fructified his thinking about religious dialogue. His exchanges with like-minded Christians also dispelled some of the terrible loneliness he had experienced in his quest to reconcile Christianity and *advaita*. We may also surmise that this period of collegial discussion, prayer, and meditation fuelled the creative surge in Abhisktananda's writing in the mid-60s. *Hindu-Christian Meeting Point* grew directly out of these meetings but *Saccidananda, Mountain of the Lord* and *Prayer* were all fashioned in the light of these gatherings.

Raimon Panikkar

Born in Barcelona in 1918 and raised in Spain by a Catholic mother and a Hindu father, Raimon Panikkar has made interreligious dialogue his life's work.[69] He was ordained a Roman Catholic priest in 1946, and was attached to the diocese of Varanasi in India where, in the 1950s, he was professor at the Kashi Hindu University. He has also held posts at universities of Madrid, Rome, Harvard, and California, and delivered the Gifford Lectures in Edinburgh in 1989. He has won many awards and is widely recognized as one of the most sophisticated advocates of interreligious dialogue. In his own life he has bridged many divides—between

East and West, India and Spain, past and present, the humanities and the sciences. In a recent interview he observed, "I consider myself 100 percent Hindu and Indian, and 100 percent Catholic and Spanish. How is that possible? By living religion as an experience rather than as an ideology."[70] Panikkar is the author of some forty books, including *The Unknown Christ of Hinduism, The Trinity and World Religions, The Silence of the Buddha, The Cosmotheandric Reality,* and *The Intrareligious Dialogue.* He now lives in retirement in Spain.

Raimon Panikkar was one of Abhishiktananda's closest friends. They met in 1957 at the Pontifical Seminary in Poona, Panikkar at that time teaching at Kashi University. Over the next decade the two spent a good deal of time together, with much "mutual listening and osmosis,"[71] discussing theology "on the road, in the sun, squeezed together in buses, in the restaurant, as well as sitting in a room."[72] Their times together included Abhishiktananda's stay with Panikkar in August 1957, and another week together in December before Panikkar left the sub-continent for the next four years. Soon after Panikkar's return they conducted the three-week pilgrimage to Gangotri, recounted in Abhishiktananda's *Mountain of the Lord.* Early in 1965 they climbed Mt Arunachala together, performing a Christian ceremony there just as they had done on the banks of the Ganges, high in the Himalayas. Abhishiktananda spent most of December that year in Varanasi. In Abhishiktananda's last years Panikkar was often away from India but they remained intimate friends and planned to spend a month together late in 1973—a plan thwarted by Abhishiktananda's heart attack. It was Panikkar who purchased the plot of land on which Abhishiktananda constructed his hermitage at Gyansu. Later Panikkar was to edit Abhishiktananda's journals for publication as *Ascent to the Depth of the Heart.* On the second anniversary of Abhishiktananda's "Great Departure" he wrote, and later published, "Letter to Abhishiktananda," one of the most moving and percipient of the many tributes paid to the departed monk.

Panikkar was important to Abhishiktananda in many ways—as an extremely well-educated, cosmopolitan Christian intellectual he was a formidable jousting partner in their lengthy discussions about matters of mutual interest; he provided a living example of the kind of interior synthesis of Christianity and Hinduism which was so attractive to Abhishiktananda; his books, especially *The Unknown Christ of Hinduism* (1964), were a powerful stimulus to Abhishiktananda's thinking about religious pluralism and reinforced the idea that Christianity (like all religions) provided only "provisional truth," an idea which for many years Abhishiktananda found profoundly disturbing.[73] It may also have been Panikkar who, along with Monchanin, aroused Abhishiktananda's momentary interest in Teilhard de Chardin. But more important than any of this was the fact that Panikkar was a steadfast and generous friend who provided Abhishiktananda with the companionship of a kindred spirit.

Bettina Bäumer

Bettina Bäumer was a young Austrian student, studying theology and philosophy in Rome under Raimon Panikkar, when she read *Ermites du Saccidânanda* (1956) in which Abhishiktananda and Monchanin gave an account of the early years of their ashram. So taken was she by this book that she resolved to go to India. Panikkar helped her to overcome various obstacles and persuaded Abhishiktananda to receive her at Shantivanam. From her arrival in 1963 Abhishiktananda recognized a kindred spirit and within a short time she had become a trusted confidante, although Abhishiktananda was always scrupulous in observing the proprieties in his friendship with the young woman. After three months, and with Abhishiktananda's encouragement, Bäumer returned to Europe to continue her studies, which now included Sanskrit and other Indological subjects, and to complete her doctorate in Munich.

Bäumer maintained a close correspondence with Abhishiktananda until returning to India in 1967 to live and work in Banaras where she was closely associated with Panikkar. During the late 60s the three spent a good deal of time together and it was during these years that her relationship with Abhishiktananda deepened. She also spent some time with him in Rishikesh. Abhishiktananda often asked her to "screen" prospective European visitors. Both Abhishiktananda and Bäumer were at this time involved with the charismatic "Harilal" (H.W.L. Poonja) who occasioned some misunderstanding between the two. (Both Abhishiktananda and Bäumer were soon to become quite disenchanted with Poonja.[74]) Bettina Bäumer also developed a close friendship with Marc Chaduc who, under Abhishiktananda's direction, spent some time in Banaras. The two went together into retreat at Bodhgaya.

At the time of Abhishiktananda's heart attack and his final illness Bäumer herself was seriously ill and unable to visit Indore. Soon after his death, she and Panikkar, while waiting several hours for a delayed train, determined to establish the Abhishiktananda Society. Bäumer succeeded Panikkar as President of the Society in 1988, a position which she still occupies. Since Abhishiktananda's death, Bäumer has become an internationally renowned scholar.[75]

Swami Chidananda

Swami Chidananda succeeded Swami Sivananda as the *ācārya* of the Sivananda Ashram in Rishikesh. He came from a wealthy family and graduated from Loyola College in Madras (now Chennai) in 1938, entering the ashram in 1943 and receiving initiation in 1949. He toured extensively in the West as a spokesman for the Divine Life Society, and was throughout his adult life interested in the issue of religious pluralism and sympathetically disposed to the other great religions—to which he often referred in his teachings. As we are told on the Sivananda Ashram website, "The glorious ideals of Lord Jesus, the Apostles, and the other Christian saints had found in his heart a synthesis [with] all that is best and noble in the Hindu culture."[76]

Chidananda and Abhishiktananda first met, at the ashram, in 1965. Abhishiktananda stayed there often and struck up a close friendship with both Chidananda and Swami Krishnananda. The former wrote of Abhishiktananda,

> It is something very wonderful and very mysterious, the way in which we both just absolutely went into a state of at-one-ment, [when] we saw each other the very first time. It was as though we had known each other always—a perfect and absolute empathy. . . . I could see from his face that an inner light had sparked in him.[77]

So impressed was Chidananda by Abhishiktananda's grasp of *advaita* that he invited him to contribute a series of articles which appeared under the title *Sannyāsa: The Call of the Desert* and which later comprised the first half of *The Further Shore*. It is clear from his references to the swami in his journal and correspondence, that Abhishiktananda held this "truly spiritual man" in the highest esteem and regarded him as one of the most authentic exponents of *advaita*. Fr Vachon, a Canadian visitor to India who met Abhishiktananda early in 1970, wrote in a letter, "He finds R. Panikkar the best man at present in Hindu-Christian dialogue. He also has much respect for Antoine, Fallon [Calcutta-based Jesuits], Griffiths. He regards Chidananda as excellent, and better than Sivananda. The swamis and *sādhus* who go to America are second-class." Vachon also reports on Abhishiktananda's characteristic wariness of European visitors, though this was often soon replaced with great warmth.[78] As we have seen, Chidananda helped devise the *dīkṣā* ceremony for Marc Chaduc and, indeed, had helped prepare him for his initiation.

Other Friends

Despite his sincere commitment to the monastic vocation and to the practice of silence and solitude, Abhishiktananda met countless individuals from both East and West during his Indian years. His letters testify to his constant comings and goings across the sub-continent and his involvement in all manner of seminars, retreats, conferences, symposia, and the like. During the Shantivanam years there was a constant stream of visitors, both Indian and European. In general, Abhishiktananda was not keen on meeting people from the West, especially those wanting to seek advice: "It is a nuisance to be so well known here," he wrote in 1967. "Here I try politely to avoid European visitors. . . . I am continually telling Westerners to go see Hindus, not people of their own race—otherwise why make the journey?"[79] Nonetheless, over the years he met many such people, some of them becoming friends. We cannot here offer any account of Abhishiktananda's relations with a myriad of people; interested readers are directed to the excellent biographies by James Stuart and Shirley du Boulay. But it is worth mentioning some of the people who, at one time or another, were close to Abhishiktananda (sometimes as correspondents): his youngest sister and intimate confidante, Marie-Thérèse; Fr Joseph Lemarié, a younger contemporary at Kergonan, later canon of Aquilea and Chartres, and lifelong correspondent; Mother Françoise-Thérèse, Prioress of Lisieux; Harold Rose, ex-Trappist novice, one-time Buddhist aspirant, and disciple of a Sufi master, with whom he first visited Tapovanam Ashram; Fr Klaus Klostermaier, author of *In the Paradise of Krishna*; Fr Dominique van Rollenghen, a Belgian Benedictine, and one of Abhishiktananda's closest friends; Mother Theophane of the Franciscan Sisters of St Mary of the Angels, a regular correspondent and one of those who nursed him through his final days at Indore; Dr Caterina ("Nuccia") Conio, professor of Indian philosophy and religion at Milan and Pisa; Dr Sara Grant, who had come to India from Scotland in 1956; Mrs Anne-Marie Stokes, a fellow-Breton resident in America and whom, after fifteen years of correspondence, Abhishiktananda was able to meet in India early in 1973; Madame Odette Baumer-Despeigne, who met Abhishiktananda in his final days and who later wrote of him most eloquently. There were countless others Abhishiktananda met in his travels, some of them well-known figures—Lama Anagarika Govinda, the Indologist Maria Bidoli, John Taylor, later the Anglican Bishop of Winchester, and Orthodox Metropolitan Anthony Bloom, to name a few. Nor should we forget the unalloyed pleasure Abhishiktananda took in the company not only of his fellow *sādhus*, but of simple and pious folk whom he met at the many holy sites he visited throughout India, and the delight he took in small children (everywhere in evidence in India!) whom he seemed to attract from the earliest days. In 1949 he had written, "I am constantly surrounded by a crowd of boys. . . . I actually had to come to India to discover how much I can be at home with a gang of urchins."[80]

Marc Chaduc and Other Disciples

In the previous chapter, it was suggested that Marc Chaduc was Abhishiktananda's only disciple, or *chelā*, in the strict sense of the word which, amongst other things, implies some sort of initiation. Chaduc was a young French seminarian who came to India expressly to sit at the feet of Abhishiktananda. They had begun corresponding in 1969 and finally met in India in October 1971. The following two years were marked by a very close relationship, the most intimate of Abhishiktananda's adult life. They conducted several retreats together and spent many hours in discussion. When apart they corresponded daily. As we have seen, Abhishiktananda was profoundly moved by Chaduc's *dīkṣā* and in his company underwent the most intense experiences at the temple at Ranagal—experiences which may well have precipitated his heart attack.

After Abhishiktananda's death, Chaduc returned to his homeland for family reasons. After a year in France he was back in India and, early in 1975, moved into a hut purchased by the Sivananda Ashram, there to undergo ten years of silence. In April 1977 Chaduc vanished. His glasses (without which he was virtually blind) were found in his hut, but of him no trace could be found. The most commonly held view is that he terminated his terrestrial existence in the rite of *jala-samādhi*, offering himself up to Mother Ganga in the manner of Swami Ram Tirth who had ended his life in this way early in the century.[81]

Chaduc was an important figure in Abhishiktananda's life for at least three reasons. Firstly, he fulfilled the role of spiritual son, and gave Abhishiktananda a warm and intimate companionship which he had only enjoyed intermittently with friends such as Panikkar and Rogers. In one of his letters Abhishiktananda wrote of "a human relation that reaches down to the most intimate depth of paternity"; the relationship with Chaduc enabled him to find that "most intimate depth of paternity" within himself. As Panikkar observed, "The strictness of your abstract ideal [of *sannyāsa*] softened in the love and warmth of that concrete encounter."[82] Secondly, Chaduc rekindled some of

Abhishiktananda's own youthful idealism and, sometimes through cruel reproaches, made Abhishiktananda himself feel that he had fallen well short of the ideals about which he had written so often and so persuasively. Here is Abhishiktananda castigating himself—rather harshly, one would have thought:

> How I wish I had the courage like him [Chaduc] to be able to go to the full extent of what is demanded by the dress I wear; and how ashamed I am of all that is unnecessary in my clothing, food, and conveniences of life. The true *sannyāsī* should have nothing, and no more, surely, should monks and nuns. . . . I shall at least have had the joy of awakening this child, and of realizing through him the ideal of which I have talked so much in my books and articles, but which alas, I have lived so little.[83]

—this from a most touching letter to his sister in which we cannot imagine him as anything other than totally sincere. Thirdly, Chaduc "taught" Abhishiktananda about the role and the responsibilities of the guru. From a letter: "It is really the *chelā* who *makes* the guru, and you have to have lived it, in order to grasp this relationship 'beyond words.'. . ."[84]

There were at least three other individuals who could at least loosely be described as disciples of Abhishiktananda: two young Hindus, Ramesh Srivastava and Lalit Sharma, who spent a good deal of time with him after 1966 and with whom he corresponded regularly, and Sister Térèse Lemoine from the Carmel of Lisieux in France who had come to India in 1965, by which time she was one of Abhishiktananda's regular correspondents. She sought a life of solitude in India and it was largely through Abhishiktananda's efforts that she was able to settle in Haridwar, near Rishikesh. Strangely, like Chaduc a year later, she disappeared from her hut in 1976, never to be seen again.[85]

Notes

1. SAC 138, DD 202.
2. L 3.8.71, 9-10.
3. Panikkar, 430 (italics mine).
4. L 22.9.73, 312.
5. L 24.1.69, 210.
6. L 13.3.67, 12.
7. L November, 1953, 66.
8. L 28,12, 52, 62.
9. D xx.
10. On Abhishiktananda's library and his reading see Friesen, 57-59.

11. Quoted in W. Perry, *Treasury of Traditional Wisdom*, 732.

12. Pr 45.

13. A. Daniélou, *The Way to the Labyrinth*, 213.

14. J.G. Weber, *In Quest of the Absolute*, 96.

15. J.G. Weber, *In Quest of the Absolute*, 97.

16. J.G. Weber, *In Quest of the Absolute*, 25.

17. J.G. Weber, *In Quest of the Absolute*, 16.

18. S. Rohde, *Jules Monchanin*, 71.

19. S. Rohde, *Jules Monchanin*, 47.

20. All passages cited in J.G. Weber, *In Quest of the Absolute*, 77-78, 82, 126. (Weber himself, writing in somewhat hagiographic mode, seems impervious to the flagrant contradictions found in these and in many other passages in Monchanin's writings.)

21. S.H. Nasr, *Sufi Essays*, 127.

22. FS 13.

23. Quoted in Panikkar, 430.

24. Monchanin's letter quoted in L 44n. See also Abhishiktananda's letter of 12.12.55 in L 87.

25. Quoted in S. Rodhe, *Jules Monchanin*, 47 L 87.

26. L 17.6.54, 72.

27. Quoted in J.G. Weber, *In Quest of the Absolute*, 119.

28. L 23.12.70, 87n.

29. See L 87-89.

30. From Abhishiktananda's Memorial Address.

31. L 10.2.53, 60.

32. Abhishiktananda, *Swami Parama Arubi Anandam*, 7-8.

33. Brahmabandhav Upadhyaya's original name was Bhavani Charan Banerji.

34. Quoted in Vattakuzhy, 70. Vattakuzhy points out that for Upadhyay "Hindu" was an ethical rather than a religious term, which allowed of such phrases as "Hindu Catholics." (Information on Upadhyay taken from Vattakuzhy, 68-73.)

35. Upadhyaya in 1899, quoted in BA 28n.

36. Quoted in Vattakuzhy, 72.

37. Quoted in Vattakuzhy, 73.

38. Quoted in Baumer-D, 316.

39. SAC 19-20.

40. SA 9.

41. L 10.2.52, 53.

42. D 2.7.71, 328.

43. F. Schuon, *Spiritual Perspectives*, 122.

44. All four excerpts are from his Diary—17.7.52; 30.3.64; 17.7.52; 26.4.64—and all quoted in J. Stuart, "Sri Ramana Maharshi and Abhishiktananda," 172-173. (These passages do not appear in *Ascent to the Depth of the Heart*.)

45. See Friesen, 67-74. The *Tripura Rahasya* was eventually translated into English by Swami Sri Ramanananda Saraswathi, first published in 1959, and

recently released in a new edition by World Wisdom, Bloomington, 2002. A translation by Swami Prabhavananda and Christopher Isherwood of *The Crest-Jewel of Discrimination* was published in 1970 (New York: New American Library).

46. See Abhishiktananda's several references to Merstone in SA.

47. Abhishiktananda's relationship with Harilal is discussed in some detail in du Boulay, 98-105.

48. As well as SA, on Poonja see Friesen, 91-93 and du Boulay, 98-105. On Poonja's later vision of Christ see L 26.1.71, 243.

49. On Mehta see Friesen, 94-96.

50. References to these individuals can be found in SA, Diary & Letters. Mahadevan's book is *Ramana Maharshi, the Sage of Arunachala*, London: Allen & Unwin, 1977.

51. Swami Nityananda Giri "Sadguru Sri Gnanananda," *Monastic Interreligious Dialogue*, Bulletin 64, May 2000. (This is somewhat different to the impression given by *Guru and Disciple* where Gnanananda seems always to be insisting on single-minded meditation as "the one thing necessary"—though this may well have been his particular message to Abhishiktananda.)

52. L 14.3.56, 90-91.

53. GD 108.

54. GD 29.

55. GD 29-30.

56. See Friesen, 103-107.

57. GD 55.

58. M. Rogers, *Abhishiktananda*, 7.

59. L 117.

60. M. Rogers, "Swamiji the Friend," 20.

61. M. Rogers, "Swamiji the Friend," 21.

62. M. Rogers, *Abhishiktananda*, 10.

63. L 17.6.59, 119.

64. On the friendship of Abhishiktananda and Rogers, see S. du Boulay, "The Priest and the Swami."

65. "Swamiji, the Friend" in Sr Vandana (ed), *Abhishiktananda: The Man and His Message*, 22.

66. On Cuttat see Stephens, 101-103 (quotation on 103).

67. For an example see HCMP 12.

68. See du Boulay, 183.

69. Panikkar's first name is variously rendered as "Raimon," "Raimondo," and "Raymond."

70. http://www.emptybell.org/panikkar.html

71. From a letter 30.12.64, cited in Friesen, 121n.

72. L 27.5.57, 104.

73. See D 24.10.66.

74. Some details of Poonja's later career and his relations with Abhishiktananda and Bäumer can be found in du Boulay, 98-105.

75. The range of Professor Bäumer's intellectual interests are evident in a recent volume, published in her honor: *Sāmarasya: Studies in Indian Arts, Philosophy, and Interreligious Dialogue* (2005), ed. Sadananda Das and Ernst Fürlinger.

76. See Friesen, 123-125, and Sivananda Ashram website: http://www.sivanandadlshq.org/saints/chida.htm

77. From Sr Vandana, "A Messenger of Light," *Clergy Monthly*, Dec 1974, 497; quoted in Friesen, 123.

78. L 225-226.

79. L 13.3.67, 190-191.

80. L 1.8.49, 25, In Stuart's biography there is a delightful photo of Abhishiktananda and some small boys outside his Gyansu hermitage, taken by Panikkar. (Photo 1 on page 6 of Illustrations.)

81. See Friesen, 120.

82. Panikkar, 448.

83. L 6.7.73, 303.

84. L 7.1.72, 259.

85. See Panikkar's introduction to *Ascent to the Depth of the Heart*, xxviii.

3

Writings

I have only one message, the message of the Absolute. It is the same message that Jesus and all the
seers have taught.

Whatever of good that is in my books stems precisely from this silence.

Abhishiktananda[1]

There can be no property in ideas. The individual
does not make them but *finds them;* let him see
to it that he really takes possession of them, and
work will be original in the same sense that the
recurrent seasons, sunset and sunrise are ever
anew although in name the same.

Ananda Coomaraswamy[2]

Abhishiktananda's vocation was realized primarily in his commitment to
the interior life and to *sannyāsa*. Certainly Abhishiktananda would not
have countenanced the thought that his spiritual practice had as one of
its ends the production of books! He shared the traditional Indian view
that books could only ever serve as signposts to the spiritual experience
itself. Nonetheless, having attained various insights, especially through
the medium of traditional Indian forms, he felt moved to share these
with his fellow-Christians of European background. In this respect,
the one theme which sounds throughout the whole corpus is the need
for the West in general and the Church in particular to be open to the
inexhaustible spiritual treasury of the Hindu tradition. As he wrote to
his friend and fellow-author, Raimon Panikkar,

> It is clear that our books . . . are not intended for Hindus. Our immediate
> role, whether or not we have sought it, is to sensitize Christian thought
> to the treasures which await it here [India], and to prepare Christians for
> dialogue. We have to be among Hindus, both physically and spiritually,
> so as to *gather* the honey for the Church and to pass it on.[3]

In this chapter we will take a conspectus of Abhishiktananda's
oeuvre, focusing on those published works in which he gives the subjects at hand his most sustained and carefully considered treatment. Our
discussion will not track the chronological appearance of these works

but rather will present them in a fashion most attuned to the themes and issues with which the present work is concerned. Nor will we make any attempt to trace the sometimes intricate pathways through which these works came to see the light of day in various translations and editions. The dates provided below signal the publication date of the first English language edition, sometimes lagging behind the French editions at a distance of some years. Readers should also bear in mind that some works were written many years before their first publication date: for example, most of *The Secret of Arunachala,* one of the author's most ravishing books, was written in the mid-50s, soon after the experiences it recounts, but was not published until 1979. Those interested in the publication history of various works are directed to James Stuart's bibliography in *Swami Abhishiktananda.*

For present purposes Abhishiktananda's writings have been divided into four categories: the major works—those published books and monographs which are amongst the author's most impressive treatments of the subject at hand and which are most likely to be of enduring interest; lesser works which are significant in Abhishiktananda's trajectory but whose subjects are better dealt with elsewhere; articles, transcripts of talks, and other pieces which are of limited interest to the general reader—and in any event, many of the more important finding their way into the books; and lastly, his most intimate writings in his journals and letters. But in all cases it is as well to bear in mind the admonition of Odette Baumer-Despeigne: "To grasp the precise significance of the thought of Henri Le Saux, it is important never to separate his writings from his personality and from the very special circumstances in which his life unfolded."[4] Of his own books Abhishiktananda had this to say:

> All is biographical—and nothing is! Everything comes from the experience of this tension [between Vedanta and Christianity], but everything has been rethought by the mind, in the halo of a double culture. The "I" naturally is literary. Who has the right to say "I," when he speaks of *advaita?*[5]

A. Major Works

Prayer (1967)

Prayer was first published in India in 1967 but only made an impact in the West when issued by SPCK in 1972. It probably remains Abhishiktananda's most widely known work. There is much in this slender but concentrated volume which might be found in any number of works by other Christian contemplatives—Thomas Merton, Henri Nouwen, Metropolitan Anthony of Sourzah come to mind. There is also a good deal that is reminiscent of Simone Weil's writings on prayer. The Christian sources on which Abhishiktananda draws will surprise no one: apart from the Scriptures (with which the author is obviously intimately familiar, the Johannine and Pauline works being amongst his favorites), Ignatius of Antioch, St John Climacus, Gregory Palamas, Augustine, Aquinas, St John of the Cross, the *Philokalia*, *The Way of the Pilgrim*. Its originality consists in the way in which Abhishiktananda gently assimilates Hindu insights and techniques into his discussion of prayer. Like many of his books it is, in the first place, directed towards Christian readers; the whole orientation of the book is uncompromisingly Christian whilst being at the same time deeply informed by the East. Abhishiktananda wrote of it, "though it is very elementary, to those who understand it conveys many things."[6] Indeed!

Abhishiktananda's keynote is evident from the opening pages:

> To live in constant prayer, to lead a contemplative life, is nothing else than to live in the actual presence of God. . . . To live in the presence of God should be as natural for a Christian as to breathe the air which surrounds him. Furthermore, to live consciously and worthily in this presence should never have for him even the appearance of a duty which he is bound to perform. . . . No, for him to live in the presence of the Almighty is a birthright; it is the deepest aspiration of his nature.[7]

The author goes on to consider prayer from various angles: its relation to reason and faith, to "works," to various other activities of the Christian life, and its place in the "universal theophany." He considers various forms of prayer—what in Christian circles is often called "meditation" (focusing the mind on God/Christ, his existence, his attributes, his love, and so on), the prayer of the affections (devotional prayer) and of petition ("the outpourings of the soul confiding all her needs to the Lord").[8] Each has its place—after all, as Frithjof Schuon remarks, "[One] of man's endowments is reasonable thought and speech; this dimension must therefore be actualized during that encounter with God which is prayer."[9] But Abhishiktananda repeatedly stresses that prayer, in its highest form, is neither an intellectual nor an emotional undertaking, these easily lapsing into mere mental activity/verbiage and sentimentalism respectively, but a *state of being* in which, through the stilling of the mind, we are most fully open to the workings of the Spirit. Ultimately we find God in silence, in the "cave of the heart":

> Man is made not merely to work with his hands and to think with his mind, but also to adore in the deep silence of his heart. Even more than

to *adore* he is called to plunge into silence and to lose himself there, unable to utter any word, not even a word of adoration or praise; for no word can express the mystery of God. . . . There the mind cannot even think or conceive a thought, for it is overwhelmed, silenced, blinded by this light.[10]

The influence of Abhishiktananda's Indian experiences is most apparent in several of his formulations; for instance, "Truly speaking, there is no outside and no inside, no without and no within, in the mystery of God and in the divine Presence," or "God has no form. He is beyond every form. Precisely for that reason he can reveal and manifest himself under any form."[11] Such themes recur in mystical literature. Compare the second formulation above with this, from the French poet and philosopher, Jean Biès, "Every form shows Him because He is in every form. None show Him because he is beyond forms."[12]

Abhishiktananda often refers to the relationship between faith and prayer, although at times they seem to be barely distinguishable—and this for good reason. From the way the word is used we can be confident that the author would accept the notion that faith is "the participation of the will in the intelligence." Therefore, "faith takes seriously the promises of God and the almost incredible revelation that we have been raised to the dignity of being children of God."[13] Schuon makes the same point even more dramatically:

One can spend a whole lifetime speculating on the suprasensorial and the transcendent, but all that matters is "the leap into the void" which is the fixation of spirit and soul in an unthinkable dimension of the Real. . . . This "leap into the void" we can call . . . "faith."[14]

How well that phrase, "the fixation of spirit and soul in an unthinkable dimension of the Real," captures the very vocation of Abhishiktananda! Prayer and faith can also be defined as "internal realities" and as "the simple acknowledgment of the presence of the Spirit in everything, everywhere and at every moment."[15] Thus,

To look with eyes enlightened by faith at trees and plants, at fruits and flowers, at birds and animals—all of them created by the Father to help and serve us and to be used by us in our ascent towards him—is also nothing less than prayer and contemplation.[16]

In this context, the boundary between "faith" and "knowledge" becomes somewhat fluid. Indeed, in another work Abhishiktananda refers to *jñāna* as "a *mysterium fidei*, a mystery of faith."[17]

Abhishiktananda surveys the history of the contemplative Christian orders, particularly the Carthusian and Carmelite, and regrets the fact that in recent times the Church has marginalized the vocation of the solitary contemplative. Here he sees an extraordinary role for the Indian Church:

> It is to be hoped that the Church of India will in the end bring to the universal Church an authentically Christian *sannyāsī* as the crowning of monastic life. Thus the Church will recover after centuries the purest traditions of the Desert and of the Hesychast movement, and at the same time drink deep at the inexhaustible sources of the Hindu ideal of renunciation in a life devoted to God alone. The Church is in the Spirit awaiting that ultimate inwardness of her life, in which she will discover the true depth of her own mystery. . . . In our day more than ever before the Church needs to hear the testimony that God is beyond all things, beyond all attempts to define him in thought or word or to reach him by activity. The Church has need of an inner silence . . . so that she may reach the fullness of the sacramental sign which she herself is.[18]

This was a plea which Abhishiktananda was to make over and over in his remaining years. Interestingly, he cites a passage from Pope Paul VI in which the pontiff affirms the indispensable role which contemplatives play in the Church, and refers to "the living water which springs up in the heart of contemplatives" and without which the souls of the faithful might "wither."[19]

The last four chapters of *Prayer* deal with yoga and prayer (particularly yogic techniques for quietening the mind), *lectio divina* and liturgical prayer, the Prayer of the Name (*nāma-japa* in Hinduism, the Jesus Prayer in the Orthodox tradition), and with "OM" and "Abba" as mantras *par excellence*. All these subjects are handled with the quiet assurance of spiritual maturity. *Prayer* is quite free of both the strident exhortations and the sentimental excesses which sometimes mar writings on this subject. As far as one can tell Abhishiktananda had not read any works by his fellow-monk, Thomas Merton. But we should not be in the slightest surprised that their message is so similar. The first few lines of *New Seeds of Contemplation* articulate precisely the central theme of *Prayer*.

> Contemplation is the highest expression of man's intellectual and spiritual life. It is that life itself, fully awake, fully active, fully aware that it is alive. It is spiritual wonder. It is spontaneous awe at the sacredness of life. It is gratitude for life, for awareness, and for being. It is a vivid realization of the fact that life and being in us proceed from an invisible, transcendent, and infinitely abundant Source. Contemplation is, above all, awareness of the reality of that Source. It knows the source, obscurely, inexplicably, but with a certitude that

goes beyond both reason and simple faith. For contemplation is a kind of spiritual vision to which both reason and faith aspire, by their very nature, because without it they must always remain incomplete. Yet contemplation is not vision because it sees "without seeing" and knows "without knowing.". . . Contemplation is also a response to a call: a call from Him Who has no voice, and yet Who speaks in everything that is, and Who, most of all, speaks in depths of our own being: for we ourselves are words of His.[20]

The Secret of Arunachala (1979)

A draft of the book was written in 1956, hard on the heels of the events which it recounts, but not finding its finished form until many years later. It recalls Abhishiktananda's formative experiences at Tiruvanna-malai in the years between 1949 and 1955, and his decisive encounter with Ramana Maharshi, the sacred mountain, and the great Temple of Siva—one which inaugurated his vocation as a Hindu-Christian *sannyāsī* and changed the trajectory of his life. During these years Abhishiktananda's many sojourns at Arunachala covered periods ranging from a few days to several months, his most extended stays coming in 1952 and 1953.

The Secret of Arunachala defies easy generic categorization, blending elements of memoir, journal, biography, travelogue, spiritual manual, mystical love-song. In this respect it is somewhat reminiscent of such classics as Marco Pallis' *Peaks and Lamas*, Anagarika Govinda's *Way of the White Clouds*, and *In the Paradise of Krishna* by Klaus Klostermaier. It might well be described as a rhapsodic paean to the three "channels of grace" which left such a profound impression on Abhishiktananda: the sage, the mountain, the temple. Certainly it is one of Abhishiktananda's most lyrical works and, perhaps better than any other, captures his abiding love of eternal India. The accounts of Ramana, the "flame-crowned mountain," and the Temple of Annamalaiyar are the cardinal points around which the book is organized, but there is much else besides. Deftly sketched portraits of some of Ramana's disciples, exem-plary and often amusing anecdotes about the many ascetics living in the mountain's network of caves, and descriptions of time-honored Saivite rituals and ceremonies all texture a narrative which never sags. It is free of the pompous solemnities which so often mar Western accounts of Vedanta, and of the gush which churns through much of the hagio-graphical literature on Ramana; Abhishiktananda's portrait of the sage is thereby all the more compelling.

Although it is little more than a vignette, Abhishiktananda's portrayal of the sage must rank as one of the most illuminating of the many written by Westerners who experienced something of his extraordinary *darśana*.[21] One might mention such figures as F.F. Humphreys, S.S. Cohen, Lanzo del Vasto, Somerset Maugham, Paul Brunton, Jean Herbert, and Arthur Osborne. Whilst leaving no doubt whatsoever about the status of Ramana, Abhishiktananda reminds us that he is only one amongst the many—albeit "the greatest belonging to our own time"—"who in the course of ages have quenched their thirst at this fountain which never ceases to flow, and in the shelter of the Mountain have discovered in the depth of their own heart the living mystery of Arunachala."[22]

After an initial tour of Arunachala—"something like Cassian's pilgrimage to the Egyptian desert of Scete"—Abhishiktananda is invited to take up occupation of one the mountain's many caves wherein he can practice austerities, living in silence and solitude. His description of this encounter with the mountain explicitly recalls Ramana's own *Marital Garland* and gives us a fair sample of Abhishiktananda's poetic style of writing:

> That was how the call of the Mountain came to me, the first of Arunachala's spell-binding wiles—the call and the wiles of a lover. . . .
> It is all up with anyone who has paused, even for a moment, to attend to the gentle whisper of Arunachala. Arunachala has already taken him captive, and will play with him without mercy until the bitter end. Darkness after light, desertion after embraces, he will never let him go until he has emptied him of everything in himself that is not the one and only Arunachala and that persists in giving him a name, as one names an other—until he has been finally swallowed up, having disappeared for ever in the shining of his Dawn-light, *Āruna*. . .[23]

Although Abhishiktananda discusses some weighty subjects the book is written with a light touch. Its considerable charm derives, in part, from Abhishiktananda's gentle irony, sometimes self-deprecatory, and from his clear-eyed but loving renditions of people and places. Amongst those making cameo appearances are several remarkable disciples—or, more precisely, followers[24]—of Ramana: Harilal W.L. Poonja, Punjabi Brahmin, ex-army officer and industrialist; Sundarammal, daughter of a wealthy Madras family who came to Tiruvannamalai in melodramatic circumstances, never thereafter leaving the precinct for the remaining fifteen years of Ramana's life; two women who lived for many years in silence, Lakshmi Devi and Radhabai Ammeyar, the "Ammal of Valadur." Other well-known figures who appear in the narrative include Ananda Mayi ("the Mother"), the scholar and biographer of Ramana, Dr T.M.P. Mahadevan, and the "Bengal tiger," A. Bose. Then too there is a larger cast of those humble and pious folk who showed Abhishiktananda himself such solicitude and hospitality during his several visits to the mountain. The author makes very little of the physical and psychological tribulations which his austerities must have entailed, and is generous in his accounts of the many colorful characters he meets on the mountain and its environs. At the same time, he is by no means oblivious to the hypocrisies and complacencies which can be found in any religious community, and sometimes unleashes a sharp and well-aimed shaft:

> There are indeed crowds of people in India who talk learnedly about *advaita*, especially in the south and in ashram circles; but they are generally the first to run to the temples to offer *pūjās* for the success of their ventures on the stock exchange or to obtain some promotion; not to mention the terrible ego-centeredness which so often accompanies the intellectual profession of the Vedanta.[25]

But such barbs are reserved for certain types rather than directed at particular individuals.

The discussion of such subjects as the Vedic hymns and myths, the doctrine of non-duality, the nature of the Self, the nature of symbolism and sacred geography, traditional architecture and iconography, is informed by Abhishiktananda's awareness that such matters cannot be *reduced* and *abstracted* to the level of *ideas* but must be *experienced* as *living realities*. Here, for example, is a characteristic passage, this one about the Vedic Revelation:

> These Vedic hymns, even when their outward meaning escapes one, have a uniquely penetrating power, at least for anyone who allows himself to be inwardly open to their spell-binding influence. We could say that, as they issue from the archetypal sources of being, so they irresistibly draw those who chant them, and equally those who hear them, into the same most secret sources of being. The mind thus finds itself carried off as if to an unknown world, a world in which however it has a marvelous sense of belonging, a world which is revealed in its very source, and yet which seems to disappear as soon as one attempts to define it in rational terms or to grasp it in concepts.[26]

Recalling his congenial philosophical discussions with a Brahmin follower of Ramana, Abhishiktananda observes,

> But now, as I look back, I cannot help smiling gently at such attempts to define in intellectual terms that which by its very nature excludes the possibility of being reduced to ideas. But even so, we have to

recognize that this has to be a starting-point for some—at least for those impenitent "Greeks" which most westerners are![27]

A scholar of comparative religion has acutely observed that,

> Religions do not all inhabit the same world, but actually posit, structure, and dwell within a universe that is their own. They can be understood not just as so many attempts to explain some common, objectively available order of things that is "out there," but as traditions that create and occupy their own universe.[28]

More than most Western pilgrims, Abhishiktananda was able to enter into the world of south Indian spirituality, to experience it directly, to live it. His descriptions of such practices as *pūjā* (worship), *japa* (invocation), *tapas* (austerities), and *pradakṣina* (circumambulation), and their place in Saivite spirituality, are those of a participant rather than a detached scholar or "spiritual tourist." The book closes with a vivid account of the Festival of Light, the Thibam of Kartikki.

Certainly there are moments when Abhishiktananda's European background and habits of mind pose some sort of obstacle or land him in difficulties—but these are rare. More remarkable is Abhishiktananda's ability to understand the spiritual ambience of southern India in its own terms. Whilst he makes some discreet references to his own religious tradition he does not view Hindu spirituality through a distorting Christian lens.

> India only reveals herself to those who are prepared to be still and over a long period to listen humbly at close quarters to the beating of her heart; only to those who have already entered sufficiently far into themselves, into their own depths, to be able to hear in the inner chamber of the heart that secret which India is ceaselessly whispering to them by means of a silence that transcends words. For silence is above all the language through which India reveals herself . . . and imparts her essential message, the message of interiority, of that which is Within.[29]

Abhishiktananda's fellow-countryman, Jean Biès, is another who has heard India's "message of interiority." He observes that "Something still exists in India that guarantees the duration of civilizations, and when forgotten, it hastens their end: the meaning of mystery and the sacred from which we have [suicidally] freed ourselves."[30] The spiritual wayfarer, seeking "the meaning of mystery and the sacred" in India, will find much to sustain and direct the quest in this marvelous book.

Guru and Disciple (1974)

Guru and Disciple hinges on Abhishiktananda's transformative encounter
with Gnanananda, and much of the book is given over to a sketch of
the swami and his teachings ("a perfect echo of the teachings of Sri
Ramana"[31]), and their immediate impact on the author. But, as with
The Secret of Arunachala, there is also a generous admixture of anecdote
and of keen observation of the life of the ashram and the surrounding
village. The book is cast in the form of a narrative about "Vanya" who
is clearly none other than Abhishiktananda himself. This device allows
Abhishiktananda to depict his experiences with a certain detachment.

Who was Sri Gnanananda? In the preceding chapter we briefly
answered this question in relation to his outer life. But here is another
answer, from Abhishiktananda himself:

> In truth the man who has realized the *ātman* is everywhere and lives
> for ever. He is the young Ramana fleeing towards Arunachala and
> he is also the priest who fed him on the way. He is the hermit who
> meditated in the forest in the days of the rajahs and he is the *sannyāsī*
> who met Auveyar. He is Yajna-valkya who revealed to King Janak the
> Upanishad of being, and he is the rishi who in primordial times heard
> the *Vedas*. Is he not Siva himself seated under the forest banyan tree...
> . He is the Without-Form Non-born, who shows something of himself
> in every form and appears afresh in every birth.[32]

As the *Katha Upanishad* has it, "He neither dies nor is born, the one
who knows. From where does he come? What will he become? non-
born, eternal, primordial, always himself!" For his followers Gnanananda was

> nothing less than the epiphany of the invisible presence, the outward
> manifestation to their human eyes of the grace and love of the Lord
> who dwells undivided both in the highest heavens and in the deepest
> depth of the heart.[33]

Although Gnanananda attracted a great many followers and was
widely revered as an authentic teacher of the wisdom of the *Upanishads*, he was little known in the West until the publication of *Guru
and Disciple*. Even today, outside south India he remains much less recognized than many of his less imposing contemporaries. It goes without
saying that he himself was quite indifferent to any kind of "fame." A
wealth of material about the *jñānī* has been gathered together by some
of his followers in *Sadguru Gnanananda: His Life, Personality, and
Teachings* (1979)—a book also, we note with interest, dedicated to
Abhishiktananda himself, with these words from the editors:

We have drawn a deep inspiration from . . . *Guru and Disciple* and we are sure that the haunting beauty and power of his exposition would capture readers' hearts as it has ours. To the hallowed memory of Swami Abhishiktananda, who could recapture the transcendent beauty of the spirit, and hold aloft the radiance of self-realization to light up the path of spiritual seekers, this book is dedicated with a profound gratitude and reverence.[34]

Such a passage serves to remind us not only of the significance of *Guru and Disciple* but of the spiritual affinity of Gnanananda and Abhishik-tananda, and of the esteem in which the French monk was held by the community at Tapovanam.

Gnanananda emerges from Abhishiktananda's pages as the "genuine article"—a fully-fledged *jñānī*, in the tradition initiated by Sankara and crowned in modern times by Ramana himself. His teachings, on Abhi-shiktananda's account, are as orthodox as one could wish. His "person-ality" is suggested by his perpetual smile, an infinite patience evinced in the gentle solicitude with which he always dealt with the simple village folk by whom he was for ever being importuned, his boundless kind-ness, especially to children, his indifference to his own material welfare. Also a man of tireless energy and vitality, quite unpredictable in his doings (often frustratingly so for his assistants!), radiating love and good humor but capable of sharp words to lazy or pretentious followers, involved in every aspect of the life of the several ashrams over which he presided. But above all a *jñānī* dedicated to the eternal message of the *Upanishads* and to the tradition of Vedanta in which those teachings were ever being actualized by those who had walked "the royal road of *dhyāna*." Like all authentic spiritual masters, Gnanananda exemplified and transmitted those qualities encapsulated in the Vedantic ternary of *sat-cit-ānanda*: a reality of Being, of intelligence and awareness, and of love-bliss-union.[35]

Guru and Disciple leaves the reader in no doubt not only about Gnanananda's status as a spiritual master but about his impact on Abhi-shiktananda:

He [Vanya] was absolutely convinced that here indeed was the guru he had so long dreamed of, the one who would enable him to leap over the crest, if only he were to agree to abandon himself to him in complete trust. . . . The guru's words rang bells within him in a way no one else's had ever done. It was as if, deep in his own heart, profound secret mysteries were coming to light which up till then had been buried in unfathomable depths. What the guru said vibrated through his whole being and the harmonies thus evoked were incomparable.[36]

In a letter from the interval between his first and second visits to Tapovanam Abhishiktananda had written, "How mysterious that Christ can take for a Christian the form of a Saivite guru!"[37] Later, in *Guru and Disciple*, he describes how his encounter with Gnanananda was "like a burn which marks one for life and leaves a permanent scar. Or like a fire which continues to burn as long as something remains to be devoured."[38]

Abhishiktananda is at pains to emphasize that his illuminations at Tapovanam had nothing to do with new *ideas* or *concepts* transmitted by the guru: he was already thoroughly versed in the traditional Upanishadic teachings. In any case he was no longer one of those "impenitent intellectuals," addicted to endless speculations and ratiocinations. At the level of the mind "he already knew everything that had been said to him here. He had read about it, heard tell of it, meditated deeply upon it."[39] In Abhishiktananda's case Gnanananda himself was ruthlessly insistent on the one thing needful—*dhyāna*:

> These discussions on wisdom and the so-called science of the Brahman are so much hot air. *Dhyāna* alone leads to the *ātman* who is *Brahman*. All the rest is just fun and games![40]

And yet, now, through the words of the guru, "an ineffable communication had been established between the master and himself in the depths of the one as of the other."[41] What Abhishiktananda *realized* at Tapovanam, more powerfully than ever before and under the influence of Gnanananda, was the reality of the Self "beyond all possible verbalization or experimentation," "an experience of totality which . . . wells up from the depths of one's being." As Abhishiktananda observes, "When this experience has hit a man one can say that he is 'done for,' at least with regard to all the ways in which he has so far sought to express himself and be aware of himself." His ego is "consumed by this implacable devouring flame."[42] In short, at Tapovanam Abhishiktananda experienced a transfiguring alchemy of the soul, triggered by his surrender to Gnanananda—one for which his long and arduous apprenticeship had prepared him. As Gnanananda was fond of saying, one can't make a fire with green wood!

This brief account of *Guru and Disciple* leaves much out of the reckoning; there is much else of considerable interest in the book—one might mention Abhishiktananda's resonant meditation on the primordial sound-syllable OM, his night-long vigil in the temple, and his ruminations on the symbolism of the Siva *liṅga*, the delicate evocation of the rituals with which the Saivite devotees greet the dawning of each new day, the pen-portraits of such figures as the faithful temple priest

Kailasandar who continues to discharge his duties though unpaid for a full year, or the impish children who scuttle about temple and ashram. Though there are many such delights, *Guru and Disciple* never achieves quite the vibrancy and charm of *The Secret of Arunachala*, perhaps because of the third-person narration. But its significance in the corpus at large can hardly be doubted, this being the book in which we are made witness to a pivotal moment in Abhishiktananda's life. As Abhishiktananda remarked,

> The meeting with the guru is the essential meeting, the decisive turning point in the life of a man. But it is a meeting that can only take place when one has gone beyond the level of sense and intellect. It happens in the beyond, in the fine point of the soul as the mystics say.[43]

More generally the book made both Indian and Western readers aware of Sri Gnanananda—that alone would ensure the book an honored place. Interestingly, Abhishiktananda himself regarded *Guru and Disciple* as his most durable and significant work, writing in the last year of his life that of all his books, it "is almost the only thing that remains afloat. All the rest consists of *nāma-rūpa* amusing itself with 'the theology of fulfilment.'"[44] We need not share this harsh judgment of his other work while saluting *Guru and Disciple* as a very fine book indeed.

Saccidananda (1974)

By the early 60s Abhishiktananda was spending more and more time at Gyansu. In his modest hermitage he plunged ever deeper into his reading of the *Upanishads* and into his meditations on Hindu-Christian themes. It was also in these years that he participated in a series of retreats and seminars, organized with Dr J.A. Cuttat, which addressed the ways in which Christianity and Vedanta might be mutually illuminating. Two books grew directly out of these experiences: *Hindu-Christian Meeting Point* and *Saccidananda*. For reasons which will be discussed later, *Saccidananda* is much the more satisfactory of the two. Both books are somewhat weakened by the theology of fulfillment to which Abhishiktananda still subscribed at that time. He also concedes that the treatment of the Trinity is still circumscribed by "the formulation of the dogma . . . which was originally worked out in terms of Greek thought."[45] The revised English language smoothed out some of the excesses of fulfillment theology, though, as the author readily concedes, the book still bears its imprint. He eventually became somewhat frustrated with his attempts at "the patching up of an old wall"[46] and spoke of the difficulty of revising "a book whose thesis one no longer accepts."[47] Starting his revisions for the English edition of *Saccidananda* (first published in French as *Sagesse hindoue mystique chrétienne*), he wrote in his journal:

> *Sagesse* is an attempt, "begging for help," "agonized," to recover one's footing when the waves—the ground-swell of *advaita* that seizes and bears all away—are carrying one off to the open sea. Why then desire at all cost to regain one's footing? The waves—just like the air— surely provide as safe a support as the sand of the shallows.[48]

Later he would write, "My whole thesis in *Sagesse* has collapsed, and in this total collapse is the awakening."[49] From Abhishiktananda's own point of view, then, *Saccidananda* is overtaken by his later writings.

Notwithstanding these skeptical qualifications on Abhishiktananda's part, for many Christian theologians it constitutes Abhishiktananda's most significant work—perhaps because it is the work in which we find his most mature Christian theology and his most considered reflections on the theme signaled by the book's subtitle, "A Christian Approach to Advaitic Experience." Fr Emmanuel Vattakuzhy calls *Saccidananda* "his most important work, containing his most mature theological thinking," while Judson Trapnell considers it "his most sustained theological work."[50] But, to deploy one of Abhishiktananda's own favorite images, the book overflows many of the limits that such a term implies.

For the moment let us attend primarily to the Introduction for the English version, written in 1971. It offers one of the author's most succinct statements about the urgent imperative of Hindu-Christian dialogue in the fullest sense of the term. Abhishiktananda opens his Introduction with some remarks about the changes which have taken place in the Church and in the world at large since the book's composition in the early 60s. As is well-known, the Second Vatican Council was a watershed in the ways in which the Church perceived its relations with other traditions. Abhishiktananda is now able to write,

> The Vatican Council took it for granted that salvation is open to any sincere man, whatever religious convictions he may or may not have, and thereby recognized the fact that only a minority of men will work out their eternal destiny with any reference to Christ's incarnation. Not only is it necessary to grant the actual existence of religious pluralism here and now, but it is also impossible to foresee a time in the historical future when Christianity might become for mankind as a whole even the predominant—let alone the only—way of realizing their transcendent vocation.[51]

This momentous development really sounded the long overdue death-knell of both "crisis theology" (all outside the Biblical revelation is "darkness and sin") and "fulfillment theology" (all religions will find their ultimate "fulfillment" in Christ).

Abhishiktananda is happy to leave theologians to wrestle with the *theoretical* problems posed for the Church by these new developments, but in this changing environment the need for "more and more intimate contacts at various levels between men of different faiths and cultures" is making itself ever more urgently felt.[52] Furthermore, real interreligious dialogue must go well beyond "relations of mutual sympathy" and beyond debate about doctrinal matters, and aim at

> a kind of inner communion at the level of the spirit, so that, even when a difference of opinion cannot be bridged at the conceptual level, both parties instinctively look for a higher and deeper insight to which their opposing ways of expressing themselves are only partial approximations.[53]

It is in this context and in this spirit that Abhishiktananda hopes the book will now be read.

Finally, in this Introduction, Abhishiktananda stresses that *Saccidananda* is not a work of systematic theology but rather,

> Its form is that of a continuous meditation, starting again and again and continually returning on itself, concerning the fundamental themes of the [Hindu-Christian] encounter. It is the meditation of one who is rooted in the spiritual and intellectual traditions of the Church, but has now come into direct contact with the intuitions of the *Upanishads* and the living experience of the sages. One cannot believe that such intuitions will not evoke wonderful echoes in the Christian soul.[54]

The contents of the book will command more detailed discussion and analysis later in this study. Suffice it for the moment to signal at least some of the subjects and themes which it unfolds: the mystery of the Absolute, "beyond all names," as it is prefigured in both the Biblical revelation and the *Upanishads;* the significance of Ramana Maharshi as a living embodiment of the wisdom of the *Upanishads;* the interior quest for the Self and the challenge posed to the monotheistic faiths by *advaita;* the Cosmic Covenant and *Sanātana dharma* (perennial or eternal wisdom); the experiential reconciliation of non-dualism and Trinitarianism; the ideal of "diversity harmonized in love, multiplicity transcended in communion"[55]; acosmism and the vocation of the *jñāni;* the nature of faith; "the bliss of the Spirit." In the course of his explorations Abhishiktananda observes that the integration of the advaitic experience into his own faith is for the Christian a necessary task. . . . If Christianity should prove to be incapable of assimilating Hindu spiritual experience from within, Christians would thereby at once lose the right to claim that it is the universal way of salvation.[56]

It is precisely this "integration of the advaitic experience" into his own Christian faith, thereby breaking a trail for other Christians, that comprises the purpose and substance of *Saccidananda*.

Towards the Renewal of the Indian Church (1970)

This book is a slightly revised memorandum written for a small group of Christians preparing for the All-India Seminar of the Roman Catholic Church in 1969. Its subject is the integration of the "cultural, religious, and spiritual heritage" of India into the life of the Church. Although offered as no more than a series of exploratory notes it is one of Abhishiktananda's most coherent and extended considerations of a subject which was one of the main preoccupations of his life in India. It is not our present purpose to consider Abhishiktananda's proposals in any detail, nor to gauge what impact this document actually had on the Church in India, but only to take note of its general thrust.

The book opens with one of Abhishiktananda's most salient themes in his writings about the Church:

> The Church is essentially a spiritual reality and Christian religion is, first of all, a living experience in the Spirit. Its source is nothing other than the inner experience of Jesus. . . . The Church is the social and human milieu in which that experience of Jesus is transmitted through all ages and to all men by the Word and the Sacraments. She is not an end in herself. She is a sign, herself a sacrament . . . just as in man the essential is the spirit, so in the Church, too, the essential is that inner reality in the heart of every man where his spirit is in direct communion with the Holy Spirit.[57]

It follows, then, that the interior life of the spirit is the most important thing in the life of both the Christian individual and of the Church itself. Indeed, *"unless such a conviction is widely disseminated, nothing worthwhile will be achieved in the Church."*[58] He reminds readers that ecclesiastical authorities have all too often been more concerned with the external aspects of the institution rather than with the work of the Spirit. This has produced "dangerous deviations," "unhealthy and superstitious use of the sacraments" and "a shameless collusion with worldly powers, either political or economical." It has also promoted "an improper rivalry" with other religions. Abhishiktananda also notes that

> We cannot indeed hide the fact in a candid examination of conscience, that too many activities in the Church directed theoretically to spread the Kingdom, are simply the self-satisfying projections in a "mythico-religious" sphere of man's insuppressible need for self-expression.[59]

Elsewhere Abhishiktananda had written, referring to both the Universal Church and the Church in India, that "The moment in history in which we are living calls us to a stern purification of all our means. . . ," a task of which he sometimes despaired.[60] For many Indians, Christians were whites who "ate meat, wore leather, and went into holy places with their shoes on."[61] However, Abhishiktananda always hoped and prayed that the Church could be redeemed by those "deep contemplative souls" who, open to the Spirit, attune the Church to that same Spirit, thus ensuring that even the most humble of worldly-inspired works in the vineyard will not be entirely devoid of spiritual fruits.

Abhishiktananda notes that the Church faces two formidable challenges in the contemporary world: on the one side by those forces in the modern Western world which consider Christianity to be, at best, no more than "a kind of fiduciary currency, lacking security, worth just the credulity of the ignorant man";[62] on the other hand there is the challenge which the civilizations of the East present out of their own spiritual experience. The confrontation with secular atheism and with Eastern spirituality together pose "the most formidable challenge the Church has ever met in the course of her history."[63] Exacerbating the difficulty of meeting these challenges is the unhappy fact that so much Christian theology is abstract, mechanical, divorced from lived experience, over-burdened with historicism. With these salutary and sometimes vinegary reflections to the forefront, Abhishiktananda turns to the question at hand: how is the Church in India to assimilate the spiritual nutrients offered by the Hindu tradition, and how, in turn, is the Church to find "the best openings through which to instill the grace of the Holy Spirit entrusted to her and consequently, the most central and far-reaching channels through which to enable divine grace to fructify a hundredfold."[64] Rather than rehearsing the details of Abhishiktananda's book, suffice it here to give a consolidated summary of those things which he urges the Church to affirm and pursue:

- the primacy of spiritual values and the centrality of contemplation to spiritual life;

- the promotion of interreligious dialogue, based on a "a common sharing of that 'awareness' within," by persons "dedicated to a life of prayer and contemplation," and in places "sanctified by the silence and meditation of holy men";[65]
- the assimilation into Christian practice of various insights and techniques derived from such traditional Indian disciplines as yoga (the control of mind and body so as to achieve that inner silence in which we answer "the call to interiority"), *nāma-japa* (invocation of the holy Name), and various austerities;
- the nurturing of the thirst, in a Christian context, for *brahmavidyā* (knowledge of the Supreme Reality) by the development of the traditional "qualifications": the ability to discriminate between things permanent and impermanent; renunciation of attachment to the fruits of action, both in this world and the hereafter; the six virtues, including the quietening of the mind, and faith in the Scriptures and the guru; the yearning for *mokṣa* (deliverance);
- the re-animation of the "cosmic covenant" within Christianity;
- the adjustment of various aspects of daily life to accord with the Indian milieu, including fasting, abstinence from flesh-eating, and the regular observance of periods of silence;
- the development of an Indian liturgy *in Sanskrit* (anything else would be "an affair of the studio, an abstract thing, a work of mere scholars"[66]);
- the integration of Hindu Scriptures and Hindu festivals into Christian worship;
- a much deeper study, particularly by the religious, of Hindu Scriptures, mythology, symbolism, iconography, the Sanskrit language, etc.; the establishment of various courses and centers to this end; such formal studies to be accompanied by regular exposure to the religious life of India by extended stays in Hindu maths, ashrams, and the like;
- the development of "a genuine Christian *sannyāsa*";
- the spread of Christian ashrams where Christian communities can live "on traditional Hindu lines" and in which "an authentic Indo-Christian spirituality, liturgy, and theology will evolve."[67]

The Mountain of the Lord: Pilgrimage to Gangotri (1966)

In June, 1964, Abhishiktananda and Raimon Panikkar (who appears in the narrative as "Sanat Kumar") walked the ancient Himalayan pilgrim route from Haridwar to Gangotri, climbing to Gomukh where the

Ganges finds one of its sources in the melting glaciers. Here, close to the abode of Lord Siva, the two Christian pilgrims celebrated the Eucharist. After farewelling his companion in Uttarkashi, Abhishiktananda returned to Gangotri to spend three weeks in total silence. These experiences are recounted in *The Mountain of the Lord*, first published in 1966 but gaining much wider circulation when it appeared in 1974 as a companion piece to "A Sage of the East," the two together comprising *Guru and Disciple*. Abhishiktananda described it as "an unmistakably Christian meditation on the theme of a Hindu pilgrimage."[68]

This short work is one of Abhishiktananda's most attractive, giving a glimpse of the existential intensity, if one may so put it, with which he lived in the two worlds of Christianity and Hinduism. The account of the outer journey, their fellow pilgrims, and the landscape through which they moved finds the author at his most poetical, though the narrative also touches on the penitential hardships of the journey. Early in the piece:

> Behold the great peaks of the Himalaya, the summit of the world, Earth's supreme effort to reach up to Heaven! Thrusting upwards to the greatest possible height, they soar towards the sky, as if to lay hold of the "waters above the firmament," of which *Genesis* speaks—to lay hold of them, and cause them to fall back to earth . . . the meeting point of the world above—that inaccessible world from which none the less we come and to which we go—with the world below in which for the time being we lead our earthly lives.[69]

For Abhishiktananda, surrounded by the sights and sounds of the Hindu faithful, experiencing the grandeur of the mountains was very much a matter of "seeing God everywhere"—not just an aesthetic pleasure but "to those who can discern everywhere the traces of God's handiwork, it [the landscape] gives a call to spiritual joy and thanksgiving."[70]

The Mountain of the Lord is not only a hymn to the sublime Himalayan peaks, symbolizing transcendence, but also to the solitaries, recluses, renunciates, "acosmics" to be found in the caves and forests on their slopes. By extension it could also be seen as an affirmation of the vocation of the solitary renunciate, whether a Christian monk in the Syrian desert, the Hindu *muni*, the Tibetan *naldjorpa* in the snowy fastness, the Taoist recluse, the shaman on a vision quest, the *staretz* of the Russian forests. Such figures are also symbolized by the mountains with their life-giving waters. "The high mountains point upwards towards heaven, stark naked, *dig-ambara*, clad in space. Such is also the monk—naked, solitary, motionless."[71] The symbolism is, of course, irresistible and one we find expressed by many contemplatives. Thomas Merton, for instance:

> The great, gashed, half-naked mountain is another of God's saints. There is no other like him. He is alone in his own character; nothing else in the world ever did or ever will imitate God in quite the same way. That is his sanctity.[72]

Later Abhishiktananda returns to his theme, calling the solitary witnesses to the Absolute "the pivots of this world, holding it steady by their own stillness within the Unmovable."[73] More than ever before, he writes, both the world at large and the Church in particular need these "immovable pillars" because "the world is more than ever carried away in the stream of events"; today

> the more urgent is the need for some at least to allow themselves to be brought by . . . the Spirit into the mystery of the Unmanifested, and [to] remain there, remote, isolated, naked, and silent, both outwardly and inwardly, before God and mankind.[74]

By so doing, the monk "bears witness to the truth that time proceeds from and returns to Eternity."[75]

After musing on the various rites of the *sādhus* and the devotions of the pilgrims, Abhishiktananda reflects that,

> It was surely fitting that a Christian also should come and worship in these high places, that he should come there to "fulfill" all signs, myths, and images, and to enable the vast sacrament of the cosmos to pass from the sign to its reality in Christ, in the Eucharist.[76]

On the Feast of the Sacred Heart, soon after sunrise, the two companions climbed to a sheltered spot and bathed in the icy waters of the glacier, thus re-enacting the primordial cosmic rite of the return to the primeval womb, the source of Being, and at the same time recalling the rite of baptism which "so powerfully symbolizes the mystery of our rebirth."[77] Then, with a little wine and a chappati of unleavened flour, the air perfumed with burning incense, with the roar of the holy river "like a mighty organ accompaniment," they celebrated the holy mystery.

> Immediately overhead we had the great heavenly luminary in whose bright light the surrounding snows were a dazzling white—the same sun which sees all that happens on the face of the earth, which enlightened the eyes of our first parents, and at which Jesus gazed as he hung upon the cross—the sun which is the ever present witness of all that is, was, or will be.[78]

And so it was that through this "final and perfect oblation," the count-less hymns and prayers of the pilgrims of the ages, their chants and devotions, their austerities and deprivations, the silence and penances of the ascetics, were all "gathered up and fulfilled in the sacrifice of the Lamb."[79]

In the end *The Mountain of the Lord* is itself a kind of prayer, rever-berating with the chants of the pilgrims and the sounds of bird and stream, set amidst the majestic Himalayan peaks, and culminating in the celebration of the sacrament. It calls to mind a passage from Frithjof Schuon in which he beautifully depicts man at prayer in the sanctuary of Nature herself:

> The saint has himself become prayer, the meeting place of earth and Heaven; and thus he contains the universe and the universe prays with him. He is everywhere where nature prays and he prays with and in her: in the peaks which touch the void and eternity, in a flower which scatters itself, or in the abandoned song of a bird.[80]

The Further Shore (1975)

The Further Shore comprises two separate works, *The Upanishads,* written in 1971 but never finally revised, and *Sannyāsa*, a series of essays written in 1973, first seeing the light of day in serialized form in *The Divine Life*, the monthly organ of the Sivananda Ashram in Rishikesh. Together these writings are the ripest fruit of Abhishiktananda's engage-ment with Indian spirituality, and can properly be regarded as his "spiri-tual testament." In this final work, completed only a few months before his passing, Abhishiktananda offers us his most seasoned reflections on many of the subjects which had preoccupied him since he first set foot on Indian soil, nearly a quarter of a century before. *The Further Shore* is the summit of his written work just as those few incandescent weeks between the *dīkṣā* of his disciple and his own "great adventure" in the bazaar of Rishikesh was to be the culmination of his existential journey in search of "the secret of Arunachala." As is suggested by the unidenti-fied writer of the Foreword (almost certainly Marc Chaduc), *Sannyāsa* is written "in letters of fire and reveals the inner fervor which consumed him to his very depths and summoned him irresistibly to an ever more acosmic life, totally absorbed in the inward vision."[81] Furthermore, it is altogether appropriate that these writings on renunciation should be published side-by-side with Abhishiktananda's last written meditation on the mystery of *Brahman*, the central theme of the *Upanishads*, these

Scriptures themselves affirming that *brahmavidyā* and *sannyāsa* are inseparable. As the *Mahānārāyana Upanishad* has it,

> That mystery of glory and immortality,
> Hidden in the depth of the heart and in highest heaven,
> Which only those can find
> Who have renounced all.[82]

These two subjects were very close to Abhishiktananda's heart: *sannyāsa* most fully expressed the ideal towards which he had been striving throughout the years in India while the *Upanishads* opened the gateway to the advaitic experience.

> His spiritual path essentially consisted in the complete appropriation of the Advaitic experience of the Upanishadic rishis, without however losing hold of his own rootedness in the Christian tradition. He made the *Upanishads* his own, and whenever he happened to comment on them, it was always with a reverent enthusiasm and in order to bring out the radiance of their marvelous intuition.[83]

Sannyāsa presents a limpid exposition of the meaning of this "sign beyond signs," particularly in the Indian tradition but also in its universality, for as Abhishiktananda so rightly claims, "The call to complete renunciation cuts across all *dharmas* and disregards all frontiers . . . it is anterior to every religious formulation."[84] He examines the way the ideal has been practiced over the centuries and considers some of the pressures and degenerations which have come with modernity. Abhishiktananda also ponders the ways in which *sannyāsa* might be assimilated into the Christian tradition to reanimate those spiritual impulses which were so evident in the flight of the Christian solitaries to the deserts of Egypt and Syria and to the forests of Russia. In one of the most arresting passages in *Sannyāsa*, Abhishiktananda explains how the ideal is actually, though paradoxically, embodied in the sacrament of the Eucharist which itself can be a "sign beyond signs."[85]

The Upanishads: An Introduction rehearses many of the themes which Abhishiktananda had explored many times previously—but here he writes with an unsurpassed clarity and power, distilling the insights of both his many years of study of these texts (the *Bṛhadāranyaka* and *Chāndogya Upanishads* being the ones which "most faithfully express Upanishadic thought in its radical purity"[86]), and of his own sometimes vertiginous experiences of *advaita*. The author contextualizes these Scriptures, explicates their controlling themes, and offers the readers various keys with which to unlock their secrets. This work also presents some wise reflections on a range of questions pertaining to the nature of religion and the so-called problems of religious pluralism. Here, for instance, is one of his last attempts to define "faith":

> Contrary to what is too often supposed, faith does not primarily consist in the mind's acceptance of certain propositions, termed "data of revelation." Faith is essentially that interior sense by which the mind penetrates obscurely into those depths of one's own being which it realizes are beyond its power to explore solely by means of thought and sense-perception.[87]

All in all, *The Further Shore*, written indeed in "letters of fire," must be one of the most stirring expressions of the universal ideal of renunciation, and of the wisdom which is its fruit. To return directly to the *Upanishads* themselves, as Abhishiktananda so frequently does in these pages: *sannyāsa* is the way to

> That mystery of glory and immortality
> Hidden in the depth of the heart, beyond the firmament,
> Which cannot be won either by ritual acts,
> Or by begetting offspring,
> Or by giving one's wealth:
> But which only they can enter
> Who have renounced all.[88]

B. Other Books

An Indian Benedictine Ashram (with Jules Monchanin) (1951)

The first edition of this booklet, written by Monchanin and Abhishiktananda, was published on 10th October, 1951, the day on which the chapel at Shantivanam was blessed. Its purpose was to acquaint readers with "the aim and *raison d'être* of the humble hermitage opened discreetly on the Kavery banks on the feast of St Benedict, the previous year."[89] Only five hundred copies were initially printed. It was expanded for the French edition, *Ermites du Saccidananda* (1956), and a revised edition of the English text appeared as *A Benedictine Ashram*, without the pleonasm of the original title. It portrays its authors' vision of a Christian ashram, and gives a lucid account of the theology underlying it. Much of the book centers on monasticism as the bridge which could link the world of Indian spirituality and the Church. Although the first chapter was written by Monchanin, it fairly represents their shared views at the time. As such it is an invaluable source on both Monchanin and Abhishiktananda, and is a landmark document in the history of the

Christian ashram movement. It provoked both excitement and disturbance in ecclesiastical circles in India and France.

Hindu-Christian Meeting Point (1969)

No book written by Abhishiktananda is without its pearls and there is
much of interest in *Hindu-Christian Meeting Point,* such as the meditations on the *Upanishads,* and the explication of certain Scriptural
passages, particularly Johannine, in an Upanishadic light. Much of
what Abhishiktananda has to say about both Christian and Hindu traditions is instructive. But, taken as a whole the book is not one of his
more commanding works. There are several readily apparent reasons
for this. Firstly, the book suffers from a certain "identity crisis": is it a
report of various intrareligious retreats and seminars concerned with
the encounter of these two traditions, striving to give a fair account
of what transpired, or is it Abhishiktananda's own responses to these
encounters? Secondly, perhaps partly as a result of the ambiguity raised
by this question, there is an unresolved tension in the book between
the fulfillment theology then very much in vogue in the Indian Church,
and an unequivocal affirmation of the wisdom literature of India and the
spiritual experience to which it testifies. Thirdly, various interrelated
questions arising out of the general theme are more decisively dealt with
in other works by Abhishiktananda—and here one is thinking primarily
of *Saccidananda* and *The Further Shore.* As to the practical questions
raised by the meeting of Hindus and Christians, both as individuals
and as collectivities, these are addressed more coherently in *Towards
a Renewal of the Indian Church.* Whilst *Hindu-Christian Meeting Point*
gives us some insights into Abhishiktananda's own spiritual experience,
it is also the least personal of his published works—and this, too, at least
in part, derives from the fact that one of its purposes is to report fairly
on the deliberations of the Cuttat Circle as a whole.

The Eyes of Light (1983)

The Eyes of Light is a posthumous compilation of several essays, some
previously unpublished, gathered together by Abhishiktananda's friend
Fr Joseph Lemarié, and appearing in the first French edition in 1979.
The opening essay, "The Experience of God in the Religions of the Far
East," is a new translation of an article which had appeared in *Cistercian Studies* in 1974. In it are to be found many of Abhishiktananda's
familiar themes about the differing but convergent spiritual/religious

traditions of East and West, including more allusions to Buddhism than we find in most of his other writings on the same subject. Other essays concern the contemplative prayer of Silence and Presence, derived from the wisdom of the *Upanishads* and constituting "India's contribution to Christian prayer," the theology of Presence (which was now over-taking the theology of fulfillment in the Indian Church), the formation of priests in the Indian Church, and spiritual childhood. The longest essay, "India and the Carmelite Order" (from *Carmel*, 1965) is another lengthy meditation on the message of the *Upanishads*, the place of contemplative monastic orders in the Church at large, and the role that the Carmelite Order might yet play in Indian Christianity. The book includes excerpts from Abhishiktananda's correspondence to Madame I. Charnelet, Mother Françoise-Thérèse, his family, Fr Lemarié, and to Father Miguel, a professed monk of the Abbey Sainte-Marie de Paris. Some fragments from his journal are also presented.

One of the most singular essays, brief though it is, is "Gandhi, Witness of the Truth," reproduced from *Annales de sainte Thérèse de Lisieux* (January 1970).[90] Abhishiktananda's reflections recall those made by the great German theologian, philosopher, and comparative religionist, Rudolf Otto. Otto claimed that people in the West mis-read Gandhi if we understand him primarily as a politician, a statesman, a doer of great deeds on the public stage; the key to Gandhi's character and his vocation is that he was a renunciate: his political activities and achievements grew out of his immediate situation; had Gandhi been in different circumstances, he would still have been a *sādhu*.[91] Abhishik-tananda hails Gandhi as a prophet and as one of those "in whom the mystery of the invisible Presence has manifested itself in the midst of their brethren with a particularly intense brilliancy."[92] This Presence, to which Gandhi often gave the name "Truth," was "a living and felt reality" in which his life was rooted and which fed all of his activities. The campaign for the liberation of his people from the foreign yoke was paralleled by the inner struggle against the ever-present enemies of the soul—"falsehood and selfishness, hatred and violence, greed."[93] Like Otto, Abhishiktananda finds something quintessentially Indian in Gandhi, without which his appeal would be quite inexplicable:

> To be sure Gandhi had his peculiarities which amused or annoyed his followers. No doubt some of his options can be debated; no doubt free India, on the whole, still remains quite far from the lofty ideal that Gandhi would have liked to inculcate in her soul. Nevertheless it was precisely the idealism of Gandhi, this sense of the absolute, of the Truth, of Love, that he derived from his contemplation of the inner mystery, his sense, in a word, of the sovereign presence of God, which

shook and drew his people, which made it attach itself to the Mahatma as to a charismatic leader, as to an emissary of God, and to follow him blindly in defiance of all obstacles. This people recognized itself in him.[94]

Thomas Merton recognized the same quality in the Mahatma:

It was the spiritual consciousness of a people that was awakened in the spirit of one person. But the message of the Indian spirit, of Indian wisdom, was not for India alone. It was for the entire world.[95]

Abhishiktananda also comments on Gandhi's attitude to religious pluralism and defends him against the absurd reproach that some Christians (both Indian and European) leveled against him, his failure to enter the Church.

Some dared even accuse him of insincerity. Had he not read the *Bible*? Had he not loudly proclaimed that the figure and the message of Christ had exercised a great influence on him? His failure to take this step may have been precisely due to the fact that Gandhi was too attached to truth, to this very truth that Jesus himself preached, to arrive at recognizing in the Church the authentic and unique messenger of this truth. . . . Perhaps it can be attributed also, and above all, to this sense of the absolute of God which is at the base of the whole religious attitude of India. God is beyond all expression, all form, all history. Saints and prophets all manifest him, each in his own way. Each one is the mystery of God become visible among men. The current of the river returns to its source, the manifestation to the unmanifest, the form to the mystery that goes beyond all form, time to eternity. Attentive to God everywhere, the sage discovers him everywhere. All signs lead to him. And he sees no reason to give privileged preference to one or the other of these signs.[96]

Furthermore, it might be added, Gandhi had no reason to abandon the "signs" of the Absolute with which the indigenous traditions of both Hinduism and Jainism had nourished his soul and which found expression in his devotion to that form of the Absolute, Rama, whose very name sprang to his lips at the moment of his death.[97]

C. Unpublished Works and Miscellanea

Amour et Sagesse (1942) (unpublished)

Written for his mother in 1942, this unpublished manuscript is an important way station on Abhishiktananda's spiritual journey. It is a deep pondering on the theme of the Trinity which Abhishiktananda regarded as the "noblest mystery" of Christianity, "so little savored" even by fervent believers.[98] It also introduces some of the mystical themes which were to sound throughout the whole *oeuvre*, and makes some reference to Indian literature, including Tagore's *Gītāñjali*. Odette Baumer-Despeigne has observed that "It is a striking fact that the Mystery of the Trinity was the subject both of the earliest writing and the last entry in his spiritual diary."[99] And indeed, there, in the final entry, we find him writing,

> The Trinity can only be understood in the experience of *advaita*. The Trinity is an experience not a *theologoumenon*. Or at least the *theologoumenon* never conveys its truth. . . . The Trinity is the ultimate mystery of oneself.[100]

In the introduction to *Amour et Sagesse*, Henri tells his mother that "I have set down nothing here except what is my own."[101] In other words, these "personal reflections on the wonderful characteristics of divine love and wisdom" came from his own experience, and were written from the heart. This was to be true of nearly all of his writings.

Guhantara: au sein du fond (1953) (unpublished)

Monchanin called this work "a spiritual essay born out of silence" while Abhishiktananda himself described it as "the direct expression of my first overwhelming experiences" (at Arunachala).[102] In the words of his biographer, "it was the first detailed articulation of the confrontation between Christianity and *advaita*."[103] It fell foul of the ecclesiastic censor in Paris, one Fr J. Guennou, who found it full of "heresies" and "redolent of relativism, modernism, quietism, modalism, and especially pantheism."[104] His report on the book was totally damning and, as James Stuart observes, "so negative as to be ludicrous"—so much so that on receiving it, after the initial shock Abhishiktananda and Monchanin could only burst into laughter.[105] *Guhantara* (which means "the dweller within the cave") was widely circulated in manuscript form amongst some of the French clergy and amongst Abhishiktananda's friends and acquaintances in India. Parts of it were published in other books and as fragments. It adumbrates some of the major themes which were to run through Abhishiktananda's works over the rest of his life. The first essay in particular, "The Special Grace of India," anticipated much of Abhishiktananda's later work in its emphasis on the interiority of Indian spirituality and in his call for the Church to heed the lessons of India in order to penetrate beyond the merely intellectual and moral dimensions of the Christian faith.

Swami Parama Arubi Anandam: Fr J. Monchanin 1895-1957 (1959)

This book was edited and largely written by Abhishiktananda—but he is nowhere mentioned by name. It comprises three parts: "glimpses of his [Monchanin's] life and ideals," written by the editor; "a garland of memories" in which we find tributes from both European and Indian friends (including Bishop Mendonça, Bede Griffiths, Raimon Panikkar, Henri de Lubac and Harold Rose); thirdly, extracts from Monchanin's writings and letters. It is a heartfelt tribute to a man with whom Abhishiktananda had shared many deep experiences, and testifies to Monchanin's many fine qualities, discussed in earlier chapters. (It is now a difficult book to locate, but well worth the effort for those interested in Monchanin.)

In Spirit and Truth: An Essay on Prayer and Life (1989)

This essay, concerned largely with the Christian path, derived from some notes written for the Carmel of Lisieux in 1961, and was first published in French as an appendix to *Eveil à soi—éveil à Dieu* (Paris: Centurion, 1971). After its translation into English by Mary Rogers it was further modified by Abhishiktananda in 1972.

D. Letters and Journal

In his Introduction to *Ascent to the Depth of the Heart: The Spiritual Diary (1948-73) of Swami Abhishiktananda (Dom Henri Le Saux)*, the editor makes the following observations:

> We cannot insist too much on the fact that this Diary, which only follows his Indian journey, embodies for Swamiji his personal monologue: he examines himself, sometimes absolutely ruthlessly, clarifies his ideas, and also challenges them. These pages reflect the central preoccupation of his whole life, on which all others converge: the Mystery of the Absolute from the perspective of *advaita*.

He also draws a telling distinction (made by the diarist himself):

> The difference between the Diary and his published writings is not only a matter of form and finish. It is also one of perspective. In his books he is aware of his role as a Christian mystic who writes chiefly for Christians (and westerners) in order to open their minds to Hindu

wisdom. In his Diary he is more and more the Hindu monk who is faced with the Christian mystery and is desperately trying to reconcile it with Vedanta. . . . This Diary is, so to speak, the laboratory of the alchemist; the forerunner of something unknown.[106]

Susan Vishvanathan has called the letters and diaries "the real *art* forms of Abhishiktananda's mysticism."[107] It might be said that in these "private murmurings of a solitary," these "pages written in the raw flesh of his being—the outpourings of his thought, the expressions of his doubts and seeking, the stammerings or the poetical flights of his ecstasies"[108]—we see Abhishiktananda strip himself naked. The *Diary*, then, is essential reading for anyone trying to retrace Abhishiktananda's existential journey. The editor concedes that the publication of such a diary might be "highly indiscreet, a kind of profanation of what . . . ought to remain hidden." But he finds some sanction in the fact that Abhishiktananda reproduced parts of his journal in his own books and especially prepared others for publication, and also anticipated the possibility of an edited publication. He also believes that Abhishiktananda's journal offers exemplary experiences for those moving across religious frontiers and "symbolizes a life lived in depth in the midst of a world that has fallen apart."[109] He also urges readers to read it in the context of Abhishiktananda's more considered and nuanced published works and in the light of his experience at large.[110]

Abhishiktananda accumulated a set of notebooks, comprising over two thousand pages which, over the years, suffered a good deal of damage from the elements. The notebooks are written in a script by no means easy to read, some of it quite indecipherable. They are littered with terms and phrases from English, Greek, Sanskrit, Latin, Tamil, and Hindi, and exhibit a "violent" disregard for grammar. The daunting task of bringing the Diary into a form that might be published was taken up by the Abhishiktananda Society which drew on the work of several people—Madame Baumer-Despeigne who typed out many of the entries, Raimon Panikkar as editor, David Fleming and James Stuart as translators. In the last chapter we noted something of the joy and fulfillment which Abhishiktananda derived from his disciple Marc Chaduc. But this relationship had at least one consequence which, on the face of it at least, was unfortunate. Abhishiktananda gave Chaduc his diary entries from November 1966 onwards, to do with as he liked. Chaduc transcribed portions of the diary and then threw away the original. As Friesen has noted, there is no reason to suppose that Chaduc's copying was anything but faithful, but the fact remains that significant portions of the diary are now lost forever.[111]

*

No less prodigious a labor was entailed in gathering together as much as possible of Abhishiktananda's vast correspondence. We have already observed that he was addicted to reading—no less to letter-writing! (In both respects he is somewhat reminiscent of his fellow-monk, Thomas Merton.) In 1974 some of Abhishiktananda's friends and associates conceived the idea of a memorial volume, under the editorship of Sr Sara Grant, which would include some excerpts from his letters. As the editor came to read through the letters drawn from fifteen separate collections, she was struck by the thought that the letters, with some judicious arrangement, might form the basis of "a vivid mosaic of Swamiji's life in India, told largely in his own words." Because of her other commitments, Sr Sara handed the task over to her colleague, Fr James Stuart. It was not until 1989 that *Swami Abhishiktananda: His Life Told through His Letters* saw the light of day as a publication of ISPCK. But Fr Stuart's labors in the intervening years had garnered a rich harvest. The book is now indispensable for anyone interested in Abhishiktananda's life in India. The letters themselves also reveal facets of Abhishiktananda's personality, his relationships and his daily doings which are either altogether absent or obscured in his other works. Fr Stuart has also done us a fine service in constructing the fullest Bibliography of Abhishiktananda.

*

All of Abhishiktananda's books contain many treasures and delights. We best appreciate each one not in isolation but when it is situated in the whole existential journey to which each book testifies at a particular moment. Each reader will respond to these works differently. For my own part I would single out four works as especially precious: *The Secret of Arunachala*—a love song to the spirit of India, a rhapsody written in a state of holy intoxication, and a profound homage to Ramana and Arunachala; *Mountain of the Lord*, a brief but poignant account of a pilgrimage, a glimpse into the density of Abhishiktananda's spiritual life, and a canticle to the Himalayan peaks; *The Further Shore*, the final distillation of Abhishiktananda's hard-earned spiritual insight and including some of the most exalted mystical passages of recent times; and *Ascent to the Depth of the Heart*, a spiritual journal of raw intensity in which a profoundly noble but troubled soul is laid bare.

A Note on Writings about Abhishiktananda

Of the several books devoted to Abhishiktananda, the first to appear was *Indian Christian Sannyāsa and Swami Abhishiktananda* (1981), by Father Emmanuel Vattakuzhy of St Joseph's Pontifical Seminary in Kerala. Originating in a doctoral thesis, it describes the place of *sannyāsa* in the Indian tradition before turning to an examination of Abhishiktananda's life in this context. It also draws out the significance of Abhishiktananda's life for the Indian Church. It was followed in 1986 by Antony Kalliath's *The Word in the Cave* which focuses on Abhishiktananda's advaitic experiences, his attempts to forge a theological reconciliation of *Advaita* Vedanta and Trinitarian Christianity, and on the theology of dialogue and religious pluralism. At that time Dr Kalliath, a Catholic theologian, was teaching in Bangalore. Both books include some historical and biographical material but are primarily theological in orientation. Sr Vandana Mataji, of the Jeevandhara Ashram in Jaiharikal, assembled some of Abhishiktananda's friends and disciples in a memorial gathering in December 1985. The occasional talks were subsequently published as a slender volume, *Swami Abhishiktananda, The Man and His Message* (1986, rev. ed. 1993), edited by Sr Vandana. Participants included Odette Baumer-Despeigne, Dr Bettina Bäumer, Fr Murray Rogers, Sr Sara Grant, and Fr George Gispert-Sauch, all of whom have also contributed to the growing periodical literature on Abhishiktananda. In *An Ethnography of Mysticism: The Narratives of Abhishiktananda* (1998) Susan Vishvanathan, an academic at Jawaharlal Nehru University in New Delhi, offers a sociological analysis of Abhishiktananda's "mystical narratives" and compares him with Simone Weil.

For those interested in the development of Abhishiktananda's spiritual life, as well as his many friendships and travels, James Stuart's *Swami Abhishiktananda: His Life Told through His Letters* (1989) complements *Ascent to the Depth of the Heart*, a selection from Abhishiktananda's journals, edited by Raimon Panikkar, and first appearing in French in 1986. Stuart's book has now been followed by Shirley du Boulay's fascinating and definitive biography, *The Cave of the Heart* (2005). It is unlikely that much useful biographical material can be added to these three well-documented books which together give us a detailed picture of a remarkable life.

No less than ten academic theses have been written on aspects of Abhishiktananda's thought. Probably the most important is John Glenn Friesen's exhaustive doctoral study, *Abhishiktananda's Non-Monistic Advaitic Experience* (University of South Africa, 2001)—a work which has been most useful in the present study, as has Fr Robert Stephens' early Masters thesis, *Religious Experience as a Meeting-Point in Religious Dialogue* (Sydney, 1984). Friesen's study is available on-line. There is a burgeoning literature on Abhishiktananda in theological and academic journals and on the internet. Odette Baumer-Despeigne, Michael Comans, George Gispert-Sauch, Klaus Klostermaier, Raimon Panikkar, James Royster, James Stuart, Judson Trapnell, Wayne Teasdale, and Edward Ulrich are among the friends, scholars, and theologians who have written interesting and provocative articles about Abhishiktananda, and more continue to appear—a welcome sign that his influence lives on. There are also several studies of Abhishiktananda in French, Italian, and German. Details of all the works mentioned above can be found in the Sources section of the present volume.

Notes

1. D 25.7.71, 332, and quoted in Friesen, 293.
2. Quoted in N. Krsnamurti, "Ananda Coomaraswamy," 172.
3. L 18.5.66, 180.
4. Baumer-D, 310.
5. L 23.1.69, 209.
6. L 8.3.68, 198.
7. Pr 2.
8. Pr 37.
9. F. Schuon, *Prayer Fashions Man*, 1.
10. Pr 28-29.
11. Pr 14, 22.
12. J. Biès, *Returning to the Essential*, 254.
13. Pr 44.
14. F. Schuon, *Logic and Transcendence*, 202.
15. Pr 11.
16. Pr 18.
17. EL 29.
18. Pr 33.
19. Pr 72-73n.
20. T. Merton, *New Seeds of Contemplation*, 1, 3.
21. Another, more detailed account of the sage, can be found in SAC, Ch 2.
22. SA 23.

23. SA 23.

24. Strictly speaking, Ramana had no disciples as such; nor did he ever refer to himself as anyone's guru. On this matter see GD 84-85.

25. SA 83.

26. SA 7-8. Readers may be interested to compare this with Bede Griffiths' equally eloquent account of "The Vedic Revelation" in *The Marriage of East and West*, 46-58.

27. SA 13.

28. W. Paden, *Religious Worlds*, 51.

29. From the original Introduction to *Guru and Disciple*, quoted in Odette Baumer-Despeigne's Introduction to *The Secret of Arunachala*, viii.

30. J. Biès, *Returning to the Essential*, 133.

31. GD 36.

32. GD 46.

33. GD 26.

34. C. Indra et al., *Sadguru Gnanananda*, vii.

35. On this subject see F. Schuon, *Logic and Transcendence*, 217.

36. GD 107.

37. L 20.1.56, 89.

38. GD 27.

39. GD 26.

40. Quoted in GD 106.

41. GD 26.

42. GD 11.

43. GD 29.

44. L 4.2.73, 286.

45. SAC xv.

46. L 18.10.72, 278.

47. L 4.2.73, 286.

48. D 25.8.70, 317.

49. L 2.2.73, 369.

50. Vattakuzhy, 83; J. Trapnell, "Gandhi, Abhishiktananda," website.

51. SAC xi.

52. SAX xiii.

53. SAC xiii.

54. SAX xiv.

55. SAC 134.

56. SAC 48-49.

57. RC 1-2.

58. RC 7 (italics mine).

59. RC 5.

60. L 14.6.66, 180.

61. Du Boulay, 60.

62. RC 10.

63. RC 10.

64. RC 26.
65. RC 21.
66. RC 46.
67. RC 74.
68. GD ix.
69. ML 6.
70. ML 14.
71. ML 48.
72. T. Merton, *New Seeds of Contemplation*, 31.
73. ML 45.
74. ML 45.
75. Ml 50.
76. ML 21.
77. ML 58.
78. ML 58.
79. ML 60.
80. F. Schuon, *Spiritual Perspectives*, 212-213.
81. Foreword, FS vii.
82. Quoted in FS ix.
83. Foreword FS ix.
84. FS 27.
85. FS 50-52. The passage in question implicitly explains why Abhishiktananda himself remained so committed to the celebration of this sacrament.
86. FS 69.
87. FS 59-60.
88. quoted in FS 51.
89. BA 1.
90. The title of this essay, as it appears in *Eyes of Light*, mis-spells the Mahatma's name as "Ghandi," a mistake repeated several times in the text. I have corrected this in the excerpts quoted.
91. R. Otto, "Gandhi, Saint and Statesman" (1933) in *Autobiographical and Social Essays*, 195-196.
92. EL 120.
93. EL 121.
94. EL 123.
95. T. Merton, *Gandhi on Non-Violence*, 5.
96. EL 123-124. In *Eyes of Light*, in the sentence "The current of the river returns to the source, the manifestation to the unmanifest," "unmanifest" appears as "manifested"—but this clearly makes no sense and must be an error which I have taken the liberty of correcting.
97. On Gandhi's relation to Hinduism see also E. Sharpe, "To Hinduism through Gandhi" and J.F.T. Jordens, *Gandhi: Conscience of India and Scourge of Orthodoxy.*
98. L 7.
99. Baumer-D, 311.

100. D 12.9.73, 388.

101. L 8.

102. Monchanin quoted in Vattakuzhy, 77; L 8.3.68, 199.

103. Du Boulay, 119.

104. D 86.

105. L 75.

106. R. Panikkar, Introduction, xiv.

107. S. Vishvanathan, *An Ethnography of Mysticism*, 100.

108. D, Editor, xv, xiii.

109. D, Editor, xvi-xvii.

110. For a provocative review of *Ascent to the Depth of the Heart*, in the form of an imaginary conversation between the reviewer and Swamji, see Sara Grant, "Time-Bomb or Tomb-Stone?"

111. Chaduc himself kept a diary which is in the custody of Madame Odette Baumer-Despeigne. She has published a few excerpts from Chaduc's diary but has not allowed anyone else to see the diary in full, perhaps because of the apparently cruel things Chaduc sometimes wrote about Abhishiktananda. Baumer-Despeigne refers to these in conversation with Susan Visvanathan in the latter's *An Ethnography of Mysticism: The Narratives of Abhishiktananda*, 98.

II

"In the Mystery of God"

Spiritual Themes in Abhishiktananda's Writings

"Spiritual experience . . . is the
meeting-place of the known and the
not-known, the seen and the not-seen,
the relative and the absolute."

4

The Monk's Vocation and *Sannyāsa*

> The call to complete renunciation cuts across all
> *dharmas* and disregards all frontiers.
>
> *Abhishiktananda*[1]

> Freedom's just another word for nothin' left to
> lose.
>
> *Kris Kristofferson*[2]

> It is not monasticism that is situated outside the
> world, it is the world that is situated outside
> monasticism.
>
> *Frithjof Schuon*[3]

Of the handful of scholars and theologians who have written in any detail about Abhishiktananda, few have given more than cursory attention to his monastic vocation, and to his writings about monasticism. His views on Vedanta and its relationship to Christianity, the Trinity, and the *Upanishads*, and on interreligious dialogue have all commanded far more attention, perhaps because it was in these fields that Abhishiktananda sometimes struck a radical note. But monasticism and the contemplative ideal provide us with the most appropriate point at which to launch our exploration of the spiritual themes which run through the *oeuvre*. After all, Abhishiktananda's life found its anchorage in his monastic vocation. Furthermore, as a contemporary scholar has observed, "It is doubtful if any Christian monk in the second half of the twentieth century has taken more seriously than Abhishiktananda the deep call to discover and explore experientially the ultimate ground that unites monks of different religious traditions."[4]

A Benedictine Ashram, jointly written by Monchanin and Abhishiktananda, opens with a beautiful statement of the monastic vocation and, in the Christian context, the Orthodox theology which informs it. Despite all the changes in Abhishiktananda's life and thinking over the next twenty-odd years I believe he would have cleaved to these words throughout, even if he may have slightly modified its theological language in his later years. It is worth reproducing here as a simple but powerful reminder of the vocation of the contemplative:

Contemplation stands supreme; viewed either from the standpoint of God or from that of Man, or from that of Holy Church. God has created the universe for His own glory, and out of love, in order to diffuse His intrinsic goodness . . . and to make intelligent creatures sharers in His eternal Bliss. Every creature is then in its own intimate way a manifestation, an ontological witness of God, a "Theophany." Everything reflects, in some measure, the divine attributes, nay participates in the divine Essence and receives its existence from the absolutely Existent. Therefore it cannot but point to God not only as its supreme Source, but especially as to its ultimate Goal. Intelligent creatures, angels and men, were created *ad imaginem et similitudinem Dei* (*Gen.* 1.26), to the image and likeness of God. Man, if we follow the hermeneutics of the Greek Fathers, is made to the image of God by his intelligence and free will, and to His likeness by grace and supernatural gifts. The dignity and happiness of man lie in this very image and likeness. His goal is to know God . . . to seek Him . . . and to love Him beyond measure. . . . Some at least of the members of society have to be deputed in the name of the rest of their brethren to a life entirely dedicated to the quest for God.[5]

Abhishiktananda's Monastic Vocation, from Kergonan to the Kavery

To claim that Abhishiktananda's vocation as a monk was the pole star of his life is not to evoke some static and unchanging ideal; Abhishiktananda's ideas were forged in the ever-changing crucible of experience, and the way in which he understood both his own vocation and that of the monk in general became ever deeper and, we might say, more universal. Later in life he was able to discern what—beyond all institutional trappings, historical accretions, cultural colorations, and religious formulations—was essential in the life of any monk at any time in any place. In his tribute to Fr Monchanin he wrote, "The monk simply consecrates himself to God."[6] This ideal never changed, but the way in which Abhishiktananda understood it and sought to live out its implications did indeed change.

From his earliest days at Châteaugiron Abhishiktananda was aflame with the desire to know, to love, to serve God. For him the Gospels demanded a life of uncompromising fidelity to God, and from his youth onwards he took with the utmost seriousness those passages in which Jesus summons his disciples "to total renunciation and the way of the Cross." In *The Further Shore* he recalls some of these passages:

Foxes have holes, and birds of the air have nests; but the Son of man hath nowhere to lay his head. . . . Let the dead bury the dead: but go thou and preach the kingdom of God. . . . No man, having put his hand to the plough, and looking back, is fit for the kingdom of God. (*Luke* 9.58-62)

Go thy way, sell whatsoever thou hast, and give to the poor, and thou shalt have treasure in heaven: and come, take up the cross and follow me. (*Mark* 10.21)

Take nothing for your journey, neither staves, nor scrip, neither bread, neither money; neither have two coats apiece. (*Luke* 9.3)[7]

In his youth and early manhood Abhishiktananda's spiritual horizon was bound by provincial Catholic piety as practiced by the French bourgeoisie, and his early years in seminary and monastery seemed to meet the demands of his vocation as he then understood it. But from the outset he believed, as he wrote in a letter of 1929, that "a monk cannot accept mediocrity, only extremes are appropriate for him."[8] By 1934, at the age of twenty-three, he was beginning to feel the call of India— which was nothing other than the invitation to a deeper commitment to his vocation as a monk. As Raimon Panikkar wrote in his "Letter," "you felt the call of India not because you were a Christian, but because you were a monk."[9] Here is Abhishiktananda writing to Fr Monchanin in 1947 about their plans for a monastic life together in India:

The point of departure should be the Rule of St. Benedict because it had behind it an extremely reliable monastic tradition which would prevent a headlong plunge into the unknown. But it must be the rule as such . . . with its original character, so flexible and universal. . . . I believe that the Benedictine Rule, in its marvelous profundity and stability, is pliant enough to dominate all these monastic forms. . . . Eighteen years of Benedictine life have deeply bound me to the *sancta regula*. . . . The observance [in the proposed ashram] will certainly be very austere, much more so than in our French monasteries. I have no objection to that. On the contrary![10]

These are not the words of a man looking to flee his monastic vows but to live them more fully. On the negative side, he rarely said anything about precisely what fuelled his dissatisfaction with monastic life at Kergonan but here and there he drops suggestive hints. This, for instance, in a letter of December 1964:

Personally I needed years to free myself (if indeed I have done so even now) from the infantilism and the lack of a sense of personal responsibility which was effectively instilled into me on the pretext of obedience.[11]

There is also no doubt that throughout his life he was often frustrated by ecclesiastical "ritualism, formalism, and intellectualism" which far from nurturing spiritual experience were a barrier to it.[12]

At the time of his arrival in India Abhishiktananda looked forward to a coenobitical rather than an eremitical life, but in the wake of his experiences at Arunachala and Tapovanam, and his immersion in Upanishadic *advaita*, the life of the *sannyāsī*, a life centered on the "inner mystery" attracted him ever more powerfully: "The inner mystery calls me with excruciating force, and no outside being can help me to penetrate it and there, *for myself*, discover the secret of my origin and destiny."[13] Eventually his ideas about the monk's vocation fused with the Hindu ideal of *sannyāsa*, and in some sense were subsumed by it. The renunciation to which one was called by *sannyāsa* was a more total and self-annihilating ideal than anything which Abhishiktananda had experienced within the Christian orders, and a more demanding call to the life of "interiority"—though, in the end, all ideas of "inner" and "outer" were burnt up in the experience of non-duality, just as the very "I" which was living out a vocation likewise disappeared. As early as 1956 he came to the realization that he must surrender his egoic investments, even in his role as a monk. From his journal:

> I have not yet managed to achieve it—the "surrender" of my "ego" as a Christian, monk, a priest. And yet I must do so. Perhaps it will then be given back to me, renewed. But meanwhile, I must leave it behind—totally—without any hope of its return. And that means absolute poverty, nakedness, hunger, fasting, a vagrant life without means of support, total solitude in heart, in body and in spirit. And still more it involves the breaking of all those bonds that are as old as myself, those bonds that are in the most secret recesses of my heart. All that superego derived from my family upbringing, from my whole training as a young child, as a young man, as a priest, as a monk.

Already he is painfully sensing that a total acceptance of *advaita* and *sannyāsa* means moving beyond his attachment to the theological formulations of Christianity:

> If one does not renounce all that one has ... — even the Jesus whom he has before his eyes. ... Even the God of Jesus, for that again is an idea which the "ego" possesses, and which prevents the "ego" from disappearing in the abyss.[14]

From Arunachala to Gyansu: Deeper into Sannyāsa

How did Abhishiktananda understand *sannyāsa?* Although Abhishiktananda recognized that the Indian tradition of *sannyāsa* allowed for the
practice of *bhakti* he believed that its highest expression entailed complete apophaticism—the giving up of all naming of either God or oneself, the commitment to "infinite silence." From his journal in 1954:

> The *sannyāsī* renounces not only the body and everything related
> to it, the entire domain of the *bahir karana* (renunciation of rights
> and freedom from all obligations); but also and likewise the entire
> *antaḥkarana*, the psychic domain, *ahamkāra* and *manas;* he renounces
> the *nāma-rūpa* (name and form) of himself and of God. *Sannyāsa*
> involves a commitment to the apophatic path.[15]

He doubted whether such an ideal had any equivalent in "ecclesial
Christianity" which "does not admit of the possibility of itself being
transcended." In this respect he discerned a yawning "abyss" between
Christianity and Hinduism in that the latter fulfilled itself in tran-
scending its own religious forms, "in orienting the best of its adepts
towards what is beyond its formulations and rites, in which alone the
Supreme Truth resides." He became keenly aware of the limitations of
Christian monasticism, at least with respect to its actual practice in the
modern world:

> Monastic profession withdraws the Christian from the world but binds
> him still more closely to the Church on pilgrimage (*viator*). Passage
> from one yoke to another. *Sannyāsa* transcends all yokes of *māyā*, all
> rights as well as all obligations . . . sets free from all rites and all Canon
> Law. *Sannyāsa* cannot be Christian.[16]

From this vantage point Abhishiktananda finds himself in a harrowing dilemma:

> From now on I have tasted too much of *advaita* to be able to recover
> the "Gregorian" peace of the Christian monk. Long ago I tasted too
> much of the "Gregorian" peace not to be anguished in the midst of
> my *advaita.*[17]

> I remain Christian so long as I have not penetrated into the
> "Darkness"—supposing that some day I penetrate that far. But is it
> still compatible with the profession of Christianity even to admit the
> simple possibility of something beyond Christianity?—Will I get out
> of this by distinguishing two levels? But even the possibility of another
> level is contradictory to Christianity. What then?[18]

However, he is able to take some comfort in the following reflections:

> Even in the context of Christian theology, each one will be judged on the conformity of his life with the ideal he has glimpsed in his own depth, and not with the ideal of some other person, or of some particular religious sect. . . . The best can easily be the enemy of the good.[19]

In the years between these journal entries of 1953-54 and his death in 1973 Abhishiktananda became ever more implacably pledged to *sannyāsa* but found a way in which to harmonize it with Christianity. His conceptual reconciliation of *sannyāsa* and Christian faith hinged on the idea that, in its deepest sense, Christian faith was a call to the "leap into the void" to which *sanyassa* also summonsed the renunciate. There is also a growing awareness of the "two levels"—in traditionalist parlance, the outer, exoteric dimension of formal religious diversity, and the inner, esoteric level where there is to be found a formless unity, what Schuon called "the transcendent unity of religions." Abhishiktananda also moved towards the view—seemingly impossible in 1954—that the Church in India might play a providential role in bringing *sannyāsa* into the universal Church. By the early 60s, when Abhishiktananda came to write *Saccidananda*, we see him venturing both a theological and an experiential synthesis of the two perspectives. He was also now able to see more clearly that no religious form, whether Christian, Hindu, or some other, had an ultimate value but that all, in the Upanishadic metaphor, were like the taper with which the fire is lit; once the fire is ablaze, the taper can be jettisoned.[20] A more theoretical way of formulating the problem is to pose the question, what is the relation between religious forms (dogmas, rites, codes, etc.) and the illuminative experience of non-duality which goes by many names—gnosis, mystical union, *jñāna*, intellection, and the like? This is a question which we will take up in much more detail in a later chapter.

Sannyāsa in "The Further Shore"

Much of what has been said already indicates the main contour lines of the ideal of *sannyāsa*. But here it is worth dwelling on Abhishiktananda's most cogent exposition, in *The Further Shore*. The call to *sannyāsa*, he tells us, is in the first place inspired by *viveka*, the ability to discriminate between the permanent and the transitory, the first requisite of the seeker of knowledge of the Real (*brahma-vidyā*). But he is at pains to make the distinction between "enchanting ideas which may inspire profound meditation or learned discussion among the initiated" and the actual raw and sometimes traumatic experience of non-duality which snatches one out of habitual modes of understanding.[21] The *sannyāsī* has but one desire, for God Alone, but not as a *deva* or celestial being who might confer favor:

> His desire for God is the desire for One who is beyond all forms, for communion with the One-without-a-second, for a joy which is beyond all sensible delights and a bliss from which has disappeared all distinction between "enjoyer" and "enjoyed."[22]

Furthermore,

> *Sannyāsīs* are their people's oblation to God, their most precious *yajña;* they are the true human sacrifice (*puruṣamedha*), victims consumed in the fire of *tapas*, their own inner oblation.[23]

In *The Mountain of the Lord*, Abhishiktananda had emphasized the role of the acosmic as witness to the Absolute:

> These acosmics are no less present to the world than are those who have been cast into the great stream of life, but their presence is at the very point from which this stream comes forth. They bear witness to the absolute, the *kaivalya*, to the Unmoving, *acala*, and do so on behalf of this world, while apparently remaining on its fringe. They are like the pivots of this world, holding it steady by their own stillness within the Unmovable.[24]

The Further Shore sketches the outlines of the renunciate's way of life with respect to the needs of the body (food, clothing, shelter), various abstinences (from idle gossip, worldly affairs, intellectual debate, unnecessary reading, and the like), the refusal to be seduced by the temptation of "gregariousness, activism, and exteriority," the practice of austerities such as fasting and silence. In his later years Abhishiktananda increasingly stressed that the final goal of the *sannyāsī* was to be "acosmic"—without name, place, possessions, without social and religious obligations, "as dead to society as the man whose corpse is being carried to the burning-*ghat*,"[25] without desire of any kind, and as if unborn. (Hence Marc Chaduc's initiatic name of Ajatananda, "Bliss-of-the-Not-born"). In the words of the *Kaṭha Upanishad*,

> He neither dies nor is born, the one who knows.
> From where does he come? What will he become?
> Non-born, eternal, primordial, always himself![26]

He found the acosmic in the Christian mystics:

> ... the Carmel—at least as it is idealized in my vision of it—is perhaps what comes closest in the Church to India's deepest aspirations: the acosmics of the Desert Fathers; the "Flee, be silent, remain at rest" of Arsenius; the *nada* of St John of the Cross; above all, the "establishment of oneself beyond oneself" of Tauler and Eckhart. That is what the Christian monk should live out in company with his advaitin brother, if he wants truly to complete in Christ the intuition of Being contained in the *Saccidananda* of the India of the rishis.[27]

In almost the last of his journal entries Abhishiktananda reflects on the "terrifying demands of non-possession in *sannyāsa*," not only the absence of possessions but rather the *impossibility* of any possession because there is no longer anyone who could be the possessor. He now understands anew that this poverty, inner as well as outer, is really the "radical starting point" of *sannyāsa*.[28]

Abhishiktananda was not so naïve as to be unaware of the pitfalls which surrounded *sannyāsa*, nor of the many abuses sheltering behind the ideal. Not the least insidious of the possible snares was what Chögyam Trungpa called "spiritual materialism"—the appropriation of "spirituality" by the ego for its own ends. Abhishiktananda regrets the kind of snobbery and elitism which has sometimes betrayed the ideal of *sannyāsa*:

> The *sannyāsī* has no place, no *loka* ... so if there is a class of *Sannyāsīs*, it is all up with *sannyāsa*! They have renounced the world—splendid! So from then on they belong to the *loka*, the "world" of those who have renounced the world! They constitute themselves a new kind of society, an "in-group" of their own, a spiritual élite apart from the common man, and charged with instructing him, very like those "scribes and Pharisees" whose attitude made even Jesus, the compassionate one, lose his temper. Then a whole new code of correct behavior develops, worse than that of the world, with its courtesy titles, respectful greetings, order of precedence, and the rest. The wearing of the saffron becomes the sign, not so much of renunciation, as of belonging to the "order of swamis."[29]

The true *sannyāsī* must, in the end, paradoxically, renounce renunciation itself, or to put it more precisely, *sannyāsa* entails the renouncing of the renouncer: "'I have renounced'? The only one entitled to pronounce it without telling a lie is no longer capable of uttering it."[30] In this sense *sannyāsa* "carries within itself its own abrogation." And here, by way of an aside, it is worth noting that the usual translation of *sannyāsa*, "renunciation," is not altogether adequate. Raimon

Panikkar draws our attention to this when writing, "The holy ascetic of Indian religiousness does not represent exclusively, and often not even mainly, an ideal of moral renunciation, but rather that of an authentic, naked, and pure life."[31]

What of the relation of *sannyāsa* to religion?

> Whatever the excellence of any *dharma*, it remains inevitably at the level of signs; it remains on *this* side of the Real, not only in its structure and institutional forms, but also in its attempts to formulate the ineffable reality, alike in mythical or conceptual images. The mystery to which it points overflows its limits in every direction. . . . All *a priori* deductions and speculations fall short of discovering the Spirit in itself beyond the level of religions. It can only be reached existentially, that is, by piercing to the very heart of the religious experience itself. . . . In every religion and in every religious experience there is a beyond, and it is precisely this "beyond" that is our goal. *Sannyāsa* is the recognition of that which is beyond all signs; and paradoxically, it is itself the sign of what for ever lies beyond all possibility of being adequately expressed by rites, creeds, or institutions.[32]

The crucial point here is that it is only through a *penetration* of religious forms—a very different matter from an impious iconoclasm in the manner of Krishnamurti and other such self-styled savants, which announces itself as being "above" forms—that the nameless reality can be reached by those prepared to pay the price of self-annihilation (i.e., the disappearance of what the "self" is imagined to be). The writings of Bede Griffiths on this matter, not surprisingly, are in complete accord with those of Abhishiktananda. Here is a passage from Fr Bede's *The Marriage of East and West*:

> A *Sannyāsī* is one who renounces the world to seek for God, but his renunciation goes far beyond what is ordinarily understood by the "world.". . . A *Sannyāsī* renounces the whole world of "signs," of appearances. . . . The Church also belongs to the world of "signs." The doctrines and sacraments of the Church are . . . signs of the divine reality. . . . The *Sannyāsī* is called to go beyond all religion, beyond every human institution, beyond every scripture and creed, till he comes to that which every religion and scripture signifies but can never name.[33]

This states the "position" the *sannyāsī* occupies vis-à-vis religion clearly enough. But certain misunderstandings inevitably arise at this point. Bede Griffiths again echoes Abhishiktananda when, drawing on his own experience of *sannyāsa*, he goes on to write,

> Yet when we say that the *Sannyāsī* goes beyond religion this does not mean that he rejects any religion. I have not felt called to reject anything

that I have learned of God or of Christ or of the Church. *To go beyond the sign is not to reject the sign, but to reach the thing signified.* . . . As long as we remain in the world we need these signs, and the world today cannot survive unless it rediscovers the signs of faith, the "Myth," the "Symbol," in which the knowledge of reality is enshrined. But equally fatal is to stop at the sign, to mistake the sign for the ultimate reality. . . . This is essentially idolatry. . . . The *Sannyāsī* is one who is called to witness to this Truth of the reality beyond the signs, to be a sign of that which is beyond signs.[34]

*

Abhishiktananda sometimes reproached himself for failing to live out absolutely the ideal of the acosmic to which he aspired, feeling that he lacked the courage to take "the final step."[35] Hence the joy he felt at Chaduc's *dīkṣā;* the disciple had outstripped the master in his commitment to *sannyāsa.* Abhishiktananda himself still owned some books and a few other paltry possessions, maintained his tiny hermitage at Uttarkashi, and cherished the human contact of his family and friends. His letters and writings testify to certain contradictory impulses in Abhishiktananda's attitude to acosmism, and it would no doubt be easy to find certain inconsistencies in his "theoretical position." However, it would be impertinent to launch any kind of "psychoanalysis" to explain the contradictions, just as it would be foolish to gather together various passages from his writings to establish his intellectual inconsistencies. What can be said without fear of contradiction is that Abhishiktananda never ceased to explore in himself all of the possibilities of his vocation, painful though this sometimes was. Further, whatever his real or imagined failings to live out *sannyāsa,* he gave us a magnificent vision of what the ideal, in its highest reaches, might actually entail.

Whilst it is impossible not to admire Abhishiktananda's aspiration to become an acosmic, it is also difficult to disagree with Raimon Panikkar who believed that Abhishiktananda had surrendered to a "certain absolutistic interpretation of monasticism" and who found Abhishiktananda's failure to realize the ideal in his own life a mark of his human warmth. Panikkar believed that monasticism's "irresistible tendency" towards "absolute acosmism," the attempt to "break all boundaries, the limitations of the body, matter, and mind as well as of the spirit," its aspiration to transcend the human condition, to be both "not human" and "not Christian"—and the latter because the Incarnation stands for the "divinization of the concrete, the limited, and even of matter and the body."[36]

In the very last of his published writings, *Sannyāsa-Dīkṣā* (the last of the five articles written for the Sivananda Ashram monthly) Abhishiktananda writes with a rhapsodic intensity which surely makes it one of the most heartfelt affirmations of *sannyāsa*. It shines with the wisdom wrested from his long pilgrimage and gives us his final, profound word on this "sign beyond signs." It is worth quoting at some length.

> *Sannyāsa* confronts us with a sign of that which is essentially beyond all signs—indeed, in its sheer transparency [to the Absolute] it proclaims its own death as a sign. . . . However the *sannyāsī* lives in the world of signs, of the divine manifestation, and this world of manifestation needs him, "the one beyond signs," so that it may realize the impossible possibility of a bridge between the two worlds. . . . These ascetics who flee the world and care nothing for its recognition are precisely the ones who uphold the world. . . . They go their way in secret. . . . But [the world] . . . needs to know that they are there, so that it may preserve a reminder of transcendence in the midst of a transient world. . . . The sign of *sannyāsa* . . . stands then on the very frontier, the unattainable frontier, between two worlds, the world of manifestation and the world of the unmanifest Absolute. It is the mystery of the sacred lived with the greatest possible interiority. It is a powerful means of grace—that grace which is nothing else than the Presence of the Absolute, the Eternal, the Unborn, existing at the heart of the realm of becoming, of time, of death and life; and a grace which is at the same time the irresistible drawing of the entire universe and its fullness towards the ultimate fullness of the Awakening to the Absolute, to the *Ātman*. This sign, this grace is supremely the *tarana*, the raft by which man passes over to the "other shore.". . . Finally, it is even the *tāraka*, the actual one who himself carries men across to the other shore, the one and only "ferryman," manifested in manifold ways in the form of all those rishis, mahatmas, gurus, and buddhas, who throughout history have themselves been woken and in turn awaken their brother-men.[37]

Contemplative Monasticism, Sannyāsa, and the Church

The more Abhishiktananda was gripped by *sannyāsa* the more he identified with the apophatic and eremitical traditions within Christian monasticism in both its Latin and Orthodox branches, turning often to the Desert Fathers of Egypt and Syria, to Pseudo-Dionysius, and to the Rhenish mystics, and cherishing the Carthusian and Carmelite Orders in the contemporary Church.[38] He also came to see St Francis of Assisi as the exemplary Christian *sannyāsī*. No longer did he see an "abyss" between Christianity and *sannyāsa*:

> The profession of a Christian monk certainly implies, at least in its roots, the full renunciation and radical transcendence which shines out so clearly in the tradition of the Hindu *sannyāsa*. . . . Above all, the call to solitude which, beginning in the fourth century, carried off so many Christians to the deserts of Egypt and Syria, and then a thousand years later, to the great forests of Central and Northern Russia, was certainly no less radical than the call of Hindu *sannyāsa*, and in its extreme form implied separation from all ecclesiastical associations and even from the sacraments. This call to solitude—alone with the Alone, alone with the alones of the One who is Alone—is still heard by Christ's disciples.[39]

Indeed, he hoped that

> The Indian Church will in the end bring to the universal Church an authentically Christian *sannyāsa* as the crowning of monastic life. Thus the Church will recover after centuries the purest traditions of the Desert and of the Hesychast movement, and at the same time drink deep at the inexhaustible sources of the Hindu ideal of renunciation in a life devoted to God alone.[40]

One of the links which Abhishiktananda now perceived between the two traditions of his "double belonging" was contemplation. Indeed, in *Towards a Renewal of the Indian Church*, he writes

> That supra-mental awareness of the Spirit within and the inner communion with Him should be considered the most important thing in the life of the individual and of the Church here below. Unless such a conviction is widely disseminated, nothing worthwhile will be achieved in the Church.[41]

This was not an idle jotting in his journal but a statement in a memorandum for participants in the forthcoming All-India Seminar of the Roman Catholic Church. In other words, we can take this as Abhishiktananda's considered position in his later years. Whilst this form of awareness was to be encouraged in all Christians it could best be nurtured within the contemplative vocations. At a time when many in the Indian Church were focusing on her social activities Abhishiktananda was adamant that contemplation must be at its very heart. He urged

> The establishment and the fostering of religious houses engaged in pure and real contemplation in silence and solitude, inside and outside. It is only from such centers that genuine contemplative life . . . can radiate and spread in the Church. . . . Let it be remembered, however, that it is

not primarily of so-called contemplative institutions that the Church is in need of above all, but contemplative men and women.[42]

He goes on to write of the two formidable contemporary challenges that the Church faces—Western atheism and Eastern spirituality. Not just the Indian but the whole Church must meet the challenge of "interiority and spiritual depth put to her by Hinduism,—by the Spirit, as we would confidently affirm, through Hinduism."[43]

> The Church here finds herself confronted, not with materialistic and secularist tendencies as in the West, but with a religious tradition deeply contemplative and spiritual. . . . Hence the necessity for the Church, both for the sake of her own spiritual awakening and for the achievement of her mission and witness in India, to take into account the essentials of the Indian contemplative tradition, to integrate them into her own patrimony, and to develop them under the guidance of the Holy Spirit to the best of her ability.[44]

Elsewhere Abhishiktananda refers to the crisis facing Christian monasticism as it "gropingly seeks to find a path forward, avoiding on one side a sterile mediaevalism, and on the other, a modernism which loses all sense of mystery."[45] He looks forward to the day when there might be a creative fusion of the tradition of the desert ("harking back to John the Baptist and the great Elijah, the typical monk-prophet of the Old Testament"), and the Indian tradition of *sannyāsa* which flowed forth from "the primeval rishis of India."[46]

No doubt Abhishiktananda would have shared Raimon Panikkar's melancholy sentiments when he addressed the Second Asian Monastic Congress (Bangalore, 1973):

> The contribution of Christian monasticism in Asia to the Church at large is minimal, not to say practically nil. Christian monasteries, where they exist, have been almost "air-lifted" *ante litteram*, so that they become enclaves, colonies of Western Christianity. In spite of strenuous effort, immense goodwill, and even holiness, the history of monasticism in Asia is a sad page in the life of the Christian Church.[47]

The two friends were deeply concerned with making the Church in India not a colonial outpost but a channel through which the spiritual riches of India could flow into the Universal Church. In this enterprise they believed the monk had a crucial role to play. One of the many recommendations Abhishiktananda makes to the Indian Church is the development of an authentic Christian *sannyāsa*. In *Renewal of the Indian Church* Abhishiktananda actually envisages the emergence of three types of Christian *sannyāsīs*: (1) pure contemplatives, men and women, both *jñānīs* and *bhaktas*, who may be solitaries or living in small groups, preferably in India's holiest places; (2) preaching *sannyāsīs—ordo predicatorum*—who, between periods of extended silence, would develop a Christian *satsang*; (3) itinerant *sannyāsīs*, Christian *parivrājas*, who would recapture the "selfsame spirit that animated Francis of Assisi and his first companions," going from "village to village in utter poverty, living on alms, singing their love for the Lord, and calling all to share in their radiating bliss."[48]

In Abhishiktananda's view (shared by Merton and many others) the monk was peculiarly well placed to act as a bridge between East and West.[49] The monastic ideal was deeply rooted in both hemispheres, and the actual spiritual experience of the monk could bypass doctrinal differences to bring the followers of various *dharmas* together. This because "the only real meeting-point between men concerned with the ultimate is in the center of the self, in 'the cave of the heart,' which is where the monk abides."[50] Monks felt a natural and spontaneous affinity:

> There is indeed a "monastic order" which is universal and includes them all. . . . It is enough that they should thus recognize each other whenever they happen to meet, and in fact those that do infallibly respond to each other. Despite all differences in observance, language, and cultural background, they perceive in each other's eyes that depth which the One Spirit has opened in their own hearts.[51]

As David Steindl-Rast (himself a Benedictine monk) has observed,

> Monks and nuns the world over speak the same language, as it were. In the things that really matter, they are often much closer to each other across religious boundaries than they are to lay people in their own respective religious groups.[52]

There are many stories about the spontaneous bond of which Abhishiktananda speaks. Three examples come readily to mind: the meetings of the Dalai Lama with Thomas Merton and Bede Griffiths, Abhishiktananda's first encounter with Swami Chidananda. Of that company of Christian monks who saw in the monastic ideal a vital link between Eastern and Western spirituality one may here mention not only Frs Monchanin and Bede Griffiths, but also such figures as Aelred Graham, Thomas Merton, William Johnston, and David Steindl-Rast. It is also a striking fact that amongst the many Eastern teachers and gurus who have made an impact in the West, some of the most revered and widely-loved have been monks—the present Dalai Lama, Thich Nhat Hanh and Shunryu Suzuki among them.

Further Reflections on Monasticism

We will conclude this chapter with a few reflections about monasticism and its place in the modern world. From Thomas Merton:

> Let us face the fact that the monastic vocation tends to present itself to the modern world as a problem and as a scandal. In a basically religious culture, like that of India, or of Japan, the monk is more or less taken for granted.[53]

But, in truth, as Frithjof Schuon reminds us, "a world is absurd exactly to the extent that the contemplative, the hermit, the monk, appear in it as a paradox or as an 'anachronism.'" It is the monk who can save us from our idolatry of "the age" because he "incarnates all that is changeless, not through sclerosis or inertia, but through transcendence."[54] It is in this sense, as well as in many others, that the monk is, in Abhishiktananda's words, the true and ultimate human oblation, his individuality consumed in God. One of the charges leveled by humanists, slaves to an ideal of utilitarian activism, is that monks are useless, perhaps worse, a breed of social parasites. In considering this shallow and impudent attitude we can do no better than turn again to Schuon:

> When anyone reproaches a hermit or a monk for "running away from" the world, he commits a double error: firstly, he loses sight of the fact that contemplative isolation has an intrinsic value that is independent of the existence of a surrounding "world"; secondly, he pretends to forget that there are escapes that are perfectly honorable and that, if it is neither absurd nor shameful to run away from an avalanche, it is no more so to run away from the temptations or even the distractions of the world. . . . In our days people are very ready to say that to escape the world is to shirk "responsibilities," a completely hypocritical euphemism that dissimulates behind "altruistic" or "social" notions a spiritual laziness and a hatred of the absolute; people are happy to ignore the fact that the gift of oneself for God is always a gift of oneself for all. It is metaphysically impossible to give oneself to God in such a way that good does not ensue to the environment: to give oneself to God, though it were hidden from all men, is to give oneself to man, for this gift of self has a sacrificial value of an incalculable radiance.[55]

No one in the East still attuned to their own religious tradition could conceive of the reproaches to which Schuon alludes, let alone take them seriously. It is a measure of the spiritually sterile climate in which many Westerners live that such prejudices can be harbored by so many. The monks and nuns of Christianity and Buddhism, the Hindu *sannyāsī* and *parivraja*, the Taoist recluse, the Zen master, the Tibetan *naldjorpa,* the Sufi contemplative, remind a forgetful world, as their predecessors have done through the ages, of the highest spiritual ideals by living as a "sign beyond signs," showing us a bridge not only between the East and West but between the manifest and the Absolute. There is no higher vocation.

*

In his writings on *sannyāsa* Abhishiktananda refers more than once to the Vedic figure of the *keśī* ("hairy one"), the one who has gone beyond all forms, all dualities, even beyond *sannyāsa* itself. In the short interval between Marc Chaduc's *dīkṣā* and his own final "Awakening," his discovery of the Grail in the Rishikesh bazaar, Abhishiktananda seems to have attained something of the state of the *keśī*. Here is how he describes it in *The Further Shore*:

> The *keśī* does not regard himself as a *sannyāsī*. There is no world, no *loka*, in which he belongs. Free and riding the winds, he traverses the worlds at his pleasure. Wherever he goes, he goes maddened with his own rapture, intoxicated with the unique Self. Friend of all and fearing none, he bears the Fire, he bears the Light. Some take him for a common beggar, some for a madman, a few for a sage. To him it is all one. He is himself, he is accountable to no one. His support is in himself, that is to say, in the Spirit from whom he is not "other."[56]

Notes

1. FS 7.
2. F. Foster and K. Kristofferson, "Me and Bobby McGee," EMI.
3. F. Schuon, *Light on the Ancient Worlds*, 121.
4. J. Royster, "Dialogue in Depth," 78.
5. BA 9-10.
6. From Abhishiktananda, "Le Père Monchanin," quoted in A. Rawlinson, *The Book of Enlightened Masters*, 148.
7. FS 50. (My quotations from the King James version.)
8. L 27.10.29, 6.
9. Panikkar, 446.
10. 18.8.47, EL 13-14.
11. L 15.12.64, 167.
12. See, for example L 15.7.66, 182-183.
13. D 19.4.56, quoted in Panikkar, 435.
14. D 6.1.56, 136.

15. D 7.1.54, 88.
16. D 9.1.54, 89.
17. D 27.9.53, 74.
18. D 26.1.54, 89.
19. D 7.4.54, 90.
20. SAC 42-43.
21. FS 3.
22. FS 5.
23. FS 14.
24. ML 44-45.
25. FS 13-14.
26. Quoted in GD 113.
27. L 26.10.59, 123.
28. L 5.7.73, 383.
29. FS 33.
30. FS 34.
31. R. Panikkar, "The Monk According to the Indian Sacred Scriptures," 253.
32. FS 26.
33. B. Griffiths, *The Marriage of East and West*, 42.
34. B. Griffiths, *The Marriage of East and West*, 43 (italics mine).
35. See Panikkar, 444-445.
36. Panikkar, 444. See also ML 51-57. The notion of acosmism is discussed in some detail in Friesen, 294ff.
37. FS 42-43.
38. See RC 130, and Pr 32-33.
39. FS 29.
40. Pr 33.
41. RC 7.
42. RC 8.
43. RC 11.
44. RC 55.
45. FS 47.
46. FS 47.
47. R. Panikkar, "The Contribution of Christian Monasticism," 74.
48. RC 76.
49. See J. Conner, "The Monk as Bridge between East and West."
50. DD 208.
51. FS 27.
52. Quoted in J. Royster, "Dialogue in Depth," 76.
53. T. Merton, *The Silent Life*, viii.
54. F. Schuon, *Light on the Ancient Worlds*, 124.
55. F. Schuon, *Light on the Ancient Worlds*, 120-121.
56. FS 38.

5

Advaita

> I have been in that heaven, the most illumined by
> light from him and seen things which to utter, he
> who returns hath neither skill nor knowledge, for
> as it nears the object of its yearning our intellect
> is overwhelmed so deeply it can never retrace the
> path it followed.
>
> *Dante*[1]

> The mystery to which [religion] points overflows
> its limits in every direction.
>
> *Abhishiktananda*[2]

Clearing the Decks

The nature of *Advaita* Vedanta, as a *theoria* and a metaphysic, has
often been misunderstood in the West, particularly by philosophers
and theologians who have sought to "explain" it within the framework of Judeo-Christian theology or, even more alarmingly, within the
categories of modern philosophy, both enterprises doomed from the
outset with the latter situated on the fringes of the absurd. "*Advaita*"
means "non-dual"; "Vedanta" signifies either "the summation of the
Vedas"—the *Upanishads*—or the philosophical/metaphysical school
or "point-of-view" (*darśana*) anchored in the Upanishadic message of
the identity of *Ātman-Brahman*, and the non-duality of the Real. The
Vedanta school, one of the six orthodox *darśanas* of Hinduism, is itself
divided into three branches, associated with Sankara, Ramanuja, and
Madhva. Western commentators sometimes err in assimilating Sankara's
doctrinal exposition and Vedanta as a whole, whilst others make the
even cruder error of collapsing Vedanta and Hinduism. But as Schuon
has remarked,

> If Hinduism is organically linked with the *Upanishads*, it is not however
> reducible to the Saivite Vedantism of Sankara, although the latter must
> be considered as expressing the essence of the Vedanta and so also of
> the Hindu tradition itself.[3]

For present purposes we can identify *Advaita* Vedanta with Sankara's metaphysic, even though Abhishiktananda himself was at pains to

emphasize that the ultimate source of the advaitic wisdom was in the intuitions of the Upanishadic seers. The essential message of *Advaita Vedanta* is pithily stated by Sankara:

> *Brahman* is real; the world is an illusory appearance;
> the so-called soul is *Brahman* itself, and no other.[4]

The Real is not "two"—strictly speaking it is not "one" either, for the category of number cannot apply to the Absolute (*Brahman*). *Advaita Vedanta* is "the most direct possible expression of gnosis": the "price," so to say, which it exacts for this directness, is its call to complete renunciation and detachment (*vairāgya*).[5]

As Abhishiktananda realized with painful clarity, the uncompromising Vedantic metaphysic poses a formidable challenge to all dualistic theologies which posit an ontological abyss between "God" and the "world," and, more specifically, for the prophetic Occidental traditions which locate the means of man's salvation in time and space—in the events and unfolding of history. Abhishiktananda states the problem in *Saccidananda*:

> However securely established in his faith a Christian may be, he cannot avoid the problem set by the fact of religious pluralism among men. . . . The challenge offered by eastern spiritual experience to Christianity, as to every form of religion and philosophy, is an ultimate one. They are pursued up to their last line of defense and compelled to face an ultimate dilemma—either to remain for ever on the level of what is multiple and relative, or to allow their identity to be dissolved in the overwhelming experience of the absolute.[6]

By the same measure, Vedanta puts the Christian claim to universality to the severest test:

> If Christianity should prove to be incapable of assimilating Hindu spiritual experience from within, Christians would thereby at once lose the right to claim that it is a universal way of salvation. . . . In its own sphere, the truth of *advaita* is unassailable. If Christianity is unable to integrate it in the light of a higher truth, the inference must follow that *advaita* includes and surpasses the truth of Christianity. . . . There is no escape from this dilemma.[7]

The extent to which Abhishiktananda succeeded in reconciling Christianity and Vedanta is a matter of some debate. His endeavors were not only a matter of trying to forge a coherent intellectual understanding of what might variously be called the Self, *Ātman-Brahman*, the Supreme Identity, God, the Godhead, the Real, or the Absolute, an understanding in which he might accommodate both his fealty to Christ and His Church, and his ever-deepening intuitions of *advaita*; it was also a matter of the utmost existential urgency, of quelling the turmoil in his soul. Consider this passage from *Saccidananda*:

> In this [advaitic] experience the supreme agony for the Christian is this—not only is he stripped of himself in his own deepest being, but literally everything is torn from him. No doubt, if it was only a question of sacrificing himself to the Lord, he would do it willingly and joyfully in the faith of the Gospel. But this radical purification seems at the same time to deprive him of the Lord himself, *his* Lord, together with the forms in which he revealed himself and even the words he has spoken to man. Further, it appears to tear him away from the Church and from the sacraments which bind him to Christ.... All his devout gestures, all his thoughts and feelings, even the noblest and purest, seem worthless.... Deep within he is no longer able to say or to understand anything except the unique and eternal *Aham*, I AM, which in its infinite solitariness reverberates deep within the Self.[8]

Abhishiktananda was impatient with the cognoscenti who could engage in subtle debate about Christian and Hindu doctrines but for whom *advaita* was never more than an abstruse theory. Abhishiktananda wanted to *live* the truths which he derived from his "double heritage." Whilst his books sometimes suggest that he had found a more or less satisfactory harmonizing of the two, his journal makes it clear that until the last few years of his life the tension between non-dualism and the doctrine of the Trinity, more generally between Vedanta and Christianity, left deep scorch marks on his psyche. The books in which he gave the problem his most extended treatment were *Hindu-Christian Meeting Point* and *Saccidananda*, both appearing in their original French editions in 1965. But even as they were going to press Abhishiktananda's thinking was going through a sea-change as he left behind the theology of fulfillment. For his most mature consideration of the subject we must turn to more fragmentary passages in his journal and to *The Further Shore*.

The whole subject of the relationship of the Vedantic doctrine of non-duality and Christianity is a veritable minefield. The debate about this issue has often been derailed by a misunderstanding of either/both *Advaita* Vedanta and Christian doctrine, and/or by a confusion of the exoteric and esoteric dimensions of the traditions in question. A great deal of mischief issues from the inability of many commentators of both East and West to situate the problem in an appropriate frame and to discern the different levels at which universal metaphysical doctrines, exoteric theological dogmas, and rational philosophical concepts are properly situated. So, our discussion of Abhishiktananda's inquiries into the possibilities of a "Christian *Advaita*" cannot proceed until we have dispelled some of the fog which has accumulated over the whole field. Our immediate task is to clarify the differences between metaphysics, theology, and philosophy. This is best done by recourse to the work of those few persons who, in recent times, have been trustworthy exegetes of the *sophia perennis*—René Guénon, Ananda Coomaraswamy, Frithjof Schuon, and other traditionalists. It is only in the light of the perennial wisdom that many of the problems confronting us can be resolved. As noted earlier, Abhishiktananda himself would have been saved much agonizing if he had been able to access these works.

The comparison of religious forms from divergent traditions is fraught with hazards. There are those who will find parallels and similarities, even identity, through facile comparisons which pay too little attention to the place of the forms in question in the larger spiritual economies to which they belong, not to mention other considerations of cultural and historical context. Myths, doctrines, rituals, codes, symbols and the like can never be understood *in vacuo*. On the other hand there are those so wedded to the conviction that their own tradition is in exclusive possession of the truth or, less immodestly, that the forms of their own faith are intrinsically superior, that they see only "opposition and mutual exclusion everywhere," quite unable to countenance the idea that, for all the diversity and variegation of religious forms, there is a necessary and Providential congruity between the metaphysical doctrines of the integral traditions. Such partisans cannot understand that the formal diversity of religions *complements* an inner unity which can only be discerned by the "eye of the heart."

Metaphysics, Theology, and Philosophy[9]

As Guénon observed more than once, metaphysics cannot properly be defined, for to define is to limit, while the domain of metaphysics is the Real, which is limitless. Consequently, metaphysics "is truly and absolutely unlimited and cannot be confined to any formula or any system."[10] Its subject, in John Tauler's words, is "that pure knowledge that knows no form or creaturely way."[11] This must always be kept in mind in any attempt at a "definition" which must needs be provisional, such as this one from Seyyed Hossein Nasr:

> [Metaphysics] is a science . . . which can only be attained through
> intellectual intuition and not simply through ratiocination. It thus
> differs from philosophy as it is usually understood. Rather, it is a *theoria*
> of reality whose realization means sanctity and spiritual perfection,

and therefore can only be achieved within the cadre of a revealed tradition. Metaphysical intuition can occur everywhere—for the "spirit bloweth where it listeth"—but the effective realization of metaphysical truth and its application to human life can only be achieved within a revealed tradition which gives efficacy to certain symbols and rites upon which metaphysics must rely for its realization.

> This supreme science of the Real . . . is the only science that can distinguish between the Absolute and the relative, appearance and reality. . . . Moreover, this science exists, as the esoteric dimension within every orthodox and integral tradition and is united with a spiritual method derived totally from the tradition in question.[12]

The ultimate reality of metaphysics is the Supreme Identity in which all oppositions and dualities are resolved, those of subject and object, knower and known, being and non-being; thus a Scriptural formulation such as "The things of God knoweth no man, but the Spirit of God" (1 Corinthians 2.11).[13]

This *sacra scientia* is rooted in the direct and immediate experience of the Real through what Eckhart and the traditionalists called the Intellect: "There is something in the soul which is uncreated and uncreatable . . . this is the Intellect."[14] If one may speak in paradox, it is that suprahuman faculty, latent within every human, which receives intuitions and apprehends realities of a supra-phenomenal order; "that which participates in the divine Subject."[15] It is an impersonal, unconditioned, receptive faculty, whence the objectivity of intellection. Marco Pallis reminds us that a belief in this transcendent faculty, capable of a direct contact with Reality, is to be found in all traditions under various names.[16] Because the metaphysical realm lies "beyond" the phenomenal plane the validity of a metaphysical principle can be neither proved nor disproved by any kind of empirical demonstration, by reference to material realities.[17] The aim of metaphysics is not to prove anything whatsoever but to make doctrines intelligible and to demonstrate their consistency.

Metaphysics assumes man's capacity for absolute and certain knowledge:

> The capacity for objectivity and for absoluteness is an anticipated and existential refutation of all the ideologies of doubt: if man is able to doubt this is because certitude exists; likewise the very notion of illusion proves that man has access to reality. . . . If doubt conformed to the real, human intelligence would be deprived of its sufficient reason and man would be less than an animal, since the intelligence of animals does not experience doubt concerning the reality to which it is proportioned.[18]

Metaphysics, therefore, is immutable and inexorable, and the "infallible standard by which not only religions, but still more 'philosophies' and 'sciences' must be 'corrected' . . . and interpreted."[19] Metaphysics can be ignored or forgotten but not refuted "precisely because it is immutable and not related to change *qua* change."[20] Metaphysical principles are true and valid once and for all, and not for this particular age or mentality, and could not, in any sense, "evolve." They can be validated directly in the plenary and unitive experience of the mystic. However, this is not to lose sight of the fact that any metaphysician will aver that every formulation is "but error in the face of the Divine Reality itself; a provisional, indispensable, salutary 'error' which, however, contains and communicates the virtuality of the Truth."[21] As Abhishiktananda remarks, "As long as man attempts to seize and hold God in his words and concepts, he is embracing a mere idol."[22] With these considerations in the foreground we can turn to a comparison of metaphysics and philosophy as it is now generally understood.

In a discussion of the Vedanta Coomaraswamy exposed some of the crucial differences between metaphysics and modern philosophy:

> The Vedanta is not a "philosophy" in the current sense of the word, but only as the word is used in the phrase *Philosophia Perennis*. . . . Modern philosophies are closed systems, employing the method of dialectics, and taking for granted that opposites are mutually exclusive. In modern philosophy things are either so or not so; in eternal philosophy this depends upon our point of view. Metaphysics is not a system, but a consistent doctrine; it is not merely concerned with conditioned and quantitative experience but with universal possibility.[23]

Modern European philosophy is dialectical, which is to say analytical and rational in its modes. From a traditional point of view it might be said that modern philosophy is shackled by a misunderstanding of the nature and role of reason; indeed, the idolatry of reason could hardly have otherwise arisen. Schuon spotlights some of the strengths and deficiencies of the rational mode in these terms:

> Reason is formal by its nature and formalistic in its operations; it proceeds by "coagulations," by alternatives and by exclusions—or, it can be said, by partial truths. It is not, like pure intellect, formless and fluid "light"; true, it derives its implacability, or its validity in general, from the intellect, but it touches on essences only through drawing conclusions, not by direct vision; it is indispensable for verbal formulations but it does not involve immediate knowledge.[24]

Titus Burckhardt likens reason to "a convex lens which steers the intelligence in a particular direction and onto a limited field."[25] Like any other instrument it can be abused. Much European philosophy, adrift from its religious moorings, has surrendered to a totalitarian rationalism, to what Blake called "Single Vision."[26] In so doing it has violated a principle which was respected wherever a metaphysical tradition and a religious framework for the pursuit of wisdom remained intact, the principle of adequation, articulated thus by Aquinas: "It is a sin against intelligence to want to proceed in an identical manner in typically different domains—physical, mathematical, metaphysical—of speculative knowledge."[27] The place of reason, of logic, and dialectic, in metaphysics is a subordinate one:

> In the intellectual order logical proof is only a quite provisional crystallization of intuition, the modes of which . . . are incalculable. Metaphysical truths are by no means accepted because they are merely logically clear, but because they are ontologically clear and their logical clarity is only a trace of this imprinted on the mind.[28]

Furthermore, as Schuon reminds us,

> Metaphysics is not held to be true—by those who understand it—because it is expressed in a logical manner, but it can be expressed in a logical manner because it is true, without—obviously—its truth ever being compromised by the possible shortcomings of human reason.[29]

Similarly Guénon:

> For metaphysics, the use of rational argument never represents more than a mode of external expression and in no way affects metaphysical knowledge itself, for the latter must always be kept essentially distinct from its formulation.[30]

Abhishiktananda well understood the limits of reason/ *eidos* and its subordinate relation to intuition (used here in its traditional Indian sense, more or less synonymous with intellection): ". . . *eidos*, proud of its worth, is generally reluctant to allow itself to be referred to its source, to intuition, that is, the fundamental, supra-mental experience and perception."[31] He further clarifies this "relation" in a passage concerning the *Upanishads*:

> In philosophy concepts and logic reign supreme; intuition can only take form if it submits to conditions established by the technical instruments of knowing. In the Scriptures also, of course, intuition is necessarily mediated through mental forms; but in this case intuition remains the governing factor from beginning to end. *Ideas, concepts, abstractions, reflections are never anything more than means of returning once more to the original intuition.*[32]

Metaphysical discernment proceeds primarily through contemplative intelligence rather than ratiocination. Metaphysical formulations depend more on symbol and on analogy than on logical demonstration, though it is a grave error to suppose that metaphysics has any right to irrationality.[33] What many modern philosophers apparently fail to understand is that thought can become increasingly subtle and complex without approaching any nearer to the truth. "An idea can be subdivided into a thousand ramifications, fenced about with every conceivable qualification and supported with the most intricate and rigorous logic but, for all that, remain purely external and quantitative for no virtuosity of the potter will transform clay into gold."[34] Analytical rationality, no matter how useful a tool, will never in itself generate metaphysical understanding. Metaphysicians of all ages have said nothing different. Sankara:

> The pure truth of *Ātman* . . . can be reached by meditation, contemplation, and other spiritual disciplines such as a knower of *Brahman* may prescribe—but never by subtle argument.[35]

The Promethean arrogance of much modernist thought, often bred by scientistic ideologies, is revealed in the refusal to acknowledge the boundaries beyond which reason and other mental operations have no competence or utility. Abhishiktananda reminds us that

> Speculative theology, however high and illuminating, remains always on the threshold of the Kingdom. It can only indicate a direction . . . and become[s] truly significant only when aiding the spirit to pass on to *the contemplation of the highest wisdom which silences the mind and transcends all its activities.*[36]

The intelligibility of a metaphysical doctrine may depend upon a measure of faith in the traditional Christian sense of "assent to a credible proposition." As Coomaraswamy observes,

> One must believe in order to understand and understand in order to believe. These are not successive, however, but simultaneous acts of the mind. In other words, there can be no knowledge of anything to which the will refuses its consent.[37]

This mode of apprehension is something quite other than the philosophical thought that "believes it can attain to an absolute contact with Reality by means of analyses, syntheses, arrangements, filtrations and polishings—thought that is mundane by the very fact of this ignorance."[38] In this context Schuon speaks of modern philosophy as "the codification of an acquired infirmity."[39]

Swami Abhishiktananda shortly before his death in December 1973
(photo Christopher Bäumer)

I

Left to right: Fr Jules Monchanin, Msgr James Mendonça, Bishop of Tiruchchirappalli (Trichinopoly), and Fr Henri Le Saux, Shantivanam, August 1950

Fr Henri Le Saux, c. 1948

Abhishiktananda, c. 1952

Fr Jules Monchanin, Easter 1957

III

Abhishiktananda at Shantivanam

IV

Abhishiktananda at Shantivanam

Abhishiktananda at Jyotiniketan Ashram,
Easter 1969 (photo Murray Rogers)

Abhishiktananda at
Jyotiniketan Ashram, 1965

Arunachala mountain

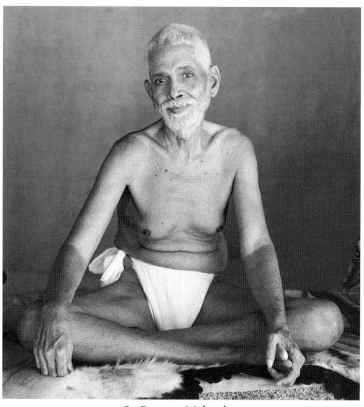

Sri Ramana Maharshi

Abhishiktananda in a cave at Arunachala

Abhishiktananda at Lakshman Jhula, Rishikesh, 1972

Swami Gnanananda

Abhishiktananda with
Bettina Bäumer

Swami Ajatananda (Marc Chaduc)

Swami Chidananda

Raimon Pannikar

Unlike modern philosophy, metaphysics has nothing to do with personal opinion, originality or creativity—quite the contrary. It is directed towards those realities which lie outside mental perimeters and which are unchanging. The most a metaphysician will ever want to do is to reformulate some timeless truth so that it becomes more intelligible in the prevailing climate.[40] A profane system of thought, on the other hand, is never more than a portrait of the person who creates it, an "involuntary memoir" as Nietzsche so nicely put it.[41]

The metaphysician does not seek to invent or discover or "prove" a new system of thought but rather to crystallize direct apprehensions of Reality insofar as this is possible within the limited resources of human language, making use not only of logic but of symbol and analogy. Furthermore, the science of metaphysics must always proceed in the context of a revealed religion, protected by the tradition in question which also supplies the necessary supports for the full realization or actualization of metaphysical doctrines. The metaphysician seeks not only to formulate immutable principles and doctrines but to live by them, to conform his or her being to the truths they convey. The pursuit of metaphysical wisdom engages the whole person or it is as nothing.[42] As Schuon states,

> The moral exigency of metaphysical discernment means that virtue is part of wisdom; a wisdom without virtue is in fact imposture and hypocrisy. . . . Plenary knowledge of Divine Reality presupposes or demands moral conformity to this Reality, as the eye necessarily conforms to light; since the object to be known is the sovereign Good, the knowing subject must correspond to it analogically.[43]

Metaphysics can be expressed visually and ritually as well as verbally. The Chinese and Red Indian traditions furnish preeminent examples of these possibilities. Moreover,

> The criterion of metaphysical truth or of its depth lies not in the complexity or difficulty of its expression, having regard to a particular capacity of understanding or style of thinking. Wisdom does not lie in any complication of words but in the profundity of the intention; assuredly the expression may according to the circumstances be subtle and difficult, or equally it may not be so.[44]

Because the fundamental distinction between reason and Intellect has been obscured in recent European thought, then similarly, "the basic distinction between metaphysics as a *scienta sacra* or Divine Knowledge and philosophy as a purely human form of mental activity has been blurred or forgotten."[45] In the field of comparative religion this has generated any amount of confusion. As Seyyed Hossein Nasr has noted, to speak of Hindu or Chinese philosophy and rationalistic European philosophy in the same breath is a contradiction in terms unless the word "philosophy" is used in two quite different senses. A failure to draw the necessary distinctions has

> made a sham of many studies of comparative philosophy and has helped to reduce to nil the real significance of Oriental metaphysics. . . . To say that this or that statement of Hegel resembles the *Upanishads* or that Hume presents ideas similar to Nagarjuna's is to fall into the worst form of error, one which prevents any type of profound understanding from being achieved, either for Westerners wanting to understand the East or vice versa.[46]

To summarize: Modern philosophy, generally speaking, is analytical, rationalistic, and quantitative; it is concerned with relationships and contingencies accessible to rational inquiry, or at least to the workings of the normal mind, these including imagination which is no less a mental process than ratiocination; philosophy is seen as progressive, autonomous, and self-validating. Metaphysics, by contrast, is concerned with supra-mundane, transcendent, and unconditioned realities; it is qualitative, symbolical, and synthetic in its modes and is rooted in certain immutable principles which could not be the product of "thinking"; it is indifferent to the question of "proofs" and the metaphysician's purpose is not the resolution of some "problem" but the demonstration of something already intellectually evident; metaphysics does not evolve or progress; it is intimately linked with spiritual disciplines and depends for its realization on the presence of elements which could only be drawn from an integral tradition; it is a practical pursuit which has as its end gnosis, transformation, and sanctification.

*

The relationship between metaphysics and theology is more subtle, complex, and problematic. Under the traditionalist view, a Divine Revelation is always the fountainhead of any orthodox religion while metaphysical insight derives from intellection. The dichotomy here is more apparent than real, Revelation taking the place of intellection for the human collectivity in question. This is a principle not easily grasped but without it the apparent antagonisms of theology and metaphysics cannot be resolved. Schuon defines the relationship between Revelation and intellection in this way:

> In normal times we learn *a priori* of divine things through Revelation, which provides for us the symbols and the indispensable data, and we

have access *a posteriori* to the truth of these things through Intellection, which reveals to us their essence beyond received formulations, but not opposing them. . . . Revelation is an Intellection in the Macrocosm, while Intellection is a Revelation in the microcosm; the *Avatāra* is the outward Intellect, and the Intellect is the inward *Avatāra*.[47]

It might be said, then, that intellection appears in a more "subjective" mode, but only with this qualification:

It is subjective because empirically it is within us. The term "subjective," as applied to the intellect, is as improper as the epithet "human"; in both cases the terms are used simply in order to define the way of approach.[48]

The traditionalists, always alert to the dangers of a reductive psychologism, insist that the truth to which intellection gives access is beyond all spatio-temporal determinations. As Schuon points out, Biblical formulations such as "the Kingdom of Heaven is within you" certainly do not mean that heaven, God, or Truth are of a psychological order but simply that access to these realities is to be found through the center of our being.[49] Religion itself, flowing from the Divine, must contain within itself principial or metaphysical knowledge but this will be veiled by the forms in question. For instance,

The message of Christ, like that of the *Bible*, is not *a priori* a teaching of metaphysical science; it is above all a message of salvation, but one that necessarily contains, in an indirect way and under cover of an appropriate symbolism, *metaphysics in its entirety*.[50]

The metaphysical emphasis varies from one tradition to another. Buddhism, for example, is primarily a spiritual therapy rather than a metaphysical system but one which of necessity requires a metaphysics while Vedanta is, in the first place, a metaphysic which implies, under the same necessity, a spiritual therapy.[51] "There is no science of the soul," says Schuon, "without a metaphysical basis to it and without spiritual remedies at its disposal."[52]

The relationship of theology to metaphysics is that of exoterism to esoterism. Exoterism is "unable of itself to take cognizance of the relationships whereby, at one and the same time, it is justified in its claims and limited in its scope."[53] Theological dogmatism is characterized by its insistence on elevating a particular point of view, or aspect of reality under a specific formal guise, to an absolute value with exclusive claims. What characterizes a metaphysical esoterism, on the other hand, is its discernment of the universal in the particular, of the essence in the form. This distinction can be hinged on the terms "belief" and "gnosis," or similarly, "faith" and "certitude." Schuon refers to the theologies as taking upon themselves the contradiction of being "sentimental metaphysics":

> Being ignorant of the differentiation of things into aspects and standpoints they have therefore to operate on the basis of arbitrarily rigid data, the antinomies of which can only be solved by going beyond their artificial rigidity; their working has moreover a sentimental slant and this is described as "thinking piously."[54]

Such remarks should not be construed as an attack on the theological perspective but only as a caution about the limits of dogmatism and the dangers of a theological totalitarianism when it enters an arena where it is inadequate. As Marco Pallis so neatly puts it,

> What one always needs to remember is that traditional forms, including those bearing the now unpopular name of dogmas, are keys to unlock the gate of Unitive Truth; but they are also (since a key can close, as well as open a gate) possible obstacles to its profoundest knowledge.[55]

In a felicitous metaphor Schuon compares the religions to the beads of a rosary, gnosis being the cord on which they are strung. In other words, the religious orthodoxies, or more specifically theologies, are only able to fulfill their function when they remain attached to the principial knowledge which is preserved in the esoteric dimension of each tradition.

The hierarchic superiority of gnosis to all other forms of knowledge and of metaphysical doctrine to all other kinds of formulations should not be allowed to obscure the interdependent relationship of the esoteric and the exoteric, of the metaphysical domain and the rest of any religious tradition. Three general points need to be made in this context, concerning the ineffectiveness of intellection outside a traditional framework, the distinction between doctrinal understanding and realization, and the relationship between metaphysical discernment and the spiritual life in general.

There are, writes Schuon,

> no metaphysical or cosmological reasons why, in exceptional cases, direct intellection should not arise in men who have no link at all with revealed wisdom, but an exception, if it proves the rule, assuredly could not constitute the rule.[56]

In more normal cases

> Intellection has need of tradition, of a Revelation fixed in time and adapted to a society, if it is to be awakened in us and not go astray.

> ... The importance of orthodoxy, of tradition, of Revelation is that the means of realizing the Absolute must come "objectively" from the Absolute; knowledge cannot spring up "subjectively" except within the framework of an "objective" divine formulation of Knowledge.[57]

Thus, although intellection can occur as "an isolated miracle" anywhere, it will have neither authority nor efficacy outside tradition.[58] (In this context the case of Ramana Maharshi is not without interest, remembering how the sage had to cast his own mystical insight into the moulds of classical Vedanta in order to be able to communicate it.)

The distinction between doctrinal understanding and even intellection itself on the one hand, and realization on the other, is a crucial one. Contemplative intelligence and metaphysical insight in themselves "do not prevent Titans from falling."[59] There must be a participation of the will in the intelligence, or as one scholar glossed Meister Eckhart, "The intellective center is not truly known without involving the volitive circumference."[60] Here the will can be defined as "a prolongation or a complement of the intelligence"[61] while intelligence itself refers to a contemplative receptivity.[62] Morality and the virtues, love, faith—these must be integrated with metaphysical insight if full realization is to occur, which is to say there must be a merging of intellectual and volitive elements in a harmonized unity. It should also be remembered that although the Intellect is

> situated beyond sentiment, imagination, memory, and reason ... it can at the same time enlighten and determine all of these since they are like its individualized ramifications, ordained as receptacles to receive the light from on high and to translate it according to their respective capacities.[63]

The spiritual life, which can only be lived in conformity with a way provided by tradition, forms both a precondition and a complement to intellection. As Aquinas put it, "By their very nature the virtues do not necessarily form part of contemplation but they are an indispensable condition for it."[64] Moreover, sanctity itself may or may not be accompanied by metaphysical discernment: one may be a saint but no metaphysician, as history repeatedly demonstrates. To expect, as a necessity, metaphysical wisdom of the saint is to confuse different modes of spiritual perfection. As Schuon reminds us,

> To say "man" is to say *bhakta*, and to say spirit is to say *jñānin;* human nature is so to speak woven of these two neighboring but incommensurable dimensions. There is certainly a *bhakti* without *jñāna*, but there is no *jñāna* without *bhakti*.[65]

The perspectives of Ramanuja and Sankara might be cited as an illustrative example of this principle.[66] For a European example of "*bhakti* without *jñāna*" one might cite St Thérèse of Lisieux—but the history of Christianity furnishes many examples.

If metaphysical discernment is to transform one's being then intellection alone is insufficient for "human nature contains dark elements which no intellectual certainty could, *ipso facto*, eliminate."[67] Here the role of faith is of critical importance:

> A man may possess metaphysical certainty without possessing "faith.". . . But, if metaphysical certainty suffices on the doctrinal ground, it is far from being sufficient on the spiritual level where it must be completed and enlivened by faith. Faith is nothing other than our whole being clinging to Truth, whether we have of truth a direct intuition or an indirect idea. It is an abuse of language to reduce "faith" to the level of "belief."[68]

The planes on which philosophy, theology, and metaphysics are situated can be identified by comparing their respective approaches to "God." For the philosopher "God" is a "problem" to be resolved rationally, as if human reason could prove no matter what!; the theologian will be less concerned with proofs, the reality of God being a revealed and thus axiomatic datum, than with belief and its moral concomitances; the metaphysician is concerned neither with rational argument nor with belief but with an intellectual evidence which brings an absolute certitude. To put it another way one might say that philosophy trades in opinions and ideas, theology focuses on beliefs and moralities, and metaphysics formulates doctrines which are the fruit of intellection. Or, again, one might say that the philosopher is intent on constructing a mental system, the theologian on discovering and living by the "will of heaven," and the metaphysician on a transformative gnosis which will conform his being to the Real.

We can recapitulate some of the central points made in our discussion of the relationships between philosophy, theology, and metaphysics through a passage from Schuon's *The Transcendent Unity of Religions*:

> Intellectual or metaphysical knowledge transcends the specifically theological point of view, which is itself incomparably superior to the philosophical point of view, since, like metaphysical knowledge, it emanates from God and not from man; but whereas metaphysics proceeds wholly from intellectual intuition, religion proceeds from Revelation. . . . In the case of intellectual intuition, knowledge is not possessed by the individual insofar as he is an individual, but insofar as in his innermost essence he is not distinct from the Divine Principle.

... The theological point of view, because it is based in the minds of believers on a Revelation and not on a knowledge that is accessible to each one of them ... will of necessity confuse the symbol or form with the naked and supraformal Truth while metaphysics ... will be able to make use of the same symbol or form as a means of expression while at the same time being aware of its relativity. . . . Religion translates metaphysical or universal truths into dogmatic language. . . . What essentially distinguishes the metaphysical from the philosophical proposition is that the former is symbolical and descriptive ... whereas philosophy ... is never anything more than what it expresses. When philosophy uses reason to resolve a doubt, this proves precisely that its starting point is a doubt it is striving to overcome, whereas ... the starting point of a metaphysical formulation is always something intellectually evident or certain, which is communicated to those able to receive it, by symbolical or dialectical means designed to awaken in them the latent knowledge that they bear unconsciously, and it may even be said, eternally within them.[69]

Our discussion of these interrelationships has necessarily had to gloss over some issues, skirt round others. Some fundamentally important principles and distinctions had to be expounded within a short compass. But two brief points. Firstly, the term "philosophy" in itself "has nothing restrictive about it"; the restrictions which we have imposed on it in this discussion have been expedient rather than essential.[70] Secondly, it must also be admitted that our discussion of the relationships of philosophy, theology, and metaphysics has been governed by some necessary oversimplifications. From certain points of view the distinctions we have established are not as clear-cut nor as rigid as our discussion has suggested. As Schuon himself writes,

In a certain respect, the difference between philosophy, theology, and gnosis is total; in another respect, it is relative. It is total when one understands by "philosophy" only rationalism; by "theology," only the explanation of religious teachings; and by "gnosis," only intuitive and intellective, and thus supra-rational, knowledge; but the difference is only relative when one understands by "philosophy" the fact of thinking, by "theology" the fact of speaking dogmatically of God and religious things, and by "gnosis" the fact of presenting pure metaphysics, for then the genres interpenetrate.[71]

Abhishiktananda and Advaita in Context

Abhishiktananda was neither a systematic theologian, nor a philosopher interested in the construction of a rationally-based "system" or "world-view" or "argument"; he *was* a Christian *mystic* who discovered in the *direct experience* of *advaita* a profound challenge both to Christian theology, at least in its exoteric form, and to his own self-understanding. His mystical intuitions were not the result of "thinking," nor of study, though each of these may well have helped to make his soul receptive to those "shattering" illuminations which he experienced at Arunachala and Rishikesh. Likewise, the *tapas* and the spiritual disciplines of prayer and meditation, conducted in silence and solitude, no doubt disposed him to be open to the message which lay hidden in the deepest recesses of the *guha*, which is nothing other than the Heart-Intellect. The "secret of Arunachala" revealed itself to a soul which was focused on "the one thing necessary" and prepared to pay the mandatory price.

Abhishiktananda's problem, to state it in over-simplified form, was this: his mystical experience, whose authenticity he could not doubt, seemed to contradict the conventional Christian theology in which he had been reared. There was nothing in his experience of the Church, nothing in its spiritual ambience, which prepared him for the abyssal experiences at Arunachala. It is true that he had a familiarity with much of the mystical literature of the Christian tradition and one can surmise that without it the experiential shock of *advaita* might have had one of several consequences: the annihilation, then and there, of his Christian faith, forever; or, a fearful retreat into the security of his former beliefs and self-understanding, and a disavowing of the experience; or, a vertiginous descent into a kind of intellectual and spiritual dizziness from which there might be no recovery. As it was, Arunachala marked the first stage of a long, lonely, and treacherous journey which Abhishiktananda undertook with remarkable daring. There is indeed something of the sacrificial heroism of the martyr in Abhishiktananda's "return to the center," and from one point of view we should perhaps not regret the fact that his spiritual odyssey was so difficult. There is a kind of fierce integrity in his refusal to abandon the Nazarene whilst retaining an unyielding grip on his inner illumination in the dark cave of Arunachala. But from another vantage point it is difficult not to feel that he would have been spared much anguish if he had had recourse to the guidance of a real Christian *jñānī*, someone with the metaphysical discernment to show him that it was never a matter of "either/or," as he at first thought, but of situating each in a framework which would give both their full due. In the early days Fr Monchanin played something of this sort of role, but in the end was not equipped to guide Abhishiktananda towards an understanding which he himself did not have (which is in no way to doubt his immense learning, sincerity, and piety).

Then too, to be sure, resort to the works of such perennialist thinkers as René Guénon and Ananda Coomaraswamy would have dispelled some of the fearsome tensions which came in the wake of Arunachala—but these were not writers in any sort of favor in ecclesiastical circles. (In his published letters there is a solitary and dismissive reference to Guénon, from which it is clear that Abhishiktananda had only a cloudy and ill-informed notion of his work.[72]) But by the end Abhishiktananda had moved to a hard-won understanding which shared a great deal of common ground with the traditionalists.

It cannot be too strongly stressed that Abhishiktananda's struggle can only be understood in the context of the times, that is to say, in a period in which Roman legalism, triumphalism, and exclusivism were the order of the day, and in which Latin theology was firmly tied to a religious historicism which identified the historical Jesus and his Church as the *only* means through which man might find salvation. At the risk of making reckless generalizations it can also be said that by this time the Western Church was suffering from a process of ossification whose origins lay as far back as the late Middle Ages when Christendom—a homogeneous civilization held together by the religious tradition—began the long process of disintegration whose end was marked by the triumph of all those anti-religious forces which comprise "modernity" (humanism, secularism, materialism, individualism, evolutionism, historicism, scientism, etc., etc.). Over a period of time, for reasons too complex to unravel here, the Church had neglected its own esoteric, mystical, and metaphysical well-springs with the inevitable result that it increasingly suffered from a kind of exoteric petrifaction, if one may so put it. In brief, the mystical/metaphysical stream of Christianity, so vital to the health of the tradition, had been forced underground. The situation in India itself was no better, the Catholic Church in the sub-continent being little more than a quasi-colonial transplant which had taken all too little notice of the spiritual habitat into which it had been imposed from without. Indeed, it many respects, in the manner of colonials, the Church in India was more "Roman" than the Romans! In the light of these general considerations we should not be surprised that Kergonan was not an altogether adequate preparation for Arunachala. Nor should we be puzzled that for many years Abhishiktananda did not understand the different levels at which a metaphysical *theoria*, a theological dogma, and a philosophical construct might best be situated and understood.

*

Several scholars and theologians have focused on the problematic relationship of Christianity and Vedanta as the locus of Abhishiktananda's most important work, and have traced his evolving trajectory in much more detail than is possible here. Readers who wish to follow step-by-step in Abhishiktananda's tracks are directed particularly to Abhishiktananda's journal and to studies by Antony Kalliath, John Glenn Friesen, Emmanuel Vattakuzhy, Michael Comans, and others. In this chapter we shall take note only of the major landmarks on this spiritual journey, paying most attention to the understanding at which Abhishiktananda arrived in his later years.

Whilst alert to the hazards of an over-tidy chronological schematization, Kalliath has persuasively suggested that Abhishiktananda's engagement with the problem moved through five phases which he summarizes as follows:

(i) 1948-1952: the initial period in which Abhishiktananda tries to understand *advaita* in terms of his own Christian consciousness; an attempt "to baptize the *advaita!*" At this time his outlook is fashioned both by the in-vogue theology of fulfillment and by a more daring attitude of inclusiveness.

(ii) 1952-1957: the years in which Abhishiktananda's direct experiences of *advaita* under the guidance of his Indian gurus—experiences of exceptional depth and intensity—trigger a crisis which it took many years to resolve. In this period Abhishiktananda begins the task of refashioning his understanding of Christianity in terms of the advaitic awakening at Arunachala. (Late in life he writes that nothing new happened after Arunachala, though his experience and understanding of *advaita* became ever deeper, culminating in the great "spiritual adventure" in the last months of his life.) In this second phase, Abhishiktananda is able to bring *advaita* and the Trinity together in his own mystical experience but is unable to reconcile them conceptually.

(iii) 1957-1962 (roughly): in these years Abhishiktananda is struggling to find an appropriate theological, conceptual, and symbolical expression of his own experience of Christian *advaita* but eventually concludes that this is impossible.

(iv) 1963-1969: the Himalayan years in which Abhishiktananda "increasingly began to interpret Reality in terms of his Self-awakening according to the *Upanishads*. Christian *mythos*, including Jesus Christ, has meaning only at the level of *nāma-rūpas* in his vision."

136

(v) 1970-1973: "Abhishiktananda rediscovers the meaning of the Christian *mythos*, but unmistakably in an advaitic light. In this rediscovery he keeps a subtle balance between the relativity and the inviolability of the Christian *mythos* in his God experience." This constitutes a "profound witness to the Hindu-Christian meeting."[73]

This schema gives a fair picture of Abhishiktananda's route in his engagement with *advaita*. Of the many questions which arise out of Abhishiktananda's experiences and his writings we will briefly consider four: 1. What did Abhishiktananda understand by the term "*advaita*"? 2. How did he understand the "relationship" between Christianity and *advaita*? 3. Was Abhishiktananda's experience of *advaita* "authentic"? 4. Was his exposition of Vedanta in conformity with that of Sankara?

Abhishiktananda's Understanding of "Advaita"

For Abhishiktananda *advaita*, in the first place, is not a recondite doctrine but an immediate *experience* of a mystery—the mystery of God, the world, and man himself. It is an "experience" like no other certainly, and one most difficult to conceptualize or communicate: "words alone will always remain powerless to convey its secret."[74] It is an "inner" awareness of the Real (Self/*Ātman-Brahman*/God/Divine Presence) in which all dualities disappear, including that of "experience" and "experiencer," of subject and object. It is quite beyond the reach of either the senses or the mind. It can only be described symbolically and metaphorically: it is a "blazing discovery," a "consuming fire," an endless "pillar of fire," "a cataclysmic transformation of being," "a shattering" of all one's previous understandings, a fathomless abyss, "an interior lightning flash." It is the discovery of the Grail, "the experience of the divine Presence in the core of both the cosmos and the human heart."[75] It is the innermost message of the *Upanishads*, the secret of Arunachala, a Return to the Source, "the ultimate awakening of the human spirit."

It is imperative to understand that Abhishiktananda uses the word "intellectual," not in the sense outlined in our discussion of metaphysics (i.e., the Heart-Intellect which apprehends the Real) but in its conventional sense—pertaining to the rational workings of the mind. His insistence that *advaita* is not an intellectual discovery means only that it is not a product of mental operations. Although Abhishiktananda does not use "intellect" in the traditional sense his references to the *guha* (the cave of the heart) make it more or less synonymous. A sample of Abhishiktananda's reflections on *advaita*:

> *Advaita* is not an intellectual discovery—but a deep-seated attitude of the spirit. Much more the impossibility of saying two than the affirmation of One.[76]

> No purely intellectual conviction obtains it, for every act of the intellect inevitably remains on the dualistic level of ordinary experience.[77]

> The advaitin theologians are just as intolerable and ineffectual as the Christian, Muslim, or Buddhist theologians, who determine truth simply by deduction from syllogisms and flat assertions. As if truth could be attained by the intellect otherwise than by using symbols— and the symbol never exhausts reality.[78]

Abhishiktananda is well aware that any purely theoretical under-standing of *advaita* can, in fact, be harmful and lead to "pride, conceit, and egoism" and to "fatal aberrations."[79] He was somewhat impatient with those for whom Vedanta was primarily a matter for endless specu-lations:

> There are in general two classes of people, both among Hindus and Christians, who are concerned with *advaita*. There are those for whom it is a magnificent idea, and there are those for whom it is an overwhelming experience in the depths of the spirit. For the first *advaita* is particularly attractive in that one can discuss it endlessly, because it defies all attempts to define it in concepts. Christians can develop an equal enthusiasm for making theoretical comparisons between the formulations of *advaita* and Christian dogma. This kind of interest always remains somewhat superficial; it is like the problems of pure mathematics, which are completely absorbing and yet commit one to nothing outside the conceptual order. However, such an *advaita* is surely not the genuine *advaita*, for *advaita* is essentially an experience. . . . As Lao Tse asked, "Is the *tao* that is talked about still the *tao*?" Spiritual problems can never be reduced to problems of the intellect.[80]

In the light of passages such as these we will not indulge in the kind of highly technical discussion of *advaita* that would seriously disturb the shade of Abhishiktananda. As well as the many traditional sources there is no shortage of such works coming from the pens of Eastern pun-dits and Western scholars alike.[81] There have also been several theses and articles devoted to Abhishiktananda's understanding of *advaita* for those looking for a more detailed analysis than is furnished here.

One important philosophical distinction made by Abhishiktananda is that *advaita*, insofar as it *can* be conceptualized, is non-dualism, not monism: "*Advaita* is certainly not the idea that there is only One."[82]

Both Robert Stephens and John Glen Friesen have characterized Abhishiktananda's conceptualization of *advaita* as "non-monistic non-duality." But in the end the experience is quite literally indescribable as it surpasses all categories:

> *Advaita* is neither a sacred nor a religious nor a supernatural nor a divine experience, because all these qualifications imply duality. It is an experience that overarches all. It is not even the supreme state of consciousness, because supreme implies comparison. It is, quite simply beyond all categories.[83]

Abhishiktananda comes to realize, after many years of perplexity, that, "The Upanishadic experience has nothing to do with any religion whatever, and still less is it a matter of mere logic or epistemology. *It is of a different order altogether.*"[84] Nor is the advaitic experience restricted to esoteric circles and the initiated, for "the spirit bloweth where it listeth." While it is true that the *Upanishads* give it an incomparable expression, *advaita* itself is not tied to the Hindu tradition but is universal, even though the "forms in which it is interpreted, the mental, linguistic, cultural, and even the religious, context in which it occurs, may vary to an infinite extent."[85] "Vedantic experience and *dharmas* belong respectively to planes which cannot be compared."[86] It stands as a challenge to all religions to "interiorize and purify" themselves.[87]

Christian Advaita?

Abhishiktananda's *Saccidananda* is subtitled *A Christian Approach to the Advaitic Experience*, presented as "a continuous meditation" from "one who is rooted in the spiritual and intellectual traditions of the Church, but has now come into direct contact with the intuitions of the *Upanishads* and the living experience of the sages."[88] He stresses that the book does not resolve the many theological problems entailed in a Christian encounter with Vedanta but hopes that it will suggest "an inward approach" and signal the real meeting-point in the "cave of the heart," wherein "all true experiences of the Spirit well up as from their source." In such a meeting the Christian, "without in the least betraying his faith," will be brought to a deeper contemplation of the divine mysteries. In 1971 Abhishiktananda wrote a new Introduction to the first English language edition of *Saccidananda*. It is one of his last statements about Christianity and *advaita*. By now he accepts two major criticisms made of *Saccidananda*: the undue influence of a theology of fulfillment in which "all the religious and spiritual experiences of mankind" are assumed to "converge" on the historical Christ and the Church; and, the reliance on a Trinitarian theology largely worked out in terms of Greek thought. By 1971 Abhishiktananda had abandoned fulfillment theology and had become more sensitive to the ways in which Christianity had been circumscribed by its historical and cultural context, particularly by the influence of Greek rationalism. He had also moved closer to understanding that metaphysical doctrines and religious dogmas are incommensurate.

Although Abhishiktananda disclaimed any attempt at a formal theological reconciliation of *Advaita* and Christian Trinitarianism, it remains true that he wrote a good deal on this subject. Here we must take some account of his principal themes without becoming entangled in the somewhat labyrinthine development of his thought. In doing so we will draw mainly on *Hindu Christian Meeting Point* and *Saccidananda: A Christian Approach to Advaitic Experience.* It should be stressed that the following account represents his thinking in the early 60s, and should not be confused with his later understanding in which he came to believe that *advaita* transcends the plane of all *dharmas*, all religious teachings.

*

At the simplest level Abhishiktananda reconciled *Advaita* and Christianity through the medium of love, the axial Christian virtue. "Not to say 'Two' in one's life, that is love."[89] The doctrine of the Trinity, understood in the light of *advaita*, "reveals that Being is essentially a *koinonia* of love."[90] The inner mystery of non-duality "flowers in communion and inter-subjectivity, revealing itself and coming to full expression in the spontaneous gift of the self to another."[91] In "the very depth" of the Upanishadic experience of identity, the Christian may discover "a reciprocity and a communion of love which, far from contradicting the *ekatvam*, the unity and non-duality of being, is its very foundation and *raison d'être.*"[92]

He also made the now familiar equation *sat-cit-ānanda*: Father-Son-Holy Spirit (Being/"I Am"/Existence-Consciousness/Intelligence-Bliss/Joy/Love), perhaps first made by Keshab Chandra Sen (1861-1907) and later by Brahmabandha Upadhyaya, Monchanin, Griffiths, and many others. There has been some debate whether this is an illegitimate and confusing appropriation or a fruitful theological synthesis—a debate into which we will not enter here.[93] Here is a passage taken from *Saccidananda* in which the ternary is considered from a Christian point of view:

Now that the Christian *jñānī* has penetrated to the heart of *Saccidananda* and experiences his "connaturality" with God, the Spirit of Wisdom makes known to him his last secrets. He now knows—

that Being, *sat*, opens itself at its very source to give birth eternally to the Son, and in him to countless creatures, each of which in its own way will for ever manifest and celebrate the infinite love and mercy of God;

that being is essentially "being-with," communion, *koinonia*, the free gift of the self and the mutual communication of love;

that self-awareness, *cit*, only comes to be when there is mutual giving and receiving, for the I only awakes to itself in a Thou;

that the supreme and ultimate felicity, *ānanda*, is fullness and perfect fulfillment, only because it is the fruit of love, for being is love.[94]

Writing a decade later Abhishiktananda puts the matter more concisely:

God then appears at the very core of one's experience where consciousness (*cit*) is identified with being (*sat*) in the infinite bliss (*ānanda*) of the Spirit, who is one only (*advaita*), one in the Father and the Son, one in God and in man, undivided *Saccidānanda.*[95]

*

In the light of his advaitic experiences Abhishiktananda had to interrogate and reinterpret all of the dogmas which had been ingrained him as a Christian. One of the most deeply entrenched was the belief in the divinity of Christ and his unique saving mission. For some time the theology of fulfillment provided a kind of life-belt for this belief. Abhishiktananda's writings in the early 60s are governed by the image of Jesus as one who awakened to the deepest mystery of the Self, simultaneously within himself and the Father. This, rather than the historical events of the Paschal mystery, constitutes the essence of Christ's saving mission:

The Paschal mystery of Redemption was accomplished at a definite time and place in the cosmos. But in reality, Redemption is neither something past nor yet to come. It is wholly and entirely realized in this present moment, in which I actually am.[96]

In *Saccidananda* Abhishiktananda argues that Christ's awakening is beyond compare:

All that the Maharishi, and countless others before him, knew and handed on of the inexorable experience of non-duality, Jesus also knew himself, and that in a pre-eminent manner.[97]

Although Christ's significance far outreaches the historical events in the life of Jesus, at this time Abhishiktananda retains his belief in Christ's uniqueness and his saving power:

> Jesus, as the perfect son of Man, *sat-puruṣa*, was the first to receive this [the full revelation of glory], and did so in the name of all men. No one can ever reach it, unless he participates in the unique experience of Jesus.[98]

The belief in the unique divinity of Jesus he later came to regard as part of the Christian *mythos*, situated at the level of *nāma-rūpa* which is annihilated in the ultimate "awakening." He had this insight as early as 1956 even if he did not realize its full implications for many years. In 1956 he had written in his journal:

> All my life, all my thought was centered for so many years on that point in space and time when Jesus appeared. And now it must be "disconnected" from space-time and centered on the eternal, the non-manifest (*avyakta*).[99]

The center of gravity of Abhishiktananda's Christian faith steadily moves away from the historical Jesus to the ontological and trans-historical Christ who becomes the inner mystery of every man, the *sat-puruṣa*, the authentic Man, the real Son of God, the archetypal Human Person. Moreover, regarding him as a *deva* could become "a wall which hinders the direct view of the Mystery of the *Brahma-ātma*."[100]

> All that Christ said or thought about himself, is true of every man. It is the theologians who—to escape being burnt, the devouring fire—have projected (rejected) into a divine *loka* the true mystery of the Self.[101]

In 1966 Abhishiktananda writes in his journal, "Christ is less real in his temporal history than in the essential mystery of my being."[102] He returns several times to the passage in John's Gospel which suggests that Jesus himself realized he must "make way," so to speak, for the Spirit: "It is good for you that I depart. If I leave you will receive the Spirit" (*John* 16.7), a verse Abhishiktananda likens to the Zen dictum, "If you meet the Buddha on the road, kill him."[103] For Abhishiktananda, Jesus was no longer the unique manifestation of God: "How could the Unlimited be limited to a single manifestation?"[104] The historical events recounted in the Gospels move into the background as Abhishiktananda comes to understand Christ as the "I AM" which is deep in every heart and which can show itself in "the dancing Siva or the amorous Krishna."[105] By the late 60s Abhishiktananda is quite clear that "Whoever, in his personal experience . . . has discovered the Self, has no need of faith in Christ, of prayer, of the communion of the Church."[106] In

1971 he writes in his journal, "My message has nothing to do with any *dharma* whatever."[107] Not long before his death he wrote these words in a letter to Murray Rogers:

> I am interested in no *christo-logy* at all. . . . What I discover above all in Christ is "I AM.". . . Of course I can make use of Christ experience to lead Christians to an "I AM" experience, yet it is this I AM experience that really matters. Christ is this very mystery "that I AM," and in this experience and existential knowledge all christo-logy has disintegrated. It is taking to the end the revelation that we are "sons of God.". . . The discovery of Christ's I AM is the ruin of any Christian theology, for all notions are burnt in the fire of experience. . . . And I find his mystery shining in every awakening man, in every *mythos*.[108]

*

The move to reconcile Christian Trinitarianism and non-duality is, conceptually, the most difficult and perhaps most tangled area of Abhishiktananda's theological thought. Wayne Teasdale has argued that Abhishiktananda's understanding of both the Trinity and the God-creature relationship is one of "qualified difference in identity":

> Difference in identity is the proper subsistence of the inner being of the Trinity. Not difference, nor identity exclusively, but difference in identity, best describes (conceptually) the way in which the Persons are united together and are distinct in their particular functions in the Divine Self-Awareness.[109]

Teasdale elaborates a theological argument to suggest that in Abhishiktananda's thought this same difference-in-identity applies to the "relationship" between God and creature. At times Abhishiktananda emphasizes the identity, at others the difference, but the sum-total, so to speak, is difference-in-identity, or perhaps we might also say, identity-in-difference. This is somewhat reminiscent of the *viśiṣṭādvaita* (qualified non-dualism) of Ramanuja, the Vaisnavite sage of the twelfth century AD. For Abhishiktananda, Christian Trinitarianism is neither dualistic nor monistic—the Real is neither "one" nor "two," nor indeed "three." Here are a few of Abhishiktananda's earlier reflections on this theme:

> God is *in* the depth of myself and God *is* the depth of myself. Deeper than my own depth.[110]

> The "authorship," the *Aham*, which governs our corporal and mental activity cannot be divided into two—God and myself. Understand this as best you can.[111]

I do not say that the human being is God or that God is the human being, but I deny that the human being plus God makes two.[112]

To find Christ is to find the self. In so far as I have contemplated in myself an image of Christ other than my own image, I have not found Christ. Christ in reality, for me, is myself—but myself "raised up," in full possession of the Spirit and in full possession by the Spirit.[113]

Of man's response to God:

It is a free and spontaneous response to God, and at the same time pure grace, pure gift of God, pure activity of the spirit in man. Who can possibly separate out and distinguish what is of God and what is of man in this essentially non-dual act in which I attain to God, attain to being, and awake to myself in the heart of God's own awakening to himself?[114]

In a letter, referring to Christianity and *advaita*, he writes, "in all this one can only give hints. It is up to each one to understand and to leap or bound beyond what is expressed. All words are deceptive."[115]

Here is a more extended passage from *Saccidananda* in which Abhishiktananda "explains" the non-duality of God-and-man and of the Trinity alike:

In the process of man's awakening to himself and to the Father, that is, of his salvation, his deification, there are not two (God and soul) working independently and complementing each other, any more than within the Trinity itself the divine Persons can be said to be independent and complementary in their being or their activity. Words cannot properly express the inner relations of God; nor can words express the no less intimate relationship between man and God. Christian faith simply makes us realize that man's freedom essentially echoes, reflects, and shares in the divine freedom, and that human freedom is grounded in the impossibility for it ever to be isolated from God's.[116]

Thus, for Abhishiktananda, the Trinity "resolves the antinomy of the One and the Many" which obsessed the thinkers of Greece, and also "the antinomy of *an-eka* and *a-dvaita*, the not-one and the not-two which obsesses the Indian seers."[117] Christ's experience actually surpasses the Vedantic experience because it recognizes distinction, not in contradiction of advaitic experience, but on its far side, as it were: for Jesus, God is *both* Other and not-Other.[118] The doctrine of the Trinity remains on the level of religious forms, but can be understood in its most universal application as

a magnificent statement, *nāma-rūpa*, of the deep experience at the same time of unity, of non-duality, and relationship. It is the realization of the eternity of my relationship with my human brother etc. But to try and produce a new Trinitarian theology only leads to dead ends. It means that one is still under the spell of *mythos* and *logos*. It is simply to replace *theos* by *theo-logia* and to confuse the idea of God with God.[119]

As was remarked earlier in this study, Abhishiktananda remained absorbed in the mystery of the Trinity until the end. It was the subject of his first serious writings and of his very last journal entry:

> The Trinity can only be understood in the experience of *advaita*. The Trinity is an experience not a *theologoumenon*. Or at least the *theologoumenon* never conveys its truth. It is only discovered in the lucidity of the inner gaze. Jesus has lived this agonizing—and fulfilling—experience of *advaita*. . . . Jesus revealed to the human being what he is, what everyone is. The Trinity is the ultimate mystery of oneself. But in the very depth of this discovery of the self-Trinity there lies the paradox: in the mystery of the non-source, who still speaks of the Source? It is only at the level of the Source, of the trickle of water springing up, that we speak of what is beyond. In the beyond there is no beyond. It simply is, *etad vai tad!* . . . The Awakening is the shining out of the splendor—in splendor—of the non-awakening, of the eternal not-born . . . a brilliance, a light, a glory that envelops everything, that transcends everything, that seizes one and takes one beyond everything.[120]

It might be said that in this mystical passage, the "formulation-structure" of the doctrine of the Trinity, the *nāma-rūpa* itself, disappears in the splendor of "the eternal not-born." As he wrote in his diary in 1966, "Dogmas, canons, rites: merely signs."[121] And this from *Hindu Christian Meeting-Point*:

> Advaita is not so much a challenge to Christian faith as a relentless reminder that God—and therefore also the acts of God—can never be wholly contained in our concepts. It is a healthy and permanently necessary reminder of the importance of the "way of negation." It condemns, and at the same time frees us from, the idolatry of the intellect, in which our laziness and pride perpetually threaten to engulf us. It rejects the self-satisfied, characteristically bourgeois, reliance on institutions and rites which, however indispensable and sacramentally effective they be, nevertheless are only signs. It delivers us from our very human tendency to transform the ineffable mystery of the Trinity into a kind of refined tritheism, or at the other extreme, into simple modalism, despite the theoretical orthodoxy of our credal statements. It also frees us from the temptation somehow to "add up" God and

ourselves, his creatures, on the grounds that we are not God—thus falling into a dualism no less contrary to our faith than monism.[122]

And, in the last year of his life, "The awakening to the mystery has nothing to do with dogmas about the Trinity, Incarnation, Redemption—nor with the golden-colored *Puruṣa* either."[123] This does not amount to a repudiation of religious formulations which remain valid at their own level—even though they occasion some impatience—but it *did* mark Abhishiktananda's discernment of the outer limit, so to speak, of all theological language and conceptualization. In brief, through mystical experience, he had moved from the domain of theology into the boundless metaphysical realm of the Real.

The Authenticity of Abhishiktananda's Advaitic Experience

Most of our discussion has assumed that Abhishiktananda did indeed have a genuine experience of *advaita*. Nonetheless, it must at least be acknowledged that there are those who either doubt or flatly deny that such was the case. One of the least sympathetic commentators to consider this question is Sita Ram Goel, the author of several articles and a book in which he attacks the whole Christian *sannyāsa* and ashram movement. His assessment of Abhishiktananda's *advaita*:

> It is highly doubtful whether, with all his study of the *Upanishads*, he ever understood what *Advaita* really means. His obstinate obsession with Jesus and the Church prevented him from breaking the barrier. . . . He remained chained to the Church to the end of his days. In the case of Henri Le Saux there was an added difficulty: he was a poet. The flow of mellifluous phrases, particularly in his native French, was mistaken by him for mystic experience. One has to read his writings in order to see how he became a victim of his own word-imageries and figures of speech. Silencing of the mind, which is a *sine qua non* for spiritual experience according to all Hindu scriptures on the subject, remained a discipline which he never learnt.[124]

On the other hand Swami Chidananda was in no doubt about the authentic *advaita* experience of both Abhishiktananda and Marc Chaduc:

> They had both gone into the realms of the Unknown, the Undefinable, the Transcendental; not drawn into "name and form" as though they had, in their aspirations, pierced "the cloud of unknowing" and had come out into the pure white light.[125]

John Glenn Friesen has probably examined this question more exhaustively than any other scholar. His conclusion is that Abhishiktananda certainly had advaitic experiences though he recalls the Vedantic distinction between *kevala* (Pure Consciousness, unqualified; sometimes also called *nirvikalpa*) and *sahaja* (the perception of Brahman in everything), and suggests that Abhishiktananda achieved the latter but probably not the former.[126] Andrew Rawlinson, author of *The Book of Enlightened Masters* and a scholar not given to hasty judgments, believes that Abhishiktananda "was realized or enlightened."[127]

Posing the question of the validity of Abhishiktananda's experience brings several considerations into play. Firstly, only a "knower of Brahman," within the framework of the guru-*chelā* relationship, is fully qualified to assess whether "another" has had an "authentic" experience. It is not up to scholars sitting in air-conditioned libraries to make definitive pronouncements on such questions, though there must be a place for the kind of provisional conjectures essayed by Friesen and Rawlinson. Secondly, it is hazardous to make even a cautious judgment on the basis of Abhishiktananda's writings alone, and those writings in translation. Some commentators have identified certain inconsistencies in Abhishiktananda's account of his experiences; these can be at least partly explained by the fact that Abhishiktananda had several advaitic experiences, each with a subtly different "flavor." Then, too, the fact that at various times he was deploying the vocabulary of different traditions also generated some anomalies. Assessing any kind of mystical experience is indeed tricky, but there are certain rule-of-thumb tests which can be brought to bear.

The mystical experience, as described by countless saints and sages through the ages, results in *absolute certitude* about the supra-sensorial Reality to which the experience gives access. It is almost always associated with *luminosity* and with *bliss*. The mystical experience-proper triggers a radical and spontaneous *self-transformation* which ineradicably changes the trajectory of the life in question. (The case of Ramana is exemplary.) The mystical experience, as opposed to a merely psychic excitation or disturbance, *annihilates egoism* as the mystic has now penetrated the veil of *māyā* and understood the nature of the Self. The "knower of Brahman" emits a *spiritual radiance* and an *equanimity* which is perfectly obvious to those who themselves have tasted the Eternal. Abhishiktananda himself tells us that

> There is in Hindu *sannyāsa* something so strong, such a burning savor
> of the Absolute, that it is irresistibly attractive to those who have

discovered within themselves that ineffable mystery to which the *Upanishads* give their insistent testimony.[128]

In Abhishiktananda's gloss of the *Īśa Upanishad*, "He who sees the *ātman* in all things, and all things in the *ātman*, does not shrink away from, refuse, reject, anything."[129] We can also recall the Biblical adage "*by their fruits shall ye know them.*" The testimony of the mystic-proper *accords with traditional sources*—Scriptures, the affirmations and negations of the saints and sages, the great doctors and pundits. In my view, late in his life Abhishiktananda passes all these "tests." He himself was not entirely free from doubt about the nature of his Arunachala adventures and it is only after the episodes with Marc Chaduc in the last three years of his life that he was able to write in his journal, "The experience of the *Upanishads* is true. *I know it.*"[130] By now he describes his earlier experiences as "glimpses," "tastes," and "touches" of the advaitic experience. At last, in 1972, he had come *fully* to know that "*Puruṣa* the color of the sun, beyond all darkness," "the full appearance of the Self."[131]

Abhishiktananda, Sankara, and Metaphysics

Sankara was not the "author" of a new "philosophy" but a metaphysician and spiritual teacher. His purpose was to demonstrate the unity and consistency of the Upanishadic teachings on *Brahman*, and to explain certain apparent contradictions "by a correlation of different formulations with the point of view implied in them."[132] Like his gurus Gaudapada and Govinda, Sankara was engaged in a metaphysical exposition of Vedanta and the development of a framework, both doctrinal and practical, for the quest of liberation. Sankara is recognized as the most authoritative exponent of the Vedanta (i.e., the *Upanishads*), one of the greatest luminaries of the whole Indian tradition. Abhishiktananda was a Christian monk who wanted to revivify Christian spirituality through the assimilation of various aspects of the spiritual heritage of India. As well as wrestling with the apparent contradictions between the Semitic tradition of prophecy and the Upanishadic emphasis on interiority and direct experience, Abhishiktananda had to find his way through a veritable thicket of modernistic fallacies, pseudo-mythologies, and scientistic shibboleths which constituted a barrier that few have been able to surmount in the modern era. Any direct comparison of Sankara and Abhishiktananda would show the same lack of a sense of proportion as evinced by Vivekananda in his imprudent equation of Jesus Christ, the Buddha, and Ramakrishna.[133] Nonetheless, this question can legitimately be posed: was Abhishiktananda's account of *advaita* consistent with that of Sankara? The short answer is no, not altogether. Michael Comans has judiciously argued that

> We should not understand him to be an *Advaitin* in the sense of a follower of Sankara. He was more in the line of Ramana and Gnanananda, for their primary concern was to direct the disciple to experience the truth of his own being and in order to do so they did not formally resort to Vedanta as a *sampradāya*, a knowledge to be communicated by means of exegesis of scripture and the study of traditional texts. . . . Perhaps it would be more accurate to say that Abhishiktananda was an *Advaitin* in the manner presented by the *Upanishads* themselves: in the manner of a seer rather than a philosopher. Thus we could say that he was not a Hindu *Advaitin* but a Christian *Advaitin* and furthermore he was *Aupanishad* (one who relies upon the *Upanishads*).[134]

As Comans indicates, insofar as Abhishiktananda drew on traditional sources in fashioning his account of *advaita*, both as an experience and as a doctrine, it was to the *Upanishads* that he turned. Panikkar and others have commented on his comparatively meager understanding of other traditional Vedantic sources. But he certainly immersed himself in the *Upanishads*, particularly the earlier ones such as the *Chāndogya*.

Put the question another way: was Abhishiktananda a metaphysician?—that is, someone who on the basis of not only their own experience but their understanding of Scripture, of doctrine, and of Tradition, is equipped to give a coherent, consistent, and authoritative exposition of universal doctrines pertaining to the Supreme Reality? Have these doctrines "incarnated" in the mind of the person in question? This question, it seems to me, must also be answered in the negative. This is no criticism of Abhishiktananda: in the end the only question that counts is whether a man has made the best of his God-given talents. But neither Abhishiktananda's particular gifts (which were formidable), nor his personality and psychic make-up, nor his peculiar circumstances on the frontier of two traditions, were conducive to a metaphysical perspective which is usually marked by a serene calm and detachment. But, a necessary caveat: the testimony of one who has direct experience of transcendent Reality, even if sometimes confused and self-contradictory in expression, will always be of interest to the metaphysician. Abhishiktananda was not a metaphysician to be compared with a Sankara, an Eckhart, an Ibn 'Arabi, a Nagarjuna. But assuredly his life and his writings are saturated with metaphysical insights.[135]

The Debate about Christianity and Advaita

The scope of the present work does not allow us to roam too far from our immediate subject. However, it is worth noting in passing that several other Christian monks and theologians have attempted to forge what has been called "Christian Vedanta" and "Christian *Advaita*." It should be said that "Christian Vedanta" is really a nonsensical term, given the primary meaning of "Vedanta"—the end or summation of the *Vedas*; "Christian *Advaita*" is much the better term as it simply suggests non-dualism considered from a Christian vantage point. But even this term is not without difficulties: *advaita* can be understood as either a "subjective" mystical *experience* or as an "objective" metaphysical *doctrine*; in either case there is nothing particularly "Christian" about it. In like manner, we cannot speak about "Buddhist Truth" as opposed to "Islamic Truth," as Truth is Truth, without qualification. Nonetheless, the term "Christian *Advaita*" has some utility if we understand it to mean *advaita* as it might be experienced or understood in Christian terms, insofar as this is possible. If we replace the term *advaita* with non-dualism, then one might adduce all manner of antecedents for the contemporary Christian interest in the subject—Pseudo-Dionysius, St Bernard, Meister Eckhart, and Nicholas of Cusa among many others.[136] But here we note in passing a few contemporary forays into this subject.

Bede Griffiths' *Vedanta and Christian Faith* (1973) marked one of his earliest excursions into the field and was followed by several other works in which he returned to the subject. His work has been closely studied, explicated, and extended by his friend and student Wayne Teasdale in *Towards a Christian Vedanta* (1987) and *Bede Griffiths: An Introduction to His Interspiritual Thought* (2003). Francis X. Clooney is one of a number of Catholic theologians conducting "experiments in comparative theology" such as can be found in *Theology After Vedanta* (1993). Other theologians and scholars who have contributed to the debate, to varying degrees, include Bradley Malkovsky (co-editor of the *Journal of Hindu-Christian Studies*), James Arraj, Raimon Panikkar, Sara Grant, Mark Sunder Rao, Bishop Lesslie Newbegin, Klaus Klostermaier, Richard De Smet, Jacques Dupuis, and John Glenn Friesen.[137]

By far the most searching and compelling work on the relationship of the Supreme Identity of Hinduism and the Christian Trinity is presented in a work as yet too little known: *Christianity and the Doctrine of Non-Dualism* by "A Monk of the West," first appearing in 1982, and in English translation in 2004. The author, Alphonse Levée in civil life, was a French lay brother of the austere Cistercian Order, whose intellectual and spiritual trajectory was decisively influenced by René Guénon, and who developed an abiding interest in the Vedanta but remained unequivocally committed to the Christian path. In his later writings he used the pseudonym "Elie Lemoine" (Elias the monk). This book offers a decisive and metaphysically acute resolution of the many perplexities and problematics with which Abhishiktananda wrestled for so many years.[138]

Notes

1. Quoted in Ram Dass, *The Only Dance There Is*, front-page.
2. FS 26.
3. F. Schuon, *Language of the Self*, 15.
4. Quoted in T.M.P. Mahadevan, *Ramana Maharshi*, 120.
5. F. Schuon, *Language of the Self*, 231n.
6. SAC 42, 45. (In the preceding sentences Abhishiktananda makes it clear that Taoism and Buddhism, as well as Vedanta, pose this challenge.)
7. SAC 49.
8. SAC 67.
9. For a fuller account of this subject see K. Oldmeadow, *Traditionalism*, Ch 8. Some of the material following is a modified excerpt from that book.
10. R. Guénon, "Oriental Metaphysics," 43-44, and *Man and His Becoming According to the Vedanta*, 14.
11. Quoted in C.F. Kelley, *Meister Eckhart on Divine Knowledge*, 4.
12. S.H. Nasr, *Man and Nature*, 81-82. See also Coomaraswamy's undated letter to "M." *Selected Letters*, 10: "traditional metaphysics is as much a single and invariable science as mathematics."
13. The Absolute may be called God, the Godhead, *nirguna Brahman*, the *Tao*, and so on, according to the vocabulary at hand. In principle there is nothing restrictive about the term "God" which infinitely surpasses the limits of theistic theologies. See F. Schuon, *Light on the Ancient Worlds*, 96-97n.
14. Quoted in M. Lings, *A Sufi Saint of the Twentieth Century*, 27.
15. F. Schuon, *Stations of Wisdom*, 88.
16. Quoted in W. Perry, *Treasury of Traditional Wisdom*, 733.
17. See R. Guénon, "Oriental Metaphysics," 53.
18. F. Schuon, *Logic and Transcendence*, 13. See also *Schuon's Esoterism as Principle and as Way*, 15ff.
19. Letter to J.H. Muirhead, August 1935, *Selected Letters*, 37.
20. S. H. Nasr, *Sufi Essays*, 86. See also F. Schuon, *Stations of Wisdom*, 42.
21. F. Schuon, *Spiritual Perspectives*, 162-163. Cf. A.K. Coomaraswamy: ". . . and every belief is a heresy if it be regarded as the truth, and not simply as a signpost of the truth." "Sri Ramakrishna and Religious Tolerance," *Selected Papers* 2, 38.

See also F. Schuon, *Sufism: Veil and Quintessence*, 2.

22. SAC 5.

23. A.K. Coomaraswamy, "Vedanta and Western Tradition," *Selected Papers* 2, 6.

24. F. Schuon, *Understanding Islam*, 24. See also *Stations of Wisdom*, 18ff.

25. T. Burckhardt, *Alchemy*, 36n.

26. For a discussion of Blake's critique of rationalism see T. Roszak, *Where the Wasteland Ends*, 142-177.

27. Quoted in S. H. Nasr, *Man and Nature*, 35.

28. F. Schuon, *Spiritual Perspectives*, 10.

29. F. Schuon, *Esoterism as Principle*, 28.

30. Quoted in F. Schuon, *Stations of Wisdom*, 29n.

31. DD 214.

32. FS 59 (italics mine).

33. F. Schuon, *Esoterism as Principle*, 28.

34. F. Schuon, *Understanding Islam*, 149.

35. Sankara's *Crest Jewel of Discrimination*, 73.

36. SAC 4 (italics mine).

37. A.K. Coomaraswamy, "Vedanta and Western Tradition," *Selected Papers* 2, 8. See also S.H. Nasr, *Knowledge and the Sacred*, 6.

38. F. Schuon, *Logic and Transcendence*, 34.

39. F. Schuon, *The Transfiguration of Man*, 4.

40. Here we are at the opposite end of the spectrum not only from the philosophical relativists but from those who hold a "personalist" or "existentialist" view of truth.

41. F. Nietzsche in *Beyond Good and Evil*, taken from *A Nietzsche Reader*, Extract 13. See also F. Schuon, *Logic and Transcendence*, 34, and *The Transfiguration of Man*, 4. (For an illuminating passage on both the grandeur and the "dementia" of Nietzsche's work see F. Schuon, *To Have a Center*, 15.)

42. See A.K. Coomaraswamy, "Vedanta and Western Tradition," *Selected Papers* 2, 9.

43. F. Schuon, *Roots of the Human Condition*, 86.

44. F. Schuon, *Understanding Islam*, 111.

45. S.H. Nasr, "Conditions for a Meaningful Comparative Philosophy," 54.

46. S.H. Nasr, "Conditions for a Meaningful Comparative Philosophy," 55, 58.

47. F. Schuon, *Esoterism as Principle*, 10. See also S.H. Nasr, *Knowledge and the Sacred*, 148-149.

48. F. Schuon, *Understanding Islam*, 57n.

49. F. Schuon, "Keys to the Bible," 356-358.

50. F. Schuon, *Logic and Transcendence*, 86 (italics mine).

51. See F. Schuon, *Spiritual Perspectives*, 55.

52. F. Schuon, *Logic and Transcendence*, 14.

53. F. Schuon, *In the Tracks of Buddhism*, 46.

54. F. Schuon, *Islam and the Perennial Philosophy*, 39.

55. M. Pallis, Foreword to W. Perry, *Treasury of Traditional Wisdom*, 10.

56. F. Schuon, *Spiritual Perspectives*, 15.

57. F. Schuon, *Understanding Islam*, 130.

58. F. Schuon, *Stations of Wisdom*, 57.

59. F. Schuon, *Spiritual Perspectives*, 138.

60. C.F. Kelley, *Meister Eckhart on Divine Knowledge*, 4. (Kelley's book clearly owes a great deal to Schuon, whose aphorisms are repeated almost word for word but nowhere in the book can we find acknowledgment of Schuon or any of the other traditionalists.)

61. F. Schuon, *Light on the Ancient Worlds*, 136. See also *Logic and Transcendence*, 199.

62. S.H. Nasr, *Ideals and Realities of Islam*, 21.

63. F. Schuon, *The Transfiguration of Man*, 25.

64. Quoted in F. Schuon, *Understanding Islam*, 133n.

65. F. Schuon, *Esoterism as Principle*, 22.

66. See F. Schuon, *Spiritual Perspectives*, 103ff.

67. F. Schuon, *Spiritual Perspectives*, 139.

68. F. Schuon, *Spiritual Perspectives*, 127.

69. F. Schuon, *The Transcendent Unity of Religions*, xxviii-xxx.

70. Schuon exposes some of the issues raised by both the ancient and modern use of the term in an essay entitled "Tracing the Notion of Philosophy," in *Sufism: Veil and Quintessence*, 115-128. See also *The Transfiguration of Man*, 3.

71. F. Schuon, *Sufism: Veil and Quintessence*, 125.

72. See L 161.

73. Kalliath, 267-268. (Dates for the last three periods are mine.)

74. FS 101.

75. The last phrase quoted in Stephens, 81. The rest of the phrases are taken from his journal; these and many others of the same kind can be found throughout his writings on *advaita*.

76. D 15.4.64, 271.

77. SAC 43.

78. D 29.11.56, quoted in Stephens, 83. (This passage is not in *Ascent to the Depth of the Heart*.)

79. Quoted in Stephens, 83, and HCMP, 78.

80. HCMP 105.

81. See works by Deutsch, Mahadevan, and Oldmeadow, listed in Sources.

82. D 15.4.64, 270.

83. D 30.11.71, quoted in Stephens, 84. (This passage is not in *Ascent to the Depth of the Heart*.)

84. FS 99 (italics mine).

85. FS 99.

86. Quoted in Stephens, 83.

87. FS 99.

88. SAC xiv.

89. D 15.4.64, 271.

90. SAC 135.

91. SAC 135.
92. HCMP 84.
93. See Stephens, 258ff.
94. SAC 176.
95. Abhishiktananda in *Clergy Monthly*, 1971, 476, quoted in Stephens, 267.
96. HCMP 91.
97. SAC 82.
98. SAC 84.
99. D 6.1.56, 137.
100. D 2.7.71, 329.
101. L 4.2.73, 287.
102. D 26.10.66, 287.
103. See Friesen, 422.
104. D 19.10.66, 284.
105. L 4.10.73, 311.
106. L 10.7.69, 217.
107. D 14.12.71, 334.
108. L 2.9.73, 310-311. These issues must also be considered in the light of Abhishiktananda's thinking about Jesus as Guru, a subject considered in Chapter 7.
109. W. Teasdale, "Abhishiktananda's Contemplative Theology," 194.
110. D 21.5.54, quoted in Stephens, 235 (italics mine).
111. D 17.7.52, quoted in Stephens, 235.
112. D 5.7.56, 151.
113. D 17.8.59, quoted in Stephens, 235.
114. HCMP 92.
115. Unpublished letter, quoted in Stephens, 237.
116. SAC 122.
117. SAC 185.
118. SAC 84-85
119. D 2.2.73, 369.
120. D 12.9.73, 388.
121. D 19.10.66, 285.
122. HCMP 96-97. ("Tritheism": accenting the distinction of the Persons in a way tantamount to affirming three Gods. "Modalism": preserving the unity of God by reducing the Persons to mere "modes" or aspects of the One. See note on page 97 of HCMP.)
123. D 2.2.73, 368.
124. Sita Ram Goel, Catholic Ashrams, quoted in M. Comans, "Swami Abhishiktananda and *Advaita*," 99.
125. From Sr Vandana, "Messenger of Light," *Clergy Monthly*, Dec 1974, 497, quoted in Friesen, 188.
126. See Friesen, 449ff, esp. 456-457.
127. A. Rawlinson, *Book of Enlightened Masters*, 149.
128. FS 43-44.

129. Quoted in J. Stuart, "Abhishiktananda on Inner Awakening," 478.

130. D 11.5.71, 348.

131. SAC 185.

132. Coomaraswamy, "Vedanta and Western Tradition," *Selected Papers* 2, 4.

133. F. Schuon: "It is unacceptable, first, because it is impossible in a truly Hindu perspective to put Buddha and Christ in a trinity to the exclusions of Rama and Krishna; secondly because Christ is foreign to India; thirdly, because, if non-Hindu worlds are taken into account, there is no reason for taking only Christ into consideration still, of course, from the point of view of Hinduism; fourthly because there is no common measure between the river Ramakrishna and the oceans that were Jesus and the Buddha; fifthly, because Ramakrishna lived at a period in the cycle which could in any case no longer contain a plenary incarnation of the great amplitude of the great Revealers; sixthly, because, in the Hindu system there is no room for another plenary and 'solar' incarnation of Divinity between the ninth and the tenth *Avatāras* of Vishnu—the Buddha and the future *Kalki-Avatāra.* 'A single Prophet,' such is the teaching of Et-Tahawi, 'is more excellent than the whole number of all the friends of God' (the saints)." F. Schuon, *Understanding Islam,* 87n.

134. M. Comans, "Abhishiktananda and *Advaita,*" 115.

135. This question will be taken up again in Chapter 10.

136. See *A Monk of the West, Christianity and the Doctrine of Non-Dualism,* 8-12.

137. Books and articles by such authors are listed under Sources, at the end of this study.

138. A review of the English translation can be found in *Sacred Web* 15, 2005.

6

The Cosmic Theophany

The day of my spiritual awakening was the day I
saw, and knew I saw, all things in God and God
in all things.

Mecthild of Magdeburg[1]

For the sage each flower is metaphysically a proof
of the Absolute.

Frithjof Schuon[2]

Every moment is a sacrament of eternity.

Abhishiktananda[3]

Abhishiktananda struggled throughout his life to overcome certain dualities, oppositions, and polarities—East and West, Time and Eternity,
Hinduism and Christianity, Trinitarianism and *advaita,* churchman and
sannyāsī, solitude and community, doctrine and experience, *jñāna* and
bhakti, mystical apophaticism and theological cataphaticism, the *via
positiva* and *via negativa.* His life can be read as the search for a synthesis
in which these could be harmonized, both experientially and intellectually. Sometimes he came to the hard-earned realization that apparent
oppositions were really complementaries, together making up a holistic
unity. One of these tensions could be formulated in any number of
ways—suggested in shorthand by terms such as world denial/world
celebration, transcendence/immanence, spirit/matter, *nirguna/saguna
Brahman, māyā/līlā.* Without discounting these creative tensions in
Abhishiktananda's life and work, in this chapter we will turn our attention to a theme which is suggested by the term "cosmic theophany,"
that is, the revelation of the Divine in that tissue of time-space relativities which make up the whole cosmos. As Mircea Eliade has stated,
"for religious man the supernatural is indissolubly connected with the
natural . . . nature always expresses something that transcends it."[4]
More specifically we will consider Abhishiktananda's reflections about
the "cosmic covenant," the nature of symbolism and sacred geography,
the sanctity of Virgin Nature, the Holy Mountain, and pilgrimage. But
before turning to Abhishiktananda's treatment of these subjects it is
necessary to clear away certain common misconceptions about religious

understandings of the natural order, particularly with regard to the two traditions to which Abhishiktananda gave his allegiance.[5]

Religion and the Natural Order

Creation myths, cosmogonies, tell of the coming into being of the cosmos, a living, organic unity displaying beauty, harmony, meaning, and intelligibility, as against the chaotic and meaningless universe of modern science. *Kosmos*, in its original Greek and in archaic times meant "Great Man" as well as "world": in the light of various cosmogonies, particularly the Greek and the Indian, this is not without significance. In the *Vedas* we have but one of many accounts of the universe being created out of *Puruṣa*, a Cosmic Man, Primordial Man, a Divine Archetypal figure.[6] One of the most beautiful expressions of the idea of an underlying harmony in the universe is to be found in the Taoist tradition and in the symbol of the *Tao* itself wherein we see the forces of *yin* and *yang* intertwined, these being the two principial forces or energies out of which the fabric of the material universe is woven. In Hinduism the harmony, order and intelligibility of the universe is signaled by the Vedic term *ṛta* which we find in the earliest Scriptures. The beneficent influences on humankind of the natural order, and the attunement of the sage to natural rhythms are *leitmotiv* in many Scriptures. By the same token, humans are enjoined to play their part in the maintenance of the cosmic order, largely through their ritual life. This idea, everywhere to be found in the archaic worlds, makes no sense from the materialistic point of view now prevailing in the West—one utterly impervious to the fact that, in Seyyed Hossein Nasr's memorable phrase, "nature is hungry for our prayers."[7]

Religious doctrines (expressed in any number of forms, not only verbal) about the relationship of the spiritual and material worlds necessarily deal with the *transcendence* and *immanence* of the Absolute (whether this be envisaged in theistic, monistic, panentheistic, or apophatic terms; God, Allah, *Brahman*, *Tao*, *Wakan-Tanka*, *nirvāna*, or whatever): the "interplay" of these two "dimensions" varies from religion to religion but both are always present. As Abhishiktananda puts it,

> The transcendence of God is the very source of his immanence; transcendence and immanence being no more than two of man's words by which he tries to indicate simultaneously the beyond-ness and within-ness of the supreme mystery, both the *rūpa* [form] and *a-rūpa* [formlessness] of being.[8]

To imagine one without the other would be akin to envisaging a circle with no center. Whatever accent a particular spiritual economy might place on these aspects of the Real the underlying principle is always the same, summed up in an old Rabbinic dictum: "The universe is not the dwelling place of God; God is the dwelling place of the universe."[9] Recall the words of Krishna in the *Bhagavad Gītā*: "By me whose form is unmanifest, all this world is pervaded; all beings abide in me, but I do not rest in them."[10] In the light of such formulations we can also dispense with the sharp dualistic separation of the "two worlds": the world of phenomena is held together by a numinous spiritual presence— indeed, without it the world of "matter" would vanish instantly and utterly. Eternity is ever-present within (so to say) the phenomenal world. Jan van Ruysbroeck referred to this inner reality as "beyond Time; that is, without before or after, in an Eternal Now . . . the home and beginning of all life and all becoming. And so all creatures are therein, beyond themselves, one being and one Life . . . as in their eternal origin."[11]

A misunderstanding which bedevils many discussions of the beliefs of non-literate and Eastern peoples alike is signaled by the term "pantheism," i.e., the worship of the natural order as coterminous with "God." This, we are sometimes told, usually by anthropologists, was the practice of such and such a "primitive" people. In reality, pantheism, if ever it existed as anything other than an anthropological fiction, could never have been more than a degenerate form of what is properly called "panentheism," which is to say a belief in the overwhelming presence of the spiritual within the natural world— a quite different matter from the pantheistic fallacy that the natural world is somehow identical with "God" Who is thereby exhausted. Black Elk, the holy man of the Oglala Indians, clearly articulated the panentheistic principle:

> We should understand that all things are the work of the Great Spirit. We should know that He is within all things; the trees, the grasses, the rivers, the mountains, all the four-legged animals, and the winged peoples; and *even more important we should understand that He is also above all these things and peoples.*[12]

The traditional mind, especially in primal societies, perceives and experiences space and time as "sacred" and "profane," which is to say that they are not uniform and homogeneous as they are for the modern scientific mind, but are *qualitatively* differentiated. A good deal of ceremonial life is concerned with *participation* in sacred time and space.[13] Through ritual one enters into sacred time, into *real* time, the "once upon a time," *illo tempore*, a time radically different from any "horizontal" duration. Likewise with sacred places, remembering that a natural site can be *made* sacred through various rituals, or it can be *recognized* as sacred—a place where the membrane, as it were, between the worlds of matter and of spirit is especially permeable. Rivers, mountains, particular types of trees, and locales related to the mythological events are sites of this sort. The sacrality of Mt Arunachala is not *conferred* but *apprehended.*

The sanctity of life itself is expressed in different ways in the various religious vocabularies. In the Judeo-Christian tradition this principle or theme begins in the affirmation in *Genesis* that man is made in the image of God, that the human being carries an indelible imprint of the Divine. As Abhishiktananda puts it, "Man's unknowable being is of the same order as God's, for man comes from God and has been created in his image."[14] Thence we have what might be called the principle of the spiritual equality of all human beings no matter what their station in life or their natural attributes and shortcomings—"all equal before God," as the Christian formula has it. The Judeo-Christian tradition has primarily affirmed the sanctity of human life, sometimes to the neglect or abuse of other life forms. One of the lessons of the great Eastern and primal religions is the principle of the moral solidarity, if one may so express it, of all living forms: in Hinduism, Buddhism, and Jainism this is embodied in the traditional Indian value of *ahiṁsā* (non-injuriousness), so magnificently exemplified by Mahatma Gandhi.

The principle of the sanctity of life, and the "moral solidarity" of living forms should not blind us to the fact that all traditional wisdoms affirm, in their different ways, that the human being is especially privileged. The human is an axial or amphibious being who lives in both the material and spiritual worlds in a way which is not quite true of other living beings, and is thus a bridge between them. Seyyed Hossein Nasr reminds us that

> Man's central position in the world is not due to his cleverness or inventive genius but because of the possibility of attaining sanctity and becoming a channel of grace for the world around him. . . . The very grandeur of the human condition is precisely that he has the possibility of reaching a state "higher than the angels" and at the same time of denying God.[15]

This religious understanding is, of course, quite incompatible with the notion that man is simply another biological organism. By the same measure, it is utterly at odds with that most elegant, seductive, and pernicious of scientistic hypotheses, Darwinian evolutionism. As Blake so well understood, "Man is either the ark of God or a phantom of the earth and of the water."[16] As "the ark of God" man is the guardian and custodian of the natural order, the pontifex, the caliph, "the viceregent of God on earth" in Koranic terms.[17]

The peculiar position of the human being is also illuminated by the traditional cosmological principle of the *microcosm/macrocosm*, expressed most succinctly in the Hermetic maxim, "as above, so below." In brief, man is not only in the universe but the universe is in man: "there is nothing in heaven or earth that is not also in man" (Paracelsus).[18] The Buddha put it this way: "In truth I say to you that within this fathom-high body . . . lies the world and the rising of the world and the ceasing of the world."[19] One of the keys to this principle resides in the traditional understanding of consciousness as being infinite, as surpassing the temporal and spatial limits of the material world—which, in fact, is nothing other than a veil of fugitive relativities, a world of appearances, a fabric of illusions, *māyā* in the Hindu lexicon.[20]

Mircea Eliade has noted how, for *homo religiosus*, everything in nature is capable of revealing itself as a "cosmic sacrality," as a hierophany. In Abhishiktananda's words, "There is no matter which does not shout aloud the presence of the spirit."[21] But in our secular age, as Eliade also observes, the universe has become "opaque, inert, mute; it transmits no message, it holds no cipher."[22] The traditional mind perceives the natural world as a teaching about the Divine Plenitude. It is so by way of its analogical participation in the Divine qualities, which is to say that natural phenomena are themselves symbols of higher realities. A symbol, properly defined, is a reality of a lower order which participates analogically in a reality of a higher order of being. Therefore, a properly constituted symbolism rests on the inherent and objective qualities of phenomena and their relation to spiritual realities. The science of symbolism proceeds through a discernment of the qualitative significances of substances, colors, forms, spatial relationships, and so on. As Schuon has observed,

> We are not here dealing with subjective appreciations, for the cosmic qualities are ordered both in relation to being and according to a hierarchy which is more real than the individual; they are, then, independent of our tastes.[23]

This kind of symbolism is an altogether different matter from the arbitrary sign systems and artificial representational vocabularies of modernity. Only when we understand the revelatory aspect of natural phenomena, their metaphysical transparency, can we fully appreciate the import of a claim such as this:

> Wild Nature is at one with holy poverty and also with spiritual childlikeness; she is an open book containing an inexhaustible teaching of truth and beauty. It is in the midst of his own artifices that man most easily becomes corrupted, it is they who make him covetous and impious; close to virgin Nature, who knows neither agitation nor falsehood, he had the hope of remaining contemplative like Nature herself.[24]

In the words of the Apostle, "The invisible things of him from the creation of the world are clearly seen, being understood by the things that are made" (Romans 1.20).

Nature, then, is a *teaching*, a primordial Scripture. To "read" this Scripture, to *take it to heart*, is "to see God everywhere," to be aware of the transcendent dimension which is present in every cosmic situation, to see, in Coleridge's marvelous phrase, "the translucence of the Eternal through and in the temporal."[25] The great Hindu saint and sage, Ramakrishna, who could fall into ecstasy at the sight of a lion, a bird, a dancing girl, exemplified this gift though in his case, Schuon adds, it was not a matter of deciphering the symbolism but of "tasting the essences."[26]

In the traditional world the natural order was never understood or studied as an autonomous and independent reality; on the contrary, the natural order could only be understood within a larger context, drawing on theology and metaphysics as well as the cosmological sciences themselves. The material world was (and is) only intelligible through recourse to first principles which could not be derived from empirical inquiry but from Revelation and gnosis:

> The knowledge of the whole universe does not lie within the competence of science but of metaphysics. Moreover, the principles of metaphysics remain independent of the sciences and cannot in any way be disproved by them.[27]

No one has stated the crucial principle here better than Sankara who taught that the world of *māyā* is not inexplicable, it is only not self-explanatory.[28] To describe the futility of a purely materialistic science (such as we now have in the West), Sankara compares it to an attempt to explain night and day without reference to the Sun. In other words, the study of the natural world is not primarily an empirical business, although it does, of course, have an empirical dimension: matter does not exist independently and its nature cannot be understood in purely material terms. This is the great dividing line between the sacred sciences of the traditional worlds and the Faustian science of our own time.

Beauty is found everywhere in the natural order as well as in the human form itself, and in sacred art. In traditional understandings there is an intimate nexus between Truth, Goodness, and Beauty. Marsilio Ficino, the Renaissance Platonist, defined beauty as "that ray which parting from the visage of God, penetrates into all things."[29] Beauty, in most traditional canons, has this divine quality. Beauty is a manifestation of the Infinite on a finite plane and so introduces something of the Absolute into the world of relativities. Its sacred character "confers on perishable things a texture of eternity."[30] Schuon:

> The archetype of Beauty, or its Divine model, is the superabundance and equilibrium of the Divine qualities, and at the same time the overflowing of the existential potentialities in pure Being. . . . Thus beauty always manifests a reality of love, of deployment, of illimitation, of equilibrium, of beatitude, of generosity.[31]

It is distinct but not separate from Truth and Virtue. As Aquinas affirmed, Beauty relates to the cognitive faculty and is thus connected with wisdom.[32] The rapport between Beauty and Virtue allows one to say that they are but two faces of the one reality: "goodness is internal beauty, and beauty is external goodness" or, similarly, "virtue is the beauty of the soul as beauty is the virtue of forms."[33] To put it another way, Oscar Wilde notwithstanding, there are no beautiful vices just as there are no ugly virtues. The interrelationships of Beauty, Truth, and Goodness explain why, in the Oriental traditions, every *Avatāra* embodies a perfection of Beauty. It is said of the Buddhas that they save not only by their doctrine but by their superhuman Beauty.[34]

Schuon gathers together some of these principles in the following passage:

> The earthly function of beauty is to actualize in the intelligent creature the Platonic recollection of the archetypes.... There is a *distinguo* to make, in the sensing of the beautiful, between the aesthetic sensation and the corresponding beauty of soul, namely such and such a virtue. Beyond every question of "sensible consolation" the message of beauty is both intellectual and moral: intellectual because it communicates to us, in the world of accidentality, aspects of Substance, without for all that having to address itself to abstract thought; and moral, because it reminds us of what we must love, and consequently be.[35]

Beauty, whether natural or man-made, can be either an open or a closed door: when it is identified only with its earthly support it leaves man vulnerable to idolatry and to mere aestheticism; it brings us closer to God when "we perceive in it the vibrations of Beatitude and Infinity, which emanate from Divine Beauty."[36]

*

Western attitudes to nature, before the onslaughts of a materialistic scientism, had been influenced by archaic pagan ideas (derived principally from Greece and from Northern Europe), Platonism and Islam, and, preeminently, the Judeo-Christian tradition. Many contemporary environmentalists point the finger at the so-called "dominion ethic" apparently sanctioned by the *Genesis* account. There is no gainsaying the fact that Christian institutions have for centuries been accomplices in an appalling environmental vandalism; one readily understands the reasons why many environmentalists resort to a clutch of clichés about the destructive influence of Christianity. Like most clichés, those bandied about by anti-religious propagandists in the environmental debate have some truth in them. However, if we look a little more closely we will find that the story is rather more complicated than is often supposed.[37]

Like all cosmogonies, the *Genesis* myth deals with the relationship of the spiritual and material. The natural world is affirmed as God's handiwork. Throughout both Testaments we are reminded that "All things were made by him; and without him was not anything made that was made."[38] Furthermore, we are to understand the Creation itself as both a psalm of praise to its Creator and as a revelation of the divine qualities. As one contemporary Christian put it, "Creation is nothing less than a manifestation of God's hidden Being."[39] In the *Psalms* we have many affirmations of this kind: "The heavens declare the glory of God; and the firmament sheweth his handiwork." We find many similar passages in the *Koran*: "The seven heavens, and the earth, and all that is therein, magnify Him, and there is naught but magnifieth his praise; only ye understand not their worship";[40] and "All that is in the heavens and the earth glorifieth Allah."[41] In fact we can find like passages in many of the great Scriptures from around the globe: thus in the *Bhagavad Gītā* the universe is celebrated as the raiment of Krishna who contains within himself all the worlds of time and space.[42]

In the *Genesis* account, the world of nature is *not* man's to do with as he pleases but rather a gift from God, one saturated with divine qualities, to be used for those purposes which sustain life and which give human life in particular, dignity, purpose, and meaning. That this stewardship ethic could degenerate into a sanction for wholesale exploitation and criminal ruination is actually a betrayal of the lessons of *Genesis*. How did this come about? The cooperative factors at work in the Western desacralization of nature are complex but we may here mention a few of the more salient: Christianity's emergence in a world of decadent pagan idolatry which necessitated a somewhat imbalanced emphasis on God's transcendence and on "other-worldliness"; the consequent neglect of those sacred sciences which might later have formed a bulwark against the ravages of a materialistic scientism; the unholy alliance of an anti-traditional Protestantism with the emergent ideologies of a new and profane world-view.[43]

Suffice it to say that all those concerned about the current "ecological crisis" would do well to ponder the implications of the following passage from Schuon:

> This dethronement of Nature, or this scission between man and the earth—a reflection of the scission between man and God—has borne such bitter fruits that it should not be difficult to admit that, in these days, the timeless message of Nature constitutes a spiritual viaticum of the first importance. . . . It is not a matter of projecting a supersaturated and disillusioned individualism into a desecrated Nature—this would be a worldliness like any other—but, on the contrary, of rediscovering in Nature, on the basis of the traditional outlook, the divine substance which is inherent in it; in other words, to "see God everywhere."[44]

Here is the same truth expressed by Black Elk in the inimitable idiom of the Lakota:

> Peace . . . comes within the souls of men when they realize their relationship, their oneness, with the universe and all its powers, and when they realize that at the center of the Universe dwells *Wakan-Tanka* [the Great Spirit] and that this center is really everywhere, it is within each of us.[45]

It is in the context of these general reflections that we now turn to Abhishiktananda's writings on various related subjects.

Abhishiktananda and Scientism

Abhishiktananda could not altogether free himself from various modernistic and scientistic ideas which sometimes contaminated his understanding of the natural world. These corrupting influences could no doubt be traced, in part, back to his childhood and formal education. In adult life he was, at different times, influenced by the pseudo-spiritual evolutionism of both Teilhard de Chardin and Aurobindo; their imprint is readily discerned in *Saccidananda*, marring what is in many respects a splendid book. He would have remained on much less treacherous ground if he had kept his eye firmly on the traditional sources, amongst which the Gospel of St John and the early *Upanishads* were the ones to which he turned most frequently. He was also, at times, susceptible to the damaging effects of the peculiarly Western malady of historicism which conspired with scientistic evolutionism to entrench the idea of Progress in the modern mentality. It is true that Abhishiktananda had no truck with many of the more absurd, grotesque, and irredeemably Eurocentric ideas which have taken shelter behind this banner, and we will find nothing of that particularly repellent variant of the ideology of Progress which found expression in the intertwined, quasi-Darwinian ideas about race and empire. Nevertheless, traces of a progressivist outlook are occasionally evident in Abhishiktananda's work—and this quite distinct from the Judeo-Christian sense of the workings of Providence in the realm of history and from any Christian eschatology. These progressivist prejudices only surface intermittently, as if Abhishiktananda had some intuitive sense that they were out of order even at the same time that part of his mind had not altogether cleared away the debris deposited there by modernity. This also generated some inconsistencies, indeed naked contradictions, in his work, and colored some of his ideas about both nature and science. However, these confusions are not our present concern, though they could not here be altogether ignored. But now we turn to some of Abhishiktananda's reflections about the various subjects we have gathered together in this chapter. His vision of the metaphysical transparency of the natural world and his immersion in the religious mythology of both West and East was far too powerful for modern, scientific ideas to no more than occasionally muddy his writing on these subjects.

Advaita, Māyā, and the Cosmic Theophany

Some readers might suppose that Abhishiktananda's ever-deeper immersion in the further reaches of Upanishadic metaphysics and his commitment to *advaita*, both philosophically and experientially, left him indifferent to the beauties of the natural world. It is often asserted that Vedantic non-dualism is "world-denying," that *māyā*, the time-space world of appearances, is a snare of illusions. This is grievously to misunderstand the case, a misunderstanding on a par with the now popular and half-baked claim that the *contemptus mundi* of Christian tradition is the principal culprit in the Western desecration of nature and root cause of the contemporary ecological crisis.

The term *māyā* has been translated, or at least signaled, by a kaleidoscopic array of terms. These can be sampled in two clusters: (a) "illusion," "concealment," "the web of seeming," "appearance," "glamour," "relativity," "classification," "contingency," "objectivization," "distinctivization," "exteriorization"; (b) "cosmic power," "divine art," "universal unfolding," "cosmic magic," "the power of Isvara," and "the principle of self-expression." Clearly there is, behind these terms, a principle of considerable subtlety. However, in these translations, we can see two strands of meaning—more or less negative in the first group, positive in the latter. The Sanskrit terms *āvarana* ("concealment") and *viksepa* ("projection") are closely associated with the notion of *māyā* and designate two aspects, or guises, of it. These twin faces of *māyā* are reflected in Hindu temple iconography and are evident in the etymology of the word. *Māyā* is linked to the root "matr": "to measure, form, build, or plan." Several Greco-Latin words are also connected with this root: "meter," "matrix," "matter," and "material."[46] On a more immediate, literal level the word refers simply to "that which" (*ya*) "is not" (*ma*).[47] In its more positive meanings we find *māyā* is etymologically related to the Assyrian *māyā* (magic) and to *māyā*-Devi (mother of Sakyamuni Buddha), Maia (mother of Hermes), and Maria (mother of Jesus).[48] Here we can detect the obvious association with the feminine and saktic pole of manifestation. As Schuon states,

> The term *māyā* combines the meanings of "productive power" and "universal illusion"; it is the inexhaustible play of manifestations, deployments, combinations, and reverberations, a play with which *Ātmā* clothes itself even as the ocean clothes itself with a mantle of foam ever renewed and never the same.[49]

The Sufic doctrine of the veil is, in some respects, analogous to the doctrine of *māyā* as articulated in the Vedanta of Sankara.

It is certainly true that there is a strain of "world-denial" in the later *Upanishads*, just as it is true that the Vedantin sees the world as an "illusion." Mircea Eliade has written of the association of *māyā* with temporality. His commentary is worth quoting at some length not only because this opens up another perspective on the questions at hand but also because it consolidates some of the points already made:

> The veil of *māyā* is an image-formula expressing the ontological unreality both of the world and of all human experience: we emphasize ontological, for neither the world nor human experience participates in absolute Being. The physical world and our human experience also are constituted by the universal becoming, by the temporal: they are therefore illusory, created and destroyed as they are by Time. But

this does not mean they have no existence or are creations of my imagination. The world is not a mirage. . . . The physical world and my vital and psychic experience exist, but they exist only in Time. . . . Consequently, judged by the scale of absolute Being, the world and every experience dependent upon temporality are illusory. . . . Many centuries before Heidegger, Indian thought had identified, in temporality, the "fated" dimension of all existence. . . . In other words, the discovery of historicity, as the specific mode of being of man in the world, corresponds to what the Indians have long called our situation in *māyā*. . . . In reality our true "Self" . . . has nothing to do with the multiple situations of our history.[50]

Just so. But we need to remember that while *māyā* is indeed "cosmic illusion,"

she is also divine play. She is the great theophany, the unveiling of God "in Himself and by Himself" as the Sufis would say. *Māyā* may be likened to a magic fabric woven from a warp that veils and a weft that unveils; she is the quasi-incomprehensible intermediary between the finite and the Infinite—at least from our point of view as creatures—and as such she has all the multi-colored ambiguity appropriate to her part-cosmic, part-divine nature.[51]

As Abhishiktananda put it, "God is everywhere, God alone is both hidden and unveiled in his manifestation."[52]

Māyā has also been called the principle of "self-expression" (i.e., of Isvara). In this context:

Creation is expression. It is not a making of something out of nothing. It is not making so much as becoming. It is the self-projection of the Supreme. Everything exists in the secret abode of the Supreme. The primary reality contains within itself the source of its own motion and change.[53]

This aspect of *māyā* also embraces the idea of *līlā* to which we will return presently. But first a digression is in order to meet possible objections to the notion that *māyā* simultaneously has both a negative and a positive character.

How is it, it may be asked, that *māyā* both conceals and projects? This is the kind of question likely to vex an either/or line of ratiocinative thought. The objection is best met by analogy:

It is very easy to label as "vague" or "contradictory" something one cannot understand. Rationalist thinkers generally refuse to admit a truth that represents contradictory aspects and that is situated seemingly beyond grasping, midway between two negative enunciations. Now there are some realities which could be formulated in no other way than this. The ray which proceeds from a light is itself light, since it illumines, but it is not the light from which it proceeded; therefore it is neither that light nor yet other than that light, though growing ever weaker in proportion to its distance from its source. A faint light is light for the darkness it illumines, but darkness for the light whence it emanates. Similarly *māyā* is both light and darkness at the same time: she is light inasmuch as being the "divine art," she reveals the secrets of *Ātmā*; she is darkness inasmuch as she conceals *Ātmā*. As darkness she is ignorance, *avidyā*.[54]

The doctrine of *māyā* helps us to develop an attitude in which the world can be rightly regarded. If we are mindful of the ephemeral nature of the world then the realm of *māyā* itself can help us in our quest—were it otherwise the Hindus would not have elaborated complex cosmological and other sciences.[55] The essential purpose of the doctrine is to free us from the noose of material existence, to deliver us from the countless solicitations of the world which only tighten the bonds of ignorance and fetter us to the samsaric wheel.

This world of *māyā* is "illusory," but not in the sense that it is a mirage or a fantasy, but in that its "reality" is only relative: it has no independence, no autonomy, no existence outside the Divine Principle Itself. The sages of both East and West have never been seduced by the idea that the material universe is a self-existing entity, which is to say that they have always understood that there is no such thing as "pure matter." Their understanding of the cosmos derives from all the sources of knowledge—mystical intuition, metaphysical *jñāna*, and the revealed Scriptures *as well as* the instruments of the mind and the senses. On the other hand, a profane, quantitative science (from whence the modern West derives its understanding of the universe), is

> a totalitarian rationalism that eliminates both Revelation and Intellect, and at the same time a totalitarian materialism that ignores the metaphysical relativity—and therewith the impermanence—of matter and the world. It does not know that the supra-sensible, situated as it is beyond space and time, is the concrete principle of the world, and consequently that it is also at the origin of that contingent and changeable coagulation we call "matter." A science that is called "exact" is in fact an "intelligence without wisdom," just as post-scholastic philosophy is inversely a "wisdom without intelligence."[56]

These passages should immunize us to the preposterous but widely-held view that the Eastern traditions are "negative," "pessimistic," "life-denying" and the like.[57] On this issue we can do no better than recall the words of Eliade when he wrote:

Perhaps more than any other civilization, that of India *loves and reverences Life, and enjoys it at every level*. For *māyā* is not [a] gratuitous cosmic illusion. . . . To become conscious of the cosmic illusion does not mean, in India, the discovery that all is Nothingness, but simply that no experience in the world of History has any ontological validity and therefore, that our human condition ought not to be regarded as an end in itself.[58]

*

We will better understand Abhishiktananda's perception of the natural world if we keep these considerations in mind. Then, too, there are several other factors which need to be highlighted. Firstly, we must not lose sight of his Christian upbringing which taught him to see the world as God's creation. We have already seen how, for Abhishiktananda, the Eucharist was the ritual means of participating "in the ascent of the whole cosmos—matter and spirit—towards its Lord."[59] Secondly, it would be wrong to think that Abhishiktananda's reading of Vedantic philosophy was ever anything more than a support for his own direct experience of the depth of the Self *and* of the world around him. As Abhishiktananda himself wrote of the mystery of the Self, although it is "unique and non-dual," yet it is "revealed in many and varied ways."[60] It should also be remembered that Abhishiktananda was less attracted to the later, more systematic and abstract *Upanishads*, finding more inspiration in the *Chāndogya* and the *Bṛhadāranyaka*, those "incomparable witnesses to the awakening of the soul to the mystery of being and of the self"[61] in which we still find much of the cosmic vision of the earliest *Vedas*. Thirdly, recall the influence of Kashmiri Saivism, the *Yoga Vāsiṣṭha*, the *Rihu Gītā*, and the *Tripura Rahasya*, all of which brought both bhaktic and tantric elements into Abhishiktananda's understanding of the tradition. The cosmology, mythology, and symbolism of Saivism all acted as a counterbalance to the more ascetical and apophatic accent of *Advaita* Vedanta, and along with the early *Vedas*, presented a vision of the cosmos which everywhere found a Divine Presence, most potently perhaps through the manifold symbolism of the *liṅga*. It is perhaps not too much to suggest that the Vedic cosmic vision (and all that flowed from it) is one of the reasons why Hinduism held a stronger attraction for Abhishiktananda than Buddhism.[62] Fourthly, while *Advaita* Vedanta was primarily a jñanic path, anchored in *dhyāna* and the "inner" realization of non-duality, the Hindu tradition has never insisted that any particular individual must practice one of the yogas exclusively. There are good grounds for supposing that Abhishiktananda's spiritual personality was a fusion of the jñanic and bhaktic types—and hence peculiarly suited to his simultaneous adherence to Vedantic, Saivite, and Christian modes. With all these considerations given their due weight let us now sample a few passages from *Guru and Disciple* which pertain to our theme, the cosmic theophany.

In recounting his experiences at Tapovanam Abhishiktananda poignantly depicts the rituals which the devotees perform each day on the river bank, just before sunrise and as the sun sets, welcoming and farewelling each day. He details the various ritual actions and gestures, then goes on to write this:

> Only those whose souls have remained totally insensitive to the mystery of the "holy lights," a mystery both inner and cosmic and to this marvelous epiphany of God in his creation, would think of labeling such rites idolatrous. This epiphany unfolds in accordance with the rhythm of time—or one might say more truly perhaps that, as it continues to unfold, it introduces this same time factor into a man's being in correspondence with the rhythm of infinite divine freedom. In fact no other country has been so intensely aware as India of the Presence—an eminently active Presence, the whole world of the divine *Shakti*, something resembling the *shekinah* of traditional Judaism.

Moreover, this Presence has been experienced since the earliest Vedic times, and is inherent in all things and

> in every phase of the life of the man, and the universe, the daily, monthly, and yearly cycles each of which depends on the phases of the heavenly bodies in which spiritual and uncreated Light manifests itself materially for the benefit of men.[63]

The Brahminical rituals are a constant reminder that "nothing is profane." Stemming from "primeval times" these rites also ensured that humankind played its part in the maintenance of cosmic order and stability. In *The Secret of Arunachala* Abhishiktananda refers to the assimilation of solar, fire, and *linga* symbolism in the holy mountain and again alludes to the symbolism of the rising and setting sun. His friend Aruneya sums up these significations in a passage which one suspects owes as much to Abhishiktananda as it does to Aruneya:

> Try to imagine what these marvelous symbols mean to us, which have been at work in the depths of our hearts for thousands of years since Vedic times. Such was Agni, celebrated by our rishis as the fire of the sacrifice, in which everything is consumed and passes over to the Beyond—and indeed there is surely something holy and sacrificial about all fire. Such was Surya, the glowing disk of the sun which every

morning emerges gloriously from the womb of the night, delivers men from darkness both within and without, and holds their attention as he climbs towards the zenith, the summit of space which symbolizes the center of the heart. These signs have been transmitted to us in our Scriptures and in the impassioned hymns of our saints.[64]

This passage reminds us that the cosmic vision of the *Vedas* centers on the Sun as the source of light—but as far more than the physical sun which we see with our sensory organ; it is the light with which the *devas* shine, the light of inner illumination. The *Gāyatrī* mantra is said by some to be the greatest verse in all of the *Vedas*: "Let us meditate on the glorious splendor of that divine light (*savitṛ*). May he illuminate our meditation."[65]

Writing of the phallic Siva-*liṅga* symbolism which many of his Western contemporaries found offensive, Abhishiktananda affirms the "incomparable dignity of the human body" and the act of procreation which is also a sign of regeneration. In the crypt of a Saivite temple he ponders the correspondences between macrocosm and microcosm, between the "inner" and "outer" worlds, and marvels at "the religious genius of India" which, through its myths, rituals, and symbolism, "untiringly invites [man] to discover in the depth of his being the freedom of the full and ultimate mystery of the self."[66] During the night he spends alone in the temple, suspended in a state which is neither sleep nor normal wakefulness, Abhishiktananda has an archetypal illumination in which every phenomenal and religious form is a vehicle for the Divine Presence:

> Everything seemed to him to be a *mūrti*, a manifestation, a revelation of God—all forms of life and all the forms, rites, hymns, and sacred formulas through which man tried to unveil and capture the mystery of the divine Presence, everything seemingly converging and flowing together, in accordance with the Hindu myth, towards the ultimate symbol of the Shiva-*liṅga*.[67]

Through his penetration of the sign of the *liṅga* Abhishiktananda understands that "there is no matter that does not shout aloud the presence of the spirit," that "the least grain of sand . . . implies the eternity and self-origination of God."[68] The *liṅga* is a symbol of "God's coming into his creation" and, by the same measure, the symbol of the creature's "departure into God." Thus the *liṅga* stands between form and non-form, "between manifestation and what can never be manifested"[69]—and, one might add, so it is with all symbols, properly understood. Abhishiktananda returns to this theme throughout his writings. A few instances:

Nothing exists that is not the sign of the Lord.[70]

God is everywhere, God alone is both hidden and unveiled in his manifestation.[71]

God is in the gently blowing breeze, in the soaring flight of the bird, in the laughter and playfulness of the child, in every movement of our bodies and minds.[72]

Nothing in creation escapes the divine presence and . . . all things are shot through and through with the sacred. This is true of all facets of nature, animal and human, feminine and masculine, in both their gracious and their awesome aspects.[73]

It should be stressed that we are not dealing here with a Wordsworthian naturism, nor with the effusions of latter-day environmentalists, but with a deep sense of the sacred "dimension" of the natural order which only comes alive when "the doors of perception" have been cleansed. This "opening" can happen in any tradition, no less in the Christian than the Hindu, but its pre-condition is a reverential disposition and the journey "inwards" which will alone attain the sacramental vision of the natural world. As Abhishiktananda writes in *Saccidananda*:

> As the soul penetrates more deeply into Jesus' "interior" or "inwardness" . . . the Spirit enables her to realize ever more inwardly the significance of the name of God [Abba], by which Jesus addressed the Father even on the Cross. Taught by Jesus, the soul discovers, or rather recovers, in this name the very mystery of the Pleroma. In it she finds the whole of creation, the entire universe visible and invisible, all humanity and every individual man, and ultimately herself. In it all things recover their meaning, their place, and their identity, within the infinite splendor of God's love.[74]

In *Saccidananda* Abhishiktananda does make a distinction between the ways in which the Hindu and Christian *jñānī* might perceive the world. For the former the world of "becoming, differentiation, and individuality" can claim "no absolute value nor ultimate importance." On the other hand, for the Christian

> the world which has been restored to him deep within God's infinite love, is full of value and significance, even at the level of temporality and diversity. It is a world called out of nothingness by the Word in creation, and out of its sinfulness by the incarnate Word at his resurrection. . . . In thus recovering his self and the world, the Christian mystic has lost nothing of what has been gained or realized by the *jñānī* in his experience of the Self. He has not stepped down from the

Real which is God to the "unreal world.". . . It is at the very heart of being itself that he has discovered the reality of time, of becoming, of particularity, and multiplicity.[75]

The Holy Mountain

Olympus, Parnassus, Helikon, Ararat, Sinai, Zion, Tabor, Horeb, the Mount of Olives, Calvary, Athos, Carmel, Monsalvat, Hira, Qaf, Hara-berezaiti, Denali, Arunachala, Chomolungma, Machapucchere, Meru, Kailas, Sri Pada, Tai Shan, Hua Shan, Fuji, Hiei, Cuchama, Uluru, Machu Picchu. Mountains have since time immemorial played a central role in the religious imagination of humankind and have forever conjured our highest aspirations, our deepest yearnings, our most noble meditations. They irresistibly suggest the *mysterium tremendum*. As Edwin Bernbaum recently wrote,

> As the highest and most dramatic features of the natural landscape, mountains have an extraordinary power to evoke the sacred. The ethereal rise of a ridge in mist, the glint of moonlight on an icy face, a flare of gold on a distant peak—such glimpses of transcendent beauty can reveal our world as a place of unimaginable mystery and splendor.[76]

Mountains not only figure prominently in the mythology and the scriptures of traditional peoples, mountain imagery saturates mystical literature from all parts of the globe. Even the secular annals of mountaineering (which only dates back to the early nineteenth century) are replete with rhapsodic paeans to the beauty of mountains and with accounts of extraordinary experiences which can, in some cases, be properly labeled as mystical. Many modern mountaineers are hard-bitten, laconic characters for whom actions speak louder than words. But many of them find themselves so transported by the grandeur and beauty of the resplendent peaks that they are moved to speak and write of them in reverential terms.[77] During the 1953 Everest Expedition, John Hunt remarked in characteristically terse fashion to his companions around a campfire at Thyangboche, "I don't mind admitting that mountains make me pray."[78]

The mountain is a multivalent symbol with a more or less inexhaustible reservoir of meanings.[79] Among the significations traditionally perceived in mountains we may here mention a few of the more universal: the mountain as Center, as the meeting place of Heaven and Earth, the *axis mundi* which runs through the three worlds, the abode of the gods and *devas*, the symbol of transcendence, the Immutable made manifest, the sacred place in which God communicates with his people, the place of transfiguration, a conduit for cosmic energies and powers, the pivot of the universe, the refuge of hermits and sages, the natural habitat of monasteries and shrines. Many of these motifs run through Abhishiktananda's writings.

As Lama Govinda observed in his captivating book about his pilgrimage in Western Tibet,

> there are some [mountains] of such outstanding character and position that they become symbols of the highest aspirations of humanity, as expressed in ancient civilizations and religions, milestones of the eternal quest for perfection and ultimate realization, signposts that point beyond our earthly concerns. . . .
>
> The power of such a mountain is so great and yet so subtle that, without compulsion, people are drawn to it from near and far, as if by the force of some invisible magnet; and they will undergo untold hardships and privations in their inexplicable urge to approach and to worship the center of this sacred power. Nobody has conferred the title of sacredness on such a mountain, and yet everybody recognizes it; nobody has to defend its claim, because nobody doubts it; nobody has to organize its worship, because people are overwhelmed by the mere presence of such a mountain and cannot express their feelings other than by worship.[80]

In the world of Tradition, mountains of this kind are part of a larger sacred geography:

> The sacred mountain, seat of the Gods, is not to be found in space, though it is visible and tangible. It is the same with Benares, or the Ganges, or the Kaaba, or Sinai, or the Holy of Holies, or the Holy Sepulcher or other places in this category. He who finds himself there is as it were gone out of space and, in a virtual sense, reintegrated in the formless Prototype of the sacred spot. Touching holy ground the pilgrim really "walks" in the formless and in it he is purified. Hence the washing away of sin in these places. . . . For the man of the golden age a mountain was in very truth an approach to the Principle.[81]

Abhishiktananda fell under the sway of mountains in two spiritually vibrant locations, Mt Arunachala in the south and, in the north, the Indian Himalaya of the Gangotri region. Both were intimately associated with Lord Siva; indeed for many devotees Arunachala *is* Siva in one of his manifold forms whilst the deity's "permanent abode" is located at the source of the Ganges. We have earlier recounted something of Abhishiktananda's shattering experiences at Arunachala. Here is one of Abhishiktananda's meditations on the impact of the mountain:

Arunachala, guru without mercy,
you deprived me of all
that until then I had loved,
of all
that until then I had enjoyed,
of all
that until then I had relied on,
the things of this world and things of the other;
you left me hanging,
free and naked,
in the solitude of the *kevala*,
in the midst of the abyss, in the depth of the heart —
Your heart, O Arunachala![82]

The Ganges doesn't have a single source but three, so the precise location of Siva's abode is, perhaps appropriately, not altogether clear. But the area bounded by Gangotri, Kedernath, and Badrinath includes the sources of the three rivers which merge to form the holy river—the Bhagirathi, the Mandakini, and the Alakanda. The whole region is therefore charged with sacred power and is home to temples and shrines which mark the end of the traditional pilgrimage route from Haridwar, the holy city on the Ganges as it emerges from the Himalayan range. Abhishiktananda traversed the entire route once, and parts of it several times. His own hermitage was located on the route, on the banks of the Ganges. In the summer months he could observe the caravanserai of devotees on their way to the temples, many of them having made very considerable material sacrifices and experiencing severe physical hardship in their determination to reach the holy sites. Abhishiktananda was deeply moved by the prayers and invocations, the chants and murmurings of the pilgrims which seemed to find an echo in the sounds of the river itself. Arunachala and Gangotri, as we have seen, were not merely places where Abhishiktananda happened to be when he underwent transformative spiritual experiences; the nature of the spiritual experience was itself provoked by these sacred sites and wedded to them. Each left its celestial melodies in Abhishiktananda's psyche and spiritual personality, if we may so express it.

Here is a small sample of suggestive excerpts from Abhishiktananda's writings, concluding with the first stanza of his own hymn to the mighty Arunachala.

Arunachala is like a lover with an irresistible appeal. I have found something there which no other place and no other being has ever been able to give me. . . . Never in my life have I felt so much at peace, so joyful, so near to God, or rather, one with God, as on this mountain.[83]

There will always be snow-capped peaks in the Himalaya which will never be reached by any man-made road . . . there will always remain forests which only eagles will ever see. In the same way, while the world lasts, there will always be some of these acosmics, naked and silent in their caves like Krishnananda whom we had visited the day before, who had entered the great silence in the year before the beginning of the first World War—who for the sake of the world itself and on behalf of those who have eyes only for outward things, have devoted themselves wholly to what is within.[84]

It is right and proper for the Christian, more than any other, to come and meditate here (the Gangotri Himalaya) on earth's ascent towards heaven through her snow-clad peaks, and on the descent from heaven of the life-giving waters in the form of dark rain-clouds—and so of the meeting of both in the mystery of those high peaks, which seize and hold on their flanks the water of heaven and then pour it out in blessing on the earth.[85]

Christ is the peak of which every earthly peak is a sign. He has that height which rises up to heaven itself to lay hold of Being and Life. In his Head he even penetrates the supreme mystery of the Father. The earth below is his footstool—or rather, the solid ground in which his roots are sunk deep within the very stuff of our human nature.[86]

Arunachala drew me into himself and taught me the secret song of silence, that which underlies all that is sung by men or by the created world, the essential hymn which no song uttered by human lips can ever adequately express.[87]

Arunachala is a symbol
and Arunachala is a Reality,
a high place of the Dravidian land,
all ruddy, *āruna*, in the rays of the rising sun,
where he is worshipped in the *liṅga* of fire,
the elemental sign of the Living God,
he who appeared to Moses in the burning bush
and on the summit of Mount Horeb,
Fire that burns and Fire that gives light,
Deus ignis consumens,
Lux mundi,
Param-jyoti,
Phos hilaron,
the joyful light of the immortal glory

of the Blessed One,
Bhagavān![88]

Notes

1. Quoted in J. and M. Fitzgerald (eds), *The Sermon of All Creation*, 22.
2. F. Schuon, *Spiritual Perspectives*, 10.
3. SAC 145.
4. M. Eliade, *The Sacred and the Profane*, 118.
5. The following section is a condensed and modified version of "'The Firmament Sheweth His Handiwork': Re-awakening a Religious Sense of Nature," in B. McDonald (ed), *Seeing God Everywhere*.
6. The term *Puruṣa* later came to also signify the Self—as Abhishiktananda often uses it.
7. S.H. Nasr, *The Spiritual and Religious Dimensions of the Environmental Crisis*, 13.
8. GD 66-67.
9. Quoted in S. Radhakrishnan, *Selected Writings on Philosophy, Religion, and Culture*, 146.
10. Quoted in B. Griffiths, *The Marriage of East and West*, 86.
11. Quoted in P. Sherrard, *Christianity: Lineaments of a Sacred Tradition*, 208.
12. J.E. Brown, *The Sacred Pipe*, xx (italics mine).
13. One of the most useful expositions of archaic understandings of sacred and profane time and space is to be found in Mircea Eliade's *The Sacred and the Profane*.
14. SAC 4.
15. S.H. Nasr, *Ideals and Realities of Islam*, 24-25.
16. Quoted in K. Raine in "The Underlying Order: Nature and the Imagination" in *Fragments of Infinity*, ed. A. Sharma, 208.
17. See J-L. Michon, "The Vocation of Man According to the Koran" in A. Sharma (ed), *Fragments of Infinity*, 135-152. See also K. Cragg, *The Mind of the Qur'an*.
18. Quoted in T.C. McLuhan, *Cathedrals of the Spirit*, 270.
19. Quoted in H. Smith, *Forgotten Truth: The Primordial Tradition*, 60.
20. Furthermore, as Lama Anagarika Govinda reminds us, "If the structure of our consciousness did not correspond to that of the universe and its laws, we should not be aware either of the universe or the laws that govern it." *Creative Meditation and Multi-Dimensional Consciousness*, 162.
21. GD 62.
22. M. Eliade, *The Sacred and the Profane*, 12-13, 178.
23. F. Schuon, *Gnosis: Divine Wisdom*, 110. The most magisterial explication of the science of symbolism in recent times is to be found in René Guénon's *Fundamental Symbols*. For brief but incisive discussions of symbolism-proper

and its relation to intellectuality, see M. Lings, *Symbol and Archetype*, and A. Snodgrass, *The Symbolism of the Stupa*, 1-10.

24. F. Schuon, *Light on the Ancient Worlds*, 84.

25. Quoted in K. Raine, *Defending Ancient Springs*, 109.

26. Frithjof Schuon, "Foundations of an Integral Aesthetics," 135n. See also C. Isherwood, *Ramakrishna and His Disciples*, 61ff.

27. S.H. Nasr, *Man and Nature*, 35.

28. See my article, "Sankara's Doctrine of *Māyā*," 131-146.

29. Quoted in R.J. Clements, *Michelangelo's Theory of Art*, 5.

30. F. Schuon, *Understanding Islam*, 48.

31. F. Schuon, *Logic and Transcendence*, 241.

32. See A.K. Coomaraswamy, "The Mediaeval Theory of Beauty" in *Selected Papers 1*, 211-20, and two essays, "Beauty and Truth" and "Why Exhibit Works of Art?" in *Christian and Oriental Philosophy of Art*, 7-22 (esp. 16-18), 102-109.

33. F. Schuon, *Logic and Transcendence*, 245-246. See also F. Schuon, *Esoterism as Principle*, 95.

34. As Schuon notes, the name "Shunyamurti"—manifestation of the void—applied to a Buddha, is full of significance; *Spiritual Perspectives*, 25n. See also *In the Tracks of Buddhism*, 121.

35. F. Schuon, "Foundations of an Integral Aesthetics," 131-132.

36. F. Schuon, "Foundations of an Integral Aesthetics," 135.

37. See Wendell Berry's essay "Christianity and the Survival of Creation" in *Sex, Economy, Freedom & Community*, 92-116.

38. *John*, I.3.

39. Philip Sherrard, *Human Image: World Image*, 152.

40. *Koran* XVII.44.

41. *Koran* LVII.2.

42. Goethe had something of the sort in mind when he wrote, "Nature is the living, visible garment of God."; quoted in V. Gollancz, *From Darkness to Light*, 246.

43. The most convincing analysis of this process is to be found in Nasr's *Man and Nature*.

44. F. Schuon, *The Feathered Sun*, 13.

45. J.E. Brown, *The Sacred Pipe*, 115.

46. A. Watts, *The Way of Zen*, 59.

47. T.M.P. Mahadevan, *Outlines of Hinduism*, 149.

48. W. Perry, *Treasury of Traditional Wisdom*, 83.

49. F. Schuon, *Logic and Transcendence*, 89n.

50. M. Eliade, *Myths, Dreams, and Mysteries*, 239-240.

51. F. Schuon, *Light on the Ancient Worlds*, 89. See also A. Lakhani, "What Thirst is For," 13-14.

52. Pr 15.

53. Radhakrishnan, *Selected Writings*, 141.

54. F. Schuon, *Spiritual Perspectives*, 100-101.

55. See S.H. Nasr, *Man and Nature*, 188-189.

56. F. Schuon, *Light on the Ancient Worlds*, 117.

57. Without pursuing the matter here, we can note that the charge of "world-denial" directed against Buddhism rests on a very partial understanding of *saṃsāra* to the neglect of its complement, *dharma*, by which is meant not simply the teachings of the Awakened One (its most familiar sense, at least to Westerners) but a pre-existent and eternal order to which these teachings testified and of which they are one expression. On this crucial point, see Philip Novak, "Universal Theology and the Idea of Universal Order," 87-88.

58. M. Eliade, *Myths, Dreams, and Mysteries*, 242-243 (italics mine).

59. SAC 59.

60. GD 9.

61. HCMP 46.

62. In a letter: "I am more Hindu than Buddhist"; this is in the course of some remarks about the "staggering" three-headed Siva at Elephanta. EL 160-161.

63. GD 54-55.

64. SA 134.

65. See B. Griffiths, *The Marriage of East and West*, 55-56.

66. GD 61.

67. GD 62.

68. GD 62-63.

69. GD 63.

70. SA 57.

71. Pr 15.

72. SAC 130.

73. GD 58-59.

74. SAC 127.

75. SAC 128-129.

76. E. Bernbaum, *Sacred Mountains of the World*, website.

77. See R. Macfarlane, *Mountains of the Mind*.

78. Quoted in W. Noyce, *South Col*, 17.

79. On the traditional symbolic vocabulary associated with mountains see M. Pallis, *The Way and the Mountain*, 13-35.

80. A. Govinda, *The Way of the White Clouds*, 198, 197.

81. F. Schuon, *Spiritual Perspectives*, 45-46.

82. SA 36-37.

83. SA 50, L 21.8.52, 57.

84. ML 41.

85. ML 21-22.

86. ML 21.

87. SA 36.

88. SA 53. (The full poem, in translation, can be found in SA 53-55.)

7

Way Stations on the Spiritual Path

A spiritual virtue is nothing other than a consciousness of a reality.

Frithjof Schuon[1]

Faith, prayer, and contemplation are the internal realities underlying the external activities of the disciple of Jesus [and] are in reality the simple acknowledgment of the presence of the Spirit in everything, everywhere and at every moment.

Abhishiktananda[2]

Abhishiktananda was not the kind to write spiritual manuals or guides, nor to build systems—metaphysical, theological, or practical. But, of course, he did write a good deal and much of his *oeuvre* bears on the spiritual path, the journey of the soul back to God. In this chapter, without attempting to impose a system where there is none or to "tidy up" his work, we shall take account of Abhishiktananda's reflections on a range of subjects which inevitably present themselves to any spiritual wayfarer. Abhishiktananda's thoughts on prayer, faith, and renunciation have been discussed earlier so here we shall do no more than again lightly touch on some of his key ideas. Some of the philosophical and mystical aspects of the spiritual path will be discussed in later chapters. The scholarly and theological focus on the subjects with which his name is now most readily associated—*advaita*, *sannyāsa*, dialogue—is natural enough. But it would be a pity if our interest in Abhishiktananda were to be confined to such themes because he had wise things to say about many other aspects of spirituality. Here we shall turn most of our attention to those insights which Abhishiktananda derived from his spiritual citizenship of Hinduism. The selection of subjects may at first strike the reader as somewhat disparate but some reflection will reveal connections perhaps not immediately apparent.

Abhishiktananda's fellow-monk and another intermediary between the spiritual universes of East and West, Thomas Merton, once observed that, "That which is oldest is most young and most new. There is nothing so ancient and so dead as human novelty. The 'latest' is always stillborn. What is really new is what was there all the time."[3] This is no less true in the spiritual domain than in any other. We should not be surprised to find that in many of his writings about both the Christian and the Hindu spiritual life Abhishiktananda is thoroughly traditional, but that he invites us to see anew what, indeed, was there all the time. Sometimes he does this by interweaving Christian and Hindu insights, not in search of any "novelty" but so that each may illuminate the other.

Faith, Prayer, Contemplation

The spirituality espoused by Abhishiktananda, in both Christian and Hindu modalities, is above all one of interiority.

> India's gift to the world is primarily that of enabling man to seize hold of the deep and indefinable mystery of his own being, the mystery of the self, "unique and non-dual," yet revealed in many and varied ways.[4]

The outer world is one in which we can find various signs, including those bequeathed to us by God in his manifold Revelations and by the holy Scriptures. But, as Abhishiktananda never tired of repeating, it is in the nature of signs that they signify something beyond themselves; that which is so signified should be our goal, not the signs themselves. In this respect it is perfectly proper to speak of Abhishiktananda as an esoterist, not in the confused sense in which the term is sometimes applied to people who are merely occultists or "psychics," but in the sense of one who has understood that the ineffable mystery towards which the signs beckon can never be exhausted by any form. Abhishiktananda wants to immerse himself directly in this mystery, beyond all names. This entails a journey "inwards," into the *guha*, the cave of the heart. In the familiar words of the *Chāndogya Upanishad*:

> In this city of *Brahman* (the heart of man)
> there is an abode, within it a small lotus flower;
> inside, a little space;
> what there is within,
> it is that which one must seek,
> which one must desire to know.[5]

In the end there is no "inner" nor "outer," no "up" nor "down," but these spatial symbols and metaphors are efficacious because they direct us to the "depths" "within" us, to the "kingdom of God" which is to be found in the center of our being, and which is not other than Being Itself. Interiority encourages a certain disposition of the soul away from that which is transient, the flotsam in the stream of Time, *māyā*.

Abhishiktananda was painfully aware of the consequences of a lack of interiority in contemporary Christianity and warned that

> So long as Christianity aims at teaching ideas about what is "outside," it will continue to fall short. Every (real) teaching contains a hidden arrow which causes the spring to flow in the depth of the heart, like the one which Arjuna released to quench the thirst of Bhisma.[6]

There is little that needs to be added to our earlier discussion of Abhishiktananda's treatment of faith, prayer, and contemplation save to remind ourselves again of his insistence that these are the indispensable staples of the spiritual life. Their attendants, so to speak, are silence and solitude. Here is a bridge between the spiritual life of the East and the West, and indeed between the primordial and the historical religions. In the words of Ohiyesa the Santee, "In the life of the Indian there was only one inevitable duty—the duty of prayer—the daily recognition of the Unseen and Eternal. His daily devotions were more necessary to him than daily food."[7] And so it is with all who walk in the ways of the Spirit.

The highest form of prayer and of worship, Abhishiktananda believed, was to be found in silence, which above all means the stilling of the mind—in the Christian context, contemplation, in the Hindu, *dhyāna*, each entailing an interior "emptying." The other mode of Christian prayer to which he was attracted through his Indian experiences was the prayer of invocation, the repetition of the Divine Name, particularly as practiced in the Jesus Prayer of the Eastern Church. Not only did such prayer have its exact parallel in Hindu *nāma-japa* ("Rama, Rama," "Hare Krishna," "Nāmah Shivaya" are its three most popular forms) but he also found some connections between the invocation of the holy name and the role of the sacred seed syllable OM in Hindu practice. In *Prayer* he finds some correspondences between "Abba" and "OM".[8] As Jesus taught us, "Hallowed be thy Name"!

Here are a few further reflections on faith, prayer, and contemplation, taken from Abhishiktananda's writings, each in itself a possible focal point for meditative prayer:

> Faith is the only way of penetrating the hidden abode of God—in the highest heaven as well as in the deepest center of our hearts.[9]

> Only faith makes possible the leap beyond—and faith rests on itself alone.[10]

> Faith is essentially that interior sense by which the mind penetrates obscurely into those depths of one's own being which it realizes are

beyond its power to explore solely by means of thought and sense-perception.[11]

To pray without ceasing is not so much consciously to *think* of God, as to act continuously under the guidance of the Spirit.[12]

Of all mantras and prayers, the invocation of the Name is the most efficient.[13]

Jñāna is an arcane knowledge, a *mysterium fidei*, a mystery of faith.[14]

Renunciation

Another keynote in all of Abhishiktananda's writings is renunciation. The one who sincerely seeks God must abandon worldly goods and values, renounce the desires of the egoic self, free himself from all attachments, comforts, and allurements, live in the most austere simplicity, and sacrifice his life to the quest. His only treasure is that in heaven, "where no thief approacheth, neither moth corrupteth"; his only desire is for God alone. Poverty, celibacy, obedience to the dictates of the Spirit, and silence are simply the outer marks of an inner renunciation. Ultimately the renouncer himself must be renounced, stripped of all sense of "I" and "mine." He must live in the spirit of Ramana Maharshi's lines:

> The ground to sleep on,
> the air to be clothed with,
> the elbow as pillow, and
> the hands a begging bowl,
> there is a feast in my heart.
> I have a smile for everybody;
> I am free from all desires.
> I am master of the world,
> and in possession of supreme joy
> because I have renounced it all.[15]

None of the austerities and disciplines of the *sannyāsī* are ends in themselves but only means to aid the soul on its journey back to God.

Morality and the Two Great Commandments

One striking feature of Abhishiktananda's writings is the scant reference to what normally comes under the canopy of "morality." Why so? Certainly not because Abhishiktananda was indifferent to the moral injunctions of the Gospels—on the contrary, he took them with the utmost seriousness, just as he did the disciplines of his monastic calling. Throughout his life in India he was, for example, quite punctilious about abstaining from flesh-eating. By all accounts, in his own person and in his activities in the world, Abhishiktananda followed the moral prescriptions of Christianity, and was not found wanting in "faith, hope, and charity." Nor was he one who, in the name of some superior knowledge, took a condescending attitude to religious forms (moral codes belonging to the world of forms). It is true that he believed that the duality of "good" and "evil" was actually transcended in the experience of *advaita* and quoted Swami Gnanananda on this subject:

> For the *jñānī* there is no longer virtue or sin, or a good deed or a bad deed. Sin, virtue, good, evil, are all related to the body, the *śarīra*, the *ahamkāra*, the consciousness of self as separate. It is only he who sees duality who sees distinction and contradiction. The *jñānī* himself is aware of things only in the non-duality of the *ātman*. Given such awareness, what could the perception of good and evil be founded upon?[16]

But this applied to the fully-fledged *jñānī* only, and is a far cry from any suggestion that morality is peripheral to the spiritual life. Those of us who have not yet reached the further shore must live in the world of forms, in the moral domain as in any other.

Three reasons might be surmised for Abhishiktananda's apparent lack of interest in morality *per se*. Firstly, he was a true follower of Christ in understanding that "all the law and the prophets" do indeed "hang on the two great commandments"—to love God and to love our neighbor. A proper understanding of these commandments as the bedrock of the moral life subsumes all else. Secondly, Abhishiktananda was perhaps offering an Indian/Hindu counterbalance to the Judeo-Christian emphasis on man's fallen state, on the volitional, penitential, and affective path to salvation. The religious perspectives of the East tend towards the view that the root of man's sufferings and troubles are not to be found in his willful sinning but in his ignorance. Jesus calls his followers to "that mysterious dignity" of being the children of God; to realize this in the depths of our being is "the one thing needful." Thirdly, Abhishiktananda realized that moral codes—be they Jewish, Christian, Brahminical or whatever—are relative and culturally conditioned, while the spiritual virtues are everywhere the same. Abhishiktananda's attention was fixed not on the regulation of man's outward behavior (moral rectitude) but on the attainment of certain states of consciousness and states of being (the virtues). He understood the truth of Frithjof Schuon's words, that "a spiritual virtue is nothing other than a consciousness of a reality." In another instructive passage Schuon has put the matter this way:

> Moralities can vary, for they are founded on social exigencies: the virtues do not vary, for they are enshrined in the very nature of man, and they are in his primordial nature because they correspond to cosmic perfections and *a fortiori*, to divine qualities. For the moralist, the good lies in action: for the contemplative it lies in being, of which action is only a possible, and at times a necessary expression.[17]

In sketching Abhishiktananda's life and surveying his written works it has been as clear as the day that he was a man consumed with the love of God. What after all is a monk but a man who consecrates his whole life to God? But we should not separate this from Abhishiktananda's love of his neighbor. Of course, Christ's two commandments are inseparable, though this should not obscure the fact that the command to love God comes first. As has often been remarked, but equally often misunderstood, it is not actually possible to observe the first commandment without in some manner observing the second. By the same token, one cannot actually observe the second without obeying the first, whatever Bertrand Russell might have to say on the subject! In any event, Abhishiktananda understood the two commandments as one.

Abhishiktananda often referred to the passages in the Gospels where, on the day of his Resurrection, Jesus appears in unfamiliar forms to Mary Magdalene, to the Apostles, and to the pilgrims to Emmaus;[18] so today he appears to us in everyman. Every human meeting is also an encounter with the divine, as is recognized in India by the traditional forms of greeting which can be assimilated under the formula "I salute the god within you." As Schuon has stated,

> Man cannot know or meet God if he has not met him in the world. He is separated from God if he denies revelation or if he does not see God in his neighbor. . . . In the neighbor God wants to be loved and heard: He wants to be loved by the charity we practice towards men and to be heard in the teachings they give us either directly or indirectly. He is hidden in our neighbor, either in the perfections which teach truth or in the troubles which call forth charity.[19]

Here is Abhishiktananda on the same subject:

> In the form of that man who stands in front of me—no matter whether he is about to bow before me or to strike me—it is Christ who wants to grow in him and in me together. . . . It is God who comes to me, in the guise of this man, so that I may help this man through my love, my respect, my service, to draw out of himself the possibilities of divine love which lie hid in his nature. Such a man may be coarse, rude, ugly,

wicked. I may have to avoid too close contact with him, not to be hurt or maimed in mind or body. I may have to threaten him, to rebuke him, I may have to claim what is due from him. Yet I can never forget that there is always in him a spark at least of divine love.[20]

Later in the same work he points out that the one who has realized the Presence within is most able to love the neighbor, realizing that all men are one, "as the Holy Spirit is one," and that for such no man can be a stranger.[21] For

> the mystery within one man's heart . . . is the mystery within every man's heart. No man is apart from others in the place in which God abides. In the very center of his heart, along with God, dwell all his brother-men and the whole creation; what has been, what is now, what is to be, even the very consummation and fulfillment of the universe is there.[22]

From these observations it is clear that every spiritual virtue is never simply a matter of the appropriate "feelings" or of "will power" but is indeed, "nothing other than a consciousness of a reality."

As we have seen, Abhishiktananda believed that the monk must consecrate himself to God and need not be involved in worldly affairs and good works. However, it would be wrong to think that he was indifferent to social abuses and injustices. He was stern in his condemnations of the Church's "shameless collusion with worldly powers, either political or economical,"[23] and of the West's exploitation of the "third world," calling for a reordering of the trade systems which allowed European powers to pay "a wretched price" for raw materials on which they then made "huge profits."[24] The *koinonia* of the Church had to be given practical expression, for, "The Church is a life conformed to the Gospel. Christians are those who love their brothers and seek to transform a civilization based on profit and egoism, which therefore is contrary to the Gospel."[25] He was often moved to compassion by the extreme poverty of many Indian villagers, and tried to live as one among them:

> One thing I have learnt in these Hindu surroundings is that one cannot be a real *sannyāsī* if one keeps anything in reserve for the morrow, be it only two annas or a handful of rice. A *samiar* should entrust himself totally to Providence.[26]

(Some members of the Church opposed the establishment of Shantivanam Ashram on the grounds that the material standard of living there was "too low"!) At times Abhishiktananda had so little money that he could not afford a little milk for his daily millet. Out of his own extremely meager material resources (from mass-stipends, in later years an intermittent trickle of royalties on his books, and occasional gifts from friends) Abhishiktananda supported a family in Tamil Nadu right up to the time of his death.[27] In a letter to Odette Baumer-Despeigne, explaining why he can no longer travel without financial assistance, he notes that more than half of his dwindling income goes to those poorer than himself.[28] The widow's mite!

Pilgrimage

Pilgrimage is a universal mode of religious experience, and there is no spiritual economy in which it does not play a part, though it is necessarily more foregrounded in some traditions than in others. No doubt the pilgrimage to Mecca, the *hajj*, is the pilgrimage *par excellence*. Doubtless, too, that pilgrimages may be undertaken for a variety of motivations—to revere a religious founder or saint, to experience the beneficent influences emanating from a sacred site, to seek healing, to expiate sins, to venerate relics, to express solidarity with the faithful in acts of communal worship at especially auspicious times and places, and so forth. Then too, there is no doubt that on occasion certain abuses accumulate around pilgrimage sites, which can become an El Dorado for charlatans and tricksters who exploit the credulity of the pilgrims. Erasmus gives us but one account of such abuses in his "Religious Pilgrimage."[29] But, no question, pilgrimage is woven into the very fabric of the spiritual quest. It is no accident that religious vocabularies of traditions the world over are permeated with the imagery of the journey, the way, the quest, the voyage, each of which may be considered as a movement from the circumference along a radius to the Center. Consider a few instances: "Tao": the Way; Jesus: "I am the Way"; the "Strait Way" of the Gospels; the "Red Road" of the Plains Indians; the "Middle Way" of the Buddha; Mahayana: "the Great Way." For the seeker, life itself is a pilgrimage in which the soul returns to its uncreate Source.

The Indian sub-continent is crisscrossed with ancient pilgrimage routes to holy mountains and temples, shrines, sculptures, groves, rivers, caves, the birthplaces of the saints and sages, tombs, the great seats of religious learning and monastic life, and other locations where the barriers between the visible and invisible worlds are more diaphanous and where the seeker may find some sort of *center*. A catalogue of such sites in India would be more or less endless, but we may mention a few of the most well-known: Mt Arunachala and its surrounding temples and ashrams, the great temple city of Madurai, Elephanta, Vrindaban,

Ayodhya, Mathura, and the holy cities of the Ganges River (Haridwar, Rishikesh, Allahabad, Banaras) and, in the Buddhist tradition, Kapilvatsu, Sarnath, Bodhgaya, and Kasanigara, to mention only those most closely associated with the life of the Awakened One.

As we have seen, by the late 1950s Abhishiktananda was increasingly drawn to the way of the wandering *sannyāsī* and to pilgrimages to India's holy sites. Even the informal, small-scale, and flexible structures of ashram life had become somewhat oppressive to him. In the years between the death of Fr Monchanin and his own passing, Abhishiktananda traveled a great deal, generally on foot or by third-class rail. He many times covered the length and breadth of the sub-continent. Much of this travel was of a purely practical kind—to attend a conference, to meet a colleague, to get medical treatment, and so on. But since his early visits to Tiruvannamalai and Tapovanam Abhishiktananda was drawn ever more deeply into the sacred geography of India and felt moved to make pilgrimages of various kinds. Mention has already been made of his several journeys in the Gangotri region, and of his return to Arunachala with Raimon Panikkar to celebrate the Eucharist on the holy mountain itself. Amongst the places to which he returned most frequently were three of the holy cities on the Ganges: Haridwar, Rishikesh, and Banaras (Varanasi).

In *The Way of the White Clouds*, his account of a pilgrimage in Western Tibet, Lama Anagarika Govinda offers the following:

> When every detail of our life is planned and regulated, and every fraction of time determined beforehand, then the last trace of our boundless and timeless being, in which the freedom of our soul exists, will be suffocated. This freedom does not consist in being able "to do what we want," it is neither arbitrariness nor waywardness, nor the thirst for adventures, but the capacity to accept the unexpected . . . it is the capacity to adapt oneself to the infinite variety of conditions without losing confidence in the deeper connections between the inner and the outer world. It is the spontaneous certainty of being neither bound by space nor time, the ability to experience the fullness of both without clinging to any of their aspects.[30]

This perhaps gives us one key to the significance of pilgrimage: it is not simply a journey to a particular destination of religious significance, but is rather a state of being and a way of living in which, at least for a time, the soul is freed of the temporal and spatial constraints which inevitably attend what is these days called "normal life." There is no doubt that Abhishiktananda was a seeker who felt increasingly frustrated by the inhibitions of an "organized" and sedentary existence, and for whom the outer physical journey was the expression of an inner freedom.

Pradakṣina

One of the practices closely associated with pilgrimage (*yātrā*) in India is *pradakṣina*, the prayerful circumambulation of a holy site, always starting in the East and moving southwards so that the site is on one's right-hand side. Abhishiktananda made many such circumambulations, perhaps most memorably the *giri-pradakṣina* of Arunachala itself, which he performed many times. In this practice he followed in the footsteps of Ramana Maharshi. It is said that the nine-mile circumambulation must be done reverently and slowly, as if "by a pregnant queen in her ninth month."[31] Abhishiktananda preferred to follow the route on moonlit nights, for at such times "the moon herself, from the height of the firmament, was making a celestial *pradakṣina* of light around the vast *Liṅga* of rock."[32] In *The Secret of Arunachala* he writes,

> As a Westerner . . . for a long time I had strong reservations on the subject of the *pradakṣina*. It seemed to me to be pure superstition and an outdated relic of ancient times and of beliefs which had long since been swept away by the stream of history. Later on, however, I understood better, and discovered here a wisdom that will endure undiminished when our so-called modern times have long been forgotten.[33]

During the *pradakṣina* the pilgrim prostrates at the cardinal points, and having completed the circuit, often proceeds to climb the mountain itself, as did Abhishiktananda, and "when he reaches the long desired summit, his heart again bids him cast himself to the ground in a final act of homage and in total self-surrender."[34] The self-surrender which pilgrimage entails, the freedom from the habitual patterns of daily life and of familiar surroundings and routines, makes the pilgrim more open to the call of the Spirit. Drawing on his own experience Abhishiktananda writes,

> A summons like that of Turinjal temple, or those of Gangotri or Kedernath may be rendered fruitless by a man's lack of courage or freedom, but nonetheless it evokes such an inner resonance that henceforth he can never again find satisfaction anywhere in the world of *māyā*. . . . Such a call pierces you to the heart, and there releases the most secret archetypes which are waiting for you in the depths of your psyche. . . . But how few there are who dare to accept themselves in their timeless mystery.[35]

Psychic Phantasmagoria and Paranormal Powers

It is well known that the psycho-spiritual disciplines of India sometimes produce extraordinary powers (*siddhis*) in their practitioners
and, indeed, that these exercise a kind of mesmeric attraction for some
Western seekers, especially the more credulous. It is also a fact that
the practice of certain sorts of austerities may give rise to all manner
of heightened and altered states of consciousness in which the aspirant
experiences such things as trances, ecstasies, visions, auditions, and
apparitions, and is able to access to a range of "paranormal" powers. It
might also be observed that there are psycho-spiritual techniques which
are practiced within the cadre of orthodox religious traditions and in
the hyperborean and primordial worlds of shamanism which do indeed
nurture extraordinary powers. Within Hinduism (and Buddhism for
that matter) the tantric traditions are of such a kind. Finally, it is indubi-
table that many of the world's greatest saints and sages evinced powers
which, to say the least of it, were far from normal. Ramakrishna is a case
in point. Swami Gnanananda, Abhishiktananda's disclaimers notwithstanding, is another. One might instance any number of examples of the
kinds of powers in question, some of them quite spectacular from the
point of view of the unenlightened, but one of the most attractive—to
be found more or less universally—is the ability to commune with animals; one might mention names such as Ramana himself, St Seraphim
of Sarov, and Crazy Horse as illustrative examples. Then, too, there is
the vexed question of drug-induced states of consciousness and the part
that they may play in the spiritual life.[36]

Although this is an interesting subject on which any amount might
be said, in the present context we confine ourselves to the observation
that Abhishiktananda's attitude to such phenomena was that, on the
whole, these things are best left to one side. As far as the vast majority
of aspirants are concerned, such powers should never be the object of
the spiritual search. In *Guru and Disciple* he reminds us that "the great
masters are continually reiterating the fact that all this [visions, psychic
powers, etc.] is absolutely secondary and has nothing to do with true
spiritual experience."[37] Here Abhishiktananda is no doubt speaking of
those subjective "productions" of the individual psyche, all too often
mistaken for the mystical state proper. In *The Secret of Arunachala* he
refers to the "great danger of being lost in those obscure and ungovern-
able regions of the psyche, where once again the ego has the mastery,
but now in highly abnormal forms."[38] As Guénon so powerfully argued
in *The Reign of Quantity*, it is one of the "signs of the times" that people

should so readily confuse the psychic and the spiritual domains, some-times elevating psychic phantasms to the plane of the spirit, sometimes dragging the things of the spirit down to a psychic level, both tendencies resulting in a "counterfeit spirituality" such as that evinced by theoso-phists, spiritualists, and occultists of various kind. Often this counter-feit spirituality takes the form of a kind of psychologism dressed up in "religious" clothes, one quite unable to distinguish between the psychic plane, the arena in which the more or less accidental subjectivities of the individual come into play in the depths of the subconscious, and the infinite realm of the spirit which, in terms of the human individual, is signaled by the capacity for the plenary experience and which is thus marked by what Schuon has called "an inward illimitability" and by transcendence.

No doubt Abhishiktananda shared the attitude of St John of the Cross, writing on "why it is undesirable to receive visions, even sup-posing they come from God":

> Faith gradually diminishes; for what is experienced through the senses detracts from faith, since faith transcends every sense. . . . Things of the senses, if they are not rejected, are an obstacle to the spirit; for the soul rests upon them and does not soar to the invisible . . . the soul becomes dependent on these phenomena.[39]

Abhishiktananda regrets the attraction of psychic "powers" for many Western seekers who have journeyed Eastwards. The confused under-standing of psychic phenomena can often serve as a serious distraction from the real work at hand; furthermore, the experiences which are sometimes engendered can be disastrous for a psyche "too feeble to bear such a shock." Most importantly, he urges us to remember that "the experience of the Self is beyond all possible verbalization and experi-mentation," one that infinitely outreaches the resources of the indi-vidual psyche; indeed, the genuine experience of the Self really means the disappearance of the phenomenal "I," the consuming of the ego by an "implacable devouring flame."[40] In brief, the "secret of Arunachala" has nothing whatever to do with the development of "powers" *per se*. On the relation of psychic phenomena to mysticism, Abhishiktananda writes:

> In speaking of mysticism it is surely unnecessary to explain that we are not now referring to those parapsychic phenomena which the ignorant frequently mistake for mysticism. The Spirit no doubt makes use of these at times to reveal his presence and activity, especially in temperaments of a certain type; but these manifestations are always incidental, and therefore essentially secondary. It is to the great

mystics that we must turn, in order to be admitted into the secrets of divine friendship. For they alone can speak of those secrets who have passed beyond all sensible experiences (visions, auditions, and similar phenomena) to the experience of a spiritual contact stripped of all forms.[41]

The Guru

In *Guru and Disciple*, Abhishiktananda wrote, 'The meeting with the guru is the essential meeting, the turning point in the life of a man.'[42] By his own reckoning, Abhishiktananda had four gurus: Ramana Maharshi, Mt Arunachala, Swami Gnanananda, and his *sadguru*, Jesus Christ. (He sometimes referred to Fr Monchanin as his guru, but here we may understand the term as a mark of courtesy for someone who was indeed, in many respects, his teacher even if the pupil soon outstripped the master.)[43] We have already considered the impact of each of these gurus on Abhishiktananda's life and thought. Here we gather together some of Abhishiktananda's more general thoughts on the role of the guru in the spiritual life, and his attempts to understand Christ as guru.

Abhishiktananda accepted the traditional Vedantic view that, in general, the experience of *advaita* could only be attained with the help of "a knower of *Brahman*," a guru who could awaken the disciple to the inner mystery of the *Ātman*. As Sankara himself wrote,

> the pure truth of *Ātman*, which is buried under *māyā*, can be reached by meditation, contemplation, and other spiritual disciplines such as a knower of *Brahman* may prescribe—but never by subtle argument.[44]

Abhishiktananda followed the orthodox Vedantic teaching that realization could never be attained by mental operations ("subtle argument"), nor by the transmission of ideas and concepts, no matter how lofty:

> The guru is certainly not some master or professor, or preacher, or spiritual guide, or director of souls who has learned from books or from other men what he, in his turn, is passing on to others. The guru is one who has himself first attained the real and who knows from personal experience the way that leads there; he is capable of initiating the disciple and of making well up from within the heart of the disciple, the ineffable experience which is his own—the utterly transparent knowledge, so limpid and pure, that quite simply, "he is."[45]

In the words of Swami Ramdas, the guru exhorts the disciple:

> Go within yourself and behold therein the splendor and glory of the eternal truth. Therein resides your ultimate home of perfect release,

happiness, and peace. Therein find the life that never fades, that never changes but ever blesses and sanctifies. Be in tune with that Reality, if you sincerely crave for the highest consummation of life.[46]

It was Swami Gnanananda who introduced Abhishiktananda to the distinction between the *guru-mūrti*, "the guru in visible form, the one who can show the way," or the *karana*-guru, the instrumental guru, and the *jñāna*- or *ātma-guru* who reveals all things.[47] In the light of realization, the *ātmā-guru*, the Self Itself, is the only guru. In Gnanananda's words,

> The real guru is *akhaṇḍa*, undivided. He is *advaita*, non-dual. He alone is the guru who can make one take the high dive. . . . The Self is visible only to the self, and the true guru is no one but "oneself" in the depth of "self."[48]

So, the encounter with the guru, and the practice of *guru-bhakti*, brings one face-to-face with oneself; such an encounter can only take place when one has gone beyond the level of "sense and intellect"; how can even the midday sun shine in a room if its shutters are closed?[49]

> What the guru says springs from the heart of the disciple. . . . When all is said and done, the true guru is he who, without the help of words, can enable the attentive soul to hear the "Thou art That," *Tat-tvam-asi* of the Vedic rishis; and this true guru will appear in some outward form or other when help is needed to leap over the final barrier.[50]

So, a paradox: how be it that the guru is within but that it is said that the disciple cannot attain realization without the help of the (outer) guru? Ramana himself taught that the guru is the "embodiment of that which is indicated by the terms *sat, cit,* and *ānanda*" (i.e. *Ātman*, the Self), which is within the disciple. But the aspirant, on account of "his acceptance of the forms of the objects of the senses, has swerved from his true state and is consequently distressed and buffeted by joys and sorrows," and so must be brought back to "his own real nature without differentiation."[51] Ramana was asked, if it be true that the guru is really one's own Self, why is it said that the aspirant cannot attain self-realization without the grace of the (external) guru? His answer:

> It is like the elephant which wakes up on seeing a lion in its dream. Even as the elephant wakes up at the mere sight of the lion, so too it is certain that the disciple wakes up from the sleep of ignorance into the wakefulness of true knowledge through the Guru's benevolent look of grace.[52]

Furthermore, the guru himself does not think of himself as "enlight-ened" and the disciple as "ignorant" because the guru abides in the reality of the one Self.[53] Many years later Abhishiktananda explained the distinction between the inner and outer guru this way:

> For the Vedantin, there is only one guru, the one who shines, not-born, in the depth of the heart. The "external" guru is only a temporary form taken by the essential guru to make himself recognized, and at the moment of recognition there is no longer either guru or disciple.[54]

Like Ramana, Abhishiktananda regarded Arunachala, to whom he wrote hymns, as his guru. The holy mountain of Siva symbolized non-duality itself, remembering that a symbol is not merely a "repre-sentation" or a kind of "stand-in" but *is* the reality symbolized on the phenomenal plane. Arunachala could simultaneously be perceived as *advaita*, the *Ātman* itself, the Immutable, and Lord Siva (here leaving aside its other significations). It thus performed the function of guru. Abhishiktananda came to understand both Ramana and the mountain as "projections" of the inner guru which is nothing other than the hidden Self in the fathomless recesses of the *guha*.

*

Since the days of Roberto Nobili (1577-1659), Christian missionaries had attempted to assimilate the Indian notions of both the guru and the *avatāra* into their own theological framework.[55] Abhishiktananda, on the other hand, in some sense took Christ out of the Judeo-Christian frame and situated him in the Hindu context. In this he was much influ-enced by his friend Raimon Panikkar and his trail-blazing work, *The Unknown Christ of Hinduism* (1974), in which it was argued that the historical person of Jesus must be distinguished from the Cosmic Christ. Through Jesus, Christians have come to know the Christ—"this Christ is the decisive reality," and not the monopoly of Christians. Abhishik-tananda was already exploring this line of thinking nearly twenty years earlier: in 1955 he had written in his diary, "Christ, the living God, does not mean for me once again Jesus of Nazareth. Christ is the mystery of my origin from God."[56] In his function of Cosmic Christ, Jesus is both the Cosmic Man, the *Puruṣa*, and "the embodiment of the unity of cre-ated being."[57] But, above all, Christ is the in-dwelling guru, not only the historical figure located in time and space.

As Catherine Cornille has suggested,

> Abhishiktananda's attempt to understand the figure of Jesus Christ through a new paradigm involved a reinterpretation, not only of

the nature and function of the figure of Jesus Christ, but also of his experience and teaching. From within the framework of *Advaita* Vedanta, Abhishiktananda comes to understand the experience of Jesus as that of *Saccidānanda*, and the expression "I and the Father are one" as expressing the awareness of non-duality of *ātman* and *Brahman*.[58]

As part of this "reinterpretation" Abhishiktananda comes to understand the Christian tradition as *Isha sampradāya*, the spiritual lineage which is maintained through the personal relationship of each adherent with Jesus as guru. He also casts Jesus in the role of the *tāraka*, the boatman who takes the aspirant to the further shore:

> Jesus effects the passing from *tamas* (darkness) to *jyoti* (light), from the *asat* (non-being) to *sat* (being), from *mṛtyu* (death) to *amṛta* (immortality).[59]

Abhishiktananda's attempt to understand Jesus Christ as guru was fuelled by several impulses, most importantly his own need to find a way of bridging the chasm between Hinduism and Christianity which he had first perceived in the wake of his Arunachala experiences. The re-thinking of Christ as guru was also one aspect of Abhishiktananda's wider project of enriching Christianity through the assimilation of aspects of Indian spirituality. Thirdly, a recasting of traditional Christology in terms of the guru would make the effulgent figure of Jesus and his universal message accessible to Hindus:

> It is possible to refuse to believe in the [unique] divinity of Christ, and in particular many are unable to accept it in the terms in which it was defined by the Church Councils. But the unique greatness of Christ's personality and his authority as a guru or spiritual leader of mankind can never be disputed.[60]

From Abhishiktananda's journal in the last year of his life:

> Christ loses nothing of his true greatness when he is delivered from the false grandeurs with which myths and theological reflection had overlaid him. Jesus is the wondrous epiphany of the mystery of Man, of the *Puruṣa*, the mystery of every human being, as the Buddha was, and Ramana, and so many others. He is the mystery of the *Puruṣa* that seeks itself in the cosmos. His epiphany is powerfully marked by the time and place of his appearance in the flesh. He came first of all for the lost ones of the house of Israel, as he himself said. Far more than being the "head" of a religion, Jesus is first of all a questioning of every human being. An examination of each one about his relation with God and with his brothers, as actually lived. Christian dogma has too often emptied Jesus and stolen him from his brothers.[61]

Beyond Words and Concepts

One motif in Abhishiktananda's writings on the spiritual path concerns the trap of an undue attachment to mental processes, "the ponderous tread of conceptual thought,"[62] to what the Romantic poets called "cerebration"—the workings of the rational, analytical, and logical mind. Abhishiktananda certainly didn't discount the capacity for thought which "can surely set man on the right track and gently indicate to the attentive soul longing for salvation how to attain it personally and experience it existentially,"[63] but he warned against the fallacy that any concept could "enclose those experiences in its definitions" or "transmit them to others." No doubt he would have endorsed Rudolf Otto's dictum (following Pascal) that, in the sphere of religion, "there are two equally dangerous extremes, to shut reason out and to let nothing else in."[64] Abhishiktananda, in consonance with the Indian tradition, accorded experience primacy over any form of conceptualization: "Reason may discuss, but experience knows."[65]

> ...the world of the East which, contrary to the Greek and Mediterranean world, has not accepted the primacy of the *eidos*, of the *logos*, of the idea. Rather, at all times, it has been directly drawn by being, life, experience in itself.[66]

Furthermore, "It is not by words that India's secret is transmittable. Words do not hold great secrets, they betray them, rather, even more than they disclose them."[67] The Western addiction to speculation, debate, argumentation, and rationalization—a malady inherited from the Greeks—too often elevates these processes into ends in themselves instead of understanding them as limited tools which have no value in themselves but only insofar as they lead to a real spiritual awakening. Even when dealing with the ultimate mysteries of the Self, of *advaita*, of voidness, the typical Westerner, "an impenitent intellectual," will not "accept defeat":

> He tries to cling to the thought of non-thought and emptiness. He expounds his ideas and exerts himself to the uttermost in his desire to understand. He cannot decide just simply to be, nor consent just to look, to receive into himself that which quite simply is. He defends himself by reference to the speculations of the Eastern exegetes, forgetting that for them speculation had no other goal than that of preparing for the awakening ... which alone has value here below. He is like the man who would not agree to breathe until he had divided up air into nitrogen and oxygen.[68]

Abhishiktananda was sometimes impatient with those theologians who would not go past the "signs" on which they were speculating but which could not themselves provide "the keys to the Kingdom" which are only yielded by "the contemplation of the highest wisdom which silences the mind and transcends all its activities."[69] He was in no danger of forgetting that,

> Reason is not Intelligence in itself, it is only its instrument, and this on the express condition that it be inspired by intellectual Intuition, or simply correct ideas or exact facts; nothing is worse than the mind cut off from its root; *corruptio optimi pessima.*[70]

In his commentaries on the Scriptures of both East and West Abhishiktananda never idolatrized the text itself, nor treated it as a handbook of logic. Indeed, he writes, "It would certainly be rash to interpret the intuitions of the apostles as though they were Aristotelian definitions. They overflow on every side the words in which they were formulated."[71]

As we have seen earlier, Abhishiktananda uses the word "faith" not only in its more conventional sense but also as an instrument of knowing; it is faith which is the only way of "penetrating the hidden abode of God—in the highest heaven as well as in the deepest center of our hearts."[72] All words are signs:

> Beyond the words and their immediate signification, it is the mystery itself latent in them that we should be eager to reach. Words and signs will of course pass into our intellect, and nest there, so to speak. . . . As signs they have finally to disappear in the thing they wanted to convey: here lies the true dignity of all signs.[73]

"As long as man attempts to seize and hold God in his words and concepts, he is embracing a mere idol."[74] The pitfalls of language, rationality, and conceptualization—of logocentrism, if you will—can often be by-passed by both myth and sacred art for these are modes of expression which do not proceed dialectically; nor are they abstract. One of Abhishiktananda's definitions of myth highlights the point: a myth is "a complex of signs and meanings which symbolize a reality so rich that it cannot be expressed directly in logical terms"[75]—somewhat reminiscent of Ananda Coomaraswamy's claim that

> The myth is the penultimate truth, of which all experience is the temporal reflection. The mythical narrative is of timeless and placeless validity, true nowhere and everywhere. . . . Myth embodies the nearest approach to absolute truth that can be stated in words.[76]

None of Abhishiktananda's remarks about the limits of reason and conceptualization should be construed to be an attack on intelligence itself with which, in the West, they are often confused. Intelligence is "a gift of God" and which "when transformed by grace" is "raised by the working of the Spirit beyond the limitations of its natural capacity."[77] Doubtless Abhishiktananda would give his heartfelt endorsement to Seyyed Hossein Nasr's observation that

> Intelligence is not what it has so often become in modern times, a mental acumen and a diabolical cleverness which goes on playing with ideas endlessly without ever penetrating or realizing them. This is not real intelligence, not contemplative intelligence which differs as much from mental virtuosity as the soaring flight of the eagle differs from the play of a monkey.[78]

Contemplative intelligence—which is really a kind of receptivity to the movement of the Spirit within—will lead us to that advaitic experience which takes us beyond all *nāma-rūpa*:

> Who will be left to raise problems on the day when he has at last discovered himself beyond the bonds and limitations of his phenomenal existence. . . ? Problems met in a dream fade automatically when one wakes up. Philosophies like theologies have no other purpose than to direct man to the knowledge that will save him. They can never enter the innermost room of the "Interior Castle"; like Moses they are forbidden to enter the Promised Land. They can only gaze at it and admire it from the distance of Mount Nebo, from the vantage-point of their discursive knowledge or even of the words in which God has enshrined his message—all of them still requiring the elucidation in the Spirit.[79]

Reading the Scriptures

The various observations mentioned above should also alert us to the openness with which we should approach Scriptures, a lesson all too often forgotten in the West where the European bias towards hyper-rationality, historicism, and logocentrism, now severed from the protective embrace of any larger and traditional religious sensibility, opens the door to the most bizarre, not to say impious, constructions (or "decon-structions," as the case may be) of Scripture. Here is Abhishiktananda on the *Upanishads*, from *Hindu-Christian Meeting Point*:

> In a word, the *Upanishads* do not seek to give information, to impart conceptual knowledge or ideas which a man only has to store away in some corner of his memory. Their aim is to help the disciple himself

to reach the fundamental experience which defies every attempt at conceptual expression, to put him into the attitude of heart and mind which will make him capable of this experience. This means freeing him from all that his reason continually superimposes on the Real, all those symbols and conceptualizations through which he imagines that he can lay hold of it and "possess" it. Thus he is gradually brought to that state of total peace and relaxation, pure receptivity and expectancy, emptied of all thought, desire, and volition, a simple transparency, which alone will permit the real to manifest itself to him in all its fullness.[80]

Because "the *Upanishads* do not offer an organized body of doctrines . . . [but] contain intuitive 'awakenings,'" they

cannot simply [be] reduced to formulas in any language whatever, for they are above all a matter of experience, a shock-treatment, an interior lightning-flash, induced by a whole series of approaches which converge from every point of the mental horizon upon this central focus of overwhelming illumination.[81]

Free from the manacles of both historicism and a flat literalism, Abhishiktananda had the gift of fathoming the depths of the Scriptures of both East and West. His manner of reading the sacred texts was much more "Eastern" than Occidental, a divergence on which Schuon comments:

[Westerners] look in a text for a meaning that is fully expressed and immediately intelligible, whereas Semites, and Eastern peoples in general, are lovers of verbal symbolism and read in "depth." The revealed phrase is for them an array of symbols from which more and more flashes of light shoot forth the further the reader penetrates into the spiritual geometry of the words: the words are reference points for a doctrine that is inexhaustible; the implicit meaning is everything, and the obscurities of the literal meaning are so many veils marking the majesty of the content.[82]

Cutting the Final Knot

This is a pervasive theme in Abhishiktananda's spiritual writings, as indeed it is in the world's Scriptures and in the world's vast treasury of mystical literature—how could it be otherwise? Rather than weaving together extracts from hither and thither let one particularly eloquent passage from Abhishiktananda suffice:

The final task in the spiritual quest is to overcome this last difference: the distinction between the goal and the way; the goal and he who is heading for it must finally disappear. In fact the man in search of the *self* is seized by a real onset of dizziness when he reaches what seems to him, from his point of view, to be the last bend in the road. He then realizes that he must henceforth renounce forever, without any possibility of turning back, everything which up till then has seemed to be the ground of his existence, which gave him being, his idea of self and his own consciousness bound to this idea of self. In the abysses of the heart to which he feels himself inexorably drawn, there is absolutely nothing he can grasp hold of or hang on to, nothing solid on which he can, so to speak, put down his foot, no air from outside in which to draw breath. It is the pure *akāśa*, infinite space, where no point can any longer be perceived, which is not bound by any horizon. . . . It is no longer even the milieu in which a man feels secure, for it has carried off the one who sought to dwell in it into the infinitude, limitlessness, and solitude. . . . As the *Upanishads* often reiterate, a man must never give up before he cuts this "final knot in the heart," *hṛdaya-granthi*, the bond which binds the Self to the conditionings of time and matter and prevents it reaching its unconfined and sovereign nature.[83]

Notes

1. F. Schuon, *Spiritual Perspectives*, 173.
2. Pr 11.
3. T. Merton, *New Seeds of Contemplation*, 107.
4. GD 9.
5. Quoted in SAC 12n.
6. L 28.5.71, 268.
7. Quoted in M. Fitzgerald (ed), *Indian Spirit*, 1.
8. See *Prayer*, Chapter 9. On the Jesus Prayer see also HCMP, 23-24.
9. Pr 9.
10. FS 38.
11. FS 59-60.
12. Pr 18.
13. Pr 58.
14. EL 29.
15. Quoted in Vattakuzhy, 130, 131.
16. GD 112.
17. F. Schuon, *Spiritual Perspectives*, 58.
18. See, for example, L 14.4.69, 212, and L 30.12.71, 260.
19. F. Schuon, *Spiritual Perspectives*, 168.
20. Pr 15.
21. Pr 23.
22. Pr 29.
23. RC 3.

24. L 178.

25. L 13.4.65, 169.

26. Abhishiktananda quoted in du Boulay, 57. Du Boulay points out that *samiar* should be *samivar*, the Tamil term for "swami."

27. L 25n. See also L 30.12.64, 169.

28. L 28.6.71, 248.

29. See "Pilgrimage," *Catholic Encyclopedia* on the New Advent website: http://www.newadvent.org/cathen/12085a.htm.

30. A. Govinda, *The Way of the White Clouds*, 60.

31. C. Cornille, *The Guru in Indian Catholicism*, 83.

32. SA 120.

33. SA 119.

34. SA 123.

35. SA 121.

36. For some discussion of this subject see my *Journeys East*, 266-268.

37. GD 10.

38. SA 80.

39. Quoted in E. Hamilton, *The Voice of the Spirit*, 48.

40. GD 11.

41. HCMP 1109. Amongst the mystics-proper whom Abhishiktananda then mentions are St John of the Cross, Teresa of Avila, Marie of the Incarnation, the Rhenish mystics Eckhart, Tauler, and Ruysbroeck "whose mysticism is especially akin to that of India," as well as Evagrius and Gregory of Nyssa.

42. GD 29.

43. Catherine Cornille lists Dr Dinshaw Mehta, the Parsi doctor, as one of Abhishiktananda's gurus, but this is to overstate the case—in this case "mentor" is probably the more appropriate term. See Cornille, *The Guru in Indian Catholicism*, 89ff. On Mehta's influence on Abhishiktananda see Friesen, 94-96.

44. *Crest-Jewel*, 43.

45. GD 29.

46. *The Essential Swami Ramdas*, 59.

47. GD 108-110.

48. GD 108-109.

49. GD 29, FS 62-63.

50. GD 30.

51. *Upadesa Manjari* ("Spiritual Instruction"), in *The Collected Works of Ramana Maharshi*, 50.

52. *Upadesa Manjari* ("Spiritual Instruction"), in *The Collected Works of Ramana Maharshi*, 51.

53. See A. Osborne, *The Teachings of Ramana Maharshi*, 97 (quoted in C. Cornille, *The Guru in Indian Catholicism*, 81).

54. L 13.11.70, 238.

55. For a rapid historical sketch see C. Cornille, *The Guru in Indian Catholicism*, 95-100.

56. D 14.8.55, 115.
57. From Abhishiktananda's journal, quoted in C. Cornille, *The Guru in Indian Catholicism*, 105.
58. C. Cornille, *The Guru in Indian Catholicism*, 101-102.
59. From Abhishiktananda's journal, quoted in C. Cornille, *The Guru in Indian Catholicism*, 102.
60. SAC 79.
61. Journal entry 2.1.73, translation from Jacques Dupuis in *Jesus Christ at the Encounter of Religions*, 80. The last four sentences—which do not appear in Dupuis—are from *Ascent to the Depth of the Heart*, 367.
62. HCMP 47.
63. GD 14.
64. Quoted in John Harvey's Preface to the second edition of *The Idea of the Holy*, xix.
65. Abhishiktananda quoted by Odette Baumer-Despeigne in P. Coff, "Abhishiktananda," 7.
66. EL 19.
67. EL 72.
68. GD 9.
69. SAC 4.
70. F. Schuon, *The Transfiguration of Man*, 57.
71. HCMP 89.
72. Pr 9.
73. Pr 46.
74. SAC 5.
75. FS 105.
76. A. Coomaraswamy, *Hinduism and Buddhism*, 6.
77. HCMP 109.
78. S.H. Nasr, *Ideals and Realities of Islam*, 21.
79. SAC 47.
80. HCMP 48.
81. FS 69, 101.
82. F. Schuon, *Understanding Islam*, 59-60.
83. GD 103.

8

Signs

The Limits of Religious Forms

The mystery to which [religion] points overflows
its limits in every direction.

Abhishiktananda[1]

Truth does not deny forms from outside but transcends them from within.

Frithjof Schuon[2]

Let us not confuse the vessel with the treasure
that it contains.

Abhishiktananda[3]

Not surprisingly, Abhishiktananda's early thinking about religion was
cast in a conventional Catholic mould: the Incarnation of Jesus Christ
was *the* pivotal moment in human history, the Redemption of sinful
mankind, "the Way, the Truth, and the Life" outside of which no man
"cometh to the Father" (*John* 14.6). In the words of *A Benedictine
Ashram*, Christ is "the center of time, the *index veri et falsi*," and His
Church is "the exclusive 'ark of salvation' through which every chosen
soul receives his call and is saved."[4] Whatever the spiritual values and
insights of other traditions, they could only find fulfillment and consummation through the Christian Revelation. This, wrote Abhishiktananda
and Monchanin, is

> the supernatural ideal which India should strive after, with the grace
> of the one Mediator, and which she should realize in her religious
> institutions as well as in the ordinary life of every one of her children—
> if she wants the riches hidden in her legacy to fructify and the noblest
> aspirations of her soul to find their full realization.[5]

As we have seen, by the end of his life Abhishiktananda had abandoned Christian exclusivism. We have already considered his changing
perception of the nature and significance of both the historical figure of
Jesus and of the Cosmic Christ. His acknowledgment that "Whoever,
in his personal experience . . . has discovered the Self, has no need of
faith in Christ, of prayer, of the communion of the Church"[6] marks the
distance he had come since co-writing *A Benedictine Ashram*.

The reasons for Abhishiktananda's changing understanding of religion are intimately related to his increasing indifference to history, to events in time, his deepening emphasis on the direct existential experience of *advaita,* and his commitment to *sannyāsa* as a mode of being which "cuts across all *dharmas* and disregards all frontiers."[7] However, it would be a grave error to suppose that this constituted a rejection of religion *per se;* rather it marked the move from an exoteric to an esoteric understanding. As Schuon reminds us,

> Exoterism consists in identifying transcendent realities with the dogmatic forms, and if need be, with the historical facts of a given Revelation, whereas esoterism refers in a more or less direct manner to these same realities.[8]

However, the picture is complicated by the fact that Abhishiktananda was not altogether immune to some of the follies of modern thought and these sometimes distorted his thinking when it veered away from traditional sources. One example: in his thinking about religion Abhishiktananda sometimes succumbed to what might be called "spiritual evolutionism," a grotesque by-product of one of the most potent pseudo-mythologies of modernity. How else can we explain a piece of foolishness such as the claim made in his journal, "The order of religion is only a practical necessity in the evolution of human consciousness."[9] In Abhishiktananda's writings one sometimes comes across an evolutionist schema in which humankind "progresses" through several "stages," marked by *mythos* (i.e., a mythological outlook expressed in narratives, images, and symbols) and *logos* and *eidos* (verbalization, conceptualization, ratiocination), towards one in which the limitations of both the mythic and logocentric outlook are overcome.[10] Now, there *may* be something in this claim if we understand it as no more than a descriptive account of a certain pattern of development, at least in the West. But to imagine that this constitutes some sort of *progressive evolution* of the spiritual possibilities of the human condition is simply to announce that one has been seduced by ideas which have no place whatever in the religious and spiritual domain. One is not in the slightest surprised that scientist thinkers such as E.O. Wilson fall into this kind of trap, but it has also ensnared many otherwise highly intelligent and gifted religious and philosophical thinkers—one may mention such figures as Vivekananda, Aurobindo, Teilhard de Chardin, Bede Griffiths, and Ken Wilber. Sometimes we find in Abhishiktananda's writings on religious forms acute metaphysical insights sitting side-by-side with assertions which one might expect from a neo-Hindu reformer or an apostle of "cosmic consciousness," but which are disturbing in a thinker who is often so perspicacious. However, it is not our purpose in this chapter to assemble a catalogue of the indiscretions, confusions, and contradictions which can be found in Abhishiktananda's writings, but to turn our attention to his many profound insights into the nature of religious forms.

Attempts to define "religion" have a long pedigree stretching back to antiquity but since the emergence in the nineteenth century of the field of inquiry variously known as "comparative religion," "the history of religions," and "religious studies," there has been a veritable flood of "definitions" and "theorizations" of religion. Many of these have produced altogether horizontal, reductive, rationalistic, and pseudo-scientific models such as those fabricated by Marx, Nietzsche, J.G. Frazer, Weber, Freud, and other thinkers who imagine that "religion" and "religious experience" can be explained in the profane categories of historicism, psychology, sociology, and modern philosophy. It is to Abhishiktananda's credit that, in general, he paid little heed to such theorizing. As we have remarked more than once, Abhishiktananda was not a systematic thinker and we will nowhere find in his writings a consolidated and systematic account of "religion." Nonetheless, it is possible to excavate from his writings an understanding which is more or less coherent. However, he himself indulged in a peculiarly modern form of reductive theorizing insofar as he attempted (not very seriously, thankfully) to develop a kind of incipient theory of religion as primarily a psychological and sociological phenomenon deriving from psychic and social "archetypes." Although his references to Jung are sparse it is not difficult to discern the Swiss psychologist's influence in some of Abhishiktananda's speculations.

In this chapter we will isolate a few of the more conspicuous themes in Abhishiktananda's later writings about religious forms, focusing on an extended passage in *The Further Shore*, highlighting his several profound insights but also drawing attention to certain obvious lacunae, ambiguities, and misconceptions. In so doing we will draw heavily on the writings of traditionalists, particularly Frithjof Schuon, whose understanding of the issues implicit in the passage surpasses that of Abhishiktananda himself.

Some of Abhishiktananda's most arresting writing on religious forms comes in his essays on *sannyāsa*. Here is a passage worth quoting at length as it articulates some key ideas from Abhishiktananda's later years, and provides several avenues into a more wide-ranging discussion of his understanding of religion:

Every great *dharma* in fact takes its rise from the awakening to the Real of some mighty personality—or it may be, of some close-knit group, as in the case of the Vedic rishis, and it develops within a social and intellectual world which is generally highly particularized. No doubt it deeply influences this world, but it is itself strongly marked by the conditioning received from this world. . . . Every *dharma* is for its followers the supreme vehicle of the claims of the absolute. However, behind and beyond the *nāma-rūpa* . . . it bears within itself an urgent call to men to pass beyond itself, inasmuch as its essence is to be a sign of the Absolute. In fact, whatever the excellence of any *dharma*, it remains inevitably at the level of signs; it remains on *this* side of the Real, not only in its structure and institutional forms, but also in all its attempts to formulate the ineffable reality, alike in mythical or conceptual images. The mystery to which it points overflows its limits in every direction. . . . The innermost core of any *dharma* explodes when the abyss of man's consciousness is pierced to its depth by the ray of pure awakening. Indeed its true greatness lies precisely in its potentiality of leading beyond itself. . . . In every religion and every religious experience there is a *beyond*, and it is precisely this "beyond" that is our goal. . . . *Sannyāsa* is the recognition of that which lies beyond all signs; and paradoxically, it is itself the sign of what for ever lies beyond all possibility of being adequately expressed by rites, creeds, or institutions. . . . The call to complete renunciation cuts across all *dharmas* and disregards all frontiers. No doubt the call reaches individuals through the particular forms of their own *dharma*. . . . In the end it is in that call arising from the depths of the human heart that all great *dharmas* really meet each other and discover their innermost truth in that attraction beyond themselves which they all share. This fundamental urge towards the Infinite is altogether beyond the reach of either sense or intellect.[11]

This passage (and many others like it in *The Further Shore*) demands the closest attention; it raises as many questions as it answers. Let us examine it in detail.

• *Every great* dharma *in fact takes its rise from the awakening to the Real of some mighty personality.* . . .

Abhishiktananda attributes the origins of religious traditions to an "awakening to the Real" of some "mighty personality" or extraordinary groups, such as the Vedic rishis. What is unstated here is whether the *dharmas* arise under the pressure of purely human initiatives or whether they spring forth from Revelations which come directly from Heaven, by way of Divine Messengers (*avatāras*) and through "events" which shatter the barriers between Heaven and Earth and so infinitely transcend the limits of Space and Time. Such Revelations take many forms: a mythology (primordial traditions), a Law and Covenant (the Sinaitic Revelation), an Incarnation (Christ), a Sacred Text (the *Koran*, the *Vedas*). Revelation is the wellspring of religion. Religions are not man-made constructions, "cultural productions," though they no doubt take on a coloring from the historical and cultural milieux in which they appear. Revelations are God's gift to humankind that we may return to Him in whose image and likeness we are made. From any particular Revelation will issue an ensemble of formal elements which together comprise a religion whose unfolding in time constitutes a tradition.

No one will doubt that the origin of any religious tradition is an "awakening to the Real," as long as we do not suppose this to be a "process" of purely human provenance. In short, the pressing question arising out of the excerpt in front of us is this: does it take proper account of Revelation? But let us pause to ask what the term "Revelation" actually entails. We shall start with a metaphorical explanation—indeed, strictly speaking, no other kind is possible. In his study of Sufism Martin Lings articulates the "idea" of Revelation in these terms:

> From time to time a Revelation "flows" like a great tidal wave from the Ocean of Infinitude to the shores of our finite world. . . . From "time to time": this is a simplification which calls for a commentary; for since there is no common measure between the origin of such a wave and its destination, its temporality is bound to partake, mysteriously, of the Eternal, just as its finiteness is bound to partake of the Infinite. Being temporal, it must first reach this world at a certain moment in history; but that moment will in a sense escape from time. "Better than a thousand months" is how the Islamic Revelation describes the night of its own advent. There must also be an end which corresponds to the beginning; but that end will be too remote to be humanly foreseeable. . . . There is only one water but no two waves are the same. Each wave has its own characteristics according to its destination, that is, the particular needs of time and place towards which and in response to which it has providentially been made to flow.[12]

This passage can be qualified by a passage from Schuon, one which should be read as a kind of addendum to the account just given:

> To say that Revelation is "supernatural" does not mean that it is contrary to nature in so far as nature can be taken to represent, by extension, all that is possible on any given level of reality; it means that Revelation does not originate at the level to which, rightly or wrongly, the epithet "natural" is normally applied. This "natural level" is precisely that of physical causes, and hence of sensory and psychic phenomena considered in relation to those causes.[13]

Furthermore,

> It has been said more than once that total Truth is inscribed, in an immortal script, in the very substance of our spirit; what the different Revelations do is to "crystallize" or "actualize," in differing degrees according to the case, a nucleus of certitudes.[14]

This leaves open the way for an understanding of Revelation compatible with whatever religious tradition is in question, not excluding Buddhism which, on the face of it at least, might appear to pose the most difficulties as far as the principle is concerned. In this context Schuon does not hesitate to speak of the Buddha's "transcendent nature . . . without which there could be no question of the efficacy of his Law nor of the saving power of his name."[15] What we can say is that Abhishiktananda's shorthand explanation of the origin of religions, in this particular passage, is not incompatible with a traditionalist understanding. But it is doubtful whether he would have accepted the manner in which Lings and Schuon put the matter. Nonetheless, it cannot be too often stated that

> Tradition cannot be improvised from human means for by the terms of a tradition the human state as such is by definition a mode of ignorance—a blindness that cannot, by merely having recourse to itself, overcome its own unknowingness.[16]

(In passing we should note another crucial point: "It is quite out of the question that a 'revelation,' in the full sense of the word, should arise in our time, one comparable, that is to say, to the imparting of the great sutras or any other primary scriptures: the day of revelations is past on this globe and was so already long ago. The inspirations of the saints are of another order."[17])

*

Abhishiktananda's passage signals the obvious fact that there have been many "awakenings to the Real"—many Revelations. But Revelation must be carefully distinguished from other intuitions and disclosures of the Divine. In the traditionalist vocabulary, "Revelation" always signifies a formal source for a whole religious tradition. When Martin Buber wrote that "Revelation is continual, and everything is fit to become a sign of revelation" he was using the word in a different sense.[18] Likewise for Archbishop Temple in writing, "Unless all existence is a medium of revelation, no particular revelation is possible."[19] Abhishiktananda said the same: "God has no form. God is beyond every form. Precisely for that reason God can reveal and manifest himself under any form."[20] The referent here, these "revelations" and "manifestations," are what Eliade calls "hierophanies" and what the traditionalists would perhaps describe as "archetypal illuminations."[21] Furthermore, Revelation-proper must be distinguished from "inspiration" which can encompass all manner of workings of divine influence. This distinction has been scrupulously preserved in the Judaic, Islamic, and Hindu traditions, which is not to suggest that it is one of which all the adherents of these traditions will be aware.[22] The neglect of this distinction in some quarters has produced abuses too numerous to catalogue here but the Protestant tendency to idolatrize Scripture is a case in point where the Revelation, Christ Himself, is confused with texts which are, in some cases, only at the level of "inspiration."

In his later writings Abhishiktananda gave the question of Revelation scanty explicit consideration. However, one of the linchpins of his earlier Christian exclusivism was the notion of the uniqueness and supremacy of the Christian Revelation over all others (insofar as they were acknowledged at all); the change in Abhishiktananda's position must necessarily have entailed a rethinking of this issue. He continued to refer to Revelation until the end of his life, sometimes in terms reminiscent of Schuon's writings on this subject and its relation to intellection. Thus, for example, Abhishiktananda in a posthumously published article,

> In the case of a divine revelation, the mind is enabled to go, in faith, beyond previous intuitions and formulations, these being at once "redeemed" and fulfilled through the grace of the Holy Spirit. If it were not so, revealed truths would remain for ever, as too often happens, extrinsic to man; they would not take root in him; they would not become integrated into his own personal and deepest experience; they would never become in him something vital. Truly, divine revelation aims at awakening and bringing to completion what had already been placed by God in seed-form in man through the very process of creation—the first step in God's call to man to participate in the divine life.[23]

• [*Every great* dharma] *develops within a social and intellectual world which is generally highly particularized.*

No one will take issue with the contention that religions develop within variegated historical and cultural contexts. What is left out of the picture here is that the Revelations are providentially fashioned in just such a way as best to meet the psychic and spiritual receptivities of the human collectivity in question, of the "particularized" world in which the Revelation manifests itself. Schuon perceives humankind neither as a monolithic psychic entity nor as an amorphous agglomerate but as divided into several distinct branches, each with its own peculiar traits, psychological and otherwise, which determine its receptivity to truth and shape its apprehensions of reality. Needless to say there is no question here of any kind of racialism or ethnocentrism which attributes a superiority or inferiority to this or that ethnic collectivity. Nor, however, is there any sentimental prejudice in favor of the idea that the world's peoples are only "superficially" and "accidentally" different. "We observe the existence, on earth, of diverse races, whose differences are 'valid' since there are no 'false' as opposed to 'true' races."[24] Each branch of humanity exhibits a psychic and spiritual homogeneity which may transcend barriers of geography and biology. To the diverse human collectivities are addressed Revelations which are determined in their formal aspects by the needs at hand. This is crucial. Thus

> what determines the differences among forms of Truth is the difference among human receptacles. For thousands of years already humanity has been divided into several fundamentally different branches, which constitute so many complete humanities, more or less closed in on themselves; the existence of spiritual receptacles so different and so original demands differentiated refractions of the one Truth.[25]

Truth is one. Revelation marks a "formalization" of Truth and thus cannot be identical with it. This distinction must be maintained if the idea of multiple Revelations is to remain intelligible:

> Truth is situated beyond forms, whereas Revelation, or the Tradition that derives from it, belongs to the formal order, and that indeed by definition; but to speak of form is to speak of diversity, and thus of plurality.[26]

In a sense the Revelations are communicated in different divine languages. Just as we should baulk at the idea of "true" and "false" languages, so we need to see the necessity and the validity of multiple Revelations.[27]

• *No doubt it* [*each* dharma] *deeply influences this* [*particularized*] *world, but it is itself strongly marked by the conditioning received from this world. . . .*

On the face of it this is a quite unexceptional claim about the reciprocal influences of "religion" and "culture," but there is a fundamental philosophical issue at stake here. It is perhaps not too much to suggest that

Abhishiktananda is at least flirting with a modernistic dichotomy which simply does not apply in any traditional world in which "religion" and "culture" are essentially inseparable. Firstly, let us accept the proposition that "In all epochs and all countries there have been revelations, religions, wisdoms; tradition is a part of mankind, just as man is part of tradition."[28] Then let us ask what is the relationship of what is generally understood by "culture" (i.e., a whole way of life of a particular people) to these "revelations, religions, wisdoms"? The answer: a traditional culture is but the manifold expression of the principial truths of the Revelation, manifested in every aspect of the world in question, through the "use of forms that will have arisen by applying those principles to contingent needs."[29]

Every *dharma* is a tradition, which can be briefly defined in the words of Marco Pallis:

> Wherever a complete tradition exists this will entail the presence of four things, namely: a source of . . . Revelation; a current of influence or Grace issuing from that source and transmitted without interruption through a variety of channels; a way of "verification" which, when faithfully followed, will lead the human subject to successive positions where he is able to "actualize" the truths that Revelation communicates; finally there is the formal embodiment of tradition in the doctrines, arts, sciences, and other elements that together go to determine the character of a normal civilization.[30]

T.S. Eliot was perfectly correct in understanding "culture" as an "incarnation" of "religion."[31]

• *Every* dharma *is for its followers the supreme vehicle of the claims of the Absolute.*

Quite so, necessarily! As each religion proceeds from a Revelation, it is, in Seyyed Hossein Nasr's words, both

> *the* religion and *a* religion, *the* religion inasmuch as it contains within itself the Truth and the means of attaining the Truth, *a* religion since it emphasizes a particular aspect of Truth in conformity with the spiritual and psychological needs of the humanity for whom it is destined.[32]

In other words each religion is sufficient unto itself and contains all that is necessary for man's sanctification and salvation. The principle of multiple Revelations is not accessible to all mentalities and its implications must remain anathema to the majority of believers. This is in the nature of things. For the normal believer of exoteric spiritual temperament, his religion is not *a* religion but *the* religion, as it must be if it is to enlist all that he is. This is why he is unlikely to sympathize with

Abhishiktananda's soliloquy, "Who is a Christian? Who is a Hindu? Who is a Muslim? I know only the children of my Father who is in heaven."[33]

From a traditionalist viewpoint, anyone today wishing to understand religion as such and the interrelationships of the various traditions must have a firm purchase on the principle of multiple Revelations. It is one which can be supported by scriptural and traditional authority though the penetration of the passages in question will again be beyond the reach of most believers. As the Semitic traditions have been the ones most prone to extravagant claims of exclusivism we shall cite but two passages from their Scriptures which are suggestive in the light of the foregoing:

> Other sheep have I which are not of this fold (*John* 10.16).

> For each we have appointed a law and traced out a path, and if God had wished, verily He would have made you one people (*Koran* V.53)

Revelation must take on some form whence we can say that it communicates truths rather than Truth, since *to form is to limit*. Nevertheless, and somewhat paradoxically, the Revelations, being of divine origin, also communicate something of the virtuality of Absolute Truth:

> Revelation speaks an absolute language because God is absolute, not because the form is; in other words, the absoluteness of the Revelation is absolute in itself, but relative *qua* form.[34]

Abhishiktananda put the matter this way: "God is the absolute. No one of his manifestations can express him completely; yet God is fully present in such manifestations."[35]

In a letter to Marc Chaduc, Abhishiktananda called religions "grandiose dream worlds," by which he did not mean that they are illusory but that, as *nāma-rūpa*, they have only a relative reality and a provisional utility. In the passage in question he goes on to say,

> But be careful not to call them dreams from the point of view of the dreamer. . . . The man who is awake marvels at the dream; in it he grasps the symbolism of the mystery. He knows that every detail has its significance. The only mistake is to want to absolutize each symbol.[36]

With the critical proviso that we discount the common assumption that dreams are of purely psychic genesis, this kind of imagery is quite adequate to its purpose even though it is only intelligible to a certain kind of spiritual sensibility. Like many of the most influential comparative mythographers of recent times—C.G. Jung, Joseph Campbell, Mircea Eliade, Heinrich Zimmer—Abhishiktananda sometimes homologizes dreams and myths, the latter being a kind of collective dream. A psychologistic reductionism often lurks in this kind of thinking and Abhishiktananda does not always manage to avoid it. Take an instance from a late letter to Raimon Panikkar:

> "salvation" means nothing—nothing real—to the humanist, any more than to the Buddhist or the Vedantin! (There is) a drive of the psyche, and to express it the mind fashions a marvelous dream. (There is) the impact of the mystery on the consciousness of a human group, and the collective psyche produces the magnificent spectacle of the myth and the *logos* . . . and then we wake up. The dream is true in the drive which gives it birth and in which it is finally absorbed.[37]

Here the dream is no longer a fertile and suggestive image but simply the product of the psyche, individual and collective. This is an unhappy instance of that modern confusion which Guénon excoriated—the confusion of the psychic and the spiritual. It also rears its head in Abhishiktananda's frequent references to archetypes in which he collapses traditional doctrines and Jungian speculations.[38] But let us return to the passage from *The Further Shore* which is not contaminated by this kind of psychologism.

• *However, behind and beyond the* nāma-rūpa *[religious forms] . . . it bears within itself an urgent call to men to pass beyond itself, inasmuch as its essence is to be a sign of the Absolute. In fact, whatever the excellence of any* dharma, *it remains inevitably at the level of signs; it remains on* this *side of the Real, not only in its structure and institutional forms, but also in all its attempts to formulate the ineffable reality, alike in mythical or conceptual images.*

This brings us to the heart of the passage in front of us. Here Abhishiktananda formulates a principle of cardinal importance. The same principle stated by Schuon:

> A religion is a form, and so also a limit, which "contains" the Limitless, to speak in paradox; every form is fragmentary because of its necessary exclusion of other formal possibilities; the fact that these forms—when they are complete, that is to say when they are perfectly "themselves"— each in their own way represent totality does not prevent them from being fragmentary in respect of their particularization and their reciprocal exclusion.[39]

Schuon uses the term "form," Abhishiktananda "sign" or "*nāma-rūpa*," but the burden of each claim is the same. Each *dharma*, each religion, each tradition, must express itself in *nāma-rūpa*, in forms, which serve two fundamental ends, flagged by the terms "doctrine" and "method":

> Every religion possesses two elements which are its basis and its foundation: a doctrine which distinguishes between the Absolute and the relative, between the absolutely Real and the relatively real . . . and a method of concentrating upon the Real, of attaching oneself to the Absolute and living according to the Will of Heaven, in accordance with the purpose and meaning of human existence.[40]

Schuon's resort to the paradoxical formulation that religion is a limited form which "contains" the Limitless, is echoed by Abhishiktananda's no less paradoxical claim that *sannyāsa* is "a sign beyond signs": "*Sannyāsa* confronts us with a sign of that which is essentially beyond all signs—indeed, in its sheer transparency, it proclaims its own death as a sign."[41] He also understands the difficulties that such expressions pose for the faithful devotee who is unable to see beyond the signs:

> It is quite difficult for the believer—without staking the value of the expression of his faith—to recognize everywhere the total mystery of this Presence. Only when the soul has undergone the experience that the Name beyond all names can be pronounced only in the silence of the Spirit, does one become capable of this total openness which permits one to perceive the Mystery in its sign . . . in the sign that reveals all and that, at the same time, points always towards the Beyond.[42]

In this recognition, Abhishiktananda believes, lies the resolution of a whole series of antinomies and the so-called problem of religious pluralism.

In highlighting both the necessity and the limits of forms, Schuon likens the religions to geometric figures. Just as it would be absurd to imagine that spatial extensions and relationships could only be expressed by one form so it is absurd to assert that there could be only one doctrine giving an account of the Absolute. However, just as each geometric form has some necessary and sufficient reason for its existence, so too with the religions.

> The differentiated forms are irreplaceable, otherwise they would not exist, and they are in no sense various kinds of imperfect circles; the cross is infinitely nearer the perfection of the point . . . than are the oval or the trapezoid, for example. Analogous considerations apply to traditional doctrines, as concerns their differences of form and their efficacy in equating the contingent to the Absolute.[43]

Each religion is indeed "a sign of the Absolute" which, through Revelation, is its origin and the goal of the spiritual method it prescribes. It

is also the case, as Abhishiktananda affirms, that each religion includes
a call to go beyond its external forms. What is perhaps not sufficiently
clear in the passage from Abhishiktananda is that this summons is only
addressed to those capable of responding, which is to say that minority
of a profoundly contemplative and jnanic disposition. The vast majority
of religious adherents cannot be *jñāna-yogis*, as the Hindu tradition well
understands; for such folk (in any tradition) any suggestion that the
religious forms are relative, provisional, and ultimately dispensable is
fraught with danger as it might allow for a descent into a sentimentalism
and subjectivism which easily falls prey to anti-traditional forces of one
kind and another. However, if gnosis as such is under consideration then
the question of religious orthodoxy cannot arise, this being a principle
which is only operative on the formal plane:

> If the purest esoterism includes the whole truth—and that is the very
> reason for its existence—the question of "orthodoxy" in the religious
> sense clearly cannot arise: direct knowledge of the mysteries could not
> be "Moslem" or "Christian" just as the sight of a mountain is the sight
> of a mountain and not something else.[44]

Nevertheless, the two realms, exoteric and esoteric, are continually
meeting and interpenetrating, not only because there is such a thing as
a "relative esoterism" but because "the underlying truth is one, and also
because man is one."[45] Moreover, even if esoterism transcends forms, it
has need of doctrinal, ritual, moral, and aesthetic supports on the path
to realization.[46]

• *The mystery to which it* [*each* dharma] *points overflows its limits in every
direction. . . . The innermost core of any* dharma *explodes when the abyss
of man's consciousness is pierced to its depth by the ray of pure awakening.
Indeed its true greatness lies precisely in its potentiality of leading beyond
itself. . . . In every religion and every religious experience there is a beyond,
and it is precisely this "beyond" that is our goal.*

Here Abhishiktananda alludes to what has been variously called intellection, gnosis, *jñāna*, *satori*, enlightenment, the plenary experience, the
"awakening" in the "abyss" which does indeed lie beyond all forms—
hence the universality of apophaticism (understanding this word in a
general sense). This is the domain of esoterism which can be entered
through the forms, *not* by some sort of iconoclastic rejection of forms.
The statements of a formal exoterism (i.e., the "outer" religion) are
partial but therapeutic truths, intimations of Truth unqualified, metaphors and symbols, bridges to the formless Reality, in Abhishiktananda's
terms, "signs," all "provisional expressions of the Real." But, for those

with eyes to see, these signs themselves, as Abhishiktananda emphasizes, point beyond or, if one prefers, "within" ("within" in two senses:
the hidden "interior" of the signs themselves, and the "within" of the
adherent, the *guha*). If "exoterism consists in identifying transcendent
realities with dogmatic forms" then esoterism is concerned "in a more
or less direct manner with these same realities."[47] Esoterism is concerned
with the apprehension of Reality as such, not Reality as understood in
such and such a perspective and "under the veil of different religious
formulations."[48] While exoterism sees "essence" or "universal truth" as
a function of particular forms, esoterism sees the forms as a function of
"essence."[49] To put it another way, *exoterism particularizes the universal,
esoterism universalizes the particular.*

> What characterizes esoterism to the very extent that it is absolute, is
> that on contact with a dogmatic system, it universalizes the symbol
> or religious concept on the one hand, and interiorizes it on the other;
> the particular or the limited is recognized as the manifestation of the
> principial and the transcendent, and this in its turn reveals itself as
> immanent.[50]

Esoterism is "situated" on the plane of mystical experience, of
intellection and realization. Abhishiktananda's later work can certainly
be understood, and applauded, as a most worthwhile attempt to "uni-
versalize" and "interiorize" the external forms of the two traditions of
which he was heir.

• Sannyāsa *is the recognition of that which lies beyond all signs; and paradoxically, it is itself the sign of what for ever lies beyond all possibility of
being adequately expressed by rites, creeds, or institutions. . . .*

This adds little to what precedes it, save to foreground *sannyāsa* as
the mode of being in which "the bureaucracy of the ego"[51] has been
dismantled and all attachments have been left behind. Here it must be
reiterated that the normal translation of *sannyāsa* as "renunciation" is
quite inadequate if that term signifies only the visible austerities which,
for example, are made through the monastic vows of poverty, obedience, and chastity. Quite clearly Abhishiktananda means much more
than this; in the end *sannyāsa*, renunciation in its full sense, entails the
renunciation of the renouncer, if one may so put it. The flame-colored
robe of the *sannyāsī* signifies the "blazing fire" in which the ego is
consumed. The true *sannyāsī* has no "supports"—

> . . . no revelation, no ecstasy, no man, no event, no *dīkṣā*, nothing
> whatever can be his support; he is founded upon himself. The inner

awakening sets him free from every bondage, and enables him to see with direct vision what the eye could never see.

He has answered the "unconditional summons to the beyond," the call of the *Upanishads* which "comes from beyond time and space."[52]

• *The call to complete renunciation cuts across all* dharmas *and disregards all frontiers. No doubt the call reaches individuals through the particular forms of their own* dharma. . . .

The first part of this formulation has been discussed in detail elsewhere. It is the sentence following which needs accenting here: "the call reaches individuals through the particular forms of their own *dharma*"—hence *the indispensability and inviolability of the forms, even for those of jnanic disposition.* It also implicitly explains why no true esoteric will ever adopt a condescending attitude to those very forms which beckoned him to that "beyond" which can never be captured in any form. Nor, as Abhishiktananda realizes, will the "knower of Brahman" be foolish enough to propose any kind of so-called "universal religion" which could never be more than an artificial and Promethean syncretism usurping the function of orthodox religious forms.[53]

The one who has penetrated religious forms, and thus gone beyond them, will not jettison them but understand and respect their function on the plane on which they are situated. Just as Sankara continued to pray to both Siva and Vishnu after "his" realization, so Abhishiktananda continued to celebrate the Eucharist until his very last days and, in the words of his disciple, "never ceased to contemplate the Mystery which has a Face even as the Gospel presents it in the person of Jesus, and at the same time the Mystery that has no face as it was revealed in the hearts of India's Rishis, the Sages of yore."[54] From Abhishiktananda's journal:

> Once you have recognized the fundamental truth of the religious myth and of the multiple forms it has taken you accept the symbolic truth of every formulation, every rite, etc., but you obstinately refuse to give them an absolute value. . . . But there is no dishonesty in taking part in a rite—for when you recognize its symbolic character, you "perform" it with still greater truth than does one who believes in the absolute value of his ritual gestures or words.[55]

Later in the same entry he writes, "There is no thought about the mystery which is not already *nāma-rūpa*, formulation."

In a letter to Marc Chaduc, written in the last year of his earthly sojourn, Abhishiktananda writes:

What a purification from all attachment is this meeting with the East, which compels us to recognize as *nāma-rūpa* all that previously we considered to be most sacred, to be the very Truth contained in "words." Later we have to be able to recognize the value of *nāma-rūpa*, *not less than we did "before," but we have discovered another level of truth*—the blinding sun of high noon.[56]

Once the awakening to the inner mystery has occurred,

> We find ourselves once more Christian, Hindu, Buddhist, for each one has his own line of development, marked out already from his mother's lap. But we also have the "smile." Not a smile which looks down condescendingly from above, still less a smile of mockery, but one which is simply an opening out, like the flower unfolding its petals.[57]

Abhishiktananda, understandably, often grew impatient with a superficial and literalist attachment to religious forms, sometimes expressed in a bogus religiosity, and always liable to be an obstacle to spiritual growth. Doubtless he would have agreed with Schuon's warning that,

> The exoteric viewpoint is, in fact, doomed to end by negating itself once it is no longer vivified by the presence within it of the esoterism of which it is both the outward radiation and the veil. So it is that religion, according to the measure in which it denies metaphysical and initiatory realities and becomes crystallized in literalistic dogmatism, inevitably engenders unbelief; the atrophy that overtakes dogmas when they are deprived of their internal dimension recoils upon them from outside, in the form of heretical and atheistic negations.[58]

On the other hand he was no less alert than Schuon to the danger of imagining that religious forms could be discarded or repudiated: "What's important . . . is to be sufficiently 'deep' in order to transcend the letter, which does not mean to reject it."[59] In a late article, after discussing the conditions in which fruitful interreligious dialogue can occur, he goes on to say,

> This does not amount to saying that formulations, structures, and rituals have to be discarded. They are necessary signs at the level of mental perception and life in society; casting them aside, except perhaps in some extreme situations—this precisely is the intuition of the Hindu *sannyāsa*—would result in depriving oneself of the normal ways of making manifest in actual life one's deep intuition of the mystery of God and man. But, in order to be true and to remain alive, those external elements must always be related in a living manner to that deep experience of which they are the sign.[60]

• *In the end it is in that call arising from the depths of the human heart that all great dharmas really meet each other and discover their innermost truth in that attraction beyond themselves which they all share. This fundamental urge towards the Infinite is altogether beyond the reach of either sense or intellect.*

This passage testifies to the outer diversity and inner unity of the *dharmas*. Their "innermost truth" constitutes the single center from which the religions emerge and "the fundamental urge towards the Infinite" signals the same center, beyond the reach of the senses and the mind alike, to which they return. As Abhishiktananda observed of religious pluralism, "diversity does not mean disunity, once the Center of all has been reached."[61] Herein lies the basis for a true spiritual ecumenicism which affirms the one Truth but which cherishes its manifold expressions. It points towards the imperatives of a properly-constituted interreligious dialogue, close to Abhishiktananda's heart and the subject of the next chapter.

Notes

1. FS 26.
2. F. Schuon, *Spiritual Perspectives*, 112.
3. HCMP 115.
4. BA 22.
5. BA 23.
6. L 10.7.69, 217.
7. FS 7.
8. F. Schuon, *Logic and Transcendence*, 144.
9. From Abhishiktananda's journal, quoted in Kalliath, 325.
10. See Abhishiktananda's article, "Archétypes religieux, expérience du soi et théologie chrétienne," in *Intériorité et révélation: essais théologiques*, Sisteron: Présence, 1982, 1970; discussed in Friesen, 256-257.
11. FS 25-27.
12. M. Lings, *What is Sufism?*, 11-12. See also S.H. Nasr, *Sufi Essays*, 30.
13. F. Schuon, *Light on the Ancient Worlds*, 35, and *Spiritual Perspectives*, 110-111.
14. F. Schuon, *Light on the Ancient Worlds*, 136. See also *Esoterism as Principle*, 10-11, and *Logic and Transcendence*, 261.
15. F. Schuon, *In the Tracks of Buddhism*, 120.
16. B. Keeble, "Tradition, Intelligence, and the Artist," 239.
17. F. Schuon, "No Activity Without Truth" in H. Oldmeadow (ed), *The Betrayal of Tradition*, 10. See also F. Schuon, *Stations of Wisdom*, 17.
18. M. Buber, *A Believing Humanism*, 113.

19. From *Nature, Man, and God*, quoted by J. Wach, *The Comparative Study of Religions*, 44.

20. Pr 14.

21. See M. Pallis, *A Buddhist Spectrum*, 152.

22. See M. Lings, *Mecca: From Before Genesis Until Now*, 1-2, and *What is Sufism?*, 25n, and F. Schuon, *Spiritual Perspectives*, 110-111, and *Understanding Islam*, 44n.

23. DD 204.

24. F. Schuon, *Gnosis: Divine Wisdom*, 32.

25. F. Schuon, *Gnosis: Divine Wisdom*, 32. For some mapping of these branches and some account of their differences see Schuon's essay "The Meaning of Race" in *Language of the Self*, 173-200. This essay should be read in conjunction with "Principle of Distinction in the Social Order" in the same volume. These essays can also be found in F. Schuon, *Castes and Races*, the latter essay appearing under the title "The Meaning of Caste."

26. F. Schuon, *Gnosis: Divine Wisdom*, 29.

27. F. Schuon, *Gnosis: Divine Wisdom*, 30. (This is not to suggest that all "religions" which claim to derive from a "Revelation" do so in fact, nor that there is no such thing as a pseudo-religion.)

28. F. Schuon, *Light on the Ancient Worlds*, 35. See also W. Perry, "The Revival of Interest in Tradition."

29. M. Pallis, *The Way and the Mountain*, 203.

30. M. Pallis, *The Way and the Mountain*, 9.

31. T.S. Eliot, *Notes Towards the Definition of Culture*, 28.

32. See S. H. Nasr, *Ideals and Realities of Islam*, 15.

33. D 26.8.63, 259.

34. F. Schuon, *Gnosis: Divine Wisdom*, 30.

35. DD 213.

36. L 30.1.73, 285.

37. L 30.1.73, 286.

38. For a detailed discussion of Abhishiktananda's "Jungian" tendencies, see Friesen, Appendix, 489-525.

39. See F. Schuon, *Understanding Islam*, 144, and *Dimensions of Islam*, 136.

40. S.H. Nasr, *Ideals and Realities of Islam*, 15.

41. FS 42.

42. EL 43-44.

43. F. Schuon, *Light on the Ancient Worlds*, 139.

44. F. Schuon, *Understanding Islam*, 139. See also *Sufism: Veil and Quintessence*, 112.

45. F. Schuon, *Esoterism as Principle*, 16.

46. F. Schuon, *Esoterism as Principle*, 29.

47. F. Schuon, *Logic and Transcendence*, 144, and *Esoterism as Principle*, 37.

48. F. Schuon, *Esoterism as Principle*, 19.

49. F. Schuon, *Esoterism as Principle*, 37.

50. F. Schuon, *Esoterism as Principle*, 37.

51. Chögyam Trungpa's phrase.
52. FS 27, 36-37, 63.
53. FS 25, 98.
54. Chaduc quoted by Odette Baumer-Despeigne in P. Coff, "Abhishiktananda" website. See also A. Sharma, "Sankara's Bhakti and Abhishiktananda's 'Adult Faith.'"
55. D 2.2.73, 369.
56. L 26.1.73, 285 (italics mine).
57. L 26.1.73, 285.
58. F. Schuon, *The Transcendent Unity of Religions*, 9.
59. EL 146.
60. DD 211.
61. SAC xiii.

9

Dialogue

Meeting in the Cave of the Heart

The only principle of interreligious dialogue is
truth; the only way it can succeed is through
love.

Abhishiktananda[1]

The real religious or theological task, if you
will, begins when the two views meet head-on
inside oneself, when dialogue prompts genuine
religious pondering, and even a religious crisis, at
the bottom of a man's heart; when interpersonal
dialogue turns into intrapersonal soliloquy.

Raimon Panikkar[2]

Any effort on behalf of truth, is never in vain,
even if we cannot measure beforehand the value
or the outcome of such an activity. . . . Every ini-
tiative taken with a view to harmony between the
different cultures and for the defense of spiritual
values is good, if it has as its basis a recognition of
the great principial truths and consequently also a
recognition of tradition or of the traditions.

Frithjof Schuon[3]

"Sannyāsīs or Swindlers?": The "Trinity from Tannirpalli" Under Attack

Late in 1986, *Hinduism Today*, a bi-monthly magazine of the Saiva Siddhanta Church, carried an article entitled "Catholic Ashrams: Adopting
and Adapting Hindu *Dharma.*" The author was Sita Ram Goel, a
member of a militant right-wing party and one-time Treasurer of the
Abhishiktananda Society, who had come to the view that the Christian
"*sannyāsīs*" of Shantivanam were frauds and swindlers whose ultimate
purpose, behind a smokescreen of rhetoric about "dialogue," remained
the conversion of Hindus to Christianity. This article proved to be the
first fusillade in a series of attacks on Christian ashrams in general and
on the "Trinity from Tannirpalli" (Monchanin, Le Saux, and Griffiths)
in particular. One Swami Devananda Saraswati of Madras, an American

convert, took up the polemical cudgels and carried the attack through the pages of the *Indian Express*. Bede Griffiths reluctantly responded to the vituperative attacks from Goel and Devananda. It would be easy to dismiss their criticisms as the churlish and spiteful outbursts of Hindu "fundamentalists," and no doubt much of what they wrote was misinformed and uncharitable; the charge that up to his dying day Abhishiktananda's driving purpose was a kind of conversion by stealth of Hindus is clearly, to say the least of it, spurious. However, some understanding of the history of Christian missionizing in India, and its auxiliary role in European imperialism, provides a context in which the attacks by Goel and Devananda become more intelligible. Long-standing European assumptions of religious, cultural, and racial superiority had come home to roost, and had inflamed Indian sensitivities to a point where umbrage might be taken on the slightest of provocations—as was the case when Swami Devananda was spurred into a polemical delirium by the ostensibly harmless but perhaps ill-considered remark of Dr Wayne Teasdale when, in a talk in Madras, he described Bede Griffiths as "Britain's appropriate gift to India." Swami Devananda fired off a letter to the *Indian Express* which, in the event, was not published but did circulate amongst some of the combatants in the ensuing imbroglio. In his letter, Devananda wrote this:

> Ten years ago I suggested to a papal nuncio that I might don a friar's habit and preach Hinduism in the Italian countryside. I was promptly warned that I would be charged with impersonating a cleric and public mischief, as Roman Catholicism was the protected state religion and in full control of Italian education. Hinduism is neither protected nor India's state religion and we find priests like Bede Griffiths in the garb of Hindu *sannyāsīs* preaching Christianity in the Tamil countryside. Bede Griffiths has no grasp at all of the Indian psyche. It must be brought to his attention that he is meddling with the soul of a very old and sophisticated people by continuing his experiments at Shantivanam.[4]

Bede Griffiths' measured reply to this letter provoked an even more hostile and embittered response from the swami:

> In that you are a Roman priest and a Benedictine monk, you cannot possibly be a *sannyāsīn*; it is verily a contradiction in terms. . . . Christianity, from its inception to today, has subsumed and subverted the deities, symbols, rituals, and philosophies of the peoples it wishes to conquer. This activity which is imperial and not spiritual, must cease before hostilities and mistrust will die; hostilities, by the way, that we never invited in the first place. By trying to justify your position as it is now, you impugn Hinduism, slur *sannyāsa*, rout reason, ruin meaning, mutilate categories, transpose symbols, deny sacred convention and

usage, profane principles, philosophize, and generally present an argument that is oxymoronic.[5]

It is not our purpose here to trace the sometimes squalid debate which ensued and which reached its culmination, on the Hindu side, with the publication of Goel's book, first published under the same title as his *Hinduism Today* article but subsequently subtitled "*Sannyāsīs* or Swindlers?" However, the episode is a salutary reminder that in India the whole question of interreligious dialogue is charged with various residual political and racial resonances which sometimes obscure and distort the spiritual purpose of such dialogue. It should also be acknowledged that some of Goel's criticisms were cogent. From an orthodox Hindu viewpoint, for example, there *was* something offensive in the assumption of the garb of the *sannyāsī* by these Western monks. None of the Tannirpalli Trinity had undergone a formal initiation (*dīkṣā*); none of them belonged to a *sampradāya* (lineage) under the authority of a recognized guru; none of them spent significant periods in traditional Hindu *maṭhas*; none of them spent much time with traditional Hindu teachers. (Abhishiktananda's close friend Swami Chidananda, whatever his merits, does not fit the bill here as the Sivananda Ashram is, in Klaus Klostermaier's words, a "modern, non-traditional outfit, geared towards a liberal clientele, including foreigners."[6]) One can also sympathize with Goel's anger over what he saw as their appropriation of Hindu rituals and symbols, and understand how this might be seen as a kind of "spiritual imperialism." As Klostermaier has remarked, genuine interreligious dialogue is no easy matter, and "presupposes on both sides a large measure of generosity, a willingness to undertake a new beginning, to break with the past, and to leave the well-trodden paths of theological stereotypes."[7] In order to understand the Indian religious climate better, before turning to Abhishiktananda's engagement with the "problem" of dialogue, it would be as well to take some note of the long history of Christian missionizing in the sub-continent.

The Background of Christian Missionizing[8]

Over the last century Christian missionaries have had a bad press. The Theosophists, the neo-Hindu reformers, Western Vedantins, fictionalists such as Somerset Maugham, historians, and the post-colonial critics, have all denounced the whole missionary enterprise. Its cooperative role in the spread of European imperialism and in the extirpation of traditional cultures has, quite properly, come under heavy fire. On the other hand, it must be recognized that the enemies of Christianity (and often of religion in general) are ever-ready to portray its representatives in the worst possible light, to attribute to them the most sinister of motives, and to sheet home to them all manner of ills. Certainly there is no hiding from the dismal fact that an arrogant and intolerant Christian exclusivism has sometimes been an accomplice in rapacious empire-building—a sad and sorry chapter in the history of Christianity. At the same time, it is worth remembering that missionaries often resisted and condemned the exploitative aspects of imperialism. Recent scholarship has only confirmed "the great variety of missionary relationships to and attitudes toward imperialism, so that no generalization, save that of variety, can be maintained."[9]

To caution that we should not be too hasty in a blanket condemnation of missionaries we need only recall the pioneering work of the Jesuits in India, Tibet, China and Japan in dispelling European ignorance about Asian religions and the cultures which were their outward expression: the legacy of men such as Fathers Nobili, Desideri, Matteo Ricci, and Francis Xavier in promoting a genuine dialogue between West and East and in opening European eyes to the spiritual riches of the East is not one that can just be waved away. Think, too, of the role of missionaries who have, in some sense, become advocates of Asian religious and philosophical traditions *against* the European values and assumptions which they themselves ostensibly represent: one may mention figures such as Dwight Goddard, Richard Wilhelm and, more recently, Klaus Klostermaier, and the missionary-sinologist, D.H. Smith. In recent times missionaries have often been in the vanguard of movements for national liberation and the achievement of human rights and social justice. So, the story of missionary activity is a complex one. We shall not here attempt any history of Western missions in India; rather, without gainsaying the sometimes disastrous effects of Christian missionizing in the sub-continent, we shall touch on some of its more positive outcomes.

Vasco da Gama arrived in the south Indian port of Calicut in 1498, and Pedro Cabral in Cochin two years later. The search for spices was soon joined by the quest for souls. The earliest European missionaries in India were Franciscans and Dominicans, soon to be followed by the redoubtable Jesuits. By the middle of the sixteenth century the Jesuits were entrenched in Goa and its hinterland, and well-advanced on their first major task—the mastery of the principal languages of the region. In 1579 the British Jesuit Thomas Stephens arrived in Goa and was soon able to produce several works in Indian languages, culminating in his 11,000-verse *Christian Purana*, "the unsurpassed masterpiece of Christian missionary literature in an Indian vernacular."[10] But it was

Father Roberto Nobili (1577-1656) who "led the missionary effort to an entirely new level of theoretical and hermeneutic awareness" and who best exemplifies "the problematic nature of the encounter between Christianity and Hinduism."[11] His efforts to find some sort of doctrinal *rapprochement* between the two traditions inevitably overstepped the ecclesiastical bounds of orthodoxy. Nobili found in the *Upanishads* a pristine monotheism and even intimations of the "recondite mystery of the most sacred trinity," discerned the "natural light" of reason in Brahminical sciences and philosophy, and argued against their dismissal by Europeans as superstitious, "as if the heathen sages were not also bringing forth valuable teachings which could likewise be of use to Christians."[12] Nobili found some precedent for his approach to Hinduism in the reception of Greek thought by the early Fathers. Nor was Nobili playing a lone hand. Heinrich Roth (1620-1668) produced the first European Sanskrit grammar, philosophical commentaries, and translations. Father J.F. Pons, another Jesuit, was probably the author of a grammar of Sanskrit in Latin in about 1733. Then, too, there were the Protestant missionary scholars such as the Dutch Calvinists Abraham Roger and Philippus Baldaeus who published Indological works in the seventeenth century, and the Moravian Bartholomäus Ziegenbalg who wrote substantial hermeneutical works on the customs and beliefs of the Hindus.

In his remarkable study of the encounter between India and Europe Wilhelm Halbfass has pointed out that the work of the missionaries of the seventeenth and eighteenth centuries laid the foundations of Indological research well before the appearance of the Asiatic Society of Bengal in 1784 and the pioneering scholarship of Jones, Wilkins, and Colebrooke, the first British Orientalists-proper. The legacy of the Jesuits was to be found not only in their texts—grammars, dictionaries, translations, commentaries, and the like—but in the collection of manuscripts and their methods of collaboration with Indian scholars.[13]

By the mid-nineteenth century the missionary ethos was increasingly influenced by the idea of fulfillment, foreshadowed in some of Nobili's writings and embryonic in the thinking of Max Müller and Monier Monier-Williams. The Scottish missionary and Indologist J.N. Farquhar was perhaps its most influential exponent. Thus, following T.E. Slater's claim that "All religions wait for their fulfillment in Christianity," Farquhar could argue that

> The Vedanta is not Christianity, and never will be—simply as the Vedanta: but a very definite preparation for it. . . . It is our belief that the living Christ will sanctify and make complete the religious thought

of India. For centuries . . . her saints have been longing for him, and her thinkers, not least the thinkers of the Vedanta have been thinking his thought.[14]

Furthermore, he added,

This is the attitude of Jesus to all other religions also. Each contains a partial revelation of God's will, but each is incomplete; and He comes to fulfill them all. In each case Christianity seeks not to destroy but to take all that is right and raise it to perfection.[15]

Christianity was to become "the crown of Hinduism" (the title of Farquhar's most influential book, published in 1913). We have already seen how fulfillment theology pervaded the thinking of Monchanin and Abhishiktananda in the 1950s. This idea was later to find an ironic echo in the neo-Hindu and Vedantin claim that all other religions and creeds are subsumed by Vedanta.

During the twentieth century many missionary societies and individual missionaries have had to come to terms with the palpable historical fact that, in India at least (and indeed most other Asian countries, the Philippines and to a lesser extent Korea, being the notable exceptions), Christian triumphalism was quite misplaced, that the rates of conversion are pitifully small, that while most Hindus are perfectly willing to accept the divinity of Christ as one *avatāra* among many, they remain quite impervious to the fulfillment theory and its many variants. So much for the kind of thinking behind Macaulay's boast in 1836 that English education would see to it that thirty years hence "there will not be a single idolater [i.e., Hindu] among the respectable classes in Bengal."[16] The general failure of Christian missionaries to win significant number of converts eventually moved the accent of mission work onto ideals of witness, service, and dialogue rather than conversion.[17] It would be a mistake to measure the validity of the missionary enterprise purely in terms of conversion rates. As Schuon has remarked,

[Christian] missionaries—although they have profited from abnormal circumstances inasmuch as Western expansion at the expense of other civilizations is due solely to a crushing material superiority arising out of the modern deviation—follow a way that possesses, at least in principle, a sacrificial aspect; consequently the subjective reality of this way will always retain its mystic meaning.[18]

Surveying over three centuries of European missionizing in India, Wilhelm Halbfass concludes:

The missionary efforts in this country can hardly be described as having been successful, and dogmatism and intolerance have frequently played a dominating role. . . . This notwithstanding, the achievements of the missionaries comprise a very important chapter in the Western encounter with Indian thought, a chapter that is exemplary from a hermeneutic standpoint and which, moreover, has had historical consequences. The missionaries have performed pioneering, detailed work in several areas. *But primarily, in spite of or perhaps precisely because of their "prejudice" and dogmatic limitations, they have also helped to define and clarify the central problems involved in approaching and understanding that which is alien.* . . . Their outstanding exponents embody a desire to understand whose singular power and problematic nature arise from their deep and uncompromising *desire to be understood.*[19]

As we have seen, the "problematic nature" of missionizing is dramatically personified in the lives and work of the three Benedictine monks who came under such heavy censure from Swami Devananda and Sita Ram Goel. Certain themes and issues circulate through the experiences and writings of each: the so-called "problem" of religious pluralism, the proper role of Christianity in India, the renewal of Christian monasticism and the revival of its contemplative and mystical heritage, the doctrinal reconciliation of a non-dualistic Vedanta with a Trinitarian Christianity, the existential problem of living out a spirituality which drew on both Eastern and Western sources. It is only in the context of a long and troubled history of the encounter between Hinduism and Christianity that we can understand Abhishiktananda's efforts to forge a new model of interreligious dialogue.

Abhishiktananda and Hindu-Christian Dialogue

Of Abhishiktananda, James Royster has written

It is, in fact, doubtful if any Christian monk in the second half of the twentieth century has taken more seriously than Abhishiktananda the deep call to discover and explore experientially the ultimate ground that unites monks of different traditions. To have profound religious experiences by means of the perspectives and practices of a tradition other than one's own is to know in one's heart, with experiential certitude and not simply intellectual opinion, that the Sacred is not confined to one's own spiritual heritage. One encounters undeniable "proof" of the non-temporal/spatial nature of the Sacred, and interreligious relationship or dialogue takes on a qualitatively new meaning. Abhishiktananda's penetration of the spiritual depths in both Hinduism and Christianity provides a revealing demonstration of transmonastic dialogue in depth.[20]

This can be endorsed without any equivocation. However, before proceeding it will perhaps be useful to distinguish five different modes of dialogue, three of which concerned Abhishiktananda deeply. Firstly, there is what Eric Sharpe has called *discursive dialogue*, the courteous and sympathetic meeting of adherents of different faiths to openly and honestly discuss their beliefs and practices. Secondly, there is what I will label "*common front*" *dialogue*, where representatives of different faiths meet together in an attempt to forge creative responses to problems of mutual concern. Such meetings may focus on the contribution the religious faiths might make to the solution of various ostensibly "secular" problems such as poverty, environmental crises, the abuse of human rights, and so on. (The Dalai Lama has been in the forefront of this kind of dialogue in recent times). Or, such dialogue might take up a more defensive posture, looking for ways to meet the challenges which face all religious traditions in the modern world—materialism, humanism, atheism, and suchlike.[21] Thirdly, there is *intrareligious dialogue*, in which persons of the same faith (though perhaps of different denominations or groups) exchange their spiritual experiences and ideas about their own tradition and its relation to other traditions. Abhishiktananda engaged in such dialogue with his Protestant friends from Jyotiniketan Ashram at Shantivanam, Nagpur, Rajpur, and elsewhere. The fourth kind of exchange might be called *experiential interreligious dialogue*, usually focusing on the interior aspects of spirituality. Such dialogue is especially favored by people of contemplative disposition and it is no surprise that monks and nuns have spearheaded this kind of dialogue in recent times. Finally, there is what we might call *interior dialogue*, or, in Panikkar's phrase, "*intrapersonal soliloquy*" wherein two faiths meet in the one human heart. Without discounting the value of the first two types of dialogue, Abhishiktananda was primarily concerned with the last three modes. Indeed, at the expense of some over-simplification, one might say that from the late 50s until his death he passed successively through the intra-religious, experiential inter-religious and interior modes of dialogue.

Generally speaking, most of the initiatives in East-West interreligious dialogue have come from the Christian side. This may be related to the keener sense in this tradition of some deficiency which might be remedied by creative intercourse with Eastern traditions. Interreligious dialogue may also be felt, perhaps subconsciously, as a kind of atonement for the historical ignominies of missionizing triumphalism and Western colonialism, and as a counter to the evangelical excesses of current day fundamentalists.[22] More positively it may derive from certain dynamic, outward-looking, and frontier-seeking tendencies in Christianity and the Western *mythos* generally.[23] On the other side, the comparative reticence of Easterners in sponsoring interreligious dialogue may stem from a post-colonial wariness of the colonizing and universalizing tendencies in Western thought whilst many Asian adherents feel no dissatisfaction with their own tradition such as might impel initiatives in this direction.

Abhishiktananda's ideas about dialogue changed under the pressure of his experiences in India. Our purpose here is not to recapitulate this history but to throw into relief certain recurrent themes and preoccupations. As in previous chapters we shall focus most directly on his later years when he reached his deepest understanding of the many awkward issues implicit in the idea and practice of dialogue. Our attention will be fixed, in the first place, on a posthumously published article in which Abhishiktananda gives one of his most considered accounts of "the depth-dimension of religious dialogue."

An Ontological and Theological Basis for Dialogue

Abhishiktananda begins his article with the observation that "Man is a social being," that there can be no "person" apart from others, and that man finds and realizes himself through his relationship and communion with others. Isolated from his fellows a man would shrink from his own humanity. In the case of the one called to a life of solitude he must have already served an apprenticeship in human fellowship, and in solitude must discover within "that center where no human being, indeed no other creature, is distant from him." Interrelationship becomes dialogue when this ontological principle of relatedness is consciously accepted and integrated:

> It is the person freely accepting its condition of being a relation, of being a thou to others; that is, accepting to live with them on the level of exchange, of symbiosis, of giving and receiving. Accepting to be a thou for the other is accepting him as an I, with all the characteristics of "I-ness" which I experience in my own person . . . recognizing the other as a subject like myself, an absolute, a universal center.[24]

In these Buberian terms, Abhishiktananda thus established an ontological rationale for dialogue: it answers to man's nature as a social being, living in conscious relationship with others. Not accidentally or fortuitously, this ontology is a reflection of a theological truth: in the Christian perspective, man's relatedness is mirrored in the "being-one-together" of the divine Persons. The Trinitarian mystery of the Godhead reveals that relatedness inheres in the very source of being. The Christian religion itself is an ongoing dialogue—between God and man, Jesus and the Father, and man and man. For Abhishiktananda dialogue is a process of *discovery* which far outreaches philosophical debate and speculation because it engages our ultimate existential concerns; it originates in the depth of our consciousness, and invites us to an ever-deepening self-awareness.

Religious Pluralism

Abhishiktananda lived through a period in which Christian attitudes to other religions were undergoing radical changes. The growing acceptance of religious pluralism was "a sign of the times which no believer should disregard." Here too Abhishiktananda finds a theological and ontological sanction for pluralism:

> Pluralism is a mark of human society, precisely because man is a being in community. Communion implies likeness but not identity. Identity suppresses communion and is the death of all relationships. Pluralism is a gift of God; it is part of the gift God makes to men in their human nature.[25]

He concedes that the challenge of religious pluralism had frightened some people into the bunkers, so to speak, protecting themselves with an aggressive fundamentalism which condemns all "others." He also recognizes that

> Another attitude, steadily on the increase and brought about precisely by the narrowness and intolerance of too many self-proclaimed believers, is a sort of estrangement from all religious forms and structures, with resort to merely personal sincerity and commitment.[26]

Nonetheless, Abhishiktananda urges Christians "to the joyful acceptance of the multiplicity of forms through which the divine Spirit brings men to the Father" and to the understanding that "God has spoken mysteriously to humankind and is still doing so in many diverse ways." Christians must recognize the Presence of the Lord "across the boundaries of their internal divisions as well as beyond the frontiers of the visible Christian fold."

Dialogue arises naturally as the "immediate consequence" of the recognition and acceptance of religious pluralism, and is a concrete way of raising that pluralism to a personal and human level:

> It is through dialogue that spiritual riches will be mutually shared, in complete disinterestedness on the part of the giver and humility on the

part of the receiver, whose roles are likely to alternate continuously in the process. Spiritual riches, even more than material riches, belong to all. They are the common property of all the children of God, and no one ever enjoys them more fully than when sharing them with his brothers.[27]

It should hardly need pointing out that this kind of acceptance of religious pluralism has nothing to do with the liberal-humanist notion of "religious tolerance." Tolerance is no substitute for a properly-constituted understanding of the inner unity of formally divergent and sometimes outwardly antagonistic religious traditions. As Coomaraswamy remarked "the very implications of the phrase 'religious tolerance' are to be avoided: diversity of faith is not a matter for 'toleration,' but of divine appointment."[28]

Meeting in the Cave of the Heart

Abhishiktananda had little interest in the kind of dialogue which focused on "structures and formulations"; such exchanges were likely to be superficial and unproductive, to end up in conceptual *cul de sacs*, and to lapse into "purely academic discussion or even an egoistic search for self-affirmation."[29] Such "dialogue" could, in fact, easily degenerate into "paralleled monologues."[30] On the formal and conceptual level the harmony of mankind is always threatened; "egoism emerges at all points, rivalry and competition set in, and with them strife." Indeed, religious disputes have perhaps been "the most potent cause of dissension and hatred among men throughout history."[31]

"*The only real meeting point between men concerned with the ultimate is in the center of the self, in 'the cave of the heart.'*"[32] Here, beyond all the differences of religious symbols and concepts, we can experience our human unity and "being-together." Indeed, the differences which are evident on the psychic, ethnic, and cultural planes, approached through the sharing of common spiritual experience, can become the very means through which we reach a new level of "being-togetherness":

> Because [such dialogue] is rooted in such solid ground, that unity, and that alone, can make room, without thereby being shaken, for the mutual otherness of all men, their cultures and civilizations. It recognizes that all are one in their origin and principle, diverse and complementary in their manifestations.[33]

This in-depth and experiential dialogue leads not to an "easy and shallow syncretism" or to "minimalism" (what has also been called "lowest common denominator" dialogue) but to "the courageous acceptance of *both the unity and the diversity* of God's creation." It will be

> a purification of each one's own faith, not indeed in its essence which is pure gold but of the alloy with which it is always mixed. It will be the *discovery of unity in diversity and diversity in unity.* From the depth at which it takes place, it will bring to light *the mutual convergence of all religions.*[34]

It follows from what has already been said that Abhishiktananda believed that any interreligious dialogue of the kind envisaged—one going well beyond friendly social relations and the expression of good will—could only be carried out by participants who had already entered the "cave of the heart." He felt that, at the very least, at least one of the partners in the dialogue must have reached these inner depths:

> If one partner lives at the level of the Spirit, he will automatically give to dialogue its proper dimension and depth; he will prevent it from staying on the plane of mere thoughts and feelings. The real meeting point between all religious-minded people can only be the place within themselves where they are on the watch for the Spirit.[35]

Interreligious dialogue, and indeed dialogue by *any* persons committed to the truth "in whatever way truth may have manifested itself in the depth of their hearts," would provide one avenue towards the solution of the many problems afflicting the world today:

> Interreligious dialogue is coming to the fore in a crucial moment of human history and the evolution of cultures, civilizations, and religions, when all previous values are being shaken and are no longer recognized, and when no one really knows what will tomorrow take the place of what is disappearing today.[36]

Abhishiktananda further insisted that interreligious dialogue should *not* "take the form of a crusade against atheism and humanism," nor be prompted merely by "a reflex of self-defense." Real dialogue can take place between all people of good will, dedicated to the truth and searching for "the means of saving the soul of mankind": "The only principle of interreligious dialogue is truth; the only way for it to succeed is love."[37]

Dialogue is the mutually enriching search for truth, for meaning and value, and for "being-together," through a new sense of interiority and a constant awareness of the Presence of God which has not been strait-jacketed into formulas, concepts, dogmas, and symbols. Abhishiktananda said,

I do not want to leave some ideas to remember, but a new interior sense, an unformulated awareness of the presence of God. The value of the words I was able to speak to you lay in their resonance rather than in their immediate meaning. Once conceptualized, this truth which I bear is no longer true.[38]

Dialogue begins and ends in "the silence of the Spirit," a silence which penetrates and enriches the words and ideas exchanged in the interval. Klaus Klostermaier, recounting his meetings with Hindu friends in Vrindaban, writes, "Strangely, my friends whom I thus met also told me that, if we sat together silently, they often understood more than if we talked."[39]

Dialogue and Theology, and the Encounter of East and West

Dialogue, Abhishiktananda argues, is integral to a full Christian theology; any theology which treats dialogue as an "appendix," a kind of optional add-on without any bearing on the substance of theology, a "superimposition" without any effect on our deepest religious convictions, has no existential value or relevance. Dialogue must be an "intrinsic component" of both theology and spirituality, particularly in the times in which we live. This kind of dialogue will inevitably lead to some theological rethinking and it may well administer some therapeutic shocks to any theology which has not yet integrated the religious "others." Furthermore, we are at a juncture in history where "Only a contemplative spirituality can be the proper foundation for a pluralistic theology."[40] Such a theology cannot simply start from conventional Christian dogmas:

> To start from Jesus within his Jewish *mythos*, and still more within the wider Mediterranean *mythos* in which the Church has projected his image, in order to establish a theology of religions (i.e. to judge everything in relation to Helleno-Judaic Christian theology and on that basis to pass judgment on the value of similar formulations or structures elsewhere) is simply false.[41]

The dialogue between Hindus and Christians will always "limp" into a "blind alley" if it is restricted to discussion of "theology, technical philosophical questions and formulations" all of which are often only the "petrified" forms of the "primordial intuitions." *Eidos*, its "extreme value" notwithstanding, is often a barrier to the kind of dialogue Abhishiktananda envisages, one rooted in the *direct experiential intuitions* themselves. Such dialogue requires a deep level of self-awareness, a freedom from cultural and religious accretions, and an unflinching openness and love for the "other." It is therefore a matter of the utmost seriousness and not to be entered into lightly or superficially: "If it does not bring me to the center of my heart, to the very source of my life and faith, it is a lie."[42] For Abhishiktananda true dialogue is not an exchange of ideas about religion but is itself a spiritual activity.

For Christians, Abhishiktananda writes, the encounter with Hinduism must be directed towards the assimilation of the advaitic experience. A merely theoretical understanding of Vedanta is of little use. Rather, *advaita* must, so to speak, infuse the Christian mode of understanding our relation with God, and be recognized as the pinnacle of human experience:

> The self-awareness of advaitic experience is the highest human experience. It must therefore be capable of being taken up [in a Christian context], redeemed and transformed by the Holy Spirit, into the very experience of divine sonship which was the foundation of Jesus' personal self-awareness, and which he imparts to all those who give their faith to him.[43]

Abhishiktananda does not hide from the fact that such "interior dialogue" can be threatening and frightening, as it challenges all of our normal securities; it operates as a kind of "searchlight," probing the furthest recesses of the soul. But it is only through such experience and self-awareness that we can enjoy the fearless freedom and joy which is our inheritance as the sons and daughters of God. The "risks" inherent in both the advaitic experience and in-depth dialogue are apparent enough in Abhishiktananda's reflections in his journal, late in his life:

> We must accept the two conflicting axes around which this inner experience has been expressed: the Abrahamic axis with its three descendants—and the Vedantin axis, with its Buddhist complement. Then we take note of the essentially *nāma-rūpa* value of all formulations-structures, whether they are Upanishadic, Buddhist, Islamic, or Christian. At that point we no longer seek to express the mystery of Jesus in Indian terms, those for example of *avatāras*, or of the *Puruṣa*, or the guru. . . . All that is a matter of correspondences between myths and *nāma-rūpa*. They only lead to dead ends. . . . The problem of the uniqueness of Jesus, the only Incarnate One, is a false problem. It arises only in the domain of *nāma-rūpas*. For the uniqueness of the Person is inaccessible, indefinable.[44]

Abhishiktananda and Gandhi on the Religious "Other"

Over the last few decades there has been much discussion about the interrelationships of the religious traditions and various models of dialogue have been widely canvassed in ecclesiastical and scholarly circles as well as "on the ground" amongst religious adherents, especially monks and nuns. It is beyond our present scope to survey these developments. Nor will we make any attempt to situate Abhishiktananda's ideas about interreligious dialogue in any theoretical framework, nor to compare them with those of other advocates of experiential dialogue—Thomas Merton, Bede Griffiths, W. Cantwell Smith, Klaus Klostermaier to name a few; these tasks have already been taken up by several scholars.[45] Rather we will simply take note of one interesting article by Judson Trapnell, who has drawn a comparison between the approaches of Mahatma Gandhi and Abhishiktananda to the religious "other"—Gandhi's "reperception" of Christianity, and Abhishiktananda's response to Hinduism.

Gandhi's engagements with Christianity are well known and need only be rehearsed in barest outline. He was raised to respect all religions but took exception to Christianity because of the disrespect for Hinduism evinced by many missionaries and Indian converts. While studying law in England and practicing it in South Africa, he read the *Bible* and was especially struck by the *New Testament* which went "straight to my heart." He studied Christian theology, attended prayer meetings and religious services, and participated in a Protestant convention, as well as developing close friendships with many Christians. He found many parallels between Christianity and his own Hindu and Jain traditions, and was eventually to affirm the essential unity of all the great religions.

Gandhi's own spiritual practice centered on *nāma-japa* which he claimed was his "surest aid" and "the best of all remedies adopted for the practice of truth and non-violence." The depth of his commitment to *nāma-japa* is evident in his final words, "Ram, Ram," as he died at the hands of an assassin. One of the three great principles which governed the whole of Gandhi's adult life, *satyāgraha* ("truth-force") was based upon a love for his opponents. (The other two were *brahmacarya*, self-control/celibacy, and *ahiṁsā*, non-injuriousness.) *Satyāgraha* was aimed at a "conversion," not in any formal religious sense, but rather "a turning of that heart [of the opponent] toward that same love through one's own suffering." He stated that the requirement of love for the other is based on "a glimpse of the *Ātma* that transcends the body," a teaching he derived from the *Gītā*. One struggles for what one believes is right and just, but without attachment to the results. Trapnell:

> Here is the necessary pole of any experiment in opening to the viewpoint of the religious "other": Not only must one attempt to understand it from inside, one must also be willing to criticize and even stand up against the other's viewpoint when what Gandhi assumed are universealizable standards of truth and justice are violated. One can understand this balance as the openness for true immersion [in the other's viewpoint] in tension with conviction about certain principles that transcend the diversity of religions. Gandhi thus exemplifies how the relativization of one's viewpoint that may occur as a result of interreligious dialogue does not need to end in relativism; the relativity of points of view may be grounded in the experience of and faith in a common absolute.[46]

On the basis of these three methods mentioned above—immersion in the viewpoint and experiences of religious others through study and friendship, spiritual praxis, and the struggle for social justice—Gandhi was able to make such statements as these:

> After long study and experience, I have come to the conclusion that (1) all religions are true; (2) all religions have some error in them; (3) all religions are almost as dear to me as my own Hinduism, inasmuch as all human beings should be as dear to me as one's own close relatives. My own veneration for other faiths is the same as that for my own faith.[47]

Gandhi's experiences enabled him to change his perception of Christianity and to move from an attitude of youthful intolerance to one of profound respect.

Unlike Gandhi, Abhishiktananda did not grow up in a climate of religious inclusiveness—on the contrary. As Trapnell remarks, "Abhishiktananda's specific struggles to reperceive the religious 'other' are indeed symptomatic of his Western Christian conditioning." Yet he was able to respond to Gandhi's invitation to all Christians, "I have no desire to dislodge you from the exclusive homage you pay to Jesus. But I would like you to understand and appreciate the other inclusive position." Each had to overcome both an interior and an external resistance to his changing understanding of religious pluralism, and their mature views only crystallized after a long period of rigorous self-discipline.

In his comparison of the transformation of Gandhi and Abhishiktananda's understanding Trapnell asks, "What, then, does this French priest teach us about the general human problem of the misperception of the religious 'other'?" His answer:

He illustrates the value of immersing oneself in the culture and religion of the "other," but also the internal resistance to changing one's point of view even in response to such broadened experience. He indicates the virtue of interreligious friendships, but also the often painful dialogue between the living lessons taught in such relationships and the assumptions, beliefs, and commitments that constitute one's pre-existing viewpoint. In addition, he argues for the deliberate yet grace-filled discipline of mystical praxis as an essential foundation for interreligious encounter. . . . Abhishiktananda thus exemplifies the possibility of reperception, but also its cost.[48]

*

The seriousness with which Abhishiktananda took the whole question of interreligious dialogue is evident in the startling and prophetic words with which he concluded "The Depth-Dimension of Religious Dialogue":

The salvation of the world and the overcoming by the Church of its present crisis will depend on all people of good will, coming together in truth and in the spirit; all men, that is, who within themselves have heard the voice of the Spirit and have not been afraid to listen to it and to abide by it.[49]

Who is to say he was wrong? His own life is an exemplary story of a man who had "not been afraid to listen," even at the cost of a long and ruthless self-interrogation and a painful stripping away of his own ingrained religious attitudes and assumptions. Abhishiktananda came together "in truth and in the spirit" with the holy men and women of India not only on the outer physical plane but in the *guha* itself. In so doing he rediscovered both God and himself. As he wrote in an unpublished letter of 1963,

The most important thing is to free oneself from everything and to bring oneself to one's own innermost center. For that, India is not essential, thank God. However I believe that according to the order of Providence, and bearing in mind the necessary sequence of time and of the growth through time of the Body of Christ towards its fullness, India by means of its age-long preparation gives to Christians in general a reminder—at once gentle and violent—that the Lord is not to be found in the place where man imagines or thinks that he is. It is only when once a man has fully left himself behind that he discovers God, and it is in him—on the other side of this preliminary loss—that he rediscovers himself in the very depth of God.[50]

Notes

1. DD 211.
2. From *The Interreligious Dialogue*, quoted in C. Cornille, *The Guru in Indian Catholicism*, 75.
3. F. Schuon, "No Activity without Truth," 13-14.
4. Quoted in Goel's website article, "*Sannyāsīs* or Swindlers?"
5. Quoted in Goel's website article, "*Sannyāsīs* or Swindlers?"
6. K. Klostermaier, "Hindu-Christian Dialogue: Revisiting the Tannirpalli Trinity's Original Vision," 5. (This article includes an informative, nuanced, and thoughtful discussion of the "*Sannyāsīs* or Swindlers" episode and avoids some of the glib sloganeering evident on both sides of the fence.)
7. K. Klostermaier, "Hindu-Christian Dialogue," 84.
8. The following section is a condensed version of part of Chapter 9 in *Journeys East*.
9. C.W. Forman, "The Growth of the Study of the Expansion of Christianity," 32. See also S. Lund, "The Christian Mission and Colonialism."
10. W. Halbfass, *India and Europe*, 37-38.
11. W. Halbfass, *India and Europe*, 38.
12. W. Halbfass, *India and Europe*, 40.
13. W. Halbfass, *India and Europe*, 45.
14. Farquhar quoted in W. Halbfass, *India and Europe*, 51.
15. Farquhar quoted in E. Sharpe, *Not to Destroy but to Fulfill*, 260.
16. *Life and Letters of Lord Macaulay*, 455.
17. For one recent and personal understanding of missionary work, quite at odds with the notion of missionizing as a form of imperialism, see Nicholas Colasuonno, "The Pilgrim Missionary."
18. F. Schuon, *Transcendent Unity of Religions*, 81.
19. W. Halbfass, *India and Europe*, 53 (italics mine except for the last phrase).
20. J. Royster, "Dialogue in Depth," 78.
21. Eric Sharpe has called this kind of exchange "secular dialogue." See "The Goals of Inter-religious Dialogue" in J. Hick (ed), *Truth and Dialogue*, 77-95.
22. See H. Coward, "Hinduism's Sensitizing of Christianity," 77.
23. See R.E. Wentz, "The Prospective Eye of Interreligious Dialogue."
24. DD 203.
25. DD 206.
26. DD 207.
27. DD 207.
28. A. Coomaraswamy, "Sri Ramakrishna and Religious Tolerance" in *Selected Papers 2*, 42.
29. DD 205.
30. HCMP 12.
31. DD 208.
32. DD 208 (italics mine).

33. DD 208.

34. DD 211 (italics mine).

35. DD 209.

36. DD 209.

37. DD 211.

38. Quoted by Odette Baumer-Despeigne in P. Coff, "Abhishiktananda," website.

39. K. Klostermaier, *In the Paradise of Krishna*, 37.

40. DD 213.

41. D 2.2.73, 368.

42. DD 14.

43. DD 216.

44. D 2.2.73, 368.

45. See works by Klaus Klostermaier, Eric Sharpe, Robert Stephens, Wayne Teasdale, Judson Trapnell, and various others, listed in Sources.

46. J. Trapnell, "Gandhi, Abhishiktananda," website.

47. Quoted in J. Trapnell, "Gandhi, Abhishiktananda," website.

48. J. Trapnell, "Gandhi, Abhishiktananda," website.

49. DD 221.

50. Unpublished letter, 3.2.63, quoted in Stephens, 60.

III

"Unity in Diversity"

Abhishiktananda in Perspective

"Real dialogue will be a purification of
each one's own faith, not indeed in its
essence which is pure gold but of the
alloy with which it is always mixed. It
will be a discovery of unity in diversity and diversity in unity."

10

Religious Pluralism and the Perennial Philosophy

> There is a universally intelligible language, not
> only verbal but also visual, of the fundamental
> ideas on which the different civilizations have
> been founded.... We need mediators to whom the
> common universe of discourse is still a reality.
>
> *Ananda Coomaraswamy*[1]

> There are those whose vocation it is to provide the
> keys with which the treasury of wisdom of other
> traditions can be unlocked, revealing to those who
> are destined to receive this wisdom the essential
> unity and universality and at the same the formal
> diversity of tradition and revelation.
>
> *Seyyed Hossein Nasr*[2]

The Collision of Religions in the Contemporary World[3]

We are living in an unprecedented situation in which the different religious traditions are everywhere impinging on each other. There has, of course, always been some intercourse in ideas and influences between the great religious cultures. Nevertheless, each civilization formerly exhibited a spiritual homogeneity untroubled, for the most part, by the problem of religious pluralism. In former times, just as man appeared as "man" and not as "yellow man" or "white man," and just as each language seemed to its practitioners to be language as such, so too each religion, for most believers, appeared as "religion" without further qualification. To choose one example from a multitude of possibilities, the Tibetans referred to their beliefs and practices not as "Mahayana Buddhism" but simply as "the way" ("*tehen*").[4] For the vast majority of believers in a traditional civilization the question of the interrelationship of the religions was one which was either of peripheral concern or one of which they remained unaware. Martin Lings:

> Needless to say our ancestors were aware of the existence of other
> religions besides their own; but dazzled and penetrated as they were
> by the great light shining directly above them, the sight of more remote
> and—for them—more obliquely shining lights on the horizons could
> raise no positive interest nor did it create problems. Today, however

those horizons are no longer remote; and amidst the great evil which results from all that has contributed to bring them near, some good has also inevitably stolen its way in.[5]

The homogeneity of Christian civilization has long since been ruptured by secularist ideologies of one kind and another. In the last few centuries European civilization has, in turn, been the agent for the disruption and sometimes extirpation of traditional cultures the world over. Comparative religion itself, as a field of study was, in part, the product of the cultural contacts to which an aggressive European imperialism gave rise. Since then all manner of changes have made for a "smaller" world, for "the global village." For some time now it has been impossible to ignore the presence of religious cultures and traditions different from our own. The interrelationships of the religions today is an issue which has taken on a new urgency in the cyclical conditions in which we live, especially for all those concerned with fostering a harmonious world community. This problem has disturbed many Christian thinkers conscious of the excesses and brutalities to which a militant religious exclusivism sometimes gave rise. Klaus Klostermaier, Cantwell Smith, Thomas Merton, Bede Griffiths, Diana Eck, and Abhishiktananda himself are amongst some of the better-known Christian writers who have recently pondered this issue.

Furthermore, in an age of rampant secularism and skepticism the need for some kind of interreligious solidarity makes itself ever more acutely felt. At a time when "the outward and readily exaggerated incompatibility of the different religions greatly discredits, in the minds of most of our contemporaries, all religion,"[6] the exposure of the underlying unity of the religions becomes an exigent task—one that can only be achieved through esoterism. The open confrontation of different exoterisms, the destruction of traditional civilizations, and the tyranny of secular and profane ideologies all play a part in determining the peculiar circumstances in which the most imperious needs of the age can only be answered by a recourse to traditional esoterisms. There is perhaps some small hope that in this climate, and given a properly constituted metaphysical framework in which to affirm the "profound and eternal solidarity of all spiritual forms,"[7] the different religions might yet "present a singular front against the floodtide of materialism and pseudo-spiritualism."[8]

The *philosophical* question of the interrelationship of the religions and the *moral* concern for greater mutual understanding are, in fact, all of a piece. We can distinguish but not separate questions about *unity* and *harmony,* too often both comparative religionists and those engaged in dialogue have failed to see that the achievement of the latter depends on a metaphysical resolution of the former question. The problem of reconciling the apparently conflicting claims of religions has too often been shelved. The principal difficulty has been succinctly stated by Seyyed Hossein Nasr:

> The essential problem that the study of religion poses is how to preserve religious truth, traditional orthodoxy, the dogmatic theological structures of one's own tradition, and yet gain knowledge of other traditions and accept them as spiritually valid ways and roads to God.[9]

Ananda Coomaraswamy, who belonged by both nativity and disposition to both the East and the West, argued that

> the only possible ground upon which an effective *entente* of East and West can be accomplished is that of the purely intellectual wisdom that is one and the same at all times and for all men, and is independent of all environmental idiosyncrasy.[10]

In a letter of 1942 Coomaraswamy wrote, "I am in fullest agreement about the necessity of recognizing a common basis of understanding, but see no basis . . . other than that of the *philosophia perennis.*"[11] Both Nasr and Coomaraswamy belong to a "school" of thinkers sometimes referred to as "traditionalists" or "perennialists." In the course of this study we have had occasion to refer frequently to the work of several other traditionalists, René Guénon, Marco Pallis, and Frithjof Schuon among them. Elsewhere I have argued that the traditionalist exposition of the *sophia perennis* furnishes the *only* completely consistent and coherent explication of the interrelationships of the great religious traditions—in other words, the *only* satisfactory basis on which to resolve the problems arising out of religious pluralism in the modern world, at least in the intellectual domain. The traditionalist outlook decisively resolves the problem spotlighted by Nasr by providing an understanding of religious pluralism which posits their inner unity but at the same time honors their diversity. Because of its premium on the "incalculable value" of religious orthodoxy, traditionalism does not threaten religious commitments—indeed it *insists* on them—but shows how the formal antinomies of different theologies can be resolved in a metaphysical synthesis, in Coomaraswamy's words, "an intellectual wisdom . . . independent of all environmental idiosyncrasy." It is beyond the compass of the present work to give a comprehensive overview of traditionalism, a task undertaken elsewhere.[12] However, in this chapter we will provide an outline of some of the principles governing the traditionalist outlook, especially those pertaining to religious pluralism. Some of these have been adumbrated elsewhere in the present study, particularly in our discussion of the interrelation of metaphysics, theology, and philosophy in Chapter 5 and in our discussion of religious understandings of the natural order, in Chapter 6, drawing heavily on both occasions on traditionalist thinkers. After some consideration of the traditionalist outlook we will turn to a more immediate and specific question: What is the relationship of Abhishiktananda's thought to perennialism?

The Traditionalist or Perennialist Perspective

In his essay "The Pertinence of Philosophy" Ananda Coomaraswamy suggested that

> if we are to consider what may be the most urgent practical task to be resolved by the philosopher, we can only answer that this is . . . a control and revision of the principles of comparative religion, the true end of which science . . . should be to demonstrate the common metaphysical basis of all religions.[13]

This is a capsule statement of the traditionalist agenda. The traditionalist perspective was first publicly articulated in the first half of the twentieth century by the French metaphysician, René Guénon. Since the time of Guénon's earliest writings a significant traditionalist "school" has emerged with Guénon, Ananda Coomaraswamy, and Frithjof Schuon acknowledged within the group as its preeminent exponents. Seyyed Hossein Nasr refers to traditionalism as "a response of the Sacred . . . to the elegy of doom of modern man lost in a world depleted of the sacred and therefore, of meaning."[14] The traditionalists, by definition, are committed to the explication of the *philosophia perennis* which lies at the heart of the diverse religions and behind the manifold forms of the world's different traditions. At the same time, they are dedicated to the preservation and illumination of the traditional forms which give each religious heritage its *raison d'être* and guarantee its formal integrity and, by the same token, ensure its spiritual efficacy. "Tradition is inextricably related to revelation and religion, to the sacred, to the notion of orthodoxy, to authority, to the continuity and regularity of transmission of the truth, to the exoteric and the esoteric as well as to the spiritual life, science, and the arts."[15]

It might be argued that "perennial philosophers" would be an apposite designation for these thinkers. They are indeed perennial philosophers but certain commentators have hastily and indiscreetly used this classification as an umbrella term to cover disparate individuals who do not belong together, thus generating considerable confusion. The traditionalists themselves have been at some pains to disassociate their vision of the perennial philosophy from those divergent points of view with which traditionalism has been conflated. There have been several attempts to reconcile formal religious antagonisms under an array of different philosophical and theological canopies—Theosophy, "anonymous Christianity," "natural religion," "universal religion," neo-Hindu Vedanta, and so on—and many of these individuals and groups have laid claim to the "perennial philosophy." One may mention such individuals as Madame Blavatsky, Aldous Huxley, and G.I. Gurdjieff. The traditionalists find all such attempts to resolve the problem of religious pluralism quite unconvincing; they are symptoms of the confusion of the times rather than an answer to it.

Traditionalism addresses itself to the inner meaning of religion through an elucidation of immutable metaphysical and cosmological principles and through a penetration of the forms preserved in each religious tradition. The sources of the traditionalist vision are Revelation, tradition, intellection, realization. It is neither a vestigial pseudo-scientific methodology nor a subjectively-determined "hermeneutic" but a *theoria* which bridges the *phenomena* and the *noumena* of religion; it takes us "from the forms to the essences wherein resides the truth of all religions and where alone a religion can really be understood."[16] It provides an all-embracing context for the study of religion and the means whereby not only empirical but philosophical and metaphysical questions can be both properly formulated and decisively answered. The traditionalists approach the issue of religious pluralism from several different angles, but always working on the basis of certain axiomatic principles. René Guénon, for instance, started from the Primordial Tradition of which the individual religious traditions are so many refractions. Here, however, as matter of expediency, we will reduce the issue of religious pluralism to one of its aspects only: the relationship of the exoteric and esoteric dimensions of religion, and, in the main, will rehearse a Schuonian explication, first articulated in *The Transcendent Unity of Religions* (1953).

The Exoteric and Esoteric Dimensions of Religion

A concept of the utmost importance in the Schuonian perspective is the distinction, first made explicit by René Guénon, between the exoteric and esoteric dimensions of any religious tradition. If the distinction is not precisely understood the traditionalist perspective on the *inner* unity of the religions cannot be fully grasped. We shall not find in the writings of the traditionalists any Procrustean attempt to affirm a unity on a plane where it does not exist nor an insipid universalism which posits a unity of no matter what elements as long as they lay some claim to being "religious" or "spiritual."

Generally we are accustomed to drawing sharp dividing lines *between* the religious traditions. The differences are, of course, palpably real and Schuon has no wish to blur the distinctions. Indeed, his vigorous defense of the principle of orthodoxy should preclude any misunderstanding on this point. However, this notwithstanding, Schuon draws another kind of dividing line which in some senses is much more fundamental—that *between the exoteric and esoteric.* A diagrammatic representation of the idea may be helpful (see Table 1). There is no question of the lines being blurred. They issue from a single point of origin and converge on their "destination," on the far side of the exoteric/esoteric divide. The apex of this diagram can be thought of as Truth, Reality, the Absolute. The point of origin and the point of "arrival" or better, fulfillment, are in fact one and the same. Below the dividing line, in the exoteric domain, we see the distinct religious traditions, each cleaving to an ensemble of formal elements deriving from a Revelation. In the esoteric domain, above the line, the different traditions converge on the Truth through a variety of means—esoteric doctrines, initiations and spiritual disciplines, intellection, the plenary experience. The necessity and the formal integrity of the different traditions is in no way compromised under this view which fully respects the formal differences between the religions on the plane where such distinctions, even antagonisms, find their proper place. It is only *through* the exoteric realm that the esoteric can be reached. The universality of every great spiritual patrimony rests "on a foundation of divinely instituted formal elements."[17] It is, of course, precisely because the formal elements of tradition are divinely instituted that the traditionalist must treat them with such respect.

Our first diagram can be complemented by another kind of representation which draws on the traditional symbolism of the circle (see Table 2). It must be noted that the exoteric domain does not derive from the esoteric but from a Revelation. This in itself is sufficient to throw out of court any suggestion that exoteric forms can be cast aside. *Within* the circumference of the formal exoterisms are to be found convergent esoterisms. At a time when it is sometimes suggested that the esoteric dimension can exist *in vacuo* or that it can be detached from the formal tradition in question, this is a point which needs some stressing.[18]

The Formal Diversity and Inner Unity of Religions

Table 1*

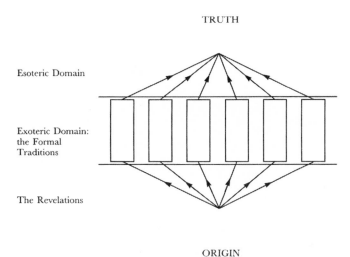

TRUTH

Esoteric Domain

Exoteric Domain:
the Formal
Traditions

The Revelations

ORIGIN

Table 2

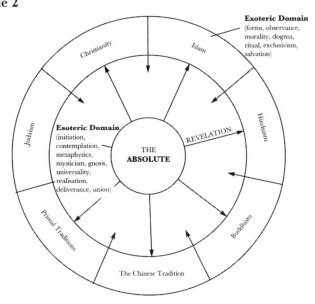

* This is a modified version of a diagram offered by Huston Smith in his Introduction to
the 1975 edition of Frithjof Schuon's *The Transcendent Unity of Religions*, xii.

In discriminating between the exoteric and the esoteric we are, in a sense, speaking of "form" and "spirit." Exoterism rests on a necessary formalism:

> Exoterism never goes beyond the "letter." It puts its accent on the Law, not on any realization, and so puts it on action and merit. It is essentially a "belief" in a "letter," or a dogma envisaged in its formal exclusiveness, and an obedience to a ritual and moral Law. And, further, exoterism never goes beyond the individual; it is centered on heaven rather than on God, and this amounts to saying that this difference has for it no meaning.[19]

It follows that exoterism must thereby embody certain inevitable and therapeutic limits or "errors" which from a fuller perspective can be seen in both their positive and negative aspects. Religion, in its formal aspect, is made up of what the Buddhists call *upāya*, "skilful means" which answer the necessities of the case, what Schuon refers to as "saving mirages" and "celestial stratagems."[20] "In religious esoterisms, efficacy at times takes the place of truth, and rightly so, given the nature of the men to whom they are addressed."[21] The limiting definitions of exoteric formalism are "comparable to descriptions of an object of which only the form and not the colors can be seen."[22] Partial truths which might be inadequate in a sapiential perspective may be altogether proper on the formal exoteric plane:

> The formal homogeneity of a religion requires not only truth but also errors—though these are only in form—just as the world requires evil and as Divinity implies the mystery of creation by virtue of its infinity.
>
> Absolute truth exists only in depth, not on the surface.
>
> The religions are "mythologies" which, as such, are founded on real aspects of the Divine and on sacred facts, and thus on realities but on aspects only. Now this limitation is at the same time inevitable and fully efficacious.[23]

In other words the forms of exoterism represent certain accommodations which are necessary to bring various truths within the purview of the average mentality. As such they are adequate to the collective needs in question. Just as there exists within each tradition an exoteric and an esoteric dimension so too there exist corresponding spiritual dispositions. It is in the nature of things that only a small minority will be blessed with the contemplative intelligence necessary to penetrate the formal aspects of religion. For the normal believer the exoteric domain is the only domain.

A specific example of an exoteric dogma might help to reinforce some of the points under discussion. In discussing the Christian dogmas about heaven and hell, Schuon has this to say:

> We are made for the Absolute, which embraces all things and from which none can escape; this truth is marvelously well presented in the monotheistic religions in the alternative between the two "eternities" beyond the grave.... The alternative may be insufficient from the point of view of total Truth, but it is psychologically realistic and mystically efficacious; many lives have been squandered away and lost for the single reason that a belief in hell and in paradise is missing.[24]

What of the attitude, so to speak, of the exoteric to the esoteric? Given the factors which have been mentioned it is not surprising that the exoteric elements in a religious tradition should be preserved and protected by representatives whose attitude to esoterism will be, at best, somewhat ambivalent, at worst openly hostile. In addressing itself to the defense of the *credo* and the forms which appear as guarantors of truth the exoteric resistance to esoterism is entirely positive. The esoteric can see and respect this guardianship of the "incalculable values" of orthodoxy. On the other hand,

> the exoteric's assessment of the esoteric is likely to be less charitable, not because exoterics are less endowed with that virtue, but because a portion of the esoteric position being obscured from him, he cannot honor it without betraying the truth he does see.[25]

It is in this context that we should understand Coomaraswamy's remark, frequently made in his correspondence with Christian "exoterics": "even if you are not on our side, we are on yours."[26] Sometimes the exoteric defendants of orthodoxy overstep themselves and in doing so beget results that are both destructive and counter-productive, especially when a religious tradition is endangered by a preponderantly exoteric outlook which "becomes crystallized in literalistic dogmatism."[27] How much of post-medieval Christian history bears witness to this truth! As to the theological ostracisms that have befallen some of the mystics and metaphysicians seeking to preserve the esoteric dimension within their respective religious traditions, Schuon reminds us of Aesop's fable about the fox and the grapes, a story which "repeats itself in all sectors of human existence."[28]

*

The supra-human origin of a religious tradition in a Revelation, an adequate doctrine concerning the Absolute and the relative, the saving power of the spiritual method, the esoteric convergence on the Unitive Truth—all these point to the inner unity of all integral traditions which are, in a sense, variations on one theme. However, there remain certain puzzling questions which might stand in the way of an understanding of the principial unity which the *religio perennis* discloses.

One frequently comes across formulations such as the following: "It is sometimes asserted that all religions are equally true. But this would seem to be simply sloppy thinking, since the various religions hold views of reality which are sharply different if not contradictory."[29] This kind of either/or thinking, characteristic of much that nowadays passes for philosophy, is in the same vein as a dogmatism which

> reveals itself not only by its inability to conceive the inward or implicit illimitability of a symbol, but also by its inability to recognize, when faced with two apparently contradictory truths, the inward connection that they apparently affirm, a connection that makes of them complementary aspects of one and the same truth.[30]

It is precisely this kind of incapacity which must be overcome if the transcendent unity of the religions is to be understood.

Let us rehearse some of the points made earlier through the following passage from Schuon:

> A religion is not limited by what it includes but by what it excludes; this exclusion cannot impair the religion's deepest contents—every religion is intrinsically a totality—but it takes its revenge all the more surely on the intermediary plane . . . the arena of theological speculations and fervors. . . . Extrinsic contradictions can hide an intrinsic compatibility or identity, which amounts to saying that each of the contradictory theses contains a truth and thereby an aspect of the whole truth and a way of access to this totality.[31]

Examples of "contradictory" truths which effectively express complementary aspects of a single reality can be found not only across the traditions but within them. One might instance, by way of illustration, the Biblical or Koranic affirmations regarding predestination and free will.[32]

From an esoteric viewpoint the exclusivist claims of one religion or another have no absolute validity. It is true that "the arguments of every intrinsically orthodox religion are absolutely convincing if one puts oneself in the intended setting."[33] If it be asked what constitutes orthodoxy, then this is the answer:

> In order to be orthodox a religion must possess a mythological or doctrinal symbolism establishing the essential distinction [between the Real and the illusory, or the Absolute and the relative] . . . and must offer a way that secures both the perfection of concentration and also its continuity. In other words a religion is orthodox on condition that it offers a sufficient, if not always exhaustive, idea of the absolute and the relative, and therewith an idea of their reciprocal relationships.[34]

Schuon restates the same principle in writing,

> For a religion to be considered intrinsically orthodox—an extrinsic orthodoxy hangs upon formal elements which cannot apply literally outside their own perspective—it must rest upon a fully adequate doctrine . . . then it must extol and actualize a spirituality that is equal to this doctrine and thereby include sanctity within its ambit both as concept and reality; this means it must be of Divine and not philosophical origin and thus be charged with a sacramental or theurgic presence.[35]

Orthodox theological dogmatisms are entitled to a kind of "defensive reflex" which makes for claims to exclusivism. However, and this is crucial,

> The exoteric claim to the exclusive possession of a unique truth, or of Truth without epithet, is . . . an error purely and simply; in reality, every expressed truth necessarily assumes a form, that of its expression, and it is metaphysically impossible that any form should possess a unique value to the exclusion of other forms; for a form, by definition, cannot be unique and exclusive, that is to say it cannot be the only possible expression of what it expresses.[36]

The argument that the different religions cannot all be repositories of the truth because of their formal differences and antagonisms rests on a failure to understand this principle. The lesson to be drawn from the multiplicity of religious forms is quite different:

> The diversity of religions, far from proving the falseness of all the doctrines concerning the supernatural, shows on the contrary the supra-formal character of revelation and the formal character of ordinary human understanding: the essence of revelation—or enlightenment— is one, but human nature requires diversity.[37]

In connection with this need for diversity, which is explained by the fact that humanity is divided into different branches, we might mention in passing Junyad's maxim that "the color of the water is the color of the vessel containing it."[38] Or, if a more abstract formulation be preferred, this from Aquinas: "the thing known is in the knower according to the mode of the knower."[39]

Religious Pluralism, Dialogue, and Comparative Religion

Firstly, it should be noted that the recognition of the proper status of traditions other than one's own depends on various contingent circumstances and does not in itself constitute a spiritual necessity. In some respects a religious intolerance is preferable to the kind of tolerance which holds fast to nothing: "the Christian saint who fights the Moslems is closer to Islamic sanctity than the philosopher who accepts everything and practices nothing."[40] Secondly, traditional orthodoxy is the prerequisite of any creative intercourse between the traditions themselves. To imagine that dialogue can usefully proceed without firm formal commitments is to throw the arena open to any and every kind of opinion and to let loose a kind of mental anarchy which can only exacerbate the problem. Thirdly, and this is the most crucial point, the question of the relationship of the religions to each other can only be decisively resolved by resort to traditional esoterisms and by the application of trans-religious metaphysical principles. But here we are back with the somewhat sensitive relationship of the exoteric and esoteric dimensions of religion. Schuon's argument, in effect, amounts to this: the problematic relationship of the esoteric and exoteric domains is more fundamental than the relationship of the traditions one to another; if this relationship were clarified and understood, then many of the questions about the interrelationship of the religious traditions would simply evaporate like the morning dew. Or, to put it differently, the "problem" of religious pluralism can only be resolved through a penetration of the exoteric barriers which each tradition has erected. In his later years Abhishiktananda understood this perfectly well.

A proper understanding of the exoteric-esoteric relationship, along with other principles which we have discussed in this study, would put an end to all the artificial and quite implausible means by which attempts have been made to reconcile formal divergences. Marco Pallis:

> *Dharma* and the *dharmas*, unitive suchness and the suchness of diversified existence: here is to be found the basis of an interreligious exegesis which does not seek a remedy for historical conflicts by explaining away formal or doctrinal factors such as in reality translate differences of spiritual genius. Far from minimizing the importance of these differences in the name of a facile and eventually spurious ecumenical friendliness, they will be cherished for the positive message

they severally carry and as necessities that have arisen out of the differentiation of mankind itself.[41]

The outlook implied in the passage from Pallis depends on a recognition of the exoteric-esoteric relationship and a subordination (*not* an annihilation) of exoteric dogmatism to the metaphysical principles preserved by traditional esoterisms. The main obstacle on this path is the tenacity with which many representatives of an exoteric viewpoint cling to a belief in the exclusive claims of their own tradition and to other "pious extravagances." Schuon goes to the heart of the matter:

> if exoterism, the religion of literalism and exclusive dogmatism, has difficulty in admitting the existence and legitimacy of the esoteric dimension . . . this is understandable on various grounds. However, in the cyclic period in which we live, the situation of the world is such that exclusive dogmatism . . . is hard put to hold its own, and whether it likes it or not, has need of certain esoteric elements. . . . Unhappily the wrong choice is made; the way out of certain deadlocks is sought, not with the help of esoterism, but by resorting to the falsest and most pernicious of philosophical and scientific ideologies, and for the universality of the spirit, the reality of which is confusedly noted, there is substituted a so-called "ecumenism" which consists of nothing but platitudes and sentimentality and accepts everything without discrimination.[42]

For many scholars and theologians the dilemma has been this: any "theoretical" solution to the problem of conflicting truth claims demands a conceptual platform which both encompasses and transcends any specific theological position; it must go beyond the premises of any particular theological outlook but at the same time not compromise the theological position to which one might adhere. Traditionalism shows the way out of this impasse. It neither insists on nor precludes any particular religious commitment. Once the necessity of orthodoxy is accepted, and the principles which govern the relationship of the exoteric and the esoteric are understood, then one can remain fully committed to a particular tradition while recognizing the limits of the outlook in question. Traditionalism requires neither a betrayal of one's own tradition nor a wishy-washy hospitality to anything and everything. The observation made by an early reviewer of *The Transcendent Unity of Religions* might be applied to traditionalism as a whole. It presents "a very concrete and specific philosophy of religion for an ecumenical age. . . . It opens one possible way for discovering a basis for coexistence for the different creeds."[43] We might add that it provides not *a* way but *the* only possible way.

We recall the words of Coomaraswamy calling for "a revision of the principles of comparative religion" whereby the discipline could serve the end of demonstrating "the common metaphysical basis of all religions."[44] The possibilities of this demonstration are more or less endless but the principles on which the undertaking can be based and the framework within which it can be pursued have been elucidated by Guénon, Coomaraswamy, Schuon, and other perennialists. Their work is there for those who seek a vision of religion adequate to the needs of the age.

In its early days the discipline of comparative religion was unable to meet this problem because it was too enmeshed in the pervasive evolutionism of the period. It also disqualified itself from a consideration of this kind of issue when it surrendered to a methodology which aped that of the natural sciences. The historical, philological, and typological approaches to religious phenomena assuredly uncovered and collated an invaluable mass of raw materials but sidestepped any questions which could only be answered from some normative base. To this day scholars have been properly sensitive to the dangers of allowing "comparative religion" to become "competitive religion," of opening the gate to an anarchic contest of conflicting truth claims, norms, and beliefs. The phenomenological approach sought to overcome the limitations of a purely descriptive approach and emphasized a more morphological study. However, once again, any questions about the truth claims of the religions or about the ways in which formal antinomies and contradictions might be resolved were ruled out of court. Today the discipline is in a state of ferment, perhaps of crisis. The apparently endless debate about methodology, about the role and purposes of the discipline go on. However, there seems to be a groundswell, in some quarters, in favor of a bolder approach to some of the questions which have previously been exiled from the domain of comparative religion. The debate is enlivened by philosophers, theologians, and others concerned with the implications of the collision of religions in the modern world. There is a good deal of talk about ecumenism and dialogue, and about fresh theological and phenomenological perspectives which might serve the ideals of world community, of interreligious understanding and the revitalization of religious and spiritual life generally.[45] From a traditionalist viewpoint, the vexed issues of ecumenism, dialogue, and the interrelationship of the religions are all strands in the same web.

It would be sanguine in the extreme to imagine that comparative religion as a discipline will harness itself to the enterprise outlined by Coomaraswamy. Nor can traditionalism reduce itself to an academic discipline. Nevertheless, there remain considerable possibilities for the discipline of comparative religion to assimilate at least something of the traditionalist outlook or to accept it as one of the perspectives from which religion can be studied—as has been shown by the work of traditionalist scholars such as Coomaraswamy, Seyyed Hossein Nasr, Joseph Epes Brown, Huston Smith, James Cutsinger, Patrick Laude, and others. This is not to deny there are some awkward questions which attend any attempt to reconcile a traditionalist vision with the demands of an impartial academic scholarship.

The claim that traditionalism is too normative to be allowed to shape academic studies is no argument at all. As currently practiced by many of its exponents comparative religion is quite clearly normative anyway. As soon as we are prepared, for instance, to talk of "sympathy," of "mutual understanding," of "world community," and so on, we have entered a normative realm. It is time scholars ceased to be embarrassed by this fact and stopped sheltering behind the tattered banner of a pseudo-scientific methodology which forbids any engagement with the most interesting, the most profound, and the most urgent questions which naturally stem from any serious study of religion. The question is not whether the study of religion will be influenced by certain norms—it will be so influenced whether we admit it or not—but to what kind of norms we are prepared to give our allegiances. The time has come to nail our colors to the mast in arguing for approaches to religion which do justice to the traditional principle of adequation, and which will help rescue the discipline from the ignominious plight of being nothing more than another undistinguished member of a disreputable family of pseudo-sciences.

The discipline of religious studies will never have any integrity so long as it is pursued as a self-sufficient, self-validating end in itself. As Klostermaier observed some time ago,

> The study of religions can no longer afford the luxury of creating pseudo-problems of its own, of indulging in academic hobbies, or of acting as if religion or the study of it were ends in themselves. The one thing that might be worse than the confusion and uncertainty in the area of religious studies would be the development of a methodology of religious studies, by scholars of religious studies, for the sake of religious studies: playing a game by rules invented by the players for the sake of the game alone.[46]

If this is not to be the fate of the discipline then, at the very least, there must be a much more radical debate about philosophical, theological, and metaphysical questions generated within the discipline. E.O. James many years ago observed that "The study of religion . . . demands both a historical and a scientific approach and a theological and philosophical evaluation if . . . its foundations are to be well and truly laid."[47] A serious consideration of the works of the traditionalists and of the whole traditionalist perspective would, at least, open the way for a fruitful reconvergence of philosophy, theology, comparative religion, and metaphysics.

Those who accept the traditionalist position can garner a richer harvest. The explication of the *sophia perennis* and its application to contingent phenomena shows the way to an outlook invulnerable to the whim and fancy of ever-changing intellectual fashions and armors one against the debilitating effects of scientism and its sinister cargo of reductionisms. It annihilates that "neutrality" which is indifferent to the claims of religion itself and removes those "optical illusions" to which the modern world is victim. For those who see religions as something infinitely more than mere "cultural phenomena," who believe them to be the vehicles of the most profound and precious truths to which we cannot and must not immunize ourselves, who wish to do justice to both the external forms and the inner meanings of religion, who cleave to their own tradition but who wish to recognize all integral religions as pathways to God, whose pursuit of religious studies is governed by something far more deep-seated than mental curiosity—for such people traditionalism can open up whole new vistas of understanding. Ultimately, for those prepared to pay the proper price, it can lead to that "light that is neither of the East nor the West."[48] A rediscovery of the immutable nature of man and a renewed understanding of the *sophia perennis* must be the governing purpose of the most serious comparative study of religion. It is, in Seyyed Hossein Nasr's words, a "noble end . . . whose achievement the truly contemplative and intellectual elite are urgently summoned to by the very situation of man in the contemporary world."[49]

Abhishiktananda, Metaphysics, and the Perennial Philosophy

Finally, we return to Abhishiktananda. Was he a metaphysician, a *jñānī* who had mastered metaphysical doctrines? Had principial and universal truths "incarnated" in his mind?[50] If by this term we mean someone like a Guénon or a Schuon, one who has a clear understanding of trans-religious metaphysical principles whereby both the outer diversity and inner unity of religious traditions can be authoritatively explained, and the various antinomies unequivocally resolved, then we cannot answer the question affirmatively without significant qualifications. Although Abhishiktananda had many of the appropriate credentials, he did not move primarily in the realm of doctrinal intellectuality. This was a matter of spiritual temperament. Throughout his life, he was in the grip of immediate and overwhelming spiritual experiences, and his principal task was the resolution *in his own person* of the apparent tensions and contradictions between Trinitarian Christianity and *Advaita* Vedanta. In the course of his struggle to solve this experiential problem Abhishiktananda developed many piercing and profound metaphysical insights—how could it be otherwise for a devotee of the *Upanishads*, one who had himself plunged into the void of *advaita* and thereby developed *viveka*, the power of discriminating between the Real and the illusory? But to be a mystic is not necessarily to be a metaphysician, as history repeatedly demonstrates. Metaphysics requires not only a contemplative and jnanic disposition but a kind of detached and synthetic intelligence which Abhishiktananda, for all his formidable gifts, did not possess. Abhishiktananda's spiritual genius manifested itself in his *being* rather than in the objectivization of metaphysical doctrine. Put another way: Abhishiktananda's medium was not doctrinal intellectuality but ontological realization (though of course the two often interpenetrate). In some respects it might be said that Abhishiktananda was essentially a *bhakta* rather than a *jñānī: bhakti* "is *a priori* not 'intellectual'; *bhakti* plumbs mysteries through 'being,' not through 'intelligence.'"[51] Nor, in the fullest sense, was Abhishiktananda a traditionalist: traditionalism is above all a metaphysical *theoria;* its leading exponents must therefore be metaphysicians. Abhishiktananda could not strictly be described as a traditionalist or perennialist if by such a term we mean one who self-consciously subscribes to the kind of exposition of the *sophia perennis* given by a Guénon, a Schuon, or a Titus Burckhardt. Nonetheless, he shared a great deal of common ground with the traditionalists. Abhishiktananda can certainly be counted in the company of those "mediators" to whom Coomaraswamy refers in the epigraph to this chapter. Part of the purpose of our discussion in this penultimate chapter is to situate the themes which run through Abhishiktananda's *oeuvre* in the context of traditionalism wherein they come into sharper focus and whereby we can better appreciate the fertility and the profundity of much of his thought.

As we have seen Abhishiktananda came to an ever-deeper understanding of the outer diversity and inner unity of religions. He did not always couch this understanding in quite the vocabulary used by traditionalists. But many of his insights are fundamentally the same. Although he never attained the clarity and precision of Schuon's exegesis of the relationship of the exoteric and esoteric aspects of religion, his writings point in the same direction. Much of his discussion of religion as *nāma-rūpa* ("formulations-structures") demonstrates his understanding of *both the relativity and the inviolability* of religious forms, even if he did not always accent the latter as heavily as do the traditionalists. Likewise, his writings about *advaita* signal a kind of esoteric insight, even though this was not a term he often used himself—indeed, when he did so it was often in a disparaging sense, referring to what might more properly be called "occultism," "spiritualism," or "psychism," according to the case at hand.[52] But there is no gainsaying the fact that Abhishiktananda *did* arrive at an understanding of "the transcendental unity of religions" which traditionalists would call "esoteric" because it is an understanding hidden from the vast majority whose disposition and sensibility are more attuned to the outward and exoteric forms of religion than to the "inner mystery." Let us state the matter slightly differently: only those of a contemplative spiritual temperament are able fully to enter the *guha*, the cave of the heart. It is also perhaps worth recalling that the very name of the *Upanishads*, the Scriptures in which Abhishiktananda immersed himself, implies an "esoteric" wisdom—"that which is heard when sitting up close" (to the guru and to the Scriptures themselves).[53] Perhaps Abhishiktananda took a somewhat sanguine view when he insisted that *anyone* could enter the *guha;* this is true in principle, to be sure, but not in fact. To understand this is not to be guilty of some sort of "elitism" or spiritual snobbery (an oxymoron in any case!), but simply to recognize palpable realities. By the same token, it bears repeating that a merely theoretical understanding of metaphysics, unaccompanied by the existential "leap into the void" and by a transformative alchemy in the soul, counts for nothing in itself—a principle on which Abhishiktananda had a very firm purchase. It explains much of his impatience with the apparently endless speculations of theologians and philosophers! At times Abhishiktananda *did* seem aware that *advaita* was not for everyone, and in one of his letters in 1966 wrote this: "in ancient times the great secret of *advaita* was restricted to those disciples whom the guru judged to be ready for it. Its wide diffusion in these days is not beneficial."[54]

A complete and firmly anchored understanding of metaphysical principles would have made Abhishiktananda quite immune to the follies of modernistic thought (whether Eastern or Western). He was unerring in his instinctive certainty that the surest guides on the spiritual path were to be found in the ancient Scriptures, in the saints and sages of yore, and in those living masters who embodied the age-old message of the rishis, quite unaffected by the grotesqueries of profane modernistic thought. However, as we have seen, Abhishiktananda was not altogether invulnerable to the seductive but confused theories and speculations of such figures as Aurobindo (himself prey to all manner of Western influences), Jung, and Teilhard de Chardin. Occasionally such thinkers seduced him into foolish and ill-considered formulations. Take this, for instance: "Teilhard's viewpoint—absolutely Pauline—is the only way to save Christianity."[55] However, from another point of view it is astonishing that Abhishiktananda was able to maintain his footing in the world of Tradition as well as he did, generally turning his back on modern theorizing in such fields as philosophy, theology, and comparative religion. All to his credit! Nonetheless, a fully-fledged metaphysician of the order of a Guénon would have had no interest in such works, save in their symptomatic aspects. Nor for a moment would such a one have entertained any kind of evolutionist schema, as Abhishiktananda sometimes applied to the development of religion itself—a field in which evolutionism becomes not merely wrong in its claims but particularly sinister in its effects. No doubt there is a certain contradiction, or at least confusion in Abhishiktananda's belief that the ancient Vedic rishis had unlocked the deepest secrets of the Self and his intermittent adherence to an evolutionistic model of religion. It is true that no religious man of any depth can swallow evolutionism unqualified, in either its biological or sociological-historicist guise. But to even flirt with evolutionist ideas (as Abhishiktananda does, for instance, in Chapters 5 and 6 of *Saccidananda*) is to betray some confusion about those immutable principles which are flagrantly violated by a pseudo-science which announces that "the flesh became Word"—for this, in a nutshell, is what the biological hypothesis amounts to. Nor would progressivist Social Darwinism, in whatever guise, cut the mustard with any traditionalist; to envisage a "new man" or a "new world" in which the wisdom of Jesus, of the Buddha, of Lao Tzu, becomes "obsolete" or "outdated" or "outgrown" is an impious absurdity of the most offensive kind. (This last observation is not directed at Abhishiktananda who was certainly not capable of this kind of foolishness, leaving it for the likes of a Vivekananda, a Gurdjieff, a Gerald Heard, or the "Aquarian Age" sentimentalists to spout such fatuities.)

How, then, are we to situate Abhishiktananda with respect to the traditionalist school? I hope that this study has demonstrated that in many ways Abhishiktananda's metaphysical intelligence, with all of the qualifications above notwithstanding, was of a rare and precious kind. His thinking was forged in the fiery crucible of his own interreligious experience and this gives his writings an urgency and existential edge unmatched by the vast majority of contemporary writers on religious and spiritual subjects. If he sometimes falls short in his understanding of both metaphysical principles and religious forms this is hardly surprising. Let us also not forget the truth of these words, from another Frenchman, "To know is not to prove, not to explain. It is to accede to vision. But if we are to have vision, we must learn to participate in the object of vision. The apprenticeship is hard."[56]

In the cases of Guénon and Schuon their grasp of metaphysical and cosmological principles seems to be more or less spontaneous, rather like the sudden solidification of certain crystalline structures. From a particular moment, their work is principially complete; thereafter it is only a matter of applying those principles which, as it were, have been grasped all at once, to the various contingent phenomena which happen to arrest their attention. Their work does not in any sense "evolve" but only ramifies. It is true that Guénon changed his mind on several significant issues—the "status" of Buddhism, most importantly. It is also true that we can occasionally discern a certain shift of emphasis in the writings of both Guénon and Schuon; Schuon's later and more sympathetic attitude to some forms of Protestantism might be adduced as an example. But, considered as a whole, it is strikingly evident that their work is informed from the beginning by a coherent set of adamantine metaphysical principles. In his reflections on René Guénon, Schuon refers to the intrinsically pneumatic or jnanic type in these terms:

> The pneumatic is in a way the "incarnation" of a spiritual archetype, which means that he is born with a state of knowledge which, for others, would be precisely the end and not the point of departure; the pneumatic does not "progress" to something "other than himself," he remains in place so as to become fully himself—namely his archetype— by progressively eliminating veils or husks, impediments contracted from the ambience and possibly also from heredity.[57]

There can be no doubt that both Guénon and Schuon himself were pneumatics in this sense. In other cases, such as that of Ananda Coomaraswamy, one sees in the early work a more or less latent understanding which is suddenly catalyzed by contact with the appropriate stimulus—in his case, the work of Guénon. This is not the sense we get in Abhishiktananda's work. True, there is a decisive moment, or series of moments, when the moulds in which Abhishiktananda's thought had been cast were shattered beyond any hope of repair—the encounters with Ramana, Arunachala, and Gnanananda. To be sure, Abhishiktananda had been hit by lightning and was not thereafter the same man. Nor was there any possibility of ignoring the illuminations in the cave, the cave of Arunachala being but the symbolic locus of the *guha*. Abhishiktananda was too courageous to countenance the idea of turning back. However, in his case, the transformation from a French priest provincial in both upbringing and outlook to a "knower of *Brahman*," embodying in his own self the timeless wisdom of the *Upanishads*, was to take up the rest of his life. Nevertheless, his ability to penetrate the religious forms of both West and East, and the progressive elimination of "husks" and "impediments" in order to "become fully himself" does suggest something of the pneumatic. Furthermore, as Barry McDonald has recently suggested, Abhishiktananda's "one-pointed dedication to his quest for the Real points to an extraordinary spiritual station, an experiential immersion in which it is difficult to distinguish between thought and being."[58]

In this study we have, for the most part, foregrounded those aspects of his work which are in conformity with traditional wisdom—after all, his inadvertencies and confusions can be of no more than passing interest. And yet, as intimated earlier, there is indeed something heroic in Abhishiktananda's search for Truth. If he was, from time to time, diverted off the path, it was certainly not through any lack of sincerity, commitment, or self-discipline. To return to the question in front of us, Abhishiktananda's "relation" to perennialism. My own view, with regard to what is most valuable and vital in Abhishiktananda's thought, is that more often than not it at least loosely conforms with traditionalist thought. Here is a tiny sample of characteristic formulations which might just as easily have come from the pen of the most thoroughly traditionalist authors:

> Diversity does not mean disunity, once the Center of all has been reached.[59]

> Truth cannot be given because it does not belong to anyone . . . truth is not the object of possession—rather, one can only be possessed by the truth.[60]

> Every *dharma* is for its followers the supreme vehicle of the claims of the Absolute.[61]

> The mystery to which [religion] points overflows its limits in every direction.[62]

> What's important . . . is to be sufficiently "deep" in order to transcend the letter, which does not mean to "reject" it.[63]

> [Religious] pluralism is a gift of God.[64]

Real dialogue will be . . . a discovery of unity in diversity and diversity in unity.[65]

He is one of those who, in many respects, is a traditionalist without knowing it, if one might put it that way; he arrived at more or the less same position by a process of trial and error, as it were. It is impossible to believe that he would not have found in the work of Schuon a resounding confirmation of his own deepest intuitions. Recourse to the traditionalist authors might well have saved him much anguish by showing him the way towards a reconciliation of the different spiritual economies which were at work in his soul, sometimes in an agonizing tension. As it was—and perhaps this was part of his special vocation and his singular achievement—he had to find his way through the labyrinth alone, although he was no doubt guided by the grace which accompanies any sincere pilgrim and which came to Abhishiktananda not only through his *sadguru*, Jesus Christ, His sacraments and His Church, but through Ramana, Arunachala, and Gnanananda, as well as through the inseparable companion in whom he put his trust throughout his Indian sojourn, the *Upanishads*. As he wrote in his journal, "The inner mystery calls me with excruciating force, and no outside being can help me to penetrate it and there, *for myself*, discover the secret of my origin and destiny."[66]

Notes

1. A. Coomaraswamy, *The Bugbear of Literacy*, 80, 88.
2. S.H. Nasr, *Sufi Essays*, 126.
3. Parts of this chapter appeared in slightly different form in *Traditionalism: Religion in the Light of the Perennial Philosophy* and in *Journeys East: 20ᵗʰ Century Western Encounters with Eastern Religious Traditions*.
4. A. Desjardins, *The Message of the Tibetans*, 20.
5. M. Lings, *Ancient Beliefs and Modern Superstitions*, 70.
6. F. Schuon, *Transcendent Unity of Religions*, xxxi.
7. F. Schuon, *Transcendent Unity of Religions*, xxxi.
8. F. Schuon, *Gnosis: Divine Wisdom*, 12.
9. S.H. Nasr, *Sufi Essays*, 127.
10. A.K. Coomaraswamy, "The Pertinence of Philosophy" in S. Radhakrishnan and J.H. Muirhead (eds), *Contemporary Indian Philosophy*, 160.
11. Letter to H.G.D. Finlayson, December 1942, *Selected Letters*, 285-286.
12. K. Oldmeadow, *Traditionalism*.
13. A.K. Coomaraswamy, "The Pertinence of Philosophy," 158-159.
14. S.H. Nasr, *Knowledge and the Sacred*, 65.

15. S.H. Nasr, *Knowledge and the Sacred*, 68.

16. S.H. Nasr, *Sufi Essays*, 38.

17. F. Schuon, *Light on the Ancient Worlds*, 137. See also S.H. Nasr, *Knowledge and the Sacred*, 293-294.

18. This kind of assumption is evident in the pretensions of people who claim to be "Sufis" without being Muslims. See S.H. Nasr, *Sufi Essays*, 169n, and *Knowledge and the Sacred*, 77.

19. F. Schuon, *Light on the Ancient Worlds*, 76.

20. F. Schuon, *Survey of Metaphysics and Esoterism*, 185n.

21. F. Schuon, *The Transfiguration of Man*, 8

22. F. Schuon, *Understanding Islam*, 80.

23. F. Schuon, *Spiritual Perspectives*, 70.

24. F. Schuon, *Light on the Ancient Worlds*, 22.

25. Huston Smith, Introduction to F. Schuon, *Transcendent Unity of Religions*, xv.

26. For one of many instances where Coomaraswamy uses this phrase see letter to Joachim Wach, August 1947, *Selected Letters*, 113.

27. F. Schuon, *Transcendent Unity of Religions*, 9.

28. F. Schuon, *Islam and the Perennial Philosophy*, 46.

29. O. Thomas, "Introduction" to *Attitudes to Other Religions*, quoted by Huston Smith, Introduction to F. Schuon, *Transcendent Unity of Religions*, iiin.

30. F. Schuon, *Transcendent Unity of Religions*, 3.

31. F. Schuon, *Islam and the Perennial Philosophy*, 46.

32. F. Schuon, *Transcendent Unity of Religions*, 4.

33. F. Schuon, *Spiritual Perspectives*, 14.

34. F. Schuon, *Light on the Ancient Worlds*, 137-138.

35. F. Schuon, *Islam and the Perennial Philosophy*, 14.

36. F. Schuon, *Transcendent Unity of Religions*, 17.

37. F. Schuon, "No Activity without Truth," 8. See also M. Pallis, *A Buddhist Spectrum*, 157.

38. Quoted in A.K. Coomaraswamy, "Sri Ramakrishna and Religious Tolerance," *Selected Papers 2*, 37.

39. A.K. Coomaraswamy, "Sri Ramakrishna and Religious Tolerance," *Selected Papers 2*, 36.

40. F. Schuon, *Logic and Transcendence*, 182. See also S.H. Nasr, *Knowledge and the Sacred*, 291, 307n.

41. M. Pallis, *A Buddhist Spectrum*, 109-110. (The essay from which this excerpt is taken can also be found in R. Fernando (ed), *The Unanimous Tradition*.) See also V. Danner, "The Inner and Outer Man" in Y. Ibish and P.L. Wilson (eds), *Traditional Modes of Contemplation and Action*, 407ff.

42. F. Schuon, *Logic and Transcendence*, 4.

43. F.H. Heinemann in *The Journal of Theological Studies* 6, 1955, 340. One might add the proviso that the kind of ecumenism envisaged would necessarily be esoteric. As Seyyed Hossein Nasr has recently pointed out "Ecumenism if correctly understood must be an esoteric activity if it is to avoid becoming the

instrument for simple relativization and further secularization." *Knowledge and the Sacred*, 282.

44. A.K. Coomaraswamy, "The Pertinence of Philosophy," 158-159.

45. On the debate about religious pluralism and dialogue: see in the Sources listed at the end of this study works by such figures as Beatrice Bruteau, Francis Clooney, John B. Cobb Jr, Pascaline Coff, Harold Coward, Jacques Dupuis, Diana Eck, Bede Griffiths, John Hick, Thomas Keating, Klaus Klostermaier, Paul Knitter, Raimon Panikkar, Eric Sharpe, and W. Cantwell Smith, as well as the various traditionalist authors mentioned in this chapter.

46. K. Klostermaier, "From Phenomenology to Meta-science: Reflections on the Study of Religion," 563.

47. E.O. James, quoted in E.J. Sharpe, "Some Problems of Method in the Study of Religion," 12.

48. From the *Koran*, quoted by S.H. Nasr, "Conditions for a Meaningful Comparative Philosophy," 61.

49. S.H. Nasr, "Conditions for a Meaningful Comparative Philosophy," 61.

50. See F. Schuon, *Spiritual Perspectives*, 11.

51. F. Schuon, *Spiritual Perspectives*, 114.

52. See L 4.5.64. 161. The same letter contains his disparaging allusion to Guénon.

53. See FS 76.

54. L 29.1.66, 177.

55. D 19.10.65, 283.

56. A. Saint-Exupery, *Flight to Arras*, 37.

57. F. Schuon, *René Guénon: Some Observations*, 6.

58. Personal correspondence with the author. October 2005.

59. SAC xiii.

60. FS 62.

61. FS 25.

62. FS 26.

63. EL 146.

64. DD 206.

65. DD 211.

66. D 19.4.56, quoted in Panikkar, 435.

11

Abhishiktananda's Gift

> The only thing you have to offer another human
> being, ever, is your own state of being.
> *Ram Dass*[1]

Abhishiktananda's life and his writings have touched many people,
both in the West and on the subcontinent. No doubt one could trace
his influence in many fields—the indigenization of the Indian Church,
monastic renewal and the revivification of contemplative spirituality,
the spread of the Christian Ashram movement, interreligious dialogue,
the fertilization of Christian theology by Eastern influences, the study
of comparative religion, and so on. And indeed, several scholars have
already charted Abhishiktananda's legacy in many of these domains.
In this concluding segment we will focus not on Abhishiktananda's
"achievements," nor track his "influence," important though these
undoubtedly are; rather we will concentrate on his *being*. His ultimate
significance rests not on what he *did*, his outer activities in the world,
but on who he *was* and, we might say, still is. As his friend Raimon
Panikkar wrote in his "Letter,"

> Your struggle . . . was not a struggle of the mind, nor of the heart.
> Your mind was far too alert and clear not to know its own limits, your
> heart too pure and unselfish to worry about itself. Your "*askesīs*," your
> struggle on the "*palestra*," [was] in the arena of being, of life, of your
> total existence.[2]

Abhishiktananda might well have said, as Gandhi did, "My life is my
message." In this concluding chapter we will weave together some
reflections about Swamiji with a few passages from one of the metaphysical and spiritual master-works of recent times, Frithjof Schuon's
Spiritual Perspectives and Human Facts.

If we share Schuon's view that "the only decisive criterion of human
worth is man's attitude to the Absolute,"[3] then Abhishiktananda's life
was exemplary. From his youth until his passing he consecrated his life
to God—in the full plenitude of that word. His earthly journey was an
unfaltering pilgrimage, a return to God Whose center is everywhere
and circumference nowhere.[4] It was a quest which Abhishiktananda
undertook with unyielding courage, fortitude, and tenacity, leaving

behind all that was not conducive to the search for God. As he himself wrote, "Spiritual experience . . . is the meeting-place of the known and the not-known, the seen and not-seen, the relative and the absolute."[5] This was no place for the faint-hearted! His spiritual heroism consisted in overcoming his very human fears to make the "leap into the void"; it was his faith which gave him courage, that "attachment with the very depths of our being to the Truth that transcends us,"[6] and the selfsame faith which motivated his austerities, his renunciation, his allegiance to *sannyāsa*. As Schuon reminds us, "Sincere and integral faith always implies renunciation, poverty, and privation, since the world—or the ego—is not God."[7] By the same token, "there is no spirituality devoid of ascetic elements."[8]

During one of his silent sojourns on Arunachala, Abhishiktananda was importuned by some pesky boys with questions about his identity. Rather than breaking his silence, he wrote down the following words: "Like you, I come from God; like you, it is to him that I am going; apart from that, nothing else matters."[9] He found God—or the Self—in the innermost chamber of the lotus in the cave of the heart. But he saw God everywhere: in his *sadguru*, Jesus Christ, in the "call of India," in his fellows, in the birds of the air and the lilies of the field. Although his life evinces some of the penitential and sacrificial character of the faith in which he was reared, Abhishiktananda's life was full of joy and a delight in all of God's creation. Little wonder that he felt such an affinity with the Saint of Assisi.

On the human level Abhishiktananda may be compared with some of the other lights of our time. In his moral seriousness, his self-interrogation, and his existential intensity, if we might so express it, he recalls Dostoevsky and Simone Weil, whilst his efforts to build a bridge between two spiritual worlds are also reminiscent of his compatriot. Less obvious but useful comparisons might also be made with Nietzsche and Wittgenstein who, whatever their deviations, exhibited a nobility—even a grandeur—of soul, a severe self-discipline, and an unswerving fidelity to the peculiar tasks to which they devoted their lives. Bettina Bäumer, who knew him better than most, has suggested that the keynote in Abhishiktananda's life and personality was *authenticity*, a term signaling his sincerity, his seriousness, his spontaneity, his lack of interest in "status" or in the trappings of "the guru."[10]

In an essay on Gandhi, George Orwell observed that all of the Mahatma's sins and misdeeds, like his worldly goods, added up to a very meager collection.[11] The same might be said of Abhishiktananda. His human faults were of a very minor order, perhaps most evident in his sometimes troubled relations with his fellow-monks at Shanti-vanam—occasional irascibility and impatience, now and then a failure to understand a point-of-view different from his own, a tendency to sometimes make harsh judgments. But these are of very little account next to his generosity and compassion, his openness, warm-heartedness, and good humor, as well as those other character traits to which we have already drawn attention.

As a bridge-builder between the spiritual traditions of West and East the most obvious comparisons are with his fellow monks, Bede Griffiths and Thomas Merton, whilst we may also remember figures such as William Johnston, Klaus Klostermaier, and Richard Wilhelm, and the great German theologian and comparative religionist, Rudolf Otto, with whom he shared an understanding of the "astonishing conformity in the deepest impulses of human spiritual experience," independent of "race, clime, and age."[12] These were all Europeans with a deep *existential engagement* with Eastern spirituality in its various forms. I am inclined to share James Royster's judgment that "It is, in fact, doubtful if any Christian monk in the second half of the twentieth century has taken more seriously than Abhishiktananda the deep call to discover and explore experientially the ultimate ground that unites monks of different traditions."[13] If we are to look for Abhishiktananda's Eastern counterparts, those who have maintained a commitment to their own patrimony but who have made a heartfelt endeavor to enter a foreign spiritual universe, we may mention Mahatma Gandhi, the current Dalai Lama, and Thich Nhat Hanh. Of course there have been a great many other Europeans who have whole-heartedly committed themselves to Eastern religious forms and spiritual practices but who less readily lend themselves to comparisons with Abhishiktananda because their engage-ments were made in the absence of any Occidental religious affiliations or because any such commitments were severed with their Eastern ini-tiations; one thinks of such figures as Sister Nivedita, Lama Anagarika Govinda, and Roshi Robert Aitken, to name just a few.

In *A Benedictine Ashram* Father Monchanin and Abhishiktananda anticipated the day when Shantivanam might open her doors to the "true sons of India, sons of her blood and sons of her soul,"

> priests and laymen alike, gifted with a deep spirit of prayer, an heroic patience, a total surrender, endowed with an iron will and right judgment, longing for the heights of contemplation, and equipped, too, with a deep and intimate knowledge of Christian doctrine and Indian thought.[14]

Do we not, in fact, have here a snapshot of Abhishiktananda himself? That he was a man imbued with the deepest "spirit of prayer" is attested by his whole life. His "heroic patience" is evident in his fidelity to the call of India, to his vocation as a monk, to his membership in the Mystical Body of Christ's Church, and in the attentive equanimity with which he awaited the messages of the Spirit. He had an "iron will," not in the service of his own ego but in the pursuit of "the one thing necessary" and in his loyalty to Truth. Few men have made a more "total surrender" than this monk who put his hand to the plough and did not look back. As a young man of eighteen, considering his monastic vocation, he had written,

> I feel myself driven by something which does not allow me to draw back or turn aside, and compels me, almost in spite of myself, to throw myself into the unknown which I see opening before me.[15]

Throughout his life he had the courage to defy convention and to surrender to the unknown. Like all mortals he made mistakes but, assuredly, in the things that matter most, he showed "right judgment." He not only longed for but attained "the heights of contemplation." He never ceased his prayerful study of the Christian Scriptures, and of the works of the great saints and doctors of the Church of whom he had the most "intimate knowledge" while his understanding of the Indian tradition came through Ramana, Gnanananda, and Arunachala, and through his immersion in the tradition's loftiest and most venerable Scriptures, the *Upanishads.* How much he loved the *Chāndogya* and the *Bṛhadāranyaka,* and what delight he took in sharing their secrets!

In 1961 Mircea Eliade wrote these words in his journal:

> My interest in Hindu philosophy and ascesis can be explained as follows: India has been obsessed by freedom, by absolute autonomy. Not in any naïve, superficial way, but with regard to the numberless forms of conditioning to which man is subjected, studying them objectively, experimentally (Yoga), and striving to find the tool that will make it possible to abolish or transcend them. Even more than Christianity, Hindu spirituality has the merit of introducing Freedom into the Cosmos.[16]

Abhishiktananda strived to attain that Freedom—not as the term is usually understood in the modern West, the freedom "to do as one likes," but the freedom of the spirit which is the birthright of the sons and daughters of God. In an essay on the renewal of contemplative spirituality in Christianity, Philip Sherrard writes of the outlook which dominates the modern World: "an activist time-bound mentality that is anti-metaphysical, anti-contemplative, and anti-symbolic" which con-fines man to a life of "frenetic activity" in the only realm of existence he knows, the temporal.[17] Abhishiktananda, on the other hand, beckons us to a contemplative spirituality wherein we discover our true nature beyond the vicissitudes of Time, "in the mystery of God."

Although it was the Sage of Arunachala who exerted such a pow-erful influence over Abhishiktananda's life, in some ways it was that other great Indian saint of modern times, Ramakrishna Paramahamsa, who might have served as a spiritual exemplar. Strangely enough, Abhi-shiktananda seems to have known little of Ramakrishna himself. The only references we find in his books, journals, and letters concern some of the more disturbing aspects of the Ramakrishna Mission, founded by the redoubtable Vivekananda against the express wishes of the Master himself. Ramakrishna might have provided an inspiration for Abhishiktananda in at least two respects. Firstly, it was Ramakrishna's "ontological plasticity" which allowed him to penetrate foreign religious forms in a more or less unprecedented fashion. As Schuon remarks,

> In Ramakrishna there is something which seems to defy every category: he was like the living symbol of the inner unity of religions; he was, in fact, the first saint to wish to penetrate foreign spiritual forms, and in this consisted his exceptional and in a sense universal mission. . . . In our times of confusion, disarray, and doubt he was the saint called to "verify" forms and "reveal," if one can so express it, their single truth.[18]

No one with any sense of proportion would want to elevate Abhi-shiktananda to the quasi-prophetic status of Ramakrishna. But is there not in Abhishiktananda's life an echo of the Paramahamsa's mission to "penetrate foreign spiritual forms" and to "reveal" the "single truth" enshrined in the two traditions to which he became heir? Ramakrishna was a Hindu *bhakta* who penetrated and "internalized" the spiritual forms of both Christianity and Islam; Abhishiktananda was a Christian monk who plunged into the boundless experience of *advaita* as extolled in the Vedanta. Secondly, as we intimated in the last chapter, there is some affinity between the bhaktic character of these two spiritual per-sonalities, Ramakrishna and Abhishiktananda, one which is expressed ontologically, in realization—in their being—rather than intellectually, in the unerring understanding and exposition of doctrinal orthodoxy in both its extrinsic and intrinsic senses.[19]

Abhishiktananda lived a life of contemplative spirituality, disci-plined by his monastic vocation—a life dedicated to prayer, solitude, and silence. Whilst it is true that Abhishiktananda often found himself embroiled in "activities" of one sort and another, he was ever replenishing his soul by drinking from "the waters of silence." As Schuon reminds us, "Love of God, far from being essentially a feeling, is that which makes the wise man contemplate rather than anything else."[20] Abhishiktananda lived a life of prayer, remembering his own words that "To pray without ceasing is not so much consciously to *think* of God, as to act continuously under the guidance of the Spirit."[21] In his wartime memoir Antoine Saint-Exupéry observes that there is "a density of being" in the monk at prayer. "He is never so much alive as when prostrate and motionless before his God."[22] Here indeed, in prayer and contemplation, Abhishiktananda himself attained the full "density of being."

Abhishiktananda's life might be considered as the living out of St Basil's four principial elements of spirituality: *separation* from the profane world, *purification* of the soul, Scriptural *meditation* which infuses the discursive intelligence with Divine Light, and unceasing *prayer*. Schuon formulates these elements in this way: "in renunciation the soul leaves the world; in purification the world leaves the soul; in meditation God enters the soul; in continual prayer the soul enters into God."[23] Renunciation, purification, meditation, prayer—the very hallmarks of Abhishiktananda's vocation, one which recalls the words of Swami Ramdas, another of India's great saints: "a sustained recollection of God, destroying all the distempers of the mind, purifies and ennobles life."[24] In the end they brought Abhishiktananda to that wisdom which is the "perfection of faith" and to that peace which "passeth all understanding."

Few have written as beautifully on prayer as Frithjof Schuon. With the example of Abhishiktananda fresh in our minds and hearts, let the following serve as our final epitaph for this pilgrim of the Absolute and man of unceasing prayer.

> Prayer—in the widest sense—triumphs over the four accidents of our existence: the world, life, the body, and the soul; or we might also say: space, time, matter, and desire. It is situated in existence like a shelter, like an islet. In it alone we are perfectly ourselves, because it puts us in the presence of God. It is like a miraculous diamond which nothing can tarnish and nothing can resist.

> Man prays and prayer fashions man. The saint has himself become prayer, the meeting-place of earth and Heaven; and thus he contains the universe and the universe prays with him. He is everywhere where nature prays and he prays with and in her: in the peaks which touch the

void and eternity, in a flower which scatters itself, or in the abandoned song of a bird.

He who lives in prayer has not lived in vain.[25]

Notes

1. Ram Dass, *The Only Dance There Is*, 6. (This Ram Dass, formerly Richard Alpert, should not to be confused with the great Indian saint, Swami Ramdas, 1884-1963.)
2. Panikkar, 447.
3. F. Schuon, *Spiritual Perspectives*, 22.
4. The phrase "Whose center is everywhere and circumference nowhere" is usually attributed to Empedocles, and has been used by St Bonaventura, Nicholas of Cusa, and other Christian writers.
5. HCMP 112.
6. F. Schuon, *Spiritual Perspectives*, 128.
7. F. Schuon, *Spiritual Perspectives*, 129.
8. F. Schuon, *Spiritual Perspectives*, 131.
9. SA 35.
10. Professor Bäumer made this observation in conversation with the author.
11. G. Orwell, "Reflections on Gandhi," *Collected Essays*, Vol. 4, 525.
12. R. Otto, *Mysticism East and West*, v.
13. J. Royster, "Dialogue in Depth," 78.
14. BA 90.
15. L 3.6.29, 4.
16. Quoted in M. Eliade, *Ordeal by Labyrinth*, 63.
17. P. Sherrard, *Christianity: Lineaments of a Sacred Tradition*, 263.
18. F. Schuon, *Spiritual Perspectives*, 115.
19. On this distinction see F. Schuon, *Language of the Self*, 1.
20. F. Schuon, *Spiritual Perspectives*, 157.
21. Pr 18.
22. A. de Saint-Exupery, *Flight to Arras*, 73.
23. F. Schuon, *Spiritual Perspectives*, 198.
24. *The Essential Swami Ramdas*, 16.
25. F. Schuon, *Spiritual Perspectives*, 212-213.

Appendix A

Chronology of Abhishiktananda's Life

1910	Born August 30th, Saint-Briac, Brittany, France
1920	First Communion; enters Minor Seminary of Châteaugiron
1925	Mother's illness; enters Major Seminary at Rennes
1926	Called to the Benedictine Order
1929	October 15th, enters the Abbey of Kergonan
1930	Birth of his youngest sister Marie-Thérèse
1931	May 17th, profession in the Benedictine Order
1934	First heard the call of India
1935	Military service
	May 30th, Solemn Profession
	December 31st, ordained as a priest
1939	Called up at outbreak of World War II
1940	Escaped enemy capture and returned to the monastery
1942	Wrote *Amour et Sagesse* for his mother
1944	Death of his mother
1947	Contact with Msgr J. Mendonça, Bishop of Tiruchchirappalli, South India
	Corresponds with Fr Monchanin
1948	Indult of Exclaustration, allowing him to leave the monastery for India
	15th August, disembarks in Colombo
1949-50	Visits to Ramana Maharshi at Tiruvannamalai
1950	With Fr Jules Monchanin, establishes Shantivanam Ashram at Kulittalai
	Death of Sri Ramana Maharshi
	December, ten day retreat at Bangalore
1952	Marie-Thérèse (sister) enters the Benedictine Abbey of Saint-Michel
1952-54	Several sojourns in the caves of Mt Arunachala
1955	Visit to Elephanta with Fr Mahieu
	Visit to Tapovanam Ashram, near Tirukoyilur, and meeting with Sri Gnanananda
1956	Second visit to Tapovanam Ashram;
	November 6th-December 8th, retreat at Kumbakonam in complete silence and isolation
1957	Travels in North India
	October 10th, death of Fr Monchanin
	December, theological conference at Shantivanam with Fr Dominique, Fr Bede Griffiths, Raimon Panikkar *et al*
1958	Another visit to Arunachala

1959 Further travels in North India; first visit to Jyotiniketan Ashram
First of several pilgrimages to Gangotri area and the source of the Ganges

1960 Becomes an Indian citizen
Visit of John Cole to Shantivanam
Shantivanam and Jyotiniketan Ashrams join in study and prayer at Shantivanam

1961 Meetings with Dr Cuttat in Delhi
Retreat/seminar at Almora
Visits to Haridwar, Rishikesh, Almora
Building of Uttarkashi hermitage
November, participation in Assembly of World Council of Churches in Delhi

1962 Inter-denominational retreat/seminar, Rajpur
Establishes small hermitage at Gyansu, near Uttarkashi, in the Himalayas

1963 Inter-denominational retreat/seminar, Nagpur

1964 Pilgrimage to Gangotri with Raimon Panikkar

1965 First meeting with Swami Chidananda, Sivanananda Ashram, Rishikesh

1968 Formally relinquishes his position at Shantivanam to Fr Bede Griffiths

1969 First contact with Marc Chaduc

1971 Chaduc arrives in India

1973 June 30th, *dīkṣā* of Marc Chaduc/Swami Ajatananda on the Ganges at Rishikesh
July, retreat at the Shiva Temple of Ranagal, near Rishikesh
July 14th, final advaitic experience and cardiac arrest, Rishikesh bazaar
December 7th, dies in Indore, buried in the cemetery of the Fathers of the Divine Word, near Indore (later moved to Shantivanam)

Appendix B

Aphorisms and Apothegms

The Mystery of the Absolute; God and Man; Truth

- God has no form. God is beyond every form. Precisely for that reason God can reveal and manifest himself under any form. (Pr 14)

- Man's unknowable being is of the same order as God's, for man comes from God and has been created in his image. (SAC 4)

- As long as man attempts to seize and hold God in his words and concepts, he is embracing a mere idol. (SAC 5)

- Jesus is God's face turned towards man and man's face turned towards God. (SA 94n)

- The call of the *Upanishads* is one which comes from beyond space and time. (FS 63)

- Christ is less real in his temporal history than in the essential mystery of my being. (D 26.10.66, 287)

- Truth cannot be given because it does not belong to anyone . . . truth is not the object of possession—rather, one can only be possessed by the truth. (FS 62)

- Reason may discuss, but experience knows. (in P. Coff)

- There is only one thing that is real, the present moment in which I am face-to-face with God. . . . I have only one sermon: "Realize what you are at this very moment." (quoted in du Boulay, 166)

- The words of the real advaitin, like those of the rishis of the *Upanishads*, are simply paradoxes, to *awaken*, not to instruct. (L 27.2.70, 226)

- The lightning flash [of Awakening] which spans the inner heaven of consciousness never has any other cause than itself; it is a grace which erupts in the depths of the soul. (FS 64)

- Like you, I come from God; like you, it is to him that I am going; apart from that, nothing else matters. (written in response to some young boys pestering him, during a period of silence, with questions about himself) (SA 35)

The Cave within the Heart

- The mystery within one's heart is the mystery within every heart. (Pr 29)

- The real yogi is one who has recovered his essential freedom, above all with regard to his own inner world of thoughts and desires. (Pr 40)

- OM is the awakening of every man in the secret of his heart, the *guha*, to the mystery that is hidden in each movement of the creation, revealing at any point of space or time its divine origin and final goal. (Pr 61)

- Every religion, in its own way . . . has assisted man to bring to expression the mystery which he bears within himself. (FS 59)

Forms and Religious Pluralism

- The mystery to which it [religion] points overflows its limits in every direction. (FS 26)

- Diversity does not mean disunity, once the Center of all has been reached. (SAC xiii)

- Every *dharma* is for its followers the supreme vehicle of the claims of the Absolute. (FS 25)

- The theologians are afraid of the assertions of the Gospels, and I had to go by way of the Hindu Scriptures in order to accept the Gospel paradoxes in their full truth. (L 29.1.72, 262)

- At the level of the Spirit every *dharma* explodes. (D 21.21.71, 335)

- There are no non-cultural religions. (L 26.1.73, 284)

- In every religious experience there is a beyond, and it is precisely this "beyond" that is our goal. (FS 26)

- *Advaita* compels the Christian to become more and more clearly and thoughtfully aware of the dimension of interiority present in his own spiritual tradition. (HCMP 107)

- *Advaita* is not opposed to anything—if it were, it would no longer be itself. (HCMP 98)

- Let us not confuse the vessel with the treasure that it contains. (HCMP 115)

- For me everything is in the *Upanishads*. But the Buddha's radically purified training is a marvelous aid for getting inside them. It is a radical deliverance from our attempts to think. (L 26.1.73, 284)

- Spontaneity has no form, not even the refusal of form. (D 14.12.72, 335)

- I am not greatly worried, when someone out of sincerity refuses to make certain gestures which no longer mean anything to him. But what I do ask of each one is to remain completely sincere with himself. (L 23.1.69, 209)

- Jesus is not the founder-head of a religion; that came later. Jesus is the guru who announces the mystery. (D 24. 7.71, 332)

- [Myth] . . . a complex of signs and meanings which symbolize a reality so rich that it cannot be expressed directly in logical terms. (FS 105)

- Myth has for its goal to transport outside of time and to allow one to live intemporality in a form that is temporal. (from "Jésus le Sauveur," quoted in Friesen, 375)

- India is much more a spiritual dimension than a geographical continent. (L 10.2.65, 168)

- Who is a Christian? Who is a Hindu? Who is a Muslim? I know only the children of my Father who is in heaven. (D 26.8.63, 259)

The Cosmic Theophany

- God is everywhere, God alone is both hidden and unveiled in his manifestation. (Pr 15)

- The least grain of sand in its very definition implies the eternity and self-origination of God. (GD 62)

- Don't worry about those who love the esoteric, who run around to ashrams and "saints." The discovery of the mystery is so much simpler than that. It is right beside you, in the opening of a flower, the song of a bird, the smile of a child! (L 4.1.0.72, 278)

- Nothing exists that is not the sign of the Lord. (SA 57)

- It is the OM that makes itself heard in the roar of the Ganges, the rustling of leaves, the chirping of birds, that is ceaselessly thrown back from the rocky cliffs, and that arouses in the *sādhu*'s heart, as it were, an infinite echo, since there it unites with the primal OM in that silence from which all words have come. (ML 26-27)

- Man is a microcosm, and only by opening up in man the foundation of his being can the Spirit transform and spiritualize the cosmos to its depths. (SAC 87)

- The present moment . . . is a "sacrament of eternity." (SAC 145)

- God is in the gently blowing breeze, in the soaring flight of the bird, in the laughter and playfulness of the child, in every movement of our bodies and minds. (SAC 130)

- There is no matter which does not shout aloud the presence of the spirit. (GD 62)

- Every place is sacred, because sacredness comes from the Self and is radiated by it. Every place in which the renouncer sits is his ashram. Every stream in which he bathes becomes for him the Ganges. (L 4.4.73, 292)

Faith, Prayer, and the Spiritual Path

- Faith is the only way of penetrating the hidden abode of God—in the highest heaven as well as in the deepest center of our hearts. (Pr 9)

- Only faith makes possible the leap beyond—and faith rests on itself alone. (FS 38)

- Faith is essentially that interior sense by which the mind penetrates obscurely into those depths of one's own being which it realizes are beyond its power to explore solely by means of thought and sense-perception. (FS 59-60)

- Of all mantras and prayers, the invocation of the Name is the most efficient. (Pr 58)

- To pray without ceasing is not so much consciously to *think* of God, as to act continuously under the guidance of the Spirit. (Pr 18)

- Not to say "Two" in one's life, that is love. (D 15.4.64, 271)

- Love is only possible for those who are in full possession of themselves. (SAC 137)

- The pearl of India will only be discovered by contemplatives. For all others it remains a sealed book. (quoted in du Boulay, 180)

- Spiritual experience . . . is the meeting-place of the known and the not-known, the seen and the not-seen, the relative and the absolute. (HCMP112)

- This experience of wisdom is the highest gift of the Spirit and the perfection of faith. (SAC 4)

- What we understand by the contemplative attitude is, before all else, an ever increasingly profound attentiveness to the inner mystery, an opening to the silence of the Spirit beyond all feelings and all thought. (EL 114)

Snares

- The intellectual temptation is as dangerous for the monk as the temptation of work. (EL 160)

- No religious man indeed wants to develop and feed his mind simply for the mind's sake alone. (Pr 45)

- After all [false] piety is perhaps the most subtle and also the surest way for the little *ego* when it has been expelled to re-establish its status and dignity. (SA 38)

- Alas, the demon of argument is perhaps the most difficult of all to exorcize! (HCMP 94)

- Whoever still retains some *ahamkāra* (egoism) should not even mention *advaita*. (L 23.1.69, 209)

- The spirit of secular activism corrodes everything. (FS 29)

The Guru

- The meeting with the guru is the essential meeting, the turning point in the life of a man. (GD 29)

- The guru, Ramana, Arunachala, and the rest, they are the outward projection of the Self, who hides himself in order to be found. (D 26.4.64; in J. Stuart, "Ramana and Abhishiktananda," 173)

- Through him shines without obstruction "the smokeless light of the *Puruṣa* who dwells within the heart." (FS 12)

- How can even the midday sun shine in a room if its shutters are closed? (FS 62-3)

- Christ, even more than a being involved in Space-Time, is that absolutely final level of consciousness, that final point beyond which nothing remains but the passage to the Father. (D 25.12.55, 132)

Silence, Solitude, *Sannyāsa*

- Silence is the truest and highest praise to the Lord, *silentium tibi laus*. (Pr 42)

- It is in the name of their brothers that men are called to solitude and the desert. (Pr 31-2)

- No society, not even a religious society, can legislate for its hermits. The most it can do is to recognize—not to bestow—their right to be "themselves," and to endorse publicly their "departure" from this world. (FS 31)

- A monk cannot accept mediocrity, only extremes are appropriate for him. (L 27.10.29, 6.)

- Those ascetics who flee the world and care nothing for its recognitions are precisely the ones who uphold the world. (FS 42)

- Human beings need *zazen*, meditation, silence, just as they need sleep. (D 3.1.73, 367)

- One who has reached the Self no longer communicates by words. What he says outwardly by words, he communicates inwardly by his silence. (D 15.3.53, 64)

- *Sannyāsa* confronts us with a sign of that which is essentially beyond all signs—indeed, in its sheer transparency, it proclaims its own death as a sign. (FS 42)

- The call to complete renunciation cuts across all *dharmas* and disregards all frontiers . . . it is anterior to every religious formulation. (FS 27)

- *Sannyāsa* is beyond all *dharma*, including all ethical and religious duties whatever. (FS 18)

- [*Sannyāsa*] is the mystery of the sacred, lived with the greatest possible interiority. (FS 43)

Beyond Words and Concepts

- It is not by words that India's secret is transmittable. Words do not hold great secrets, they betray them, rather, even more than they disclose them. (EL 72)

- . . . the world of the East which, contrary to the Greek and Mediterranean world, has not accepted the primacy of the *eidos*, of the *logos*, of the idea. Rather, at all times, it has been directly drawn by being, life, experience in itself. (EL19)

- The *Upanishads* cannot simply [be] reduced to formulas in any language whatever, for they are above all a matter of experience, a shock-treatment, an interior lightning-flash, induced by a whole series of approaches which converge from every point of the mental horizon upon this central focus of overwhelming illumination. (FS 101)

- It would certainly be rash to interpret the intuitions of the apostles as though they were Aristotelian definitions. They overflow on every side the words in which they were formulated. (HCMP 89)

- People are on the lookout for ideas, but I would like them to realize that to hold their peace is what they need. (L 1.6.73, 300)

- The *Upanishads* do not offer an organized body of doctrines . . . they contain intuitive "awakenings." (FS 69)

- Speculative theology, however high and illuminating, remains always on the threshold of the Kingdom. It can only indicate a direction . . . and become[s] truly significant only when aiding the spirit to pass on to the contemplation of the highest wisdom which silences the mind and transcends all its activities. (SAC 4)

- People argue about Jesus—it is easier than to let yourself be scorched by contact with him. (L 16.1.73, 283)

- Men are drawn to ashrams in order to learn to read in their own depths, not in books. (SA 21)

- *Jñāna* is an arcane knowledge, a *mysterium fidei*. (EL 29)

The Church

- The Church has to be multiform. It was providentially born in a Semitic environment, but is not bound to it. The child does not remain in the cradle indefinitely. (L 12.7.64, 164-165)

- One evening . . . seated here besides the Ganges, I was thinking about the [Vatican] council, and was suddenly seized with uncontrollable laughter. (L 24.10.66, 186)

- When seen from the Himalayas, how mean and petty sound the arguments of radicals and reactionaries alike! (quoted in du Boulay, 237)

- The Church of the poor ought to be, not a Church that gives to the poor, but one which lives its poverty. (L 15.12.64, 167)

- I am thinking of all the harm that is done to the Gospel here, when it is preached by people who have behind them all the prestige, money, science, and technology of the west. (L 24.10.66, 186)

- What's important in the Church and everywhere is to be sufficiently "deep" in order to transcend the letter, which does not mean to "reject" it. (EL 146)

- The Church is like an immense tree which provides shelter and food for all sorts of birds. (Pr 50)

Dialogue

- [Religious] pluralism is a gift of God. (DD 206)

- The only principle of interreligious dialogue is truth. (DD 211)

- Spiritual riches, even more than material riches, belong to all. They are the common property of the children of God, and no one ever enjoys them more truly than when sharing them with his brothers. (DD 207)

Glossary of Frequently Used Sanskrit and Hindi Terms

advaita	non-duality, both as doctrine and as experience
ashram	spiritual community gathered around a guru
Ātman	the Self; one with *Brahman*, the Supreme Reality
avatāra	"descent"; an incarnation of a deity
bhakti	loving devotion
Brahman	the Absolute, the One, the Real, the Supreme Identity
chelā	disciple
darśana	the radiant Presence of a saint; also vision or point of view
dharma	a religion (the sense in which Abhishiktananda most often uses the term); duty or vocation; a norm of religious or social life
dīkṣā	initiation
dhyāna	meditation, contemplation
guha	the "cave of the heart"
jñāna	knowledge of the Real
karma	work, action; the accumulated effect of past deeds
liṅga	the phallic stone symbol of Siva
maṭha	monastery, religious community, center of learning
māyā	illusion, relativity, temporality
nāma-rūpa	"name" and "form"
nāma-japa	repeated invocation of the Holy Name
Puruṣa	the Primordial, Archetypal, and Cosmic Man; also the Self, the *Ātman*
rishi	a sage of old (usually of Vedic times)
saccidānanda	Being (*sat*)-Awareness (*cit*)-Bliss (*ānanda*); the Vedantic ternary applied to *Ātman-Brahman*
sadguru	real or ultimate guru
sādhu	renunciate
śakti	divine energy pervading the cosmos; the creative Feminine Principle

sannyāsa	the ideal and practice of complete renunciation
sannyāsī	renunciate
tapas	austerities (silence, solitude, fasting, etc.)
yoga	union; psycho-spiritual discipline; one of the Indian philosophical schools
Vedanta	"the end or summation of the *Vedas*"; the *Upanishads*; the non-dualistic school of Indian philosophy and metaphysics, primarily associated with Sankara

For a glossary of all key foreign words used in books published by
World Wisdom, including metaphysical terms in English, consult:
www.DictionaryofSpiritualTerms.org.
This on-line Dictionary of Spiritual Terms provides extensive
definitions, examples and related terms in other languages.

Sources

A. Abhishiktananda: A Select Bibliography

Initial dates are those of first publication, usually in French; other dates are those of the editions actually consulted during research. For full bibliographical details and publication history see James Stuart, *Swami Abhishiktananda: His Life Told through His Letters*, 329-339.

Books and Monographs

1951 *A Benedictine Ashram*. Douglas: Times Press, 1964 (written with Fr Jules Monchanin).

1956 *Ermites de Saccidânanda*. Tournai: Casterman, 1956.

1959 *Swami Parama Arubi Anandam: Fr J. Monchanin 1895-1957*. Tannirpalli: Saccidananda Ashram, 1959 (edited and largely written by Abhishiktananda).

1965 *Hindu-Christian Meeting Point*. Delhi: ISPCK, 1976.

1965 *Saccidananda: A Christian Experience of Advaita*. Delhi: ISPCK, 1984.

1966 *Mountain of the Lord: Pilgrimage to Gangotri*. Delhi: ISPCK, 1990.

1967 *Prayer*. London: SPCK, 1972.

1969 *The Church in India: An Essay in Self-Criticism*. Madras: CLS, 1969.

1970 *Towards the Renewal of the Indian Church*. Ernakulam: KCM, 1970.

1970 *Guru and Disciple*. London: SPCK, 1974 (comprises "A Sage from the East," first published 1970, and "Mountain of the Lord," 1966).

1975 *The Further Shore*. Delhi: ISPCK, 1975.

1978 *The Secret of Arunachala*. Delhi: ISPCK, 1997.

1982 *Intériorité et révélation: essais théologiques*. Sisteron: Presence, 1983.

1983 *The Eyes of Light*. Denville: Dimension Books, 1983.

1986 *Ascent to the Depth of the Heart: The Spiritual Diary (1948-1973) of Swami Abhishiktananda (Dom Henri Le Saux)*, ed. Raimon Panikkar, tr. David Fleming and James Stuart. Delhi: ISPCK, 1998.

1989 *In Spirit and Truth: An Essay on Prayer and Life*. Delhi: ISPCK, 1989.

Select Articles

1958 "Christian *Sannyasis*." *Clergy Monthly Supplement*, 4:3, 106-113.

1958 "Le Père Monchanin." *La Vie Spirituelle*, 98, 71-95.

1967 "A Letter from India" (with C.M. Rogers). *One in Christ*, 3, 195-199.

1967 "Baptism, Faith, and Conversion." *Indian Journal of Theology*, 16:3, 189-203.

1968 "The Church in India: A Self-Examination." *Religion and Society* (Bangalore), 15:3, 5-19.

1969 "An Approach to Hindu Spirituality." *Clergy Review* (London), 54:3, 163-174.

1970   "Communication in the Spirit." *Religion and Society*, 17:3, 33-39.
1971   "Yoga and Christian Prayer." *Clergy Monthly*, 35:11, 472-477.
1973   "Theology of Presence as a Form of Evangelization in the Context of Non-Christian Religions." In *Service and Salvation*, ed. J. Pathrapankal. Bangalore: Theological Publications, India, 407-417 (reproduced in *The Eyes of Light*).
1973   Foreword to James Borst, *A Method of Contemplative Prayer*. Bombay: Asian Trading Corporation, 1973, reprinted by Society of St Paul, Newcastle, Australia, 1979, 7-11.
1974   "The *Upanishads* and Advaitic Experience." *Clergy Monthly*, 38:11, 474-486 (reproduced in *The Further Shore*).
1974   "The Experience of God in Eastern Religions." *Cistercian Studies*, 9:2-3, 148-157.
1981   "The Depth Dimension of Religious Dialogue." *Vidyajyoti*, 45:5, 202-221.

About Abhishiktananda

Books

Conio, Caterina. *Abhishiktananda: Sulle frontiere dell'incontro cristiano-indù.* Assisi: Citadella Editrice, 1984.

Davy, M-M. *Henri Le Saux, Swami Abhishiktananda, le Passeur entre deux rives.* Paris: Editions du Cerf, 1981.

du Boulay, Shirley. *The Cave of the Heart: The Life of Swami Abhishiktananda.* Maryknoll, NY: Orbis, 2005.

Grant, Sara. *Lord of the Dance: Swamiji, the Man.* Bangalore: Asian Trading Corporation, 1987.

Hackbarth-Johnson, Christian. *Interrelgiöse Existenz, Spirituelle Erfahrung und Identität bei Henri Le Saux (O.S.B.) Swami Abhishiktananda (1910-1973).* Frankfurt a.M.: Peter Lang, 2002.

Kalliath, Antony. *The Word in the Cave: The Experiential Journey of Swami Abhishiktananda to the Point of Hindu-Christian Meeting.* New Delhi: Intercultural Publications, 1986.

Rogers, Murray and David Barton. *Abhishiktananda: A Memoir of Dom Henri Le Saux.* Oxford: SLG Press, Convent of the Incarnation, 2003.

Stuart, James. *Swami Abhishiktananda: His Life Told through His Letters.* Delhi: ISPCK, 2000.

Vandana (Sister Vandana Mataji) (ed.). *Swami Abhishiktananda: The Man and His Message.* Delhi: ISPCK, 1993, rev. ed.

Vattakuzhy, Emmanuel. *Indian Christian Sannyasa and Swami Abhishiktananda.* Bangalore: Theological Publications in India, 1981.

Visvanathan, Susan. *An Ethnography of Mysticism: The Narratives of Abhishiktananda.* Rashtrapati Nivas Shimla: Indian Institute of Advanced Study, 1998.

Articles and Book Chapters

Arraj, James. *Christianity in the Crucible of East-West Dialogue* (published together with *God, Zen, and the Intuition of Being* as *Inner Explorations, Volume IV: East-West Contemplative Dialogue*). Inner Growth Books and Videos, 2001, Ch 2. (also on the internet).

Baumer-Despeigne, Odette. "The Spiritual Journey of Henri Le Saux-Abhishiktananda." *Cistercian Studies*, 18, 1983, 310-329.

—"The Spiritual Way of Henri Le Saux/Abhishiktananda." *Bulletin of Monastic Interreligious Dialogue*, 48, October 1993, 20-25.

Bruteau, Beatrice. "In the Cave of the Heart: Silence and Realization." *New Blackfriars*, July-August 1984, 3011-319.

Coff, Pascaline. "Abhishiktananda: An Interview with Odette Baumer-Despeigne." *Bulletin of Monastic Interreligious Dialogue*, 48, October 1993, 53-60 (also on internet).

Comans, Michael. "Swami Abhishiktananda (H. Le Saux) and *Advaita*: The Account of a Spiritual Journey." *Indo-British Review*, 19:1, 1993, 99-116 (also in Geoffrey A. Oddie, ed. *Religious Traditions in South Asia: Interaction and Change*. Surrey: Curzon Press, 1998, 107-124).

Cornille, Catherine. *The Guru in Indian Catholicism*. Louvain Theological and Pastoral Monographs, No 6. Louvain: Peeters Press & W.B. Eerdmans, 1991, 75-118.

Dupuis, Jacques. *Jesus Christ at the Encounter of World Religions*. Maryknoll, NY: Orbis, 1991, 67-90.

Edwards, Felicity. "Spiritual Experience in Three Contemporaries: Dom Henri Le Saux, Vandana Mataji RSCJ, and Fr. D.S. Amalorpavadass, and its Significance for Interreligious Dialogue and Social Responsibility." In John W. De Gruchy (ed), *Religion and the Reconstruction of Civil Society*. Pretoria: University of South Africa, 1995, 75-89.

Gillespie, George. "The Language of Mysticism." *Indian Journal of Theology*, 32:3-4, 1983, 45-62.

Gispert-Sauch, George. "Exploring the Further Shore." *Vidyajyoti*, 40, 1976, 502-506.

— "The Spirituality of Swami Abhishiktananda." *Ignis Studies*, 10, 1985, 41-47.

Goel, Sita Ram. *Catholic Ashrams: Sannyasis or Swindlers?* New Delhi: Voice of India, 1994, rev. ed.

Grant, Sara. "Time-Bomb or Tombstone? Reflections on the Private Journal of Swami Abhishiktananda." *Vidyajyoti*, 52, 1988, 83-97.

Klostermaier, Klaus. "Hindu-Christian Dialogue: Revisiting the Tannirpalli Trinity's Original Vision." *Hindu-Christian Studies Bulletin*, 16, 2003, 3-11.

Malkovsky, Bradley. "*Advaita* Vedanta and Christian Faith." *Journal of Ecumenical Studies*, 36:3-4, Summer-Fall 1999, 397-422.

Nicholl, Donald. *The Beatitude of Truth*. London: Dartman Longman Todd, 1977, Ch. 16, 216-222.

Oldmeadow, Harry. "Jules Monchanin, Henri Le Saux/Abhishiktananda and the Hindu-Christian Encounter." *Australian Religion Studies Review*, 17:2, 2004, 98-113.

Panikkar, R. "Letter to Abhishiktananda." *Studies in Formative Spirituality*, 3:3, 1982, 429-451.

Royster, James E. "Abhishiktananda: Hindu-Christian Monk." *Studies in Formative Spirituality*, 9:3. November 1988, 309-328.

—"A Dialogue in Depth: A Monastic Perspective." *Quarterly Review*, 9:2, Summer 1989, 75-92.

Sharma, Arvind. "Sankara's *Bhakti* and Swami Abhishiktananda's 'Adult Faith.'" *Journal of Dharma*, 15, 1990, 240-244.

Schmalz, Mathew N. "The Return from the Further Shore: Theological Implications of Christian *Sannyasa.*" *Koinonia*, 5, Fall 1993, 191-217.

Stephens, Robert. "Abhishiktananda: The Benedictine Swami." *Tjurunga: An Australasian Benedictine Review*, 31, 1986-87, 72-79.

Stuart, James. "Swami Abhishiktananda." *Clergy Monthly*, 38:2, February 1974, 80-82.

—"Sri Ramana Maharshi and Abhishiktananda." *Vidjajyoti*, April 1980, 167-176.

—"Abhishiktananda on Inner Awakening." *Vidjayjoti*, 46, 1982, 470-484.

—"The Religious in the Church, as seen by Swami Abhishiktananda." *Vidjayjoti*, 57, 1993, 401-413.

Teasdale, Wayne. "Abhishiktananda's Contemplative Theology." *Monastic Studies*, Autumn 1982, 179-199.

—"Abhishiktananda's Mystical Intuition of the Trinity." *Cistercian Studies*, 1, 1983, 60-75.

Trapnell, Judson B. "Two Models of Christian Dialogue with Hinduism: Bede Griffiths and Abhishiktananda." *Vidjayjoti*, 60, 1996, 101-110.

Ulrich, Edward T. "Swami Abhishiktananda's Interreligious Hermeneutics of the *Upanishads.*" *Hindu-Christian Studies Bulletin*, 16, 2003, 22-29.

—"Swami Abhishiktananda and Comparative Theology." *Horizons: The Journal of the College Theology Society*, 31: 1, 2004, 40-63.

Wilfred, Felix. "Widening the Horizons: D. Swami Abhishiktananda." In *Beyond Settled Foundations: The Journey of Indian Theology*. Madras (University of Madras), 1993, 53-60.

Theses

Bailey, Casey. *Three Roman Catholic Approaches to the Self in Hindu-Christian Dialogue: Abhishiktananda, Panikkar, and Griffiths*. MST thesis, Jesuit School of Theology at Berkeley, 1984.

Friesen, John Glenn. *Abhishiktananda's Non-Monistic Advaitic Experience*. PhD thesis, University of South Africa, 2001 (on internet).

Kalliath, Antony. *Self-Awakening: An Analytico-Critical Study of the Religious Experience of Swami Abhishiktananda in the Context of Hindu-Christian Meeting*. ThD thesis, Pontificia Universitas Gregoriana, 1991.

Kuttianimattathil, Jose. *Practice and Theology of Interreligious Dialogue: The Trajectory Undertaken by the Indian Church since Vatican II*. Rome (Gregorian University), 1994, see pp. 31-38.

Laure Olive-Stehli, Laure. *Jules Monchanin and Henri Le Saux, Two Catholic Priests in India: A Psychobiographical and Transpersonal Approach*. MA thesis, California Institute of Integral Studies, 1997.

Pascual, Martin A. *Faith Expressions of Mother Teresa and Swami Abhishiktananda: Toward a Constructive Understanding of Catholic Mission in India.* Thesis, Harvard University, 1996.

Spence, Roger Earl. *Interiority in the Works of Abhishiktananda and Ken Wilber.* PhD thesis, Graduate Theological Union, 1987.

Stephens, Robert. *Religious Experience as a Meeting-Point in Dialogue: An Evaluation of the Venture of Swami Abhishiktananda.* MA thesis, Sydney University, 1984.

Ulrich, Edward Theodore. *Swami Abhishiktananda's Interreligious Hermeneutics of the Upanishads.* PhD Thesis, Catholic University of America, 2001.

Yesurathnam, R. *An Examination of Swami Abhishiktananda's Dialogical Theory.* DTh thesis, Serampore University, 1987.

*

See also *Setu: Bulletin of the Abhishiktananda Society*, ed. Bettina Bäumer, 25 issues.

*

Internet Resources

Website of the Abhishiktananda Society: http://www.upanishad.org/lesaux/abhisociety.htm.

Website on Monchanin and Le Saux: http://monchaninlesaux-lyon.cef.fr/.

Amaladoss, Michael. "Double Religious Belonging and Liminality" (from *Vidyajyoti*, January 2002). http://www.sedos.org/english/amaladoss_8.htm.

Bäumer, Bettina. "Abhishiktananda and the Challenge of Hindu-Christian Experience." MID Bulletin, Issue 64 (May 2000) 34-41. http://www.monasticdialog.com/bulletins/64/Challenge_Hindu_Christian.htm.

—"Swami Abhishiktananda/Henri Le Saux OSB, Pilgrim and Hermit: A Bridge between Hinduism and Christianity." http://www.monasticdialog.com/bulletins/72/baumer.htm.

Bowe, Peter. "Keeping Faith with Interfaith: Searching for 'God' in a Pluralist World." http://www.interfaith-center.org/keepingfaithwithinterfaith.htm.

Coff, Pascaline. "Dialogue with Eastern Religions." http://www.mkzc.org/dialog1.html.

Cozzanni, Bernardino. "Inculturation of Monastic Values at Saccidananda Ashram." http://www.bedegriffiths.org/golden/gs_4.htm.

du Boulay, Shirley, "The Priest and the Swami." http://www.thetablet.co.uk/.

Friesen, John Glenn. "Abhishiktananda: Hindu Advaitic Experience and Christian Beliefs." *Hindu-Christian Studies Bulletin*, 11, 1998. http://www.sandiego.edu.

Gerry, Frank. "The Johannine *Upanishads*." http://www.christianmeditation-australia.org/cmcweekend.doc.

Ishpriya, Sister. "Begging in Another Temple." http://www.dimmid.org/ data/09/ED3_BeggingAnotherTemple.htm.

Malkovsky, Bradley. "*Advaita* Vedanta and Christian Faith." *Journal of Ecumenical Studies*, June 22, 1999. http://static.highbeam.com/j/ journalofecumenicalstudies/june221999/advaitavedantaandchristianfaith/

Painadath, Sebastian. "The Spiritual and Theological Perspectives of Ashrams: A Tribute to Santivanam, 50 Years." http://www.sedos.org/english/ sebastian.htm.

Trapnell, Judson. "Abhishiktananda's Contemplative Vocation and Contemporary India." http://www.infinityfoundation.com/mandala/s_es/s_es_ trapn_vocation.htm.

—"Gandhi, Abhishiktananda, and the Challenge of Reperceiving the Religious 'Other.'" http://www.infinityfoundation.com/mandala/s_es/s_es_trapn_ gandhi.htm.

Video

Patrice Chagnard. *Swamiji, un voyage intérieur.* Paris, 1984, 86 min.

B. Other Sources

—"Pilgrimage." *Catholic Encyclopedia,* on the New Advent website: http:// www.newadvent.org/cathen/12085a.htm.

A Monk of the West. *Christianity and the Doctrine of Non-Dualism,* tr. Alvin Moore Jr and Marie M. Hansen. Hillsdale, NY: Sophia Perennis, 2004.

Bäumer, Bettina and John R. Dupuche (eds.). *Void and Fullness in the Buddhist, Hindu, and Christian Traditions.* New Delhi: D.K. Printworld, 2005.

Baumer-Despeigne, Odette. "A Way of Initiation." In B. Bruteau (ed.), *The Other Half of My Soul: Bede Griffiths and the Hindu-Christian Dialogue,* 42-63.

Bernbaum, Edwin. *Sacred Mountains of the World.* Berkeley: University of California Press, 1998. See also: http://www.mtnforum.org/resources/library/ berne98a.htm.

Berry, Wendell. *Sex, Economy, Freedom, and Community.* New York: Pantheon, 1993.

Biès, Jean. *Returning to the Essential.* Bloomington: World Wisdom, 2004.

Brown, Joseph Epes. *The Sacred Pipe.* Baltimore: Penguin, 1971.

Bruteau, Beatrice (ed.). *The Other Half of My Soul: Bede Griffiths and the Hindu-Christian Dialogue.* Wheaton: Quest, 1994.

Buber, Martin. *A Believing Humanism.* New York: Simon & Schuster, 1967.

Burckhardt, Titus. *Sacred Art in East and West.* Bedfont: Perennial Books, 1967.

—*Alchemy: Science of the Cosmos, Science of the Soul.* Baltimore: Penguin, 1972.

Clements, R.J. *Michelangelo's Theory of Art.* New York, 1941.

Clooney, Francis. *Theology After Vedanta.* Albany: SUNY, 1993.

—"No Other Name? A Survey of Christian Attitudes Toward the World Religions." *Religious Studies Review,* 15:3, July 1989, 198-203.

Cobb, Jr, John B. *Beyond Dialogue: Toward a Mutual Transformation of Christianity and Buddhism*. Philadelphia: Fortress Press, 1982.

—"Christianity and Eastern Wisdom." *Japanese Journal of Religious Studies*, 5:4, December 1978, 285-298.

Colasuonno, Nicholas. "The Pilgrim Missionary." *Studies in Formative Spirituality*, 13:3, November 1992, 273-288.

Conner, James. "The Monk as Bridge between East and West." In B. Bruteau (ed.), *The Other Half of My Soul*, 80-97.

Conner, Tarcisius. "Monk of Renewal." In P. Hart (ed.), *Thomas Merton, Monk*, 173-194.

Coomaraswamy, Ananda. *Coomaraswamy 1: Selected Papers; Traditional Art and Symbolism*, ed. Roger Lipsey. Princeton: Bollingen Series, Princeton University, 1977.

—*Coomaraswamy 2: Selected Papers, Metaphysics*, ed. Roger Lipsey. Princeton: Bollingen Series, Princeton University, 1977.

—*Christian and Oriental Philosophy of Art*. New York: Dover, 1956.

—*The Bugbear of Literacy*. London: Perennial Books, 1979.

—*What is Civilization? and Other Essays*. Ipswich: Golgonooza Press, 1989.

—*Hinduism and Buddhism*. New Delhi: Munshiram Manoharlal, 1995.

—*Selected Letters of Ananda Coomaraswamy*, ed. Rama P. Coomaraswamy and Alvin Moore Jr. New Delhi: Indira Gandhi National Center, 1988.

—"The Bugbear of Democracy, Freedom, and Equality." *Studies in Comparative Religion*, 11:3, 1977, 133-158.

—"The Pertinence of Philosophy." In S. Radhakrishnan and J.H. Muirhead (eds.), *Contemporary Indian Philosophy*. London: Allen & Unwin, 1952, rev. ed.

Coomaraswamy, Rama P. "Who Speaks for the East?" *Studies in Comparative Religion*, 11:2, Spring 1977, 85-91.

Coward, Harold. *Hindu-Christian Dialogue: Perspectives and Encounters*. Maryknoll, NY: Orbis, 1989.

—"Hinduism's Sensitizing of Christianity to its own Sources." *Dialogue and Alliance*, 7:2, Fall-Winter 1993, 77-85.

Cragg, Kenneth. *The Mind of the Qur'an: Chapters in Reflection*. London: Allen & Unwin, 1973.

Daniélou, Alain. *The Way to the Labyrinth: Memories of East and West*. New York: New Directions, 1987.

Danner, Victor. "The Inner and Outer Man." In Y. Ibish and P.L. Wilson (eds.), *Traditional Modes of Contemplation and Action*. Tehran: Imperial Iranian Academy of Philosophy, 1977.

Das, Sadananda and Ernst Fürlinger (eds.). *Sāmarasya: Studies in Indian Arts, Philosophy, and Interreligious Dialogue* (in honor of Bettina Bäumer). New Delhi: D.K. Printworld, 2005.

Desjardins, Arnaud. *The Message of the Tibetans*. London: Stuart & Watkins, London,1969.

Deutsch, Eliot. *Advaita Vedanta: A Philosophical Reconstruction*. Honolulu: University of Hawaii, 1973.

Deutsch, Eliot and Rohit Dalvi (eds.). *The Essential Vedanta: A New Source Book of Advaita Vedanta*. Bloomington: World Wisdom, 2004.

du Boulay, Shirley. *Beyond the Darkness: A Biography of Bede Griffiths.* London: Rider, 1998.

Eck, Diana. *Encountering God: A Spiritual Journey from Bozeman to Banaras.* Boston: Beacon, 1993.

Eliade, Mircea. *The Sacred and the Profane.* New York: Harcourt Brace Jovanovich, 1959.

—*Myths, Dreams, and Mysteries.* London: Collins, 1972.

—*Ordeal by Labyrinth: Conversations with Claude-Henri Rocquet.* Chicago: University of Chicago, 1982.

Eliot, T.S. *Notes Towards the Definition of Culture.* London: Faber, 1962.

Fernando, Ranjit (ed.). *The Unanimous Tradition.* Colombo: Sri Lanka Institute of Traditional Studies, 1991.

Fitzgerald, Judith and Michael. *The Sermon of All Creation: Christians on Nature.* Bloomington: World Wisdom, 2005.

Fitzgerald, Michael. *Indian Spirit.* Bloomington: World Wisdom, 2002.

Forman, Charles W. "The Growth of the Study of Christian Expansion." *Religious Studies Review*, 13:1, 1987, 30-33.

France, Peter. *Hermits: The Insights of Solitude.* London: Pimlico, 1996.

Gollancz, Victor (ed.). *From Darkness to Light.* London: Gollancz, 1964.

Govinda, Anagarika. *Foundations of Tibetan Mysticism.* London: Rider, 1969.

—*The Way of the White Clouds.* Boulder: Shambhala, 1970.

— *Creative Meditation and Multi-Dimensional Consciousness.* Wheaton: Quest, 1976.

Griffiths, Bede. *Vedanta and Christian Faith.* Los Angeles: Dawn Horse Press, 1973.

—*Return to the Center.* London: Collins, 1976.

—*The Marriage of East and West.* London: Collins, 1982.

—*Christ in India: Essays Towards a Hindu-Christian Dialogue.* Springfield: Templegate, 1984.

Guénon, René. *Introduction to the Study of Hindu Doctrines.* London: Luzac, 1945.

—*The Crisis of the Modern World.* London: Luzac, 1975.

—*Man and His Becoming According to the Vedanta.* New Delhi: Oriental Books Reprint Co., 1981.

—*The Reign of Quantity and the Signs of the Times.* Ghent: Sophia Perennis et Universalis, 1995.

—*Fundamental Symbols.* Cambridge: Quinta Essentia, 1995.

—"Oriental Metaphysics." In J. Needleman (ed.), *The Sword of Gnosis.* Baltimore: Penguin, 1974, 40-56.

Halbfass, Wilhelm. *India and Europe: An Essay in Philosophical Understanding.* Delhi: Motilal Banarsidass, 1990.

Hamilton, Elizabeth. *The Voice of the Spirit: The Spirituality of St John of the Cross.* London: Darton, Longman & Todd, 1976.

Hart, Patrick (ed.). *Thomas Merton, Monk.* New York: Doubleday, 1976.

Hick, John (ed.). *Truth and Dialogue: The Relationship of the World Religions.* London: Sheldon, 1974.

—and Paul Knitter (eds.). *The Myth of Christian Uniqueness.* London: SCM, 1988.

Indra, C.T. et al. *Sadguru Gnanananda: His Life, Personality, and Teachings.* Bombay: Bharatiya Vidya Bhavan, 1979.

Isherwood, Christopher. *Ramakrishna and His Disciples.* Calcutta: Advaita Ashrama, 1974.

Jordens, J.F.T. *Gandhi: Conscience of India and Scourge of Orthodoxy.* Canberra: Australian National University, 1991.

Keating, Thomas. "Meditative Technologies: Theological Ecumenicism." In B. Bruteau (ed.), *The Other Half of My Soul,* 112-125.

Keeble, Brian. "Tradition, Intelligence, and the Artist." *Studies in Comparative Religion,* 11:4, 1977, 235-250.

Kelley, C.F. *Meister Eckhart on Divine Knowledge.* New Haven: Yale University, 1977.

Klostermaier, Klaus. *In the Paradise of Krishna.* Philadelphia: Westminster Press, 1969.

—"Hindu-Christian Dialogue: Its Religious and Cultural Implications." *Sciences Relgieuses/Studies in Religion,* 1:2, 1971, 83-97.

—"From Phenomenology to Meta-science: Reflections on the Study of Religion." *Studies in Religion,* 6:4, 1976-1977, 551-564.

—"All Religions are Incomplete—Complementarity as Theoretical Model to Guide the *Praxis* of Interreligious Dialogue." *Dialogue & Alliance,* 7:2, Fall-Winter 1993, 60-76.

Kṛṣnamurti, N. "Ananda Coomaraswamy." In S.D.R. Singam (ed.), *Ananda Coomaraswamy: Remembering and Remembering Again and Again.*

Lakhani, Ali. "What Thirst is For." *Sacred Web,* 4, December 1999, 13-14.

Lings, Martin. *What is Sufism?* London: Allen & Unwin, 1975.

—*Symbol and Archetype: A Study of the Meaning of Existence.* Cambridge: Quinta Essentia, 1978.

—*Ancient Beliefs and Modern Superstitions.* London: Allen & Unwin, 1980.

—*Mecca: From Before Genesis Until Now.* Cambridge: Archetype, 2004.

Lund, Søren. "The Christian Mission and Colonialism." *Temenos,* 17, 1981, 116-123.

Macaulay, Thomas B. *Letters of Lord Macaulay.* London: Longman, 1876.

Macfarlane, Robert. *Mountains of the Mind: A History of a Fascination.* London: Granta, 2004.

McLuhan, T.C. *Cathedrals of the Spirit: The Message of Sacred Places.* Toronto: HarperPerennial, 1996.

Mahadevan, T.M.P. *Outlines of Hinduism.* Bombay: Chetana, 1956.

—*Ramana Maharshi: The Sage of Arunachala.* London: Allen & Unwin, 1977.

Manavath, Xavier. "Summary of Books Relevant to Spiritual Formation and the Hindu-Christian Dialogue." *Studies in Formative Spirituality,* 11:3, November 1990, 425-438.

Merton, Thomas. *The Silent Life.* New York: Farrar, Straus & Giroux, 1957.

—*New Seeds of Contemplation.* New York: New Directions, 1961.

—*Gandhi on Non-Violence.* New York: New Directions, 1965.

—*The Asian Journal of Thomas Merton,* ed. Naomi Burton, Patrick Hart, and James Laughlin. New York: New Directions, 1972.

—*Thoughts on the East,* ed. George Woodcock. New York: New Directions, 1995.

Michon, Jean-Louis. "The Vocation of Man According to the Koran." In Arvind Sharma (ed.), *Fragments of Infinity: Essays in Religion and Philosophy*. Bridport: Prism, 1991.

Nasr, Seyyed Hossein. *Ideals and Realities of Islam*. London: Allen & Unwin, 1966.

—*Man and Nature: The Spiritual Crisis of Modern Man*. London: Allen & Unwin, 1968.

—*Sufi Essays*. London: Allen & Unwin, 1972.

—*Knowledge and the Sacred*. New York: Crossroad, 1981.

—*Religion and the Order of Nature*. New York: Oxford University, 1996.

—*The Spiritual and Religious Dimensions of the Environmental Crisis*. London: Temenos Academy, 1999.

—"Conditions for a Meaningful Comparative Philosophy." *Philosophy East and West*, 22:1, 1972, 53-61.

Neihardt, John. *Black Elk Speaks*. London: Abacus, 1974.

Nietzsche, Friedrich. *A Nietzsche Reader*, ed. R.J. Hollingdale. Harmondsworth: Penguin, 1977.

Newbigin, Lesslie. "A Christian Vedanta?" http://gospel-culture.org.uk/1992.htm.

Nityananda Giri, Swami. "Sadguru Sri Gnanananda." *Monastic Interreligious Dialogue*, Bulletin 64, May 2000, website.

Novak, Philip. "Universal Theology and the Idea of Universal Order." *Dialogue & Alliance*, 6:1, Spring 1992, 82-92.

Noyce, Wilfrid. *South Col*. London: William Heinemann, 1954.

Oldmeadow, Kenneth ("Harry"). *Traditionalism: Religion in the Light of the Perennial Philosophy*. Colombo: Sri Lanka Institute of Traditional Studies, 2000.

Oldmeadow, Harry. *Mircea Eliade and Carl Jung: "Priests without Surplices"?*, Department of Arts, La Trobe University Bendigo, 1995 (Studies in Western Traditions: Occasional Papers, 1).

—*Journeys East: 20th Century Western Encounters with Eastern Religious Traditions*. Bloomington: World Wisdom, 2004.

— (ed.), *The Betrayal of Tradition*. Bloomington: World Wisdom, 2004.

—"Sankara's Doctrine of *Maya*." *Asian Philosophy*, 2:2, 1992, 131-146.

—"'The Firmament Sheweth His Handiwork': Re-awakening a Religious Sense of the Natural Order." In Barry McDonald (ed.), *Seeing God Everywhere*. Bloomington: World Wisdom, 2003, 29-50.

Orwell, George. *The Collected Essays, Journalism, and Letters of George Orwell, Volume 4: In Front of Your Nose, 1945-1950*. Harmondsworth: Penguin, 1970.

Osborne, Arthur. *Ramana Maharshi and the Path of Self-Knowledge*. London: Rider, 1970.

—(ed.), *The Collected Works of Ramana Maharshi*. Tiruvannamalai: Sri Ramanasramam, 1979.

Otto, Rudolf. *Mysticism East and West: A Comparative Analysis of the Nature of Mysticism*. New York: Meridian Books, 1957.

—*The Idea of the Holy*. London: Oxford University Press, 1958.

—*Autobiographical and Social Essays*, ed. Gregory D. Alles. Berlin: Mouton de Gruyter, 1996.

Paden, William. *Religious Worlds.* Boston: Beacon, 1988.

Panikkar, Raimon. "The Contribution of Christian Monasticism in Asia to the Universal Church." *Cistercian Studies,* 9:2-3, 73-84.

—"The Monk According to the Indian Sacred Scriptures." *Cistercian Studies,* 9: 2-3, 1974, 253-255.

—"Inter-Religious Dialogue: Some Principles." *Journal of Ecumenical Studies,* 12, 1975.

—"A Tribute" (to Bede Griffiths). In Beatrice Bruteau (ed.), *The Other Half of My Soul: Bede Griffiths and the Hindu-Christian Dialogue,* 30-33.

Pallis, Marco. *Peaks and Lamas.* London: Readers Union/Cassell, 1948.

—*The Way and the Mountain.* London: Peter Owen, 1960.

—*A Buddhist Spectrum.* London: Allen & Unwin, 1980.

Perry, Whitall. *Challenges to a Secular Society.* Washington DC: Foundation of Traditional Studies, 1996.

—"The Revival of Interest in Tradition." In R. Fernando (ed.), *The Unanimous Tradition,* 3-16.

—(ed.), *A Treasury of Traditional Wisdom.* London: Allen & Unwin, 1971.

Prabhavananda, Swami and Christopher Isherwood (eds.), *Shankara's Crest Jewel of Discrimination.* New York: Mentor, 1970.

Radhakrishnan, Sarvepalli. *Selected Writings on Philosophy, Religion, and Culture,* ed. Robert McDermott. New York: E.P. Dutton, 1970.

Raine, Kathleen. *Defending Ancient Springs.* Ipswich: Golgonooza, 1985.

—"The Underlying Order: Nature and the Imagination." In A. Sharma (ed.), *Fragments of Infinity,* 198-216.

Ralston, Helen. *Christian Ashrams: A New Religious Movement in Contemporary India.* Lewiston, NY: Edwin Mellen, 1987.

Ram Dass. *The Only Dance There Is.* New York: Anchor/Doubleday, 1974.

Ramdas, Swami. *The Essential Swami Ramdas,* ed. Susanaga Weeraperuma. Bloomington: World Wisdom, 2005.

Rawlinson, Andrew. *The Book of Enlightened Masters: Western Teachers in Eastern Traditions.* Chicago: Open Court, 1997.

Redington, James. "The Hindu-Christian Dialogue and the Interior Dialogue." *Theological Studies,* 44, 1983, 587-603.

Rodhe, Sten. *Jules Monchanin: Pioneer in Hindu-Christian Dialogue.* Delhi: ISPCK, 1993.

Roszak, Theodore. *Where the Wasteland Ends.* New York: Doubleday, 1972.

Sankara. *Crest Jewel of Discrimination,* tr. and ed. Swami Prabhavananda and Christopher Isherwood. New York: Mentor, 1970.

Saint-Exupéry, Antoine de. *Flight to Arras.* Harmondsworth: Penguin, 1961.

Saraswati, Ramanananda (tr.). *Tripura Rahasya.* Bloomington: World Wisdom, 2002.

Schuon, Frithjof. *Language of the Self.* Madras: Ganesh, 1959.

—*Stations of Wisdom.* London: Perennial Books, no date; reprint of John Murray ed., London, 1961.

—*Light on the Ancient Worlds.* London: Perennial Books, 1966.

—*Spiritual Perspectives and Human Facts.* London: Perennial Books, 1967.

—*In the Tracks of Buddhism.* London: Allen & Unwin, 1968.

—*Dimensions of Islam.* London: Allen & Unwin, 1969.

—*The Transcendent Unity of Religions.* New York: Harper & Row, 1975.

—*Logic and Transcendence.* New York: Harper & Row, 1975.

—*Understanding Islam.* London: Allen & Unwin, 1976.

—*Islam and the Perennial Philosophy.* London: World of Islam Festival, 1976

—*Gnosis: Divine Wisdom.* London: Perennial Books, 1979.

—*Esoterism as Principle and as Way.* London: Perennial Books, 1981.

—*Sufism, Veil and Quintessence.* Bloomington: World Wisdom Books, 1981.

—*Castes and Races.* London: Perennial Books, 1982.

—*Survey of Metaphysics and Esoterism.* Bloomington: World Wisdom Books, 1986.

—*The Essential Writings of Frithjof Schuon,* ed. S.H. Nasr. New York: Amity House, 1986.

—*To Have a Center.* Bloomington: World Wisdom Books, 1990.

—*The Feathered Sun.* Bloomington: World Wisdom Books, 1990.

—*Roots of the Human Condition.* Bloomington: World Wisdom Books, 1991.

—*The Transfiguration of Man.* Bloomington: World Wisdom Books, 1995.

—*The Eye of the Heart.* Bloomington: World Wisdom Books, 1997.

—*René Guénon: Some Observations.* Hillsdale, NY: Sophia Perennis, 2004.

—*Prayer Fashions Man: Frithjof Schuon on the Spiritual Life,* ed. James S. Cutsinger. Bloomington: World Wisdom, 2005.

—"Foundations of an Integral Aesthetics." *Studies in Comparative Religion,* 10:3, 1976, 130-135.

—"No Activity without Truth." In Harry Oldmeadow (ed.), *The Betrayal of Tradition.* Bloomington: World Wisdom, 2005, 3-14.

Sharma, Arvind (ed.). *Fragments of Infinity: Essays in Religion and Philosophy.* Bridport: Prism, 1991.

Sharpe, Eric J. *Faith Meets Faith: Some Christian Attitudes to Hinduism in the Nineteenth and Twentieth Centuries.* London: SCM, 1977.

—*The Universal Gita: Western Images of the Bhagavadgita.* London: Duckworth, 1985.

—"To Hinduism through Gandhi." In *The Wisdom of the East.* Sydney: ABC, 1979, 52-63.

—"Some Problems of Method in the Study of Religion." *Religion* 1:1, 1971.

—"The Goals of Interreligious Dialogue." In J. Hick (ed.), *Truth and Dialogue: The Relationship of the World Religions.* London: Sheldon,1974, 77-95.

Sherrard, Philip. *The Rape of Man and Nature.* Colombo: Sri Lanka Institute of Traditional Studies, 1987.

—*Human Image: World Image.* Cambridge: Golgonooza Press, 1992.

—*Christianity: Lineaments of a Sacred Tradition.* Brookline: Holy Cross Orthodox Press, 1998.

Singam, S. Durai R. (ed). *Ananda Coomaraswamy: Remembering and Remembering Again and Again.* Kuala Lumpur: privately published, 1974.

Smith, Huston. *Forgotten Truth: The Primordial Tradition.* New York: Harper & Row, 1976.

Snodgrass, Adrian. *The Symbolism of the Stupa.* Delhi: Motilal Banarsidass, 1992.

—*Architecture, Time, and Eternity: Studies in the Stellar and Temporal Symbolism of Traditional Buildings,* 2 volumes. New Delhi: P.K. Goel/Aditya Prakashan, 1990.

Teasdale, Wayne. *Bede Griffiths: An Introduction to his Interspiritual Thought.* Woodstock, VT: Skylight Paths, 2003.

—"*Sannyasa:* The Primordial Tradition of Renunciation—A Radical Monastic Proposal." *Cistercian Studies Quarterly,* 31:1, 1996, 75-93.

—"Bede Griffiths as Visionary Guide." In B. Bruteau (ed.), *The Other Half of My Soul: Bede Griffiths and the Hindu-Christian Dialogue,* 2-25.

—"Christianity and the Eastern Traditions: The Possibility of Mutual Growth." In B. Bruteau (ed.), *The Other Half of My Soul: Bede Griffiths and the Hindu-Christian Dialogue,* 126-163.

Thomas, Philipos. "Christian Ashrams and Evangelization of India." *Indian Church History Review,* 11, 1977.

Trapnell, Judson B. *Bede Griffiths: A Life in Dialogue.* Albany: SUNY, 2001.

—"Bede Griffiths, Mystical Knowing, and the Unity of Religions." *Philosophy and Theology,* 7:4, Summer 1993, 355-379.

—"Multireligious Experience and the Study of Mysticism." In B. Bruteau (ed.), *The Other Half of My Soul: Bede Griffiths and the Hindu-Christian Dialogue,* 198-223.

Vandana, Sr Mataji. *Gurus, Ashrams, and Christians.* Delhi: ISPCK, 1988.

—*Christian Ashrams: A Movement with a Future?* Delhi: ISPCK, 1993.

—"Spiritual Formation in Ashrams in Contemporary India." *Studies in Formative Spirituality,* 11:3, November 1990, 355-379.

Wach, Joachim. *The Comparative Study of Religions.* New York: Columbia University Press, 1958.

Watts, Alan. *The Way of Zen.* Harmondsworth: Penguin, 1972.

Weber, J.G. *In Quest of the Absolute: The Life and Work of Jules Monchanin.* Kalamazoo: Cistercian Publications, 1977.

Acknowledgments

The following people have been immensely helpful in many different ways and I am beholden to them.

Bettina Bäumer
Michael Fitzgerald
Barry McDonald
Peter Oldmeadow

I am also most grateful to the following for their support and assistance.

Jean Biès
Rodney Blackhirst
Nicholas Colloff
Shirley du Boulay
Alvaro Enterria
Loris Ferguson
Ranjit Fernando
the late Fr Bede Griffiths
Susana Marin
Clinton Minnaar
Russell Oldmeadow
John Penwill
the late Professor Eric Sharpe
Wolfgang Smith
Mary-Kathryne Steele
Robert Stephens
Christine Street
Trish Waddington
Stephen Williams

I warmly thank all of my family for their unfaltering love and encouragement, and I dedicate this book to my wife Rose.

Biographical Note

HARRY OLDMEADOW is Coordinator of Philosophy and Religious Studies in the Department of Arts, La Trobe University, Bendigo, Australia. He studied history, politics, and literature at the Australian National University, obtaining a First Class Honors degree in history. In 1971 a Commonwealth Overseas Research Scholarship led to further studies at Oxford University. In 1980 he completed a Masters dissertation on the traditionalist or perennialist school of comparative religious thought. This study was awarded the University of Sydney Medal for excellence in research and was later published under the title *Traditionalism: Religion in the Light of the Perennial Philosophy* (2000). His principal intellectual interests include not only the traditionalist school of thinkers but the mystical and esoteric dimensions of the major religious traditions, especially Christianity, Hinduism, and Buddhism. He also has an abiding interest in the primal traditions of the American Plains Indians and the Aborigines of Australia. His latest works include *Journeys East: 20th Century Western Encounters with Eastern Religious Traditions* (World Wisdom, 2004), *The Betrayal of Tradition: Essays on the Spiritual Crisis of Modernity* (World Wisdom, 2005), and *Light from the East: Eastern Wisdom for the Modern West* (World Wisdom, 2007). Over the last decade he has published extensively in such journals as *Sacred Web*, *Sophia*, and *Vincit Omnia Veritas*. He currently resides with his wife on a small property outside Bendigo.

Index

Titles in the Perennial Philosophy Series by World Wisdom